ENCYCLOPEDIA OF LANGUAGE AND EDUCATION

Encyclopedia of Language and Education

VOLUME 7: LANGUAGE TESTING AND ASSESSMENT

The volume titles of this encyclopedia are listed at the end of this volume.

Encyclopedia of Language and Education

Volume 7

LANGUAGE TESTING AND ASSESSMENT

Edited by

CAROLINE CLAPHAM

Lancaster University
England

and

DAVID CORSON

The Ontario Institute for Studies in Education
University of Toronto
Canada

KLUWER ACADEMIC PUBLISHERS

DORDRECHT / BOSTON / LONDON

Library of Congress Cataloging-in-Publication Data

```
Language testing and assessment / edited by Caroline Clapham and David
Corson.
     p.   cm. -- (Encyclopedia of language and education ; v. 7)
   Includes bibliographical references and index.
   ISBN 0-7923-4702-1 (alk. paper). -- ISBN 0-7923-4596-7 (set : alk.
paper)
   1. Language and languages--Ability testing.   I. Clapham,
Caroline.   II. Corson, David.   III. Series.
P53.4.L376   1997
418'.0076--dc21                                              97-30205
```

ISBN 0-7923-4934-2 (PB)   ISBN 0-7923-4702-1 (HB)
ISBN 0-7923-4936-9 (PB-SET)   ISBN 0-7923-4596-7 (HB-SET)

Published by Kluwer Academic Publishers,
P.O. Box 17, 3300 AA Dordrecht, The Netherlands

Sold and distributed in the U.S.A. and Canada
by Kluwer Academic Publishers,
101 Philip Drive, Norwell, MA 02061, U.S.A.

In all other countries, sold and distributed
by Kluwer Academic Publishers Group,
P.O. Box 322, 3300 AH Dordrecht, The Netherlands

Printed in the Netherlands (on acid-free paper)

TABLE OF CONTENTS

VOLUME 7: LANGUAGE TESTING AND ASSESSMENT

Section 2: Methods of Testing and Assessment

Section 3: The Quantitative and Qualitative Validation of Tests

Section 4: The Ethics and Effects of Testing and Assessment

(

GENERAL EDITOR'S INTRODUCTION

ENCYCLOPEDIA OF LANGUAGE AND EDUCATION

This is one of eight volumes of the Encyclopedia of Language and Education published by Kluwer Academic. The publication of this work signals the maturity of the field of 'language and education' as an international and interdisciplinary field of significance and cohesion. These volumes confirm that 'language and education' is much more than the preserve of any single discipline. In designing these volumes, we have tried to recognise the diversity of the field in our selection of contributors and in our choice of topics. The contributors come from every continent and from more than 40 countries. Their reviews discuss language and education issues affecting every country in the world.

We have also tried to recognise the diverse interdisciplinary nature of 'language and education' in the selection of the editorial personnel themselves. The major academic interests of the volume editors confirm this. As principal volume editor for Volume 1, Ruth Wodak has interests in critical linguistics, sociology of language, and language policy. For Volume 2, Viv Edwards has interests in policy and practice in multilingual classrooms and the sociology of language. For Volume 3, Bronwyn Davies has interests in the social psychology of language, the sociology of language, and interdisciplinary studies. For Volume 4, Richard Tucker has interests in language theory, applied linguistics, and the implementation and evaluation of innovative language education programs. For Volume 5, Jim Cummins has interests in the psychology of language and in critical linguistics. For Volume 6, Leo van Lier has interests in applied linguistics and in language theory. For Volume 7, Caroline Clapham has interests in research into second language acquisition and language measurement. And for Volume 8, Nancy Hornberger has interests in anthropological linguistics and in language policy. Finally, as general editor, I have interests in the philosophy and sociology of language, language policy, critical linguistics, and interdisciplinary studies. But the thing that unites us all, including all the contributors to this work, is an interest in the practice and theory of education itself.

People working in the applied and theoretical areas of education and language are often asked questions like the following: 'what is the latest research on such and such a problem?' or 'what do we know about such

C. Clapham and D. Corson (eds), Encyclopedia of Language and Education,
Volume 7: Language Testing and Assessment, ix–xi.
© *1997 Kluwer Academic Publishers. Printed in the Netherlands.*

and such an issue?' Questions like these are asked by many people: by policy makers and practitioners in education; by novice researchers; by publishers trying to relate to an issue; and above all by undergraduate and postgraduate students in the language disciplines. Each of the reviews that appears in this volume tries to anticipate and answer some of the more commonly asked questions about language and education. Taken together, the eight volumes of this Encyclopedia provide answers to more than 200 major questions of this type, and hundreds of subsidiary questions as well.

Each volume of the Encyclopedia of Language and Education deals with a single, substantial subject in the language and education field. The volume titles and their contents appear elsewhere in the pages of this work. Each book-length volume provides more than 20 state-of-the-art topical reviews of the literature. Taken together, these reviews attempt a complete coverage of the subject of the volume. Each review is written by one or more experts in the topic, or in a few cases by teams assembled by experts. As a collection, the Encyclopedia spans the range of subjects and topics normally falling within the scope of 'language and education'. Each volume, edited by an international expert in the subject of the volume, was designed and developed in close collaboration with the general editor of the Encyclopedia, who is a co-editor of each volume as well as general editor of the whole work.

The Encyclopedia has been planned as a necessary reference set for any university or college library that serves a faculty or school of education. Libraries serving academic departments in any of the language disciplines, especially applied linguistics, would also find this a valuable resource. It also seems very relevant to the needs of educational bureaucracies, policy agencies, and public libraries, particularly those serving multicultural or multilingual communities.

The Encyclopedia aims to speak to a prospective readership that is multinational, and to do so as unambiguously as possible. Because each book-size volume deals with a discrete and important subject in language and education, these state-of-the-art volumes also offer authoritative course textbooks in the areas suggested by their titles. This means that libraries will also catalogue these book-size individual volumes in relevant sections of their general collections. To meet this range of uses, the Encyclopedia is published in a hardback edition offering the durability needed for reference collections, and in a future student edition. The hardback edition is also available for single-volume purchase.

Each state-of-the-art review has about 3000 words of text and most follow a similar structure. A list of references to key works cited in each review supplements the information and authoritative opinion that the review contains. Many contributors survey early developments in their topic, major contributions, work in progress, problems and difficulties, and future directions for research and practice. The aim of the reviews, and of the Encyclopedia as a whole, is to give readers access to the international literature and research on each topic.

David Corson
General Editor Encyclopedia of Language and Education
Ontario Institute for Studies in Education of the University of Toronto
Canada

INTRODUCTION

Volume 7 of the Encyclopedia of Language and Education addresses the evaluation of the language proficiency of first and second language users. It forms an integral part of this encyclopedia because assessment, in some form or other, plays an essential part in language education and research.

The volume is divided into four parts, the first of which covers the assessment of single language skills such as reading and writing. This is followed by a section containing reviews of different methods of testing such as integrated testing, performance testing, and the testing of language for specific purposes. Two succeeding reviews, which discuss the assessment of the linguistic proficiency of children, are followed by ones on self-assessment, aptitude testing and the assessment of speech and language disorders. The third part of the volume discusses methods of validating tests using qualitative or quantitative methods, and the final part addresses the ethics and effects of testing and assessment.

CURRENT TRENDS IN TESTING AND ASSESSMENT

For the assessment historian, this volume provides a bird's eye view of current trends in assessment. A similar volume produced ten years ago would have concentrated more on receptive and integrative methods of assessment, and would have focused on the use of new psychometric methods for analysing objectively-marked tests. Now, though, there is more interest in methods of evaluating the productive skills of writing and speaking, and in assessing the validity and reliability of such methods (see, for example, the reviews by Rubin and Schramm, and Cumming). (Basically, a valid test is one that provides accurate information about the trait being measured; for more about this see the section on validity below. A reliable test is one that gives the student a consistent mark, regardless of such factors as choice of examiner, or place or time of assessment.) There is also interest in investigating the different abilities or traits of which language skills are composed (see, for example, the reviews by Weir, Buck and Bachman), and an increasing concern with assessing how well such traits are measured (see, for example, the reviews by Cumming, Fulcher and Pollitt).

C. Clapham and D. Corson (eds), Encyclopedia of Language and Education,
Volume 7: Language Testing and Assessment, xiii–xix.
© *1997 Kluwer Academic Publishers. Printed in the Netherlands.*

FIRST AND SECOND LANGUAGE ASSESSMENT

It is unusual for a book on the assessment of linguistic proficiency to bring together reviews relating to both the L1 and the L2. Since there may be major differences in the processes involved in the acquisition of first and second languages, it might be expected that the authors of the L1 and L2 reviews would approach assessment in different ways. However, although they draw on almost wholly different sets of references, their interests tend to be very similar. For example, Purves and Cumming (L1 and L2 Writing) both report an increasing interest in portfolio assessment; and Rubin and Schramm, and Fulcher (L1 and L2 Speaking) focus on rating scales and ways of improving marker reliability. The most striking difference between the reviews in the two areas is that in the reviews on reading, Vincent (L1) focuses on children's initial literacy, whereas Weir (L2) concentrates on the processes involved in reading for academic purposes.

TESTING AND ASSESSMENT

The reviews in this volume relate to both 'testing' and 'assessment'. However, these two terms are difficult to define. Although it is common to use 'assessment' as a superordinate term covering all forms of evaluation, the terms 'testing' and 'assessment' can also be used interchangeably, or can be used as contrasting terms: 'tests' tend to be designed for large numbers of students, are often for gatekeeping purposes, and, in the case of schools, may be imposed by outside authorities; 'assessments', on the other hand, tend to be carried out on a one-to-one basis, and frequently involve exploratory methods of evaluation which, rather than assigning scores to students, diagnose problems and encourage student motivation. However, usage varies from individual to individual. The fact that the contributors to this volume use the terms in different ways emphasises differences in viewpoints and also the tension between requirements for student grading and/or institutional accountability and teachers' concerns for the development of their individual students. The terms in themselves, though, are, of course, unimportant. What is important is that although large scale and small scale assessments are constrained by different administrative practicalities, they must all be as fair as possible to those they affect. This means that the constructors of all methods of assessment must strive to make these as valid and reliable as possible.

In this introduction, since it seems impossible to distinguish fully between the two terms, I use the terms 'assessment' and 'testing' with both their superordinate and subordinate meanings.

The rest of this introduction highlights those areas which seem to be attracting most interest at the moment.

VALIDITY

Over the years views of validity have changed. The 1954 American Psychological Association Standards (described in Davidson, Turner and Huhta's review) cited four kinds of validity: content, construct, concurrent and predictive validity. Content and construct validity related respectively to the content of test items and the linguistic theory on which the test was based; concurrent and predictive validity related to comparisons of students' test results with external criteria such as other test results or teachers' rankings. By the 1966 edition, concurrent and predictive validity had been conflated into criterion-related validity, and in the 1975 edition all four were subsumed under the single heading of construct validity. (For more about changing views of validity, see Banerjee and Luoma's review.) Most of the reviews in the first three sections of this volume are concerned, either implicitly or explicitly, with aspects of this construct validity. However, not everyone uses the same terminology: Weir, and McNamara both refer to content validity, Oscarson refers to concurrent validity, and Cumming to predictive validity. Some of the authors refer to construct validity in its all-encompassing meaning (see, for example, Bachman and Eignor, and Rea-Dickins); and some leave validity implications to be inferred.

In 1989, Messick published an influential paper in which he added a new dimension, 'consequential validity', to the existing view of construct validity. Consequential validity relates to the effects, both intended and unintended, of a test on all those on whom it impinges. (For a clear and concise description of what Messick had in mind, see his 1996 article in *Language Testing*.) As the reviews in Section Four of this volume show, there has recently been a surge of interest in issues relating to test impact, accountability and ethics. This increased concern is not, of course, limited to assessment, but is prevalent throughout the field of education. A few years ago, as Norton and Hamp-Lyons point out in their reviews on accountability and fairness, there were few papers on the subject but now such papers are presented at all the major applied linguistics conferences. Similarly, Wall shows how interest in washback has grown in the last few years, and Davidson, Turner and Huhta chart the spread of documentation relating to standards and codes of practice.

The current concern with construct validity, together with the recent availability of computer-based analysis techniques, has led to an increased interest in the qualitative and quantitative validation of tests. As the review by Banerjee and Luoma shows, qualitative studies using such methods as think-aloud protocols, classroom observations and linguistic analyses of students' writing and speaking are mushrooming. Quantitative methods of test validation, too, have changed in the past few years. Bachman and Eignor describe how recent developments in areas such as performance assessment and computer adaptive testing have led to advances in Item

Response Theory applications, and how increased interest in construct validation has encouraged a greater use of factor analysis and the development of more sophisticated methods of structural equation modelling. They also describe current quantitative attempts to attach proficiency descriptors to scores on scales.

With the increase in the use of single tasks to assess students' performance, especially in the areas of writing and speaking, has come an increased concern with the generalisability of results. Purves, Fulcher, and McNamara, among others, discuss the importance of being able to generalise from performance on a single task to a student's wider linguistic proficiency, and Bachman gives an introduction to generalisability theory and the uses to which it can be put.

The availability, too, of comparatively user-friendly Rasch analysis computer programs has led many researchers to apply Rasch multi-faceted measurement to the analysis of rater performance (see Pollitt's review), and this, together with the increased interest in more open-ended methods of assessment, has led to greater interest in the construction and uses of rating scales for assessing compositions and interviews (see the reviews by McNamara, Pollitt and Bachman). Fulcher, and Lynch and Davidson discuss the need for rating scales to be devised empirically, and Purves, Cumming, and Rubin and Schramm describe research into the validity and reliability of existing rating scales.

TEST METHODS

Although the emphasis in this volume is on tests of production, there is some discussion of other kinds of testing. For example, Weir discusses the pros and cons of multiple choice and short answer questions in reading tests, and Weir, Buck, and Read discuss integrative tasks such as cloze and dictation. In addition Buck discusses the difficulties involved in designing listening tasks that test what we know about listening. Tasks for testing writing and speaking are described in many reviews, with Cumming, and Purves, for example, discussing composition tasks, and Banerjee and Luoma describing ways of discovering the effects on students' speech of different elicitation techniques. There is also interest in what McKay, and Lynch and Davidson call 'alternative methods of assessment' by which they mean classroom-based evaluation such as portfolio assessment (see also Purves, Rubin and Schramm, and Cumming), and classroom observations (see Rea-Dickins and Rixon). Several reviews discuss ways of making tests as similar to 'real life' as possible: Douglas shows that the aim in Language for Specific Purposes tests is to make tasks as authentic as possible and to take account of the interaction between language knowledge and specific purpose content knowledge; McNamara describes the work-sample approach to performance testing which aims at a realistic representation of real world tasks; and Lewkowicz shows how test writers attempt to simulate real life by integrating tests of different linguistic skills such as reading, listening and writing. In direct contrast to this, Rea-Dickins and Read focus on the separate testing of grammar and vocabulary respectively: Rea-Dickins looks at existing ways of assessing grammar and shows how difficult it is to test it 'communicatively'; Read discusses ways of testing vocabulary width and depth, and considers the importance of context in lexical assessment. The authors inquire into the roles of grammar and vocabulary in the assessment of language skills, and both seek fuller information about the underlying constructs. (The use of 'construct' in this context refers to the combination of traits or abilities of which an individual's knowledge of grammar or vocabulary is composed.)

LANGUAGE CONSTRUCTS

This search for a deeper understanding of language constructs is a common theme throughout this volume. In his review on aptitude testing, for example, Cascallar calls for a greater understanding of the components of language proficiency; and Weir, focusing on the abilities involved in reading, discusses the variations in readers' interpretations according to such factors as their purposes for reading, and their background knowledge. All the reviews on testing specific skills include pleas for more research into the construct of the skill being tested.

SELF-ASSESSMENT

As learners are encouraged to be more concerned with setting their own language learning goals, the role of self-assessment becomes increasingly important. Oscarson points out that self-assessment may be more useful in day-to-day teaching than in 'high-stakes tests', and describes research into ways of helping students to assess their own L2 skills. Piolat describes another aspect of self-assessment. She bases her review on the field of cognitive psychology, and describes how L1 writers assess and revise their written texts. She describes the differences between the revision processes of novice and experienced writers, and calls for more research into writers' self-assessments as they write in different genres.

SPEECH AND LANGUAGE DISORDERS

An interesting new field of assessment research is covered by Baker and Chenery. In a review which comes, at least in part, from the field of speech pathology, they describe different types of speech and language disorder, listing existing ways of assessing them, and commenting on the strengths and weaknesses of these procedures.

COMPUTER-BASED TESTING

In their review on computer-based assessment, Gruba and Corbel mainly concentrate on computer adaptive testing. Neither they nor the other contributors to this volume focus on computer test tasks since, in spite of past expectations of a boom in computer-based testing, few novel computer test types have yet been devised. However, it seems likely that over the next few years the explosion in computer accessibility, memory and sophistication will transform methods of testing and assessment. Buck, for example, refers to the potential use of multi-media input for listening tests: the use of film and good sound effects will enable listening tests to incorporate those visual stimuli which comprise so important a part of some aspects of listening (see Bostrom's review). However, before launching too swiftly into computer-based assessment it is necessary to investigate what exactly is being tested. McNamara points out, for example, that although there have been attempts to present reading tests on computers it is not yet known whether the processes involved in reading on screen and on paper are truly equivalent: although a computer-administered test of reading should be able to replicate computer users' real world computer reading, it may not be a substitute for a more conventional paper-based test.

FUTURE DIRECTIONS

This brings us back to the call for more research into language constructs. As more becomes known about the factors underlying the different linguistic skills, and as computer-testing finally becomes more prevalent, it seems likely that researchers will focus more attention on *how* the skills of reading, writing, listening and speaking should be assessed. In addition, there is likely to be more emphasis on performance testing and alternative methods of assessment, with, perhaps, more emphasis on the reliability of such measures. There is sure too to be more research into test impact and the ethics of assessment, and more research into the effects of assessment on peoples of different ages and cultures.

We shall know soon enough how accurate these predictions are, but of one thing we can be certain: as Spolsky points out in *Measured Words* (1996), developments in testing wax and wane, so that over the next few years some aspects of assessment will fall out of favour, while others will be newly reinvented.

ACKNOWLEDGEMENT

The editors would like to thank the Lancaster University Language Testing Research Group for their ideas about which aspects of language testing and assessment should be covered in this volume.

Caroline Clapham

Section 1

Testing Language Skills

DENIS VINCENT

THE TESTING OF READING IN THE MOTHER TONGUE

INTRODUCTION

Reading is probably more often tested than any other skill in education systems which practice educational testing and assessment. However, it is important to distinguish between the reading 'tests' and other means whereby reading ability is assessed. Any task or procedure which elicits information about a person's reading ability could be loosely regarded as a 'test' of reading. However, there is an important distinction to be made between reading tests (and certain testing techniques) which are the products of empirical development procedures and a broad range of informal classroom assessment practices which teachers may use – as well as tests – to obtain information about how well individuals or groups of learners are performing.

The development and use of formalised tests is a well documented activity with accounts in the academic and professional literature. Moreover, the tests or test procedures themselves are usually published and available for public scrutiny. In contrast, informal, local practices by individual teachers are more elusive although in practice there may be considerable similarities in content. For example, the cloze procedure is used widely in both formal empirically-developed standardized tests and teacher devised versions (Rye, 1982). It is of course quite reasonable for teachers to model their own local informal assessment practices on the content of published or public examples. In fact, there is also influence in the other direction. Test developers may well seek to model their tests on naturally occurring classroom practices.

However, for the reasons given above, this account will concentrate primarily on examples of tests (and to a lesser extent testing techniques) which are formalised and exist in some published form.

Formalised reading tests can vary considerably in format, design and approach but a typical standardised test might consist of printed texts or tasks to be used to assess reading performance and a manual for administering, marking and scoring and interpreting the test. The tasks themselves may be either silent (written) or oral. The former will normally be designed for simultaneous use with groups of readers. In many English-speaking countries tests for use in schools and colleges are marketed by commercial publishers although national governments and regional administrations are also significant clients for the development and use of reading tests. Tests

C. Clapham and D. Corson (eds), Encyclopedia of Language and Education,
Volume 7: Language Testing and Assessment, 1–10.
© *1997 Kluwer Academic Publishers. Printed in the Netherlands.*

have also been central to international studies comparing literacy in different countries (Elley, 1994) although in many respects the testing of reading is an insular activity embedded in national/local concerns. It is notable, for example, that reading tests in English rarely transfer across national boundaries. (For the testing of L1 reading in languages other than English, see the reviews in Section Five of Volume 2.)

As well as specific formal tests, a number of test-like techniques and methods for assessing reading exist which are published or are sufficiently well-documented to be regarded as established procedures. Miscue analysis (Gollasch, 1982; Arnold, 1992) and 'think-aloud protocols' (Brown & Lytle, 1988) are important examples of such methods. (For more about reading test techniques see Weir's review in this volume.)

This review does not describe the classroom methods used by reading teachers informally to assess reading achievement. This is not to say that teachers' normal classroom practices do not provide valuable models for the design of formal tests and testing procedures. Indeed, there is a significant body of thought about educational assessment generally which challenges the role of testing in favour of broader modes of assessment which emphasise:

- the teacher's role as a gatherer of evidence about, and as an observer of, performance in authentic contexts;
- the teacher's capacity to make valid (and reliable) professional judgements about reading attainment if suitable frameworks or structures are provided.

This approach is most firmly established in the USA, and the International Reading Association and the National Council of Teachers of English (1994) have produced a policy document which applies such thinking to the assessment of literacy. Gipps (1994) provides a useful general account of how this 'performance assessment' movement has developed in the USA and notes that, independently, there have been similar initiatives in Britain. Harrison & Salinger (1997) contains a number of accounts by British and US contributors of the development of reading assessment schemes along such lines. It remains to be seen how far such forms of assessment will become established.

USES OF READING TESTS

There are four main types of reading test user:
1. administrators;
2. researchers;
3. clinicians/psychologists;
4. teachers.

Administrators

Administrators usually have simple and clearly-defined purposes for testing reading. They need system-wide regular information about the functioning of the education services and institutions for which they are responsible. Numeracy and general cognitive ability/intelligence are also often part of such agenda but it is nevertheless literacy, and reading in particular, which is most frequently the focus of concern. Public account-ability over standards of literacy is a central (and controversial) function, as is the need to monitor standards and evaluate the impact of organisational or curriculum changes. Data from reading test surveys can also inform decisions about the allocation of resources although evidence from one major British study (Gipps et al., 1983) revealed that this is not always done efficiently. One of the most effective functions of testing is screening for children who are failing to progress in learning to read or are at risk of doing so. Testing is sometimes mandated on a system-wide basis for this purpose.

Researchers

In reading research, and indeed in educational research more generally, test results are one of the most common forms of dependent variable. This is particularly the case in evaluation studies and method/treatment com-parisons where the effectiveness of a particular intervention in method or curriculum may be ultimately judged by its effects on learners' standard-ised test scores. In fact, much of what is known or believed about reading rests on the assumption that 'reading' is synonymous with 'reading test performance'.

Clinicians

It is common practice to include tests of reading where a child is referred for clinical assessment, either because there is a particular difficulty with literacy learning or because there is some other reason for a general edu-cational assessment to be made. Clinicians such as reading specialists or educational psychologists will normally use individually-administered tests at this point, although they may also refer to previously-obtained group test results. In cases of reading difficulty, the initial purpose of testing will be to establish the severity of the reading problem and whether it is at all exceptional, when considered in relation to other tests of intellectual ability. At a further stage, tests and testing techniques may be used to investigate the nature of a reading problem more deeply.

Of the special challenges which face the testing of reading, the identi-fication or diagnosis of specific reading difficulty (or dyslexia) is perhaps the most formidable. Although there is widespread popular acceptance of the existence of such a condition, a definitive and accepted test for it has yet to be devised. The established clinical practice in assessing possible cases of dyslexia is (a) to exclude possible social and emotional factors which might account for failure in learning to read and (b) to establish a discrepancy between intelligence (as measured by a standardised individual test) and attainment (again normally assessed by standardised testing). Stanovich (1992) has argued that the intelligence-attainment discrepancy criterion is a theoretically flawed basis for distinguishing between dyslexics and other 'common or garden' backward readers and suggests that a test which measured discrepancy between reading comprehension and listening comprehension would be a better criterion. 'Dyslexic' readers would be those, if any, who were unable to read material they were able to understand verbally. Such a procedure would also have considerable merits for clinical and classroom use, although it remains to be seen whether test developers will succeed in meeting the considerable challenge of creating such an instrument.

Teachers

The use teachers make of reading tests is not as simply typified as it is for the previous three types of user. On the one hand, most of the managerial, evaluative and clinical functions discussed above are encountered at school or classroom level. As managers, teachers need feedback about the literacy levels and progress of class groups and individual learners, they may need to evaluate their own practice, they will need to screen and to make clinical assessments of failing readers. Testing is a powerful tool for all of these important purposes and suitable examples are readily available commercially to teachers in many countries. However, teachers in practice remain divided and ambivalent over testing. While some teachers may indeed be able and willing to use the 'technology' of testing in these ways, others may consider that such tests are nothing but an unwelcome externally-imposed burden.

WHAT DO READING TESTS MEASURE?

The content and format of reading tests are diverse (see below) and the aspects of reading which test developers have sought or claimed to measure have also been wide-ranging. Farr & Carey (1986) produced a definitive review of the testing of reading which dealt with published standardised reading tests used in primary and secondary education in the USA. In their analysis they identify the following categories:

- comprehension;
- word recognition skills and vocabulary;
- study skills;
- rate.

This is a representative, if broad, indication of what reading tests cover. It does not include attitudinal or motivational variables in reading, although Pumfrey (1986) reviews an extensive research literature providing considerable support for the claim that reading attitudes can be measured.

Within the categories used by Farr and Carey there is considerable variation. For example, tests have been developed which break down the skills underlying word recognition into visual, auditory and phonic components (e.g. Daniels & Diack, 1958). Similar attempts have been made to create batteries of tests designed to differentiate between higher order comprehension skills (e.g. Vincent & de la Mare, 1986). Tests based on such multi-faceted models of reading skill aim to provide teachers with profiles of readers' relative strengths and weaknesses in different aspects of reading. However, empirical studies have consistently shown that different types of reading tests tend to be substantially intercorrelated and test-based research has yet to verify theoretical descriptions of reading in terms of separate component skills. (For more about the reading process, see the review by Goodman in Volume 2.)

ORIGINS OF READING TESTS

The insularity of reading tests noted above is strongly exemplified in the way reading tests have developed over time in different countries. For example, in the USA the testing of reading was pioneered in the first half of the 20th Century by researchers such as Edward Thorndike, Arthur Gates and William Gray. There is little evidence to suggest their work had any practical impact on the testing of reading in Britain however, where Cyril Burt, Phillip Ballard and Fred Schonell were responsible for developing the first published reading tests.

Although mother tongue reading tests produced in one country are rarely adopted in another there are certain common cross-national influences which have probably affected their development. In particular, the testing of reading has been very much part of a larger mental and psychological measurement movement (Linn, 1993). This has led to the creation of the technology of psychometrics which is applied in a similar fashion by constructors of reading tests in different countries and languages.

Another important common factor has been the need felt by governments and administrators for information about the literacy levels being attained in school systems. Psychometric tests of reading have provided an efficient and powerful tool for this purpose.

However, a systematic documentation or analysis of such tendencies and influences have yet to be undertaken. A compilation of historical accounts of how the testing of reading has evolved in different countries is long overdue!

CONTEMPORARY MODES OF TESTING READING

The content and design of reading tests are usually determined by the circumstances in which the development work is undertaken. While the format and purpose of some reading tests have been largely determined by their constructors, it is increasingly common for tests to be the product of commercial, political or administrative initiatives. For example, where a test is to be developed to assess reading attainment amongst children following a nationally or locally prescribed reading curriculum the specification for the test design and content is likely to be determined by the form or content of the curriculum in question.

Bormuth (1970) and Carver (1992) have suggested theoretical models for the design of reading tests and Carver has applied his model in a series of empirical studies. There are also texts written for practitioners which seek to provide frameworks for the selection and use of reading tests (e.g. Pumfrey, 1977; Vincent, 1985). However, in practice there is no widely-accepted body of reading test theory which can be regarded as a standard classification of reading tests as they now exist. Nevertheless, some analysis can be made in terms of function, mode, level of text and basis for scoring/marking:

1. Function: normative/norm-referenced (standardised)/criterion-refer-enced/diagnostic
   It will be clear from previous paragraphs that the normative function predominates in the testing of reading. Commentary upon criterion-referenced reading tests is to be found in Vincent (1985) and in Lynch and Davidson's review in this volume. Diagnostic testing of reading is discussed by Turner (1997).
2. Mode: individual (oral)/group (silent); timed (speed test)/untimed (power test)
   There are some fundamental differences in the conditions under which reading can be tested. Tests designed for individual administration normally focus on oral reading while tests designed for group admin-istration invariably require silent written responses. The majority of reading tests are untimed 'power' tests which differentiate reading ability through tasks or questions representing a gradient of increas-ing difficulty. Relatively few reading tests have measured rate of reading. Although functionally important for mature reading, speed is not normally significant in initial teaching curricula. Farr & Carey (1986) provide a useful review of US reading rate tests.

3. Level of text or content: pre-reading (non-textual)/word /sentences/
   continuous texts
   Even a brief inspection of a representative cross-section of published
   tests will reveal a striking diversity of content. This reflects the great
   range of age and reading levels which testing can cover. The pre- and
   initial reading stages have been particularly active areas for test development. Early tests were concerned with 'reading readiness', testing
   cognitive, perceptual, motor and linguistic developments thought to
   be necessary for success in learning to read. Typically, these employed pictorial material, symbols and diagrams rather than written
   language. Subsequently the focus shifted to testing early linguistic
   awareness and the development of concepts relating to the nature and
   purpose of print (Downing, Schaefer & Ayers, 1993; Clay, 1979).
   The simplest tests of early reading itself consist of lists of words of
   graded difficulty. Typically, the words are read aloud and the number
   of correct decodings are scored. Comprehension via word-picture
   matching items may also be tested. Graded word reading lists are
   a popular testing medium and can provide norms across a wide age
   range. However, reading lists of unrelated words have been widely-
   criticised for reducing reading to 'barking at print'.
   Sentence-based tests provide a somewhat more sophisticated level of
   assessment. Again, oral and silent modes are possible; the latter may
   well employ a multiple-choice completion format (e.g. The cup / and
   / with / under / is / on the table.).
   Both word- and sentence-lists tests have psychometric advantages:
   statistically reliable tests capable of discriminating over wide attainment ranges can be constructed – albeit at the risk of adopting a
   trivialised or distorted definition of reading. By basing testing on
   continuous and connected texts greater authenticity is achieved, arguably making it possible to assess readers' ability to respond to
   features of text beyond the sentence level.
4. Marking and interpretation: objective/judgmental
   A powerful factor in determining the nature of a reading test is the extent to which it can be objectively marked and scored so that decisions
   about the correctness/appropriateness of responses are automatic and
   independent of judgement or interpretation by human assessors. Traditionally, administrators (and researchers) have favoured such tests:
   time and cost in administering, marking and scoring tests are minimised; results are quantifiable and publicly perceived as impartial
   and unbiased.
   Such considerations carry less weight where testing is initiated by
   practitioners for teaching purposes. There is greater scope for sacri-
   ficing objectivity in exchange for greater richness of insight into the
   nature of the reading process. This involves making assessments from

within structured procedural frameworks. Typically these require administration and/or scoring and interpretation skills to be developed through training, practice and experience. Standardised individual reading tests, published Informal Reading Inventories (most common in the USA) or the national curriculum standard assessment tasks used in England and Wales are contrasting examples. In theory, once individuals are trained to administer and mark such tests they will not vary significantly from one another. Thus the results for any particular reader should not depend upon the identity of the person who assessed them. However, as in practice there is likely to be some inter-tester variation, the assessments should be considered semi-objective rather than fully objective.

PROBLEMS AND DIFFICULTIES

The previous sections have sketched out a map of the prevailing model of reading testing. This treats reading as a measurable and predictable psychological process which can be reliably and representatively sampled through performance on generally simple tasks such as reading aloud a list of graded words or answering multiple-choice comprehension questions. Historically, educators have relied upon the technology of mental measurement – psychometrics – to assess reading and the content of existing reading tests has been shaped to fit the psychometric model. However, for those concerned with the curriculum, matters of test content and format are increasingly problematic because of the pressure for what is tested to become what is taught. It will be evident that what has been outlined above does not amount to a curriculum for reading.

The testing of reading is a conservative enterprise. The 'end-users' of reading tests have not traditionally been eager clients for innovation. In the final paragraph of their book Farr and Carey (1986) note with regret the lack of change in test use over the preceding 50 years. Any future changes in the testing of reading will have to take place in spite of these attitudes.

FUTURE DIRECTIONS

Developments in Information Technology (IT) have already affected the way reading is tested and may continue to do so. The already highly-developed optical document reading and scanning technology for rapid processing of group reading test papers is likely to become increasingly flexible and versatile, possibly extending to recognition of hand-written responses.

Of greater interest could be developments in computer-mediated reading assessment, in which tasks are presented via non-print media, such as display screens and audio, with oral and written/keyed responses being recorded and analysed directly by the administering computer. In certain areas of educational assessment computer-mediated testing is already well-established, particularly in the form of computer adaptive testing (CAT) in which the response to earlier questions or tasks determines which questions will be presented subsequently. (For more about CAT see the review by Gruba and Corbel in this volume.) Bunderson, Inouye & Olsen (1993) optimistically review these general developments although whether there will be significant advantages over conventional modes of administration for reading in particular remains to be seen. The area in reading which is most likely to profit from CAT is the assessment of word-recognition processes in failing readers. Here assessment focuses on responding to letter strings and single word tasks (e.g. Snowling & Goulandris, 1996). In clinical settings there may be advantages in employing CAT to carry out the assessment.

The impact of IT in the mainstream assessment of reading is less easy to foresee. At a theoretical and pedagogical level it would be necessary to create 'expert systems' for assessing normal reading processes in ways which could beneficially be implemented in computer form. Schwartz (1984) presents an early attempt at this but subsequent progress has been very modest. (For more about IT and literacy see the review by Abbott in Volume 2.)

Foreseeable advantages are thus speed, clerical convenience and volume of data handling but these are generic to educational assessment rather than reading-specific. It is questionable whether such developments would mean reading per se would be better assessed. Institutions concerned with teaching initial literacy are probably the least well-equipped to conduct computer-mediated testing on a viable scale. This has provided little incentive for the necessary test or application development work.

There are also cultural difficulties. Reading is still predominantly a paper and print based activity and the value of transferring texts normally encountered in this way to screen displays for assessing the capacity to read them is far from self-evident. However, the ways in which the use of IT could change and re-define literacy itself will present educators, and ultimately test developers, with entirely new challenges.

University of East London, England

REFERENCES

Arnold, H.: 1984, *Diagnostic Reading Record*, Hodder & Stoughton, Sevenoaks.
Ballard P.B.: 1923, *The New Examiner*, University of London Press Ltd, London.
Bormuth, J.R.: 1970, *On the Theory of Achievement Test Items*, University of Chicago Press, Chicago, IL.
Brown, C.S & Lytle S.L.: 1988, 'Merging assessment and instruction: Protocols in the classroom', in S.M. Glazer, L.W. Searfoss, & L.M. Gentile (eds.), *Reexamining*

Reading Diagnosis: New Trends and Procedures, International Reading Association, Newark, NJ.

Bunderson, C.V., Inouye, D.K. & Olsen J.B.: 1993, 'The four generations of computerized educational measurement', in R.L. Linn (ed.), *Educational Measurement* (third edition), American Council on Education and The Oryx Press, Phoenix, AZ.

Burt C.: 1962, *Mental and Scholastic Tests* (fourth edition), Staples Press, London.

Carver, R.P.: 1992, 'What do standardised tests of reading comprehension measure in terms of efficiency, accuracy and rate?' *Reading Research Quarterly* 27(4), 346–359.

Clay, M.: 1987, *The Early Detection of Reading Difficulties* (third edition), Heinemann, Auckland, New Zealand.

Daniels, J.C. & Diack, H.: 1958, *The Standard Reading Tests*, Granada Publishing, St Albans, England.

Downing, J. Schaer, B. & Ayres, D.A.: 1993, *LARR Test of Emergent Literacy*, NFER-Nelson, Slough.

Elley W.B. (ed.): 1994, *The IEA Study of Reading Literacy: Achievement and Instruction in Thirty-Two School Systems*, Elsevier Science Ltd/Pergamon, Oxford.

Farr, R. & Carey, R.F.: 1986, *Reading: What Can be Measured?* (second edition), International Reading Association, Newark, NJ.

Gipps, C.V.: 1994 *Beyond Testing: Towards a Theory of Educational Assessment*, The Falmer Press, London.

Gipps, C.V. Steadman, S., Blackstone, T. & Stierer, B.: 1983, *Testing Children: Standardised Testing in Schools and LEAs*, Heinemann, London.

Gollasch, F.V. (ed.): 1982, *Language and Literacy: The Selected Writings of Kenneth S. Goodman* (Volume I), Routledge & Kegan Paul, Boston, MA.

Harrison, C. & Salinger, T.: 1997, *International Perspectives on Reading Assessment: Theory and Practice*, Routledge, London.

International Reading Association and National Council of Teachers of English: 1994, *Standards for the Assessment of Reading and Writing*.

Linn, R.L.: 1993, *Educational Measurement* (third edition), American Council on Education and The Oryx Press, Phoenix, AZ.

Pumfrey, P.: 1977, *Measuring Reading Abilities: Concepts, Sources and Applications*, Hodder & Stoughton, London.

Pumfrey, P.: 1986 'Measuring attitudes towards reading', in D. Vincent, A.K. Pugh, & G. Brooks (eds.), *Assessing Reading: Proceedings of the UKRA Colloquium on the Testing and Assessment of Reading*, Macmillan, Basingstoke.

Schonell F.J. & Schonell F.E.: 1960, *Diagnostic and Attainment Testing* (fourth edition), Oliver and Boyd, Edinburgh.

Schwartz, S.: 1984 *Measuring Reading Competence: A Theoretical-Prescriptive Approach*, Plenum Press, New York.

Snowling, M. & Goulandris N.: 1995 'Assessing reading skills', in E. Funnell & M. Stuart (eds.), *Learning to Read: Psychology in the Classroom*, Blackwell, Oxford.

Stanovich, K.E.: 1992, 'The theoretical and practical consequences of discrepancy definitions of dyslexia', in M. Snowling & M. Thomson (eds.), *Dyslexia: Integrating Theory and Practice*, Whurr, London.

Turner, M.: 1997, *The Psychological Assessment of Dyslexia*, Whurr, London.

Vincent, D.: 1985, *Reading Tests in the Classroom: an Introduction*, NFER-Nelson, Slough, England.

Vincent, D. & de La Mare, M.: 1986, *The Effective Reading Tests*, NFER-Nelson, Slough, England.

ALAN C. PURVES*

THE ASSESSMENT OF WRITING IN THE MOTHER TONGUE

Written Composition is an ill-defined domain. If one looks at the kinds of measures of writing performance used by schools and universities, not to mention national boards of education, from the perspective of assessment theory, the current practice is haphazard and atheoretical. There have been several efforts at mapping the domain through an examination of writing tasks and through an examination of perceived criteria for good writing, but in general these have been ignored in many practical assessments of student performance. The problems in writing assessment are similar to those in the assessment of any form of performance: the selection of representative tasks to sample the breadth of the domain, the conditions under which the assessment takes place, and the nature of the criteria and judging of the performance of the students.

EARLY DEVELOPMENT

Writing and composition have formed a part of the assessment of learning from the time of the earliest Chinese Civil Service Examinations. But until the past century writing was seen as a medium of examination rather than as an end. That is to say, examinations were set in various subjects and the candidates were asked to compose extended answers to the questions. The responses were judged by experts in the subject who commented on both the knowledge and writing skills of the candidate. This situation still obtains in the school-leaving and university entrance examinations of many countries around the world.

During the course of the twentieth century, however, attention turned to composition as a subject in itself. The practice in most countries was for some central group to set a common topic for the students, establish the time and conditions for the assessment, and then judge the resulting compositions. In general the group was composed of experts and teachers, and the judgment was often done by individual markers operating alone with only a minimal rubric. The judges, it was considered, had, after all, set topics and marked papers for decades in their classrooms, and the situation of the large examination differed little from that of the classroom.

---

* It is with great regret that the publishers have to announce that Alan Purves did not live to see the publication of this review.

C. Clapham and D. Corson (eds), Encyclopedia of Language and Education,
Volume 7: Language Testing and Assessment, 11–19.
© *1997 Kluwer Academic Publishers. Printed in the Netherlands.*

Such methods of assessment remained the norm in many countries around the world, for either school matriculation or university entrance.

In the United States, the assessment of writing as a subject of its own came into sharp focus in the 1930s; groups of markers or raters began to be assembled and some attention was paid to uniformity or reliability. In general, however, although the assessment of writing was practiced extensively by university committees and national or regional boards, it did not come to be the object of serious study until the 1950s. This was partly because changes in the populations seeking admission to further education made it necessary to have measures of language familiarity and proficiency. As a result many of the tests prepared through the 1940s and 1950s were multiple-choice measures of grammatical concepts and usage and there was little measurement of the ability to write extensively. After a series of studies of the validity of these measures, however (see Braddock, 1963 for a summary of several of these studies), there came to be an increasing demand for direct measures of writing. This cry has been generally heeded in the United States, and indirect measures are now used mainly for preliminary screening or as a supplement.

Study in composition has, in the past, focused primarily on the nature of the scoring of writing performance. To a lesser extent there has been research on the nature of the task, and it is only recently that there have been studies of the conditions under which the writing takes place.

MAJOR CONTRIBUTIONS

Among the early research studies in writing assessment, two stand out, both of them conducted in the early 1960s in the United States. One study (French et al., 1961) looked at the way in which different raters examined and judged compositions. A set of compositions was given to groups of raters, who came from a variety of professions; for example, there were English teachers, editors, lawyers, business people, and teachers of other subjects. Each group had to decide which of nine categories (performance levels) a composition belonged to and had to place that composition physically in the appropriate pile. Each group then commented on why they had rated it as they did. No composition was placed in fewer than five piles, and the comments revealed that different groups applied or emphasized different criteria. From the study the researchers concluded that a composition could be judged on the basis of content, development, organization, style, wording, and mechanics. A group of raters or judges then looked at a sample of compositions, developed a scoring scale, and selected a set of compositions that illustrated each of the defined performance levels. The scale was then applied to the larger body of compositions using some form of multiple marking.

This study has been emulated and refined in a number of different ways, and has spawned two major approaches to the systematic grading of a composition.

One such approach is called the 'holistic' approach. Although at first it may appear to be like general impression marking, it takes into account the major factors that French et al. found and derives from these a scoring scheme that focuses on a weighting of the factors. It may call for the marker to give separate marks for each factor selected, an approach often referred to as 'modified holistic', or 'analytic'. Alternatively, the scheme may create a score description noting the combination of the factors that constitute that score category. Many types of holistic schemes have been developed, but it is not yet known whether there can be any sort of generalization across schemes (Purves, 1992a). (For more about holistic and analytic methods of marking see the review by Cumming in this volume.)

The second approach to scoring was established by Lloyd-Jones in the 1970s (see Cooper & Odell, 1977) and was derived from an examination of the rhetorical demands of the topic. This was followed by the focusing on a set of factors that were considered a priori to form a criterion for successful performance on the topic. The scoring scheme was based upon rhetorical theory, and often focused upon the modes of discourse that were used to generate the specifications for the assessment itself. These modes of discourse were generally based on the work of currently fashionable rhetoricians, particularly Moffett, Kinneavy, and Britton. See Britton, Burgess, Martin, McLeod & Rosen, 1975; Kinneavy, 1971; Moffett, 1968 Thus, if an assignment or task was considered a narrative, the scoring would be based on the degree to which writers adhered to the general conventions of narrative.

There is also a third approach to scoring, the 'traditional' approach, where an expert marker assesses a composition according to general impression; this method is often used in examinations. The expert marker selects a number of compositions which she or he deems superior, a number that are 'fair', and a number that are 'poor'. There may be some discussion of the qualities that lead to the rating, but in general they remain undefined. The raters are then asked to examine these 'range finders', and to make as quick a judgment as possible on each of the subsequent compositions in the set. The experience of leaders in this process is that the longer a rater looks at a particular composition, the more likely the score is to vary from the first impression. This impression scoring can be highly reliable, but the approach has been severely criticized by those who advocate the other two.

The second study (Godschalk, Coffman, and Swineford, 1968), took up the issue of reliability and validity more extensively. The study sought to determine whether a single composition scored using the general impression method could predict the scores given to a body of compositions written by the same student. The students also took a multiple-choice vocabulary examination (the SAT-V). The vocabulary test proved to be the best predictor of the broader composition score, but this study set forth a number of prediction and reliability studies that were conducted over the next decade. The best summary studies were conducted in the 1980s (Breland, 1983; Breland & Young, 1984). These showed that the best estimate of a student's writing performance could be derived from multiple observations involving a variety of tasks and judged by a variety of raters.

In the 1980s, the International Association for the Evaluation of Educational Achievement (IEA) conducted a study of written composition in the mother tongue that involved students and teachers in a large number of countries (for the final assessment, the countries included Chile, England, Finland, Germany [Hamburg], Hungary, Indonesia, Italy, Netherlands, New Zealand, Nigeria, Sweden, Thailand, The United States, and Wales). The study covered both research into the assessment of writing and a study of comparative achievement (Gorman, Purves & Degenhart, 1988; Purves, 1992a). (Various national reports of this study are cited in Purves, 1992b.)

For the study there needed to be common tasks across countries and cultures and therefore there had to be a common depiction of the domain of writing, standard administrations, and a common scoring rubric. Analysis of current theories of composition and contemporary rhetorics as well as analysis of the tasks submitted from each of the countries show that a writing task may be considered to provide a cognitive problem for the writer or to offer the writer a discourse function which has to be met. In the array of cognitive problems, the writer may see herself as transcribing material where the form and the content are given or are available in long-term memory (reading or lecture notes, certain lists, stream-of-consciousness journals); organizing or reorganizing known or available material (writing reports, directions, narratives, and the like); inventing new material, or transferring it into new structures.

The discourse functions that may underlie a writing task are: the metalingual, where the discourse is designed primarily to help the writer learn; the expressive or emotive, where the writer is seeking to express her opinions or feelings; the referential, where the writer is aiming at presenting information clearly; the conative, where the writer is seeking to convince or persuade the reader; the poetic, where the writer is focusing on the text as an object to delight or please the reader, and the phatic, where the aim is to keep writer and reader in touch.

But the assignment of a composition consists of more than cognitive demand and discourse function. The IEA study identified 15 dimensions of a composition assignment:

A. Instruction
B. Stimulus
C. Cognitive demand
D. Purpose
E. Role
F. Audience
G. Content
H. Rhetorical specification

I. Tone, Style
J. Advance Preparation
K. Length
L. Format
M. Time
N. Draft
O. Criteria

The research team also explored the characteristics of the criteria by which compositions are judged. Replicating the French study internationally, the research team found the same set of factors with one exception, an additional affective response to the writer or the composition. Based on this analysis, the project used a scoring scheme that included each of the factors as well as a general impression score. The use of separate factor scores allowed for the comparison of factors across compositions (since each student wrote on three topics selected from the domain). The result of the study showed that despite attempts to create a standard scoring system, scores for a student's performance tended to vary according to the topic. More particularly, raters tended to display cultural biases when rating compositions, so that the application of a scoring scheme and scale tended to produce task-specific and situation or culture-specific scores. This finding tends to corroborate other studies of writing assessment as well as findings in other fields of performance assessment – such as competitive athletics and the arts. Other studies demonstrate the strong influence there is on scoring of external factors such as whether the texts are word-processed or hand-written, the color of the ink (which may produce a gender bias on the part of the raters), and the conditions under which the scoring sessions take place (see Wolfe et al. as well as a variety of articles in *Writing Assessment*). The nature of writing assessment is most carefully studied in a recent work by Li (1996), who looked at expert judges in China and the United States and studied their comments on papers written by students from each culture. The judges' comments indicated that their judgments of writing were deeply rooted in their culture's religious practices and beliefs, philosophical and intellectual history, and traditions of taste, as well as in the patterns of rhetoric and language.

The upshot of this research is simply to confirm that performance in writing and the judgment of performance in writing are both situated within a given culture and in particular circumstances so that the assessment is generally local rather than universal. Any claims that a particular writer is good or bad must be seen in a relative rather than an absolute sense.

WORK IN PROGRESS

Despite this rather gloomy finding for many of those involved in writing assessment, the search goes on for some sort of magic metric and there have been countless studies looking at issues of task specification, scoring, and reliability. Another feature of writing assessment that sheds light on the problematic nature of writing assessment relates to the conditions of testing and administration. The IEA comparative study showed that there existed great national differences in the use of time and the expectations of school writing. In some countries, secondary school students had less than an hour in which to produce a finished essay; in others they might be allowed four or five hours. Clearly the norms and expectations of both teachers and students differed widely according to the different settings. With more time, students might be expected to revise and edit rather than present a first draft.

Concern about this, and the difficulty in generalizing from such a limited sample has led to an interest in portfolio assessment, based on a collection of classroom work. Portfolios may, of course, be defined in a number of different ways, but they generally comprise selections of a given student's work over a period of time, and demonstrate performance in a variety of rhetorical types and genres. A number of studies have examined various aspects of portfolios as an assessment device; many of them have dealt with the issue of task variation and scoring (See Black et al., 1994; Calfee & Perfumo, 1996). In general the attempts to derive a generalizable score from these that can compare performance on disparate works by different people in different contexts have not proved particularly convincing. As Calfee and Perfumo (1996) report, the schools and classes that use portfolios are enthusiastic, yet attempts to standardize grades across classrooms have produced inconsistent results, and teachers' judgments are often descriptive and narrative, and cannot be assessed statistically. (For a description of students' assessment of their own writing, see Piolat's review in this volume.)

This finding raises the issue as to whether in the judgment of writing performance, the issue is less one of reliability or validity than it is one of trust. In many forms of performance assessment outside of education (such as dressage, ice skating, and piano), the tasks and the conditions of performance are standardized, but the judges are not checked by statistical means. Their scores are considered to be valid because they are experts and their judgments, albeit inconsistent from performance site to performance site, are accepted as expert. Perhaps this approach should be adopted for the assessment of writing, and no attempt should be made to achieve some sort of statistical purity.

PROBLEMS AND DIFFICULTIES

In writing at school, students are asked to demonstrate: 1. their articulateness according to certain conventions; 2. their fluency or the ability to produce writing on demand; 3. their flexibility in moving from genre to genre; and 4. their ability to write appropriately, suiting what is written to the norms of the genre and the situation. Students also need to show competence in the motor acts required in producing text, and the skills required for producing discourse. Writing in school has to follow particular conventions, and the conventions appropriate in one subject are not always those in another, but students may be apprenticed to five or six rhetorical communities within one day or one week.

When teachers around the world assess student writing, they are looking at two aspects of the student's performance: the ability to produce a comprehensible text, and the ability to produce effective discourse. In judging the first ability, they comment upon handwriting and neatness, spelling, punctuation, and grammar. In judging the second, they comment on the quality of the content, the organization and structure, and the style. The first tends to be a relatively stable feature in any writer and allows for some form of common measurement. The latter, however, is, as research has consistently shown, much more culture and task specific. Since policy makers tend to seek whatever measure is brief, reliable, and inexpensive, many are tempted to require tests to measure students' ability to produce comprehensible text, although such an ability is not what is valued in the writing curricula of most countries. In addition, the ability to produce comprehensible writing is becoming less of a problem as the use of word processors becomes more widespread. The problems of judging effective discourse may be incompatible with the desire for efficiency in measurement, but the search for better and more convincing ways to use human judges needs to continue.

FUTURE DIRECTIONS

Writing is a socially situated act and therefore responds to social pressures. It also responds to the various technologies for storing and retrieving natural language. Most writing assessment has until now examined the performance of students composing in a limited amount of time using pencil or pen and paper. However, new writing technologies are beginning to come into play as are the new forms of writing generated by those technologies. Assessment research and the practitioners of assessment are beginning to acknowledge these phenomena, but there have been few attempts to conduct assessment on-line or using word processors (see Huot, 1996). Such will be the trend of the future, and although the technology may change the issues of task assignment, conditions of writing and scoring will remain paramount and probably intractable (See the review by Gruba and Corbel in this volume).

The Scribes, Inc., New York, USA

REFERENCES

Black, L. Daiker, D., Sommers, J., & Stygall, G. (eds.): *New Directions in Portfolio Assessment: Reflective Practice, Critical Theory, and Large-Scale Scoring*, Heinemann Boynton/Cook, Portsmouth NH.

Braddock, R., Lloyd-Jones, R., & Schoer, L.: 1963, *Research in Written Composition*, National Council of Teachers of English, Champaign, IL.

Breland, H.M.: 1983, *The Direct Assessment of Writing Skill: A Measurement Review*, Educational Testing Service, Princeton, NJ.

Breland, H.M. & Young, J.W.: 1984, *Combined Approaches in the Assessment of Writing Samples*, Paper read at Annual AERA, New Orleans.

British National Writing Project: 1987, *Ways of Looking at Children's Writing: The National Writing Project Response to the Task Group on Assessment and Testing*, School Curriculum Committee Development Publications, London.

Calfee, R. & Perfumo, P. (eds.): 1996, *Writing Portfolios in the Classroom: Policy and Practice, Promise and Peril*, Lawrence Erlbaum Associates, Mahwah, NJ.

Cooper, C. & Odell, L. (eds.): 1977, *Evaluating Writing: Describing, Measuring, Judging*, National Council of Teachers of English, Urbana, IL.

Freedman, S., Greenleaf, C., & Sperling, M.: 1987, *Response to Student Writing* (Research Report Number 23), National Council of Teachers of English, Urbana, IL.

French, J.W., Diederich, P.B., & Carlton, S.: 1961, *Factors in the Judgment of Written Composition*, Educational Testing Service, Princeton, NJ.

Godschalk, F.I., Coffman, W.E., & Swineford, F.: 1966, *The Measurement of Writing Ability*, College Entrance Examination Board, New York.

Gorman, T.P., Purves, A.C., & Degenhart, R.E. (eds.): 1988, *The IEA Study of Written Composition: The International Writing Tasks and Scoring Scales*, International Studies in Educational Achievement Vol. 5, Pergamon Press, Oxford, England.

Gubb, J., Gorman, T., & Price, E.: 1987, *The Study of Written Composition in England and Wales*, NFER-Nelson, Windsor.

Hillocks, G.: 1986, *Research on Written Composition: New Directions for Teaching*, National Conference on Research in English, Urbana, IL.

Huot, B.: 1996, 'Computers and assessment: Understanding two technologies', *Computers and Composition* 13, 231–244.

Li, X-M.: 1996, *"Good Writing" in Cross-Cultural Contexts*, SUNY Press, Albany, NY.

Purves, A. & Takala, S. (eds.): 1982, 'An international perspective on the evaluation of written composition', *Evaluation in Education: An International Review Series*, Vol 5, No. 3. Pergamon Press, Oxford.

Purves, A.C. (ed.): 1988, *Writing Across Languages and Cultures: Issues in Contrastive Rhetoric*, Sage Publications, Newbury Park, CA.

Purves, A.C. (ed.): 1992a, *The IEA Study of Written Composition: Education and Performance in Fourteen Countries*, Pergamon Press, Oxford, England.

Purves, A.C.: 1992b, 'Reflections on assessment and research in written composition', *Research in the Teaching of English* 26, 108–122.

Ruth, L., & S. A. Murphy, S.A.: 1986, *Designing Writing Tasks for the Assessment of Writing*, Ablex, Norwood, NJ.

Wolfe, E., Bolton, S., Feltovich, B. & Welch, C.: 1993, *A Comparison of Word-Processed and Hand-Written Essays from a Standardized Writing Assessment*, The American College Testing Program, Iowa.
Witte, S.P., Cherry, R., Meyer, P., & Trachsel, M.: 1994, *Holistic Assessment of Writing: Issues in Theory and Practice*, Guildford Press, New York.

ROBERT N. BOSTROM

THE TESTING OF MOTHER TONGUE LISTENING SKILLS

One can test 'listening' in a number of ways depending on how the activity is defined. It is not uncommon for individuals in an interaction to believe an interactant has 'listened', regardless of the outcome of the listening process. An individual may end an interview by saying 'Thanks for listening' – in the belief that the other person has been paying attention – when the only response that person has made is to stay awake. But if we set out to demonstrate that one person had listened to another, we need some external indication that 'listening' has occurred – if one individual states 'please don't smoke' and the second individual lights a cigarette, we may well assume that the second individual was not listening.

Testing listening, then, involves some kind of external response, and the nature of the response depends on what we think the process entails. In addition, testing listening is usually carried out because we assume that individuals differ in their ability to listen. Often we are concerned about deficiencies in listening ability because we feel that this deficiency may hamper academic performance, or the quality of a relationship. Clearly the first task in testing is to decide what we think good listening should be. Our ideas about good listening have changed a good deal in the last few years, and consequently the activities that we think would test listening have changed also.

EARLY HISTORY

The definition of 'listening' has grown out of the cognitive tradition that has dominated Western educational thought since Greek and Roman times. Initially listening and reading were simply assumed to be different ways of acquiring and retaining information. The discovery that persons skilled in reading were not necessarily skilled listeners (and vice versa) led researchers to examine the processes separately.

The earliest attempts at measuring listening simply consisted of composing a segment of prose – usually a short essay – which contained a number of factual details, and then reading it aloud; the auditors were expected to remember the 'facts'. This kind of listening 'test' was exactly the same as a test of 'reading comprehension', except that the material was presented orally (Brown & Carlsen, 1955; Nichols, 1947). A 'good' listener was therefore defined as one who remembered many facts; a poor one remembered few. Since these facts were presented in short lectures,

C. Clapham and D. Corson (eds), Encyclopedia of Language and Education,
Volume 7: Language Testing and Assessment, 21–27.
© 1997 Kluwer Academic Publishers. Printed in the Netherlands.

this assessment came to be called 'lecture' listening. The Brown-Carlsen listening test used this technique and for many years was the principal listening test used in research. A variety of other tests were used from time to time, but all of them assumed that the 'lecture' model was the best definition of listening. (For a discussion of the difference between spoken and written texts, see Buck's review in this volume.)

The 'operational definition' of listening ability, therefore, was the ability to remember the content of a short piece of prose delivered orally. Listening was assumed to be a skill separate and distinct from other communication skills, and its improvement in an academic setting was considered an important educational outcome (Becker & Dallinger, 1961). Almost all 'listening' research done in Europe and Australia adopted this common sense belief. But this belief was challenged by Charles Kelly (1965, 1967), who demonstrated that testing for retention following a lecture was substantially the same as testing for intelligence. Kelly's research showed that those who remembered many facts presented from a lecture also scored high on IQ tests. Low scorers on lecture tasks similarly did poorly on IQ tests. Kelly concluded, reasonably enough, that 'listening ability' was not different from the cognitive ability that we call intelligence, and that this finding apparently invalidated studies using this technique, and called into question the notion that there was a separate characteristic called 'listening ability'.

Although memory for the content of spoken discourse might be one of the factors involved in efficient listening, researchers have come to realise that listening is more complex than they had thought. For example, many writers (Burgoon, 1994; Burns & Beier, 1973; Leathers, 1979) pointed out that a good listener could detect affective cues about the speaker's state of mind, rather than the content of the message. It was typical to call this 'interpersonal' listening, looking for affective rather than factual content. Of course, the speaker's affective state is importantly influenced by his or her relationship with the interactant. An early test of interpersonal listening was the Jones-Mohr Listening Test (Watson & Barker, 1984). In this test, speakers used vocal intonations to indicate various affective states, and respondents were asked to identify the states. However, this procedure lacked a theoretical basis and this contributed to the subsequent lack of interest in the test.

The next development in testing followed the development of new cognitive models, specifically inspired by research in memory. These models are the basis of today's testing of listening.

MAJOR CONTRIBUTIONS

Research into memory demonstrates that memory has different components. Most of us think that we simply remember or do not remember something. Actually memory varies widely. Sometimes we briefly remember information presented to us and then forget it. Cognitive researchers have called this 'short-term' memory. Memory that persists is usually called 'long-term', and various researchers have posited a number of intermediate processes. Memory for words is different from memory for images and events.

Since listening seems to make use of memory in a fundamental way, a productive approach to measuring listening might be based on models of memory. If 'listening skill' is not the same as intelligence, then examining different kinds of listening tasks might provide information about how listening works, a useful guide to aspects of the listening process The use of memory as a model led to the hypothesis that verbal decoding can be divided into three components: short-term listening, short-term with rehearsal, and lecture listening (Bostrom & Waldhart, 1980, 1988; Bostrom, 1990). This approach led to the development of The Kentucky Comprehensive Listening Test (KCLT). This test does not present an essay accompanied by a series of questions. Instead, in one section of the test, responses are elicited immediately after the information has been presented. In a second section a response is elicited after a significant pause has occurred, using 'rehearsal' listening. Two further sections contain a traditional lecture test and a test of affect detection. Research has shown that the varying aspects of listening differentiated among one another (Bostrom & Waldhart, 1980), and further, that short-term listening seemed to have little relationship to cognitive abilities such as intelligence.

Good short-term listeners apparently perform better in oral situations (Bostrom & Waldhart, 1980). This finding has been replicated in a number of different settings. In a study of 'managerial effectiveness', short-term listening skill was demonstrated to be the best discriminator between good and poor branch managers in banks (Alexander, Penley, & Jernigan, 1992). In another setting, short-term listening was the best single predictor of upward mobility in the organization (Sypher, Bostrom, & Seibert, 1989). Other communicative abilities were important, but this measure of listening was the strongest predictor. In an interview study, Bussey (1991) found that those with good short-term skills asked more questions of their interviewees than did those with poor short-term skills. Comparisons of other listening phenomena, such as accelerated speech (King & Behnke, 1989) provide strong evidence for the claim that short-term listening is qualitatively different from long term, and investigation of short-term listening in interpersonal settings indicates that it is importantly related to other interpersonal abilities.

Though the KCLT does have an interpretive component, many researchers felt that affective messages were more important than it seemed to indicate. The Watson-Barker Listening Test (WBLT) contains more interpretive material. Developed in 1983, the WBLT lays a greater emphasis on interpersonal relationships than does the KCLT, and further includes 'instruction- following' (Watson & Barker, 1983). This test includes short-term retention as a separate scale but, unlike the KCLT, does not test short-term with rehearsal. A video version of the WBLT is available, and this test is particularly suited to listening training in applied situations.

Educational Testing Service has developed an examination to assess the general fitness of candidates for teaching positions, and this test is used in a large part of the United States as a screening examination. This test was formerly known as the National Teacher Examination, but is now called the 'Praxis' test. The test has three main portions: competency in teaching content (for example, someone who wishes to teach chemistry must demonstrate knowledge of chemistry), knowledge of a 'professional' nature, such as how schools are administered and organized, and finally, communication skills. Communication skills involve writing, reading, and listening. The listening test assesses retention of content, the ability to draw inferences from dialogues, and retention from long paragraphs. Many of these scales are similar to those in the KCLT and the WBLT. Some items reflect short-term listening (short statements and answers), others interpretive listening (the affective content of statements or dialogues), and others 'lecture' listening (responding to 'talks'). However, the Praxis test scores only 'statements and questions', 'dialogues' and 'talks'.

WORK IN PROGRESS

There are a number of important information sources in interpersonal interactions that are not typically included in contemporary tests. They include non-verbal signals and schematic (or cultural) listening. Work is in progress in assessing this type of 'listening'.

A substantive body of research clearly indicates that individuals vary in their ability to decode the non-verbal cues present in interpersonal exchanges (Burgoon, 1994). Often when non-verbal signals contradict the verbal ones, individuals accept the non verbal as a more valid expression of the true feelings of the interactant (Burgoon, 1994; Leathers, 1979). Most investigations of non-verbal cues center on visual displays, such as facial expression, posture, and the like. Others have investigated 'vocalic' messages, such as pitch, intonation, and inflection. Visual cues have typically been shown to be of greater influence than the vocalic ones in most situations. However, some studies show that vocalic cues are of more use in detecting deception than visual ones (Littlepage & Pineault, 1981; Streeter et al., 1977).

Recently, however, Keely-Dyreson et al. (1991) examined decoding differences in isolation. They compared the ability of respondents to decode visual cues with their ability to decode vocal cues, and found that visual cues were more accurately perceived than vocal ones. Some gender differences were also observed. In short, the division of messages into 'verbal' and 'non-verbal' categories may be too simple. Visual and vocal cues, both of which have been categorized as non-verbal messages, would seem to differ in important ways. Comparisons of decoding abilities are rare. What the relationships might be among visual/non verbal decoding ability, vocal/non-verbal decoding ability, and verbal decoding ability is not known.

In summary, decoding of non-verbal messages is an important aspect of all interactions, and this decoding usually involves visual and aural cues. Research indicates that visual cues are decoded with much greater accuracy and that the ability to decode vocalic messages is not nearly as good as most persons suppose. Lateral asymmetry of brain function may well be an unsuspected contributor to the lack of accuracy in vocalic decoding. Vocalic decoding is important because in mediated communications, such as the telephone, and in some other circumstances, visual cues are not available, and it may be impossible to observe facial expressions and other body movements.

Another way of examining the acquisition of information may involve the use of schemata (Fitch-Hauser, 1990). Richard Mayer (1983) notes that schemata underlie almost all important cognitive activities, and it is clear that whether these are called 'schemata', 'frames', or 'scripts', the comprehension of spoken or written messages is affected by the activation of background knowledge (see, for example, Bracewell, Fredericksen, & Fredericksen, 1982). It is clear that interpreting a prose passage is quite often impossible without knowledge of the 'big picture' in the situation.

Thain (1994) has used aspects of schema theory in formulating his definition of 'authentic' listening. Thain reasons that many aspects of listening skill involve 'pure traits' such as memory and vocabulary, but these must be integrated if the entire message is to be understood. He presents an example of a situation in which decoding cannot take place without a larger understanding of the situation involved. Usually these situations stem from particular cultural understandings, such as sport or business. Thain is hoping to develop a measure that will test both L1 and L2 listening, and plans to use it for assessment in the U.S. military's language education program.

PROBLEMS AND DIFFICULTIES

As we review the history of listening research, we see that traditional studies of communication have centered on linguistic competence – understandably, since it has taken place in the traditional 'learning paradigm' of the Western world. The cognitive/linguistic approach has affected our basic orientation to almost every effort to study communicative competence. Unfortunately, sometimes, this is just not adequate. The study of communication often needs to focus on behaviour, on relationships, and on affect. Traditional studies in listening assessment have not examined the overall communicative process, but have focused primarily on individual differences in the processing of orally presented symbols.

FUTURE DIRECTIONS

Clearly it is time to take another look at research in listening as a whole. Definitions of listening began with a concern with symbolic processing (synonymous with intelligence) and were later supplemented with other aspects, such as attitudes. Memory models were introduced, with an emphasis on schemata of various types. If we look carefully at all the previous research in listening, we can see that the one common element in all of these different approaches has been information processing. This common thread is strong enough for us to say that the best definition of listening is the acquisition, processing, and retention of information in the interpersonal context (Bostrom, 1996). This is a much more inclusive definition, but has a number of advantages. One advantage of using this more inclusive model of listening is that visual stimuli are just as important as aural stimuli. The inclusion follows logically from integrating interpretive, relational, and behavioural aspects of communication.

University of Kentucky, USA

REFERENCES

Alexander, E.R., Penley, L.E. & Jernigan, I.E.: 1992, 'The relationship of basic decoding skills to managerial effectiveness', *Management Communication Quarterly* 6, 58–73.

Bostrom, R.N.: 1990, *Listening Behavior: Measurement and Applications*, Guilford, New York.

Bostrom, R.N. & Bryant, C.: 1980, 'Factors in the retention of information presented orally: The role of short-term memory,' *Western Speech Communication Journal* 44, 137–145.

Bostrom, R.N. & Waldhart, E.S.: 1980, 'Components in listening behavior: The role of short-term memory', *Human Communication Research* 6, 211–227.

Bostrom, R.N. & Waldhart, E.S. : 1988, 'Memory models and the measurement of listening', *Communication Education* 37, 1–18.

Bostrom, R.N.: 1996, 'Memory, cognitive processes and the process of listening', In O.G. Hargie (ed.), *Handbook of Communication Skills*, Routledge, London, 237–258.

Bracewell, R.J., Fredericksen, C.H. & Fredericksen, J.D.: 1982, 'Cognitive processes in composing and comprehending discourse', *Education Psychologies* 17, 146–164.

Burgoon, J.: 1994, 'Nonverbal signals,' in Knapp, M. & Miller, G. (eds.), *Handbook of Interpersonal Communication* (2nd edition), Sage, Beverly Hills, CA, 344–393.

Burns, K. & Beier, E.: 1973, 'Significance of vocal and visual channels in the decoding of emotional meaning', *Journal of Communication* 23, 118–130.

Bussey, J.: 1991, 'Question asking in an interview and varying listening skills', Paper delivered at the Annual Meeting of the Southern Communication Association, Tampa, Florida.

Educational Testing Service.: 1984, *Test Analysis: Core Battery*, Unpublished statistical report. Educational Testing Service, Princeton, NJ.

Fitch-Hauser, M.: 1990. 'Making sense of data: constructs, schemas, and concepts', in R. Bostrom (eds.), *Listening Behavior: Measurement and Applications*, Guilford, New York, 76–90.

Kelly, C.: 1965, 'An investigation of the construct validity of two commercially published listening tests', *Speech Monographs* 32, 139–143.

Kelly, C.: 1967, 'Listening: A complex of activities or a unitary skill?', *Speech Monographs* 34, 455–466.

King, P.E. & Behnke, R.R.: 1989, 'The effect of compressed speech on comprehensive, interpretive, and short-term listening', *Human Communication Research* 15, 428–443.

Leathers, D.: 1979, 'The impact of multichannel message inconsistency on verbal and nonverbal decoding behaviors', *Communication Monographs* 46, 88–100.

Littlepage, G.E. & Pineault, M.A.: 1981, 'Detection of truthful and deceptive interpersonal communications across information transmission modes', *The Journal of Social Psychology* 114, 57–68.

Loftus, G. & Loftus, E.: 1976, *Human Memory: The Processing of Information*, Wiley, New York.

Mayer, R.: 1983, *Thinking, Problem Solving, and Cognition*, Freeman, San Francisco.

Nichols, R.: 1947, 'Listening: Questions and problems,' *Quarterly Journal of Speech* 33, 83–86.

Sypher, B.D., Bostrom, R.N., & Seibert, J.H.: 1989, 'Listening, communication abilities, and success at work', *Journal of Business Communication* 26, 293–303.

Thain, J.W.: 1994, 'Improving the measurement of language aptitude: the potential of the L1 measures', Paper presented at the Language Aptitude Improvement Symposium, Washington, D.C.

Thomas, L.T. & Levine, T.R.: 1994, 'Disentangling listening and verbal recall: Related but separate constructs?' *Human Communication Research* 21, 103–127.

Watson, K.W. & Barker, L.L.: 1983, *Watson-Barker Listening Test*, Spectra Associates, Inc., Auburn, Alabama.

Watson, K.W. & Barker, L.L.: 1984, 'Listening behavior: Definition and measurement', in R.N. Bostrom (ed.), *Communication Yearbook Eight*, Sage, Beverly Hills, 178–197.

DONALD L. RUBIN AND GEORGE SCHRAMM

THE TESTING OF FIRST LANGUAGE SPEAKING SKILLS

The capacity to speak in one's native language is a biological endowment. In many respects, the effectiveness of even very young, unschooled children to express their communicative intentions orally is quite awe-inspiring. Indeed, children who fail spontaneously to develop highly accurate articulation, fluent production, and mainly unobtrusive vocal characteristics are regarded as having communication disorders. In fact, the most institutionally well-entrenched programs of oral language assessment are those which seek to screen and diagnose speech pathologies, rather than to document normative proficiency in oral communication competence. (For more about the assessment of speech disorders, see Baker & Chenery's review in this volume.)

Because speech is a primal and nearly irrepressible faculty, relatively little demand for native language oral communication assessment – as compared to the tremendous demand for literacy assessment – has been manifest. In the absence of obvious evidence to the contrary, it is generally assumed that all native speakers are competent speakers. It is only with the advent of more sophisticated and rigorous concepts of speaking competence that inquiry into the testing of speaking has become an active field (Goulden, 1992). Concomitantly, a heightened sensitivity to the contribution of speaking competence to various kinds of effectiveness has increased the demand for oral communication assessment among educators and employers.

A second factor generally militating against the testing of speech is the inherent difficulty in assessing spoken language. Speech is a fast-fading medium; even audio or video recordings do not freeze oral performance parameters in an easily scannable and rescannable, comprehensive fashion. Because speech assessment cannot be freed from real-time constraints, it is inherently labor intensive and expensive. Moreover, if inter-rater subjectivity is an obstacle to the reliable and valid assessment of writing performance, it is much more so in speaking assessment. That is because extraneous but potent factors like physical appearance and vocal personality cues are so salient in speech. Thus the testing of speaking presents particularly demanding logistical and psychometric challenges.

One final impediment to testing speech performance is more attitudinal than theoretic or technical. The act of speaking in the presence of others is the ultimate act of self presentation. Small wonder that anxiety about public speaking is often rated as more severe than fear of personal violence.

C. Clapham and D. Corson (eds), Encyclopedia of Language and Education,
Volume 7: Language Testing and Assessment, 29–37.
© *1997 Kluwer Academic Publishers. Printed in the Netherlands.*

To evaluate someone's speech, therefore, is particularly face-threatening. Students, employees, and professionals whose oral competence we might wish to certify are loath to subject themselves to such ego-threatening scrutiny. By the same token, teachers, supervisors, and other assessors who might feel comfortable rendering rigorous judgment in other testing domains can be far more reluctant and less candid in assessing speech.

Nevertheless, much interesting and useful work in the testing of speaking has taken place over the past quarter century. Most of this work has taken place in the English speaking world, though many notable projects in non-English speaking nations have been mounted (e.g., van Gelderen, 1994). Much of the best work in the testing of speaking has taken place in the context of the assessment of English as a second language (e.g., Lantolf & Frawley, 1985). (For more about L2 testing of speaking, see Fulcher's review in this chapter.)

Moreover, well-validated techniques for evaluating managerial communication in organizational settings have long included such oral-based exercises as leaderless group discussion and intensive interviews, often administered in assessment centers (Crooks, 1976). Similarly, performance testing in many professional licensure examinations (e.g., attorney or school principal) may sample and assess task-specific speaking skills (Campbell, 1992). Professional and organizational assessment, however, also lie outside the practical ken of this review.

The particular focus of this article, then, is the testing of nonpathological aspects of speaking ability among native speakers of English mainly in educational contexts.

EARLY DEVELOPMENT

By the mid-Sixties, progressive British educators had developed a notion of 'oracy' as a skill domain that deserved attention in primary and secondary schools, in tandem with more typical curricula in reading and writing. James Britton (1970), for example, introduced educators to the notion that 'talk is the sea upon which all else floats'. British educators desiring to encourage the teaching of oracy hoped that large scale assessment in spoken English would have a 'washback' effect on classroom practices (Wilkinson, 1968). As a consequence, British educators have long and varied experience with oral components of first the Certificate of Secondary Education (CSE) and General Certificate of Education (GCE), and now the General Certificate of Secondary Education (GCSE) examinations (Hitchman, 1968; Taylor, 1983; Jenkins & Cheshire, 1990).

In the United States, as a result of the Basic Skills legislation of the late Seventies (Elementary and Secondary Education Act Title II) kindergarten through 12th grade (K-12) curriculum developers were charged to think about the value of oral communication in social, educational and professional settings. This legislation sought to ensure higher standards of achievement by establishing a core of common skills wherein speaking and listening skills were treated as significant academic competencies and more than just the precursors to literate behavior.

In response to the Basic Skills movement in the U.S., The Committee on Assessment and Testing (CAT) of the Speech Communication Association (SCA) developed conceptual definitions of communication competence and of appropriate assessment strategies. From the beginning, this project adopted a developmental perspective and an orientation toward *functions* of communication (e.g., informing, persuading, ritualizing). Subsequently, a set of assessable speaking and listening competencies for high school students was derived (Bassett, Whittington & Staton-Spicer, 1978). The framework for the assessment of communication competence encompassed the domains of (A) communication codes, (B) oral message evaluation, (C) speech communication skills, and (D) human relations. SCA's CAT subsequently promulgated testing policy statements, 'Criteria for Evaluating Instruments and Procedures for Assessing Speaking and Listening' and 'Criteria for the Assessment of Oral Communication'. These policies promote the view that tests of oral communication should be independent of literacy skills, should sample a range of tasks from high to low interaction among examinees and/or between raters and examinees, and should be performance-based. (See Backlund & Morreale, 1994 for a history of further developments and for more information about other documents produced by this movement.)

MAJOR CONTRIBUTIONS

One important development from the SCA competencies project was the construction of the Communication Competence Assessment Instrument (CCAI) by R. Rubin (1982). The CCAI (which also includes a test of listening) is the most widely used and most thoroughly validated measure of college-level speaking proficiency. Using a combination of interview and reporting elicitation tasks, the CCAI samples 19 skills in speaking, listening, and interpersonal communication. The CCAI has recently been adapted for use with secondary school populations (R. Rubin, Welch, & Buerkel, 1995).

Another project supported by the CAT focused on public speaking as a distinct domain of communication competence. This project ultimately resulted in the publication of *The Competent Speaker*, a theory-driven tool for the assessment of public speaking behaviors (Morreale, et al., 1993). This instrument consists of eight primary rating scales: (1) chooses and narrows a topic, (2) selects a purpose that is appropriate for the audience and occasion, (3) selects situationally appropriate supporting material,

(4) organizes appropriate material for the situation, (5) uses situationally appropriate language, (6) varies vocal properties to heighten and maintain interest, (7) uses appropriate pronunciation and grammar, and (8) supports the message with physical behaviors. Each rating dimension is subdivided into more atomistic components, and three different levels of proficiency for each scale are described. (For more discussion about rating scales, see Fulcher's review in this volume.)

D. Rubin & N. Mead (1984; see also Morreale & Backlund, 1996) classified such formal, large-scale oral communication assessment procedures according to (1) type of response measured (rater marking as opposed to actual audience effect), (2) content of the assessment instrument (speech situation sampled, evaluation criteria adopted), (3) administrative feasibility, and (4) target populations and potential sources of bias. Underhill (1987), in contrast, describes oral exercises that, without the benefit of long-term validation studies, can be used to develop local small scale speaking tests which, with less formal psychometric foundation, can sometimes be deployed in schools and classrooms. Underhill discusses (a) test types – including self assessment, direct interview, and tests for which the learner prepares ahead; (b) elicitation techniques – including discussion/conversation, oral report, role-play, and using a picture story; and (c) marking systems – including rating scales and impression marking.

Much of Underhill's (1987) analysis is linked to practices of the British GCSE exams and their precursors, which have long included oral components (Jenkins & Cheshire, 1990; Wilkinson, 1968). Perhaps because the GCSE exams are under the decentralized oversight of semi-autonomous examining boards, their practices are diffuse, and sometimes appear ill-developed from both theoretic and psychometric perspectives (Taylor, 1983), as well as from the perspectives of educators involved in preparing students and administering the tests (e.g., Philips, 1989). In the case of the CSE, up to 30% of exam scores was derived from tests of oral performance (Taylor, 1983). Likewise it is impossible to pass the current GCSE without achieving a passing mark in the oral section (Jenkins & Cheshire, 1990). Practices among the various examination boards have ranged from 'unmoderated' assessments of conversation and reading discussions to highly structured sets of reporting, story telling, and other speech tasks.

Thus the GCSE exams represent the most ambitious experiment to date in testing native (also non-native) English speaking skills. With few exceptions, unfortunately, little programmatic evaluation of the GCSE exams has been disseminated. Little reliable information is available either about the propriety (validity) of their resulting certification outcomes, or about any 'washback' influences on classroom practices in oral communication instruction (see Wall & Alderson, 1993). (For more about washback, see the review by Wall in this volume.)

WORK IN PROGRESS

Many U.S. educators are convinced that assessment can play a powerful washback role in promoting oral communication instruction (Rubin & Mead, 1984). For that reason, keen attention is devoted to tracking the progress of large school systems as they implement speech assessment programs. One of the more promising of such projects was undertaken by the Massachusetts Board of Education (Massachusetts Department of Education, 1979). Intended for students in grades 7–10, the assessment plan called for classroom pre-screening of students' oral skills. Students who required further assessment would be subjected to a series of structured tasks designed to elicit a variety of communication behaviors. The project eventually foundered, mainly on the issue of feasibility and financial support rather than because of any psychometric issue. Still, the Massachusetts project suggested that with sufficient commitment, large-scale speech assessment in the public schools was possible.

The most recent survey of policies for testing speaking skills in U.S. public schools (Litterst, VanRheenen & Casmir, 1994) reveals that about one-third of educational jurisdictions are engaged in innovative projects, but that these remain largely at the developmental stage. In Arizona, for example, speaking and listening are to be assessed at the local (school district) level. In Minnesota, proposed graduate requirements will mandate that students demonstrate 'speaking clearly for academic, technical, and personal purposes and with a variety of audiences'. In North Carolina, a proposed senior year (12th grade) state-wide examination calls for students to engage in a 'demonstration project', which culminates in an oral presentation before a review panel.

PROBLEMS AND DIFFICULTIES

The threats to reliability and validity of speech assessment are well understood (see reviews in Rubin & Mead, 1984; Spitzberg & Hurt, 1987; Stiggins, Backlund & Bridgeford, 1985; Underhill, 1987). Especially because oral communication is so rich in terms of nonverbal information, judging a speech performance is intermeshed with all the complexities and distortions of interpersonal perception. Inter-rater reliability in this domain is notoriously fragile and subject to interference from raters' perceptions of speaker physical attractiveness (Ambady & Rosenthal, 1993). The raters' prior knowledge and interest in the speaker's topic can also introduce extraneous variance to the scoring (Miller, 1964). Stabilizing effects of rater training upon inter-rater reliability are not well established in this domain.

Variations in students' speech topics (whether assigned or self-selected), interview probes, and even variations among interviewers may affect the reliability of speech assessment; this is a psychometric issue that has been barely broached in the assessment of first language proficiency. In addition, any oral performance so directly reflects the student's affective state (as well as more stable personality and skill traits), that it is subject to considerable intra-individual variation. Thus test-retest reliability of test-takers' performance in oral assessment is another issue that demands further investigation.

The validity of speech assessments suffers from a lack of construct definition. Speech performance testing which seeks to assess a broad, functional, communication competence should involve more than a narrowly focused examination of linguistic ability or assessment of a single communicative context such as public speaking. For example, most spoken discourse is not monologic; it is interactive. Hence some educators (e.g., D. Rubin & Mead, 1984) have argued that speaking and listening skills should not be measured in isolation from each other, as is mainly the case at the moment. Considerable controversy also attends considerations of the validity of formal speech assessments for students of varying ethnic (Powell & Avila, 1986) and personality (Alexander, 1988) profiles. Evaluation criteria that reward traits like volubility, explicitness, or directness are almost certain to be culture-bound (D. Rubin, 1986). Finally, criterion measures for establishing concurrent validity of speech assessment instruments are not well-established (see R. Rubin, 1985).

Beyond psychometric adequacy of speaking measures looms the problem of feasibility in large-scale oral assessment. All performance testing is labor intensive – for administrators, raters, and test-takers alike. Speech tests are especially so. Speech forms like story telling or interview responses are not group administrable, in the sense that students must perform sequentially rather than simultaneously. Even group discussion tasks carry a high price in terms of time-per-examinee, as well as threats to the independence of each students' individual rating. In addition, speech must be rated in real time. For high-stakes testing, each student should be assessed by at least two raters, and performances must be audio- or video-taped. It has been estimated that a single direct assessment of speech performance requires at least .2 personnel hours per performance for rating alone (cited in Rubin & Mead, 1984). Small wonder that large-scale assessment of speaking has been pursued so infrequently. (Listening assessment does not share these feasibility disadvantages. It can be machine scored, group administered, and requires no real-time raters. Therefore it has been adopted more widely, at least in the U.S.; see Litterst, et al., 1994.) (For more about the testing of listening see the chapters by Bostrom and Buck in this volume.)

FUTURE DIRECTIONS

Two related movements, one focusing on educational standards, the other focusing on portfolios as assessment tools, will determine the direction of educational assessment during the rest of this century, and the field of speech assessment will flourish or flounder depending on the success with which it can align itself with these movements. In the U.S., the standards movement seeks to identify rigorous but achievable objectives within each content area that can serve as the fulcrum for a consensus among educators. In 1996 a joint enterprise of the (U.S.) National Council of Teachers of English and the International Reading Association promulgated a set of educational standards in reading and language arts not unlike those of the Basic Skills legislation. While speaking (and listening) are named in several of the later standards, the document seemed largely aimed at improving literacy instruction. That same year SCA issued 'Speaking, Listening, and Media Literacy Standards for K-12 Education'. Among the standards cited in this document are student demonstrations of 'communication strategies to enhance relationships and resolve conflict' which employ 'language that clarifies, persuades and/or inspires while respecting the listeners' backgrounds ...;' as well as a demonstrated understanding of 'the role of communication in the democratic process'.

Standards such as these are intended not merely to express a consensus about educational philosophy, but deliberately to govern assessment practices. In particular, the standards movement is linked to the trend toward authentic (or alternative) assessment (Herman, Aschbacher & Winters, 1992). In most educational settings, authentic assessment means collecting multiple performance artifacts over time, allowing for realistic student preparation away from the test site and time, allowing for collaborations between students, allowing students to select their own artifacts to be assessed, and using assessment as an opportunity to encourage students to reflect on their processes of learning and growth. This is the essence of portfolio assessment. (For more about portfolio assessment see the chapters by Purves and Cumming in this volume.)

Can speech performance be captured in portfolios? With increasing access to technology, it is not difficult to imagine students collecting audiotapes of oral reports or videotapes of group meetings (or digitized computer multimedia files), and then unifying them with a reflective introduction. Other artifacts which might belong in a speech performance portfolio could include listener response forms, meeting agendas and minutes, planning notes and outlines, and visual aids used in conjunction with oral presentations (Arneson, 1994). New Standards, a consortium of state and large urban school districts headquartered at the Center for Education and the Economy, has begun to develop portfolio exemplars that include evidence of proficiency in oral communication at elementary, middle, and high school levels. It is quite possible that alternative assessment of speech might mitigate many of the problems associated with traditional oral assessment. A portfolio is a means of collapsing real-time performance and encapsulating multiple performance samples. As such, portfolio assessment could help alleviate some of the feasibility limitations that have hampered oral assessment. Almost certainly, the use of portfolios in oral communication assessment would promote the washback effect that testing speaking skills should be able to exert on the content of classroom instruction.

The University of Georgia, USA

REFERENCES

Alexander, J.: 1988, 'Oral communication – a survey of teachers' attitudes', *The Use of English* 39(3), 11–18.
Ambady, N. & Rosenthal, R.: 1993, 'Half a minute: Predicting teacher evaluations from thin slices of nonverbal behavior and physical attractiveness', *Journal of Personality and Social Psychology* 64, 431–441.
Arneson, P.: 1994, 'Assessing communication competence through portfolios, scoring rubrics, and personal interviews', in S. Morreale & M. Brooks (eds.), *Assessing College Student Competency in Speech Communication: 1994 SCA Summer Conference Proceedings and Prepared Remarks*, Speech Communication Association, Annandale VA, 115–123.
Backlund, P.A. & Moreale, S.P.: 1994, 'History of the speech communication association's assessment efforts and present role of the committee on assessment and testing', in S. Morreale & M. Brooks (eds.), *Assessing College Student Competency in Speech Communication: 1994 SCA Summer Conference Proceedings and Prepared Remarks*, Speech Communication Association, Annandale VA, 9–16.
Bassett, R.E., Whittington, N., & Staton-Spicer, A.: 1978, 'The basics in speaking and listening for high school graduates: What should be assessed?', *Communication Education* 27, 293–303.
Britton, J.: 1970, *Language and Learning*, Penguin Books, Harmondsworth, UK.
Campbell, J.O.: 1992, 'The opportunities of changing technology for performance assessment', in J. Pfeiderer (ed.), *What We Can Learn From Performance Assessment for the Professions: Proceedings of the 1992 ETS Invitational Conference*, Educational Testing Service, Princeton NJ, 69–76.
Crooks, L.A.: 1976, 'The selection and development of assessment center techniques', in J.L. Moses & W.C. Byham (eds.), *Applying the Assessment Center Method*, Pergamon Press, New York, 69–88.
Goulden, N.R.: 1992, 'Theory and vocabulary for communication assessment', *Communication Education* 41, 258–269.
Herman, J.L., Aschbacher, P.R., & Winters, L.: 1992, *A Practical Guide to Alternative Assessment*, Association for Supervision and Curriculum Development, Alexandria, VA.
Hitchman, P.J.: 1968, 'CSE tests in spoken English', *Educational Research* 20, 218–225.
Jenkins, N. & Cheshire, J.: 1990, 'Gender issues in the GCSE oral English examination: Part I', *Language and Education* 4, 261–292.
Lantolf, J. & Frawley, W.: 1985, 'Oral proficiency testing: A critical analysis', *The Modern Language Journal* 69, 337–345.
Litterst, J.K., VanRheenen, D., & Casmir, M.H.: 1994, 'Practices in statewide oral com-

munication assessment: 1981–1994', in S. Morreale & M. Brooks (eds.), *Assessing College Student Competency in Speech Communication: 1994 SCA Summer Conference Proceedings and Prepared Remarks*, Speech Communication Association, Annandale VA, 187–215.

Massachusetts Department of Education.: 1979, *Assessment of Speaking Skills State Test, Secondary level*, Author, 350 Main Street, Malden MA, 02148.

Miller, G.R.: 1964, 'Agreement and the grounds for it: Persistent problems in speech rating', *The Speech Teacher* 13, 257–261.

Morreale, S.P. & Backlund, P.: 1996, *Large Scale Assessment of Oral Communication* (second edition), Speech Communication Association and ERIC Clearinghouse on Reading and Communication Skills, Annandale, VA.

Morreale, S.P., Moore, M.R., Taylor, K.P., Surges-Tatum, D., & Hulbert-Johnson, R.: 1993, *"The Competent Speaker" Speech Evaluation Form*, Speech Communication Association, Annandale, VA.

Philips, C.: 1989, 'Imaginary gardens with real toads', *The Use of English* 40(2), 65–69.

Powell, R. & Avila, D.: 1986, 'Ethnicity, communication competency, and classroom success: A question of assessment', *Western Journal of Speech Communication* 50, 269–278.

Rubin, D.L.: 1986, ' "Nobody play by the rules he know": Cultural interference in classroom questioning events', in Y.Y. Kim (ed.), *International and Intercultural Communication Yearbook*, Sage, Beverly Hills, 158–177.

Rubin, D.L. & Mead, N.: 1984, *Large Scale Assessment of Oral Communication Skills: Kindergarten Through Grade 12*, ERIC/RCS and Speech Communication Association, Annandale, VA.

Rubin, R.: 1982, 'Assessing speaking and listening competence at the college level: the communication competence assessment instrument', *Communication Education* 31, 19–32.

Rubin, R.: 1985, 'The validity of the communication competence assessment instrument', *Communication Monographs* 52, 173–185.

Rubin, R., Welch, S., & Buerkel, R.: 1995, 'Performance-based assessment of high school speech instruction', *Communication Education* 44, 30–39.

Spitzberg, B. & Hurt, H.: 1987, 'The measurement of interpersonal skills in instructional contexts, *Communication Education* 36, 28–45.

Stiggins, R., Backlund, P., & Bridgeford, N.: 1985, 'Avoiding bias in the assessment of communication skills', *Communication Education* 34, 135–141.

Taylor, B.: 1983, 'CSE oral assessment: A consideration of practice', *Uses of English* 35(1), 49–64.

Underhill, N.: 1987, *Testing Spoken Language: A Handbook of Oral Testing Techniques*, Cambridge University Press, Cambridge.

van Gelderen, A.: 1994, 'Prediction of global ratings of fluency and delivery in narrative discourse by linguistic and phonetic measures – oral performances of students aged 11–12 years', *Language Testing* 11, 291–319.

Wall, D. & Alderson, J.C.: 1993, 'Examining washback: The Sri Lankan impact study', *Language Testing* 10, 41–69.

Wilkinson, A.: 1968, 'The testing of oracy', in A. Davies (ed.), *Language Testing Symposium: A Psycholinguistic Approach*, Oxford University Press, London, 117–205.

C.J. WEIR

THE TESTING OF READING IN A SECOND LANGUAGE

A direct reading test should reflect as closely as possible the interaction that takes place between a reader and a text in the equivalent real life reading activity. However, in real life, reading purpose, background knowledge, formal knowledge, and various types of language knowledge may all interact with text content to contribute to a reader's text comprehension.

It is the current belief of reading test developers that they need to make sure they do not artificially constrain the processing options available to the test taker either through presenting inappropriate *performance conditions* relating to the texts' topic, length, discoursal structure etc., or through restrictive, insufficient or ill conceived sampling of the *operations* (activities) the reader is asked to perform on the text (Weir, 1993). Although full genuineness of text or authenticity of task is likely to be unattainable in the second language reading tests we develop, we still need to select appropriate texts, to be read for realistic purposes, and we expect the reader to extract an agreed level of meaning under specified performance conditions.

EARLY DEVELOPMENTS

The importance of reading in second language learning has long been recognised. Howatt (Howatt, 1984, pp. 152–156) cites the work of Marcel (1853) who stressed the primary importance of reading in language learning. Pugh (1978, p. 20) notes that from about 1910 there was an increased interest in comprehension exercises on texts requiring close careful reading. He contrasts this with an American interest in the speed of silent reading which is noticeable by its absence in the British literature of the first half of this century.

Slow silent reading was a feature of many of the second language tests produced in the earlier part of the twentieth century. Spolsky (1995, p. 41) cites Handschin (1919) as one of the first publishers of silent tests of reading comprehension in French and Spanish and provides details of others in the early post World War I period. The University of Cambridge Local Examinations Syndicate (UCLES) was also using a reading test for EFL candidates in the early part of this century with the Cambridge Proficiency Test making a first appearance in the UK in 1913.

Most of these early tests had certain characteristics in common: they did not use 'authentic' texts or tasks (for a discussion of authenticity in

C. Clapham and D. Corson (eds), Encyclopedia of Language and Education,
Volume 7: Language Testing and Assessment, 39–49.
© *1997 Kluwer Academic Publishers. Printed in the Netherlands.*

testing, see Buck's review in this volume); they were not overtly based on any theoretical view of underlying reading processes; texts were not selected with the target situation of candidates in mind; test items were not designed in any principled fashion; and no need was felt to demonstrate statistical properties such as reliability.

Spolsky (1995) describes how traditional tests, usually employing short answer questions (SAQs), were largely supplanted by rational-empiricist objective measures, most commonly multiple choice questions (MCQs), because of their superior reliability and psychometric qualities.

Until the early 1980s, much of the discussion about the testing of reading in TESOL focused on *how* we were going to test it. The concern was largely with the test formats we might employ and the reliability of these measures.

We now seem to be entering a 'post modern age' (Spolsky, 1995) as concern mounts that, although objective reading tests may be reliable, they may not be delivering valid information on the abilities we seek to measure. We appear to be moving away from the 'rationalist-empiricist' measurement era (Spolsky, 1995, p. 1). The SAQ format is now regaining currency as test constructors attempt to rectify its earlier deficiencies by using techniques such as mindmapping (forming a consensus framework of the main ideas and important details a reader might be expected to extract from a text (Sarig, 1989)) and introspection (Faerch & Kasper, 1987; Storey, 1995) to establish what is to be tested and to ensure that that is indeed what is being tested. The humanistic-descriptive approach such systems embody, with its concern for what we are measuring, is now supported and enhanced by an additional concern for the accuracy and replicability of measurement (Spolsky, 1995, p. 5). Statistical validation through internal consistency estimates, correlational data and factor analysis is now proving useful in the validation of such tests.

TEST METHODS

Choosing test formats

In the latter part of this century the three principle methods of testing reading comprehension have been the cloze procedure, MCQs and SAQs. However, all these methods have their drawbacks.

Cloze

Despite arguments in favour of cloze procedure's efficiency and reliability, a number of doubts have been expressed concerning its validity as a device for testing the global comprehension of a text. One of its main flaws is that it seems to produce more successful tests of syntax, lexis and comprehension at the local or sentence level, than of reading comprehension in general or of inferential or deductive abilities. (For more about its limitations see Alderson, 1978; Bernhardt, 1991; Taylor, 1953; and Weir, 1990, 1993).

Multiple Choice Questions

One of the problems with using MCQs to test reading is that by providing possible answers alongside the questions, testers may themselves adversely affect students' performance. Not only do the distractors present choices that otherwise might not have been thought of, but we do not know whether a candidate's failure is due to lack of comprehension of the text or of the question. In addition, a candidate may get an item right by eliminating wrong answers, which is a different skill from that of being able to choose the right answer in the first place (Weir, 1990). Another possible problem is one of passage independence. Bernhardt (1991, p. 198) cites evidence of candidates being able to determine answers without reading the passage. There is also some concern that students' scores on multiple-choice tests can be improved by training in test taking techniques and that such improvement reflects an enhanced ability to do multiple choice tests rather than any increase in language ability. The measurement of the reading trait, therefore, may be contaminated by the method employed. (For more about problems with MCQs, see Heaton, 1975; Weir, 1990, 1993; and West, 1991.)

Short Answer Questions

Another form of muddied measurement occurs if language abilities other than reading are being tested. With SAQs students have to supply their own answers, and there is some concern that if candidates are required to use their own words rather than language supplied in the text, the item may be significantly more difficult than it would be otherwise (Pollitt & Hutchinson, 1986). Furthermore, it might be testing writing as well as reading. There is accordingly interference with the measurement of the intended construct.

In an attempt to avoid this contamination of scores, several Examination Boards in Britain have included tasks which require information from written texts to be translated into a non-verbal form, e.g., by labelling a diagram, completing a chart or numbering a sequence of events. These can be useful test tasks, but a good deal of care needs to be taken that the task the students have to complete does not itself complicate the process or detract from the authenticity of the experience. There is also a danger that in order to fit more neatly into such formats, texts are sometimes expressly written for this purpose, and thus the authenticity of the task is compromised.

One advantage of SAQs, though, is that as answers are not provided one can be more certain that if a student gets the answer right, this must be because the student has understood the text. Furthermore, texts can be selected to match performance *conditions* appropriate to any level of student, and the format allows the testing of all the *operations* that might be required in a test of reading (see Weir, 1993 for a discussion of SAQs advantages and disadvantages and advice on their construction).

Text selection

In the past, reading texts were often short and in many cases artificially constructed (West, 1991). In the current 'orthodoxy' texts tend to be genuine and undoctored and as far as possible are selected according to the appropriacy for the target situation needs of the test takers (see Weir, 1993 for discussion of performance conditions to be taken account of in the design of reading tests). However, it is not always easy to determine which texts are most appropriate for which test takers. Though there is some evidence that test performance is enhanced by background knowledge in the content area of a reading comprehension passage (Alderson & Urquhart, 1983) the evidence is not conclusive (see Clapham, 1996; Ja'far, 1992; and Koh, 1985). Douglas discusses this in his review in this volume.

TEST VALIDATION METHODS

If the focus for questions is determined in a principled fashion, for example, by mindmapping, as described above, idiosyncrasy in content selection can largely be avoided. The immediate recall protocols advocated by Bernhardt (1991, pp. 200–210) for testing individuals might alternatively be used to help decide on what a candidate should be able to take away from a text.

The content validity of a test can be further investigated by a scrutiny of the test content by experts and by asking appropriate readers to introspect on their test taking processes as they take the test. The use of both these methods will enhance the probability that in the final test the required operations are being tested (Storey, 1995). Introspection in particular can illuminate the extent to which the behaviour elicited by test items equates with the behaviour that the theory based model identifies as being representative of the real reading which occurs outside of the test itself. Storey (1995) shows how introspective validation can help identify the proportions of construct-relevant and construct-irrelevant variance generated by test items. (For more about qualitative methods of test validation, see Banerjee and Luoma's review in this volume.)

WORK IN PROGRESS: THE READING CONSTRUCT

In the 1980s concern switched away from *how* to test reading towards a concern with *what* it is we are trying to test; a concern with the nature of the reading construct itself.

Williams and Moran (1989, p. 224) report on the apparent consensus among writers of teaching materials on the multi-dimensional nature of reading comprehension. The writers seem to accept that reading can be broken down into 'underlying skills components' for the purposes of teaching and testing – a view shared by many language teachers and testers (Grabe, 1991, p. 382). A recent four – level version of such a breakdown for testing purposes is provided in Table 1 below, based on Weir, 1993.

TABLE 1. Summary Checklist of Operations in Reading

Level A: Reading expeditiously for global comprehension

> **Search reading** i.e. locating information quickly and selectively on predetermined topic(s) relevant to predetermined needs (e.g. answering questions on the main idea(s) of the text).

> **Skimming** i.e. looking through a text quickly and selectively to identify the main idea(s) and the discourse topic as efficiently as possible.

Level B: Reading expeditiously for local comprehension

> **Scanning** i.e. looking quickly through a text to locate a specific phrase, word or number.

Level C: Reading carefully for global comprehension

> Reading carefully to establish accurate comprehension of the explicitly stated main ideas the author wishes to convey (might include tracing the development of an argument, reducing what is read to an outline of the main points).

> Making propositional inferences. The reader uses explicit statements in the text to come to a conclusion that is not explicitly stated, without recourse to knowledge from outside the text.

Level D: Reading carefully for local comprehension

> At some level all of the above might include knowledge of the following more specifically linguistic contributory skills, or they can be tested discretely:

> Understanding the syntactic structure of a sentence and clause.
> Understanding lexical and/or grammatical cohesion.
> Understanding lexis/deducing meaning of lexical items from morphology and context.

The multi-divisible and unitary views of reading

It is current practice among many test-developers, when constructing test items relating to a text, to focus on the reading components in Table 1 above, either singly or in combination, even though the sum of these parts – the answers to these test items – might not necessarily equate fully with what the reader would normally take away from the text.

If specific skills components or strategies could be clearly identified as making an important contribution to the reading process, then it would of course be at least possible, if not necessary, to test these and to use the composite results for reporting on the reading proficiency revealed. However, despite the wide-spread influence of a multi-divisible view of reading on current testing and teaching practice, caution needs to be exercised as little empirical evidence has as yet been offered in its support.

A substantial number of studies have claimed that it is not possible to differentiate between reading ability components, either through empirical demonstration of the separate functioning of such components when these are operationalised in language test items, or through the judgement of experts on what the focus of such test items actually is (e.g. Alderson, 1990; Alderson & Lukmani, 1989; Carver, 1992; Lunzer et al., 1979; Rosenshine, 1980; Rost, 1993). However, although almost all of the quantitative studies seem to suggest that in general it may not be possible to identify multiple, separate reading ability components, there is one factor, vocabulary, which is consistently distinguished from general reading comprehension. Given that most of the factor analyses in the above studies produced more than one significant factor, it would be difficult to maintain that reading is a unitary ability (see Rost, 1993 in particular).

There is, in addition, a disturbing corollary to the fully unitary argument which deserves serious attention from all involved in developing language tests. If there are no discernible components in reading – i.e., if reading is unidimensional – it should not really matter how we test it, or what operations we try to assess. The inability to provide consistent or conclusive empirical evidence (either quantitative or qualitative) for the separability of components might well encourage us to utilise test formats with a specifically linguistic focus (Level D type operations in Table 1 above). Items focusing on the microlinguistic level are relatively easy to construct, administer and mark, frequently have respectable reliability estimates, and seem to correlate fairly highly with more global tests of reading comprehension.

However, it would seem imprudent to test only specifically linguistic Level D operations if we wish to make direct statements about a candidate's overall reading ability. Tests focusing on Level D microlinguistic elements may well correlate quite highly with other reading tests which measure global comprehension more directly, but correlations of .8 still leave a third of the test variance unaccounted for, so performance on one test does not tell us everything about performance on the others. In addition, in a number of studies, microlinguistic items do appear to load on a different factor from careful or search reading for main ideas. This suggests that the items are measuring something different. Level D microlinguistic elements seem to contribute to Level A and C activities, but on their own may not constitute an adequate predictor of those abilities.

There is also some evidence that expeditious (quick, purposeful and efficient) reading (for example, search reading, skimming) may not involve exactly the same abilities as reading carefully (Pugh, 1978). Investigations into overseas students' abilities (Beard, 1972; Weir, 1983) indicate that for many readers, reading quickly and efficiently (Level A operations) posed greater problems than reading carefully and efficiently (Level C operations). Empirical evidence is also emerging that items testing search reading for main ideas may load on a different factor from items testing careful reading for main ideas. Many of the studies reporting reading as a unitary activity are based on tests which contain no sections or items testing the ability to process text quickly and efficiently for main ideas, and these studies, therefore, may not be in a position to make the claims that they do.

Equally serious problems may arise in accepting unthinkingly a multi-divisibility view. In the past, broadly sampling components across Levels A–D seemed a sensible course of action for assessing reading comprehension. Test constructors attempted to sample across the range of hypothesised operations in order to take an adequate sample of a construct that could be labelled reading (Weir, 1983, 1990). However, doubts now arise concerning the relative contribution of components to the measurement of the construct of reading, at least in terms of the relationship between Level D and the other three levels (Alderson & Lukmani, 1989, p. 269; Weir & Porter, 1994). Weir and Porter noted that there were a number of students who were able to cope with reading passages and questions at the global level, but who could not cope with test items focusing on microlinguistic items at the local level, that is cohesive devices, lexis and structural elements.

In proficiency tests of L2 reading, the issue of validity is crucial given the use to which the results of such tests are normally put. If items with a specific local linguistic focus are used in the measurement of reading ability, and if the results are then used to decide who may embark on further study or enter the professions, the results might be unfair. Those students who can understand almost all the main ideas and important information in a passage but who are unsure about the meaning of particular lexical items or cohesion devices – items selected for inclusion perhaps subjectively or idiosyncratically – may not pass through the entrance gate which the test embodies.

With evidence against both the unitary view of reading ability on the one hand, and the multi-divisible view on the other, it is important for those concerned with language test development to reflect critically on the ramifications of operationalising either in reading tests.

The reader

As well as the text and task based factors discussed above we also need to consider the readers themselves. Urquhart (1987) makes an important distinction between 'comprehensions' and 'interpretations' when he refers to two specific sets of differences between readers' approaches to reading. He says that different 'comprehensions' arise from different and consciously adopted *purposes*, which lead the reader to read a text differently at different times. These comprehensions are comparatively easy to test. Most reading tests contain a variety of test items which either require gist extraction or more careful and detailed study.

'Interpretations', on the other hand, hardly feature in most published reading tests, nor is it easy to see how they could be included. They arise from a different kind of reader input, and the answers to such test questions will vary from reader to reader. Urquhart argues that it is essential to consider the relationship between text, reader and comprehension, since this relationship has a major bearing on testing, and on the limits of testing. He argues that there has been for some time a consensus in the field of reading theory that every text is incomplete, and that it has to be converted into meaningful discourse by the reader. This in turn entails variety in interpretation by different readers, governed by factors such as background knowledge, formal knowledge and the relationship adopted by the reader to the text. Readings may differ according to the reader's culture, either ethnic or professional, or according to the reader's different knowledge or preoccupations.

Because of the difficulty of testing 'interpretations', we may have to limit ourselves to testing 'comprehensions', in which case we must accept that we will only be able to assess a limited part of reading ability, information retrieval from the text rather than from pragmatically inferred meaning beyond the text.

FUTURE DIRECTIONS

The argument as to whether reading is multi-divisible, or whether it is an indivisible, unitary process, is still unresolved. If a fully unitary view is to be clearly rejected, future research will need to demonstrate the consistent presence of at least a second component in repeated analyses of test results across a range of samples of English as a second or other language candidates. Secondly, future research will need to investigate whether such components are identifiable. Finally it will have to establish the extent to which each component has a meaningful effect on the measurement of reading comprehension. How much of the overall variance does each component explain in a reading test?

The wholesale adherence to either the unitary or the multi-divisible view may be problematic. For further investigation of these matters, it will be necessary firstly to develop tests which are maximally valid tests of the skill components at the four levels (through systematic a priori validation including mindmapping of target texts by language and subject specialists, expert judgement, student introspection and statistical analysis) and secondly to investigate the performance on the resulting tests of students at a variety of ability levels.

There is some doubt about the status of items which focus on specifically linguistic operations at Level D as part of the assessment of a candidate's general reading ability. As a matter of urgency, it is necessary to investigate whether testing at Level D does in fact contribute any valid information about a candidate's ability to handle Level A, B and C activities. We must address the implications of emerging evidence that there may be groups of candidates who are capable of operating at Levels A and C but who are severely disadvantaged by test items which focus on Level D.

In testing reading we might be best served by establishing the test population's purposes for reading and investigating the ability of test takers to achieve these (Pugh, 1978, p. 78). These purposes relate closely to the strategies and skills involved in search reading, skimming, scanning and careful reading listed in Table 1 above. The purposeful nature of these strategies and skills for expeditious and careful reading, and the fact that they result in the achievement or non-achievement of a measurable product, makes them suitable for testing.

Systematic research may help us better to understand what reading involves and will enrich the descriptions that can be made available. A focus on the criterial and measurable components of reading ability may enable us to move away from an unhelpful single grade in reading tests, and away from single reading tests, to a situation where a diagnostic profile of criterial skills and strategies arising out of a range of measures becomes a possibility (Spolsky, 1995).

University of Reading, England

REFERENCES

Alderson, J.C.: 1978, *A Study of the Cloze Procedure with Native and Non-Native Speakers of English*, Unpublished Ph.D. thesis, University of Edinburgh, Edinburgh.
Alderson, J.C.: 1990, 'Testing reading comprehension skills (part one)', *Reading in a Foreign Language* 6(2), 425–438.

Alderson, J.C. & Lukmani, Y.: 1989, 'Cognition and reading: Cognitive levels as embodied in test questions', *Reading in a Foreign Language* 5(2), 253–270.

Alderson, J.C. & Urquhart, A.H.: 1983, 'The effect of student background discipline on comprehension: A pilot study', in A. Hughes & D. Porter (eds.), *Current Developments in Language Testing*, Academic Press, London, 121–127.

Beard, R.: 1972, *Teaching and Learning in Higher Education*, Penguin Books Ltd., Harmondsworth.

Bernhardt, E.B.: 1991, *Reading Development in a Second Language: Theoretical, Empirical and Classroom Perspectives*, Norwood, Ablex Publishing Corporation, NJ.

Carver, R.P.: 1992, 'What do standardised tests of reading comprehension measure in terms of efficiency, accuracy and rate?' *Reading Research Quarterly* 27, 347–359.

Clapham, C.: 1996, *The Development of IELTS: A Study of the Effect of Background Knowledge on Reading Comprehension*, Cambridge University Press, Cambridge.

Faerch, C. & Kasper, G. (eds.).: 1987, *Introspection in Second Language Research*, Multilingual Matters Ltd., Clevedon, Avon, England.

Grabe, W.: 1991, 'Current developments in second language reading research', *TESOL Quarterly* 25(3), 375–406.

Handschin, C.H.: 1919, *Handschin Modern Language Tests, Test A*, World Book Company, Yonkers, New York.

Heaton, J.B.: 1975, *Writing English Language Tests*, Longman, London.

Howatt, A.P.R.: 1984, *A History of English Language Teaching*, Oxford University Press, Oxford.

Ja'far, W.: 1992, *The Interactive Effects of Background Knowledge on ESP Reading Comprehension Proficiency Tests*, Unpublished Ph.D. thesis, CALS, University of Reading, Reading, UK.

Koh, M.Y.: 1985, 'The role of prior knowledge in reading comprehension', *Reading in a Foreign Language* 3, 375–380.

Lunzer, E., Waite, M., & Dolan, T.: 1979, 'Comprehension and comprehension tests', in E. Lunzer, & K. Gardner (eds.), *The Effective Use of Reading*, Heinemann Educational, London, 37–71.

Marcel, C.: 1853, *Language as a Means of Mental Culture and International Communication; or, Manual of the Teacher and the Learner of Languages*, Chapman and Hall, London.

Pollitt, A. & Hutchinson, C.: 1986, 'The validity of comprehension tests: What makes questions difficult?', in D. Vincent, A.K. Pugh & G. Brooks (eds.), *Assessing Reading*, Macmillan Education Ltd., Basingstoke.

Pugh, A.K.: 1978, *Silent Reading*, Heinemann Educational, London.

Rosenshine, B.V.: 1980, 'Skills hierarchies in reading comprehension', in R.J. Spiro, B. Bruce & W. Brewer (eds.), *Theoretical Issues in Reading Comprehension*, Lawrence Erlbaum Associates, Hillsdale, NJ, 535–554.

Rost, D.H.: 1993, 'Assessing the different components of reading comprehension: Fact or fiction', *Language Testing* 10(1), 79–92.

Sarig, G.: 1989, 'Testing meaning construction: Can we do it fairly?', *Language Testing* 6(1), 77–94.

Spolsky, B.: 1995, *Measured Words: the Development of Objective Language Testing*, Oxford University Press, Oxford.

Storey, P.: 1995, *Investigating Construct Validity through Test Taker Introspection*, Unpublished Ph.D. thesis, CALS, University of Reading, Reading, UK.

Taylor, W.L.: 1953, 'Cloze procedure: A new tool for measuring readability', *Journalism Quarterly*, 415–433.

Urquhart, A.H.: 1987, 'Comprehensions and interpretations' *Reading in a Foreign Language* 3(2), 387–409.

Weir, C.J.: 1983, *Identifying the Language Needs of Overseas Students in Tertiary Educa-*

tion in the United Kingdom, Ph.D. thesis, University of London, Institute of Education, London.

Weir, C.J.: 1990, *Communicative Language Testing*, Prentice Hall, London.

Weir, C.J.: 1993, *Understanding and Developing Language Tests*, Prentice Hall, London.

Weir, C.J. & Porter, D.: 1994, 'The multi-divisible or unitary nature of reading: The language tester between Scylla and Charybdis', *Reading in a Foreign language* 10(2), 1–20.

West, R.: 1991, 'Developments in the testing of reading', *English as a World Language* 1(1), 60–70.

Williams, E. & Moran, C.: 1989, 'Reading in a foreign language at intermediate and advanced levels with particular reference to English', *Language Teaching* 22(4), 217–228.

TEACHING GRAMMAR IN A SECOND LANGUAGE

ALISTER CUMMING

THE TESTING OF WRITING IN A SECOND LANGUAGE

The testing of second-language writing has been a principal concern of educators over the past two decades, particularly in relationship to the use of English and French in universities, colleges and schools. Many academic, professional, technical, and vocational fields have required people to demonstrate their writing competence in diverse languages taught throughout the world, and recently the writing of expository or narrative compositions has come to be considered an exceptionally important indicator of students' proficiency or achievement in English and French as second languages, particularly as an indicator of the capacity of students to function effectively in these languages in academic contexts. The qualities of second-language writing that have prompted this focal status, however, also represent major areas of recent theoretical controversy, empirical research, and debate concerning educational policies. The integrated, holistic nature of composition writing requires students to make effective use of varied, complex aspects of language proficiency in a purposeful manner. Composition writing represents a 'real' academic task, while providing, for the purposes of assessment, direct evidence of individual students' language performance. The tasks generally require students to produce texts that can be readily evaluated impressionistically on a variety of features whilst the results can be related to normative standards and documented for further analyses.

EARLY DEVELOPMENTS

The evaluation of written compositions has for centuries served as a routine form of integrated language assessment (Kelly, 1969, pp. 156–171). Recent commentators (e.g., Hamp-Lyons, 1991, p. 7) have observed how tests from the 1950s to the 1970s tended to adopt a 'structuralist-psychometric' orientation. For example, they evaluated second-language students' knowledge of writing indirectly by using discrete test items that assessed knowledge of particular linguistic features, such as grammatical or stylistic choices or errors, or specific composing behaviors, such as spelling or editing. Influential authorities in language testing at this time, such as Lado (1961) and Harris (1969), advocated specifying test items in this manner because of the objectivity and control that could be exercised. In doing so, they espoused methods of testing that were compatible with lock-step approaches to language instruction, such as grammar-translation

C. Clapham and D. Corson (eds), Encyclopedia of Language and Education,
Volume 7: Language Testing and Assessment, 51–63.
© 1997 Kluwer Academic Publishers. Printed in the Netherlands.

or audio-lingual teaching methods, which sequenced the presentation and practice of specific aspects of a language to be taught, and thus tested. (For more about the assessment of grammar, see Rea-Dickins' review in this volume.) However, these same authorities also recommended assessing writing directly and holistically, by, for example, utilizing 'short compositions on assigned topics ... of thirty minutes duration each' in which 'style and content are graded as well as mechanics' (Lado, 1961, p. 256, and similarly, see Harris, 1969, pp. 69–71, 77–80, as well as Henmon, 1929, and discussions by Spolsky, 1995, pp. 43–45, 223–226).

From the late 1970s onwards, several interrelated influences have helped to give written composition its current status in evaluation practices, and have ensured that most comprehensive testing of language proficiency for academic purposes now requires learners to demonstrate that they can write extended stretches of meaningful, literate discourse in the language being evaluated. One influence on this was the theoretical conceptualization of language proficiency above and beyond the conventional elements of vocabulary and grammar, at the level of text-discourse or rhetoric. This influence was signalled by Kaplan's widely-cited (1966) analysis of rhetorical differences in essays written by students at an American university with different cultural backgrounds. Similarly, the International Association for the Evaluation of Educational Achievement (IEA) conducted international comparative studies of achievement in English as a Foreign Language (Lewis & Massad, 1975) and French as a Foreign Language (Carroll, 1975) in a variety of countries. The IEA project established standards for test development and validation based on J.B. Carroll's model of language skills (e.g., Carroll, 1975), which viewed writing as one of four basic, integrated language skills (the others being reading, oral production and auditory comprehension). It also provided a model set of prompted writing tasks which, as Wolf (1992) has observed, formed an early type of performance testing. At about the same time, the direct assessment of writing became the widely-accepted norm for evaluation practices in English mother-tongue writing in schools and universities (see Purves' review in this volume). Within several years, many second-language educators, adopting a communicative orientation to language instruction, explicitly advocated testing students' performance on realistic, communicative tasks such as composition or letter writing (e.g., Canale, 1981; Morrow, 1979). This emerging perspective was supported by several extensive needs analyses that found the successful writing of essays, examinations, and other kinds of texts to be integral to routine performance in second language academic contexts (e.g., Bridgeman & Carlson, 1983; Kroll, 1979; Weir, 1983).

MAJOR CONTRIBUTIONS

By the 1990s, perspectives and publications on second-language writing had proliferated to the point that Hamp-Lyons (1991) was able to edit an extensive volume on fundamental issues related to evaluation in this area. In particular, six influential projects in the early 1980s established ratings of students' written compositions as the pervasive, conventional means of assessing second-language writing. Each project produced, from compelling theoretical rationales and extensive pilot research, descriptive criteria in the form of scales for rating second-language writing. These offered simple analytic frameworks that appealed to many educators' needs to view students' second-language writing comprehensively, holistically, in a standard way, over a full range of proficiency levels (typically sequenced from initial competence to native-like mastery of writing). These criteria and scales had an apparent authoritative coherence which helped demarcate the range of possible performances in writing a second language that students might display, and thus helped raters conceptualize normatively individuals' levels of writing proficiency. Each of these projects conceptualized the large-scale testing of second-language writing in a similar manner: students perform specific, brief (e.g., lasting about 30 minutes) composition tasks; the results are then judged impressionistically and reliably (ideally with about 80% agreement) by trained raters using a common scale (or set of scales) with descriptive criteria and anchor papers displaying model compositions at each reference point on the scale (i.e., essentially as advocated two decades earlier by Lado, 1961, pp. 256–260 and in the 1920s by Henmon, 1929, as described by Spolsky, 1995, pp. 43–46). The six projects nonetheless differed in three fundamental ways. Culturally, they addressed differing contexts for language education. Politically, different institutions, agencies or professional organizations promoted them. Technically, they differed in whether they treated the construct of second-language writing proficiency holistically (i.e., as a single entity, and thus as a single scale that integrates the principal traits of students' texts, based on readers' general impressions of the texts) or as multiple traits (i.e., as component sets of skills, and thus as separate scales representing analytically distinct traits that can be evaluated independently and can be presumed to vary according to individual writers on such traits as rhetorical organization, vocabulary choice, or ideational content) (see Hamp-Lyons, 1991, pp. 241–276; Weir, 1990, pp. 63–68). This technical distinction has, in testing practice, also been commonly called a difference between holistic rating (which assesses all aspects of a written composition together based on raters' overall impressions in reference to a single scale) and analytic rating (which asks raters to judge specific traits of students' writing separately and to mark each trait independently according to a set of unique scales). As Hamp-Lyons (1991) has argued, however, the term multiple-trait is preferable to analytic because all impressionistic ratings of compositions, including holistic scales, require raters to perform analyses.

Holistic rating scales appeared in: B. Carroll's (1980) English Language Testing Service (ELTS) test scales for adults writing in English as a second or foreign language for academic and professional purposes in Britain and elsewhere; the American Council on the Teaching of Foreign Languages' scales for secondary-school students in the U.S. learning languages such as French, German, or Spanish (ACTFL, 1986, and earlier versions from 1981); and Educational Testing Service's (1992, and earlier versions from 1986) Test of Written English for compositions written by overseas students of English intending to study in universities or colleges in North America (as an adjunct to the Test of English as a Foreign Language, see Stansfield & Ross, 1988, Spolsky, 1995, pp. 327–331). Multiple-trait (or analytic) rating scales appeared in Jacobs, Zinkgraf, Wormuth, Hartfiel and Hughey's (1981) ESL Composition Profile for essays written by adult learners of English as a Second Language at North American universities or colleges (using the rating criteria: content, organization, vocabulary, language use, and mechanics) and the Royal Society of Arts' scales (1980 and subsequent versions developed and administered by the University of Cambridge Local Examinations Syndicate) for judging various communicative writing tasks (such as writing messages, letters, sets of instructions, or reports) in English as a Foreign Language (using the rating criteria: accuracy, appropriacy, range, and complexity). These five projects established scales that raters might apply generically across various writing tasks, though often within a single task-type such as an essay, narrative or report. In contrast, the scales developed between 1983 and 1985 by Dickson, Boyce, Lee, Portal, Smith, and Kendall (1987) for surveys of 13-year-old British children's proficiency in French (and for related tests of German and Spanish) resembled primary-trait scoring (see Hamp-Lyons, 1991, pp. 246–247) in that a unique, holistic scale was defined empirically for each separate writing task they administered (e.g., giving personal information, describing a place), recognizing its unique contexts and content. Only the ESL Composition Profile and the Test of Written English focused solely on writing; the other four projects considered writing in conjunction with scales for other skill areas such as oral communication (on which considerably more research had been done), reading, and listening comprehension.

WORK IN PROGRESS: PROBLEMS AND DIFFICULTIES

Considerable research in the past decade has addressed a common set of concerns raised in the development or administration of these six projects or various new ones akin to them. These issues have centered on: the reliability of scoring procedures, the selection of composition tasks, the validation of the construct of second-language writing proficiency or achievement, and the attempt to make the assessment of second-language writing more relevant to educational purposes.

Reliability of Scoring

Most research on the evaluation of second-language writing has focused on establishing the reliability of scoring among pools of raters (e.g., Cushing-Weigle, 1994; Shohamy, Gordon & Kraemer, 1992; Stansfield & Ross, 1988). Because of the reliance on human interpretation in rating compositions impressionistically, this is perhaps the major area of controversy in writing test development and administration at the moment. Test development projects have tended to address this matter by carefully refining their descriptive criteria and their procedures for scoring, by training and maintaining pools of raters, and by establishing consistent agreement among these raters (i.e., inter-rater reliability). However, analysts such as Hamp-Lyons (1990), Henning (1991) and Raimes (1990) have pointed out that establishing and maintaining inter-rater agreement is only a minimum step toward reliability. Indeed, if test analysts focus on inter-rater agreement alone (i.e., as a simple calculation of agreement within a pool of raters on each test administration), their analyses may neglect actual differences in reliability among raters, for example, differences over time and over geographic locations. For instance, a simple calculation of agreement among raters at one test administration in one location may not be able to account for differences among raters at other times or other places. Polio (1997) has reviewed various studies of writing in second languages, demonstrating that practices for estimating reliability for measures of linguistic accuracy among raters of composition in this research is often inadequate or imprecise. Inter-rater reliability therefore needs to be complemented in testing practice by other analyses such as test-retest reliability or internal consistency estimates (as well as construct validation – see below). Similarly, several researchers have determined that different populations of raters, such as English instructors with orientations to mother-tongue, foreign-language or second-language instruction, may exercise differing expectations in evaluating second-language compositions. This tendency raises concerns over which (or whose) values should be promoted as standards for effective writing in a second language (see Kobayashi & Rinnert, 1996; Song & Caruso, 1996 for recent studies).

Selection of Composition Tasks

A second frequent concern is the selection of composition tasks to be evaluated and the conditions under which examinees do such writing.

Many second-language tests require examinees to compose one or two brief texts (presumably for reasons of efficiency in terms of testing time and scoring costs). But considerable controversy exists about this practice. One question is whether such tasks can solicit sufficient indications of students' writing proficiency, given the well-demonstrated differences in performance across different writing tasks or topics. A second controversy is over whether such tasks correspond realistically to real-world writing demands, particularly where academic tasks might typically be done over periods of weeks or months (Hamp-Lyons, 1990; Raimes, 1990; Wall, 1982). Given these concerns about performance variables related to writing assessment, authors such as Kroll and Reid (1994) have proposed guidelines for the preparation and evaluation of instructions and prompts for assessing second-language writing. Such guidelines can help reduce the range of performance variables that might appear in writing tasks on a composition test, ensuring that the writing solicited is what the testers have intended and that the conditions posed for the students are clearly prescribed. Such concerns also raise questions about the predictive validity of brief compositions if used, for example, for purposes of admissions to academic programs or for certification of professional competence. Moreover, in technical terms, a single composition task in effect forms a test consisting of a single item (albeit a large, comprehensive one). This makes it difficult to claim that such a test elicits an adequate sample of the broad domain of second-language writing. A related concern is whether writing should be tested in isolation, as was proposed in Carroll's (1975) model of language skills, and as is frequently done in practice, or whether students' second-language literacy should be assessed in a more integrative fashion, by, for example, testing reading and writing together (as attempted by Carson, Carrell, Silberstein, Kroll, & Kuehn, 1990). (See also Lewkowicz's review in this volume.)

Construct Validation

Several researchers have begun to probe into issues of construct validation that underlie concerns about reliability in scoring or the representativeness of the writing tasks used in testing. Such research involves investigating fundamental aspects of second-language writing proficiency or achievement. Four research areas have emerged, each contributing in different ways to our knowledge of the central construct evaluated in tests of second-language written composition. One area has focused on the characteristics of written texts that second-language learners produce in tests, a second on the decisions and criteria that raters utilize to form their evaluation judgments, a third on empirically validating scales and criteria used for scoring, and a fourth on specifying models of second-language writing proficiency or achievement. Research in these areas is still preliminary but of considerable importance in refining what is meant by testing second-language writing (Connor-Linton, 1995; cf. Huot, 1990 for an analogous position on the evaluation of mother-tongue writing).

Characteristics of written texts
Recent research on composition text features has focused on identifying the specific textual characteristics that distinguish examination composi-tions written by adult learners at one level of proficiency in English from those written at higher or lower levels. As Homburg (1984) proposes, an objective basis (i.e., in the linguistic or rhetorical features of students' texts) might thus be discovered which could justify the constructs un-derlying raters' impressionistic scoring of second-language compositions. Studies pursuing such analyses have found, for example, in various con-texts, significant differences in learners' morphology, rather than syntax (Bardovi-Harlig & Bofman, 1989), accurate use of articles (Cumming & Mellow, 1996), metadiscourse markers (Intaraprawat & Steffensen, 1995), vocabulary (Laufer & Nation, 1995), rhetorical framing (Tedick & Math-ison, 1995), and various indices of clause structures (Homburg, 1984; Ishikawa, 1995; Perkins, 1980). As each of these researchers has ac-knowledged, however, the contexts investigated in their studies were too restricted to be of general significance in defining developmental sequences in second-language writing which might substantively inform testing prac-tices, though this is a future possibility. Research of this type has scarcely begun to evaluate the diverse writing produced in different educational contexts, by different populations of learners. Nor has it begun to evaluate the different types of writing produced for the different task-types that are associated with second-language learning internationally, such as: high school learners of English as a Second Language (e.g., Tarone, Downing, Cohen, Gillette, Murie & Dailey, 1993); university students of French as a Foreign Language (e.g., Kern & Schultz, 1992); or primary school students in various types of Bilingual (e.g., Carlisle, 1989) or Immersion (e.g., Harley, Allen, Cummins & Swain, 1990) programs. Research of this type may, in the future, lead to useful specifications of second language development in the context of written compositions, which could inform specifications for language tests. But for now the range of variables and contexts of language development to be considered seems daunting. Per-haps the one finding from such studies with immediate implications for testing is that simple tallies of students' errors are inadequate as indicators of second-language writing proficiency (see review by Rifkin & Roberts, 1995); that is, many more text variables (such as those listed above), in addition to students' grammatical errors, need to be accounted for in assessing written compositions in a second language.

Raters' decisions and evaluation criteria
A different line of research has investigated the judgment processes of
raters of second-language compositions, studying the thought processes
and decisions that skilled raters make while evaluating second-language
compositions. Such studies have typically used think-aloud protocols to
generate verbal accounts of the aspects of students' texts that raters attend
to while judging them, as well as the criteria they cite in forming their
judgments. For example, Cumming (1990) found 28 distinct strategies
that experienced evaluators used frequently when interpreting and judging
ESL compositions. Vaughn (1991) described various similar criteria cited
in the think-aloud protocols she gathered from raters. In addition to contributing to construct validation, such descriptions improve the training of
novice raters by clarifying the subtle, otherwise implicit, decision making
processes of skilled raters (Cumming, 1990; Cushing-Weigle, 1994).

Empirical validation of scales
A third approach to the construct validation of tests of second-language
writing has involved empirically scaling, using methods such as Rasch
analysis, the scores obtained for specific populations of learners (e.g., as
described above for Dickson, Boyce, Lee, Portal, Smith, & Kendall's study
in Britain). (For more about Rasch Analysis see the reviews by Pollitt and
McNamara in this volume.) Surprisingly, despite the recent proliferation
of scales for assessing second-language writing, very few of these scales
have been subjected to the rigorous empirical analyses needed to verify that
they correspond to the writing of specific populations of language learners.
Tyndall and Mann Kenyon (1996) describe a prototypical approach in their
development of a new holistic rating scale at one university. They used
multi-faceted Rasch analyses to assess the distribution of ratings made in
terms of each raters' consistency and relative severity (in respect to other
raters) and to discover whether the raters' placement of students on the scale
were well separated and defined. Hamp-Lyons & Henning (1991) describe
an alternative approach to empirical verification, comparing scores for
different populations of ESL learners and aspects of ESL writing on a
multi-trait rating scale.

Models of second-language writing proficiency
Of immediate relevance to the construct validation of second-language
writing tests is research proposing descriptive and explanatory models of
student achievement in respect to second-language writing. Although at a
preliminary stage of inquiry, such research attempts to define theoretically,
and to verify empirically, those aspects of their second-language writing
that learners are able to improve on and to show how such improvement
might vary according to the educational experiences students have had,
their individual backgrounds, and their uses of the language. Certain

conceptual models have been proposed for second-language writing development (e.g., Valdes, Haro & Echevarriarza, 1992) or second-language literacy generally (e.g., Hornberger, 1989). Sasaki and Hirose (1996) present a promising approach to model-building, with obvious relevance to test design, in their specification and evaluation of a causal path model of explanatory variables that accounted for variance in the essay scores of adult Japanese learners of English. Similarly, Silva's (1993) synthesis of empirical research to date has taken a major step forward in identifying the aspects of second-language writing that uniquely distinguish it from writing in the mother tongue. (For more about recent research into mother tongue and second language writing, see Grabe & Kaplan, 1996.)

Relevance to educational purposes
Perhaps the chief problem with current approaches to testing second-language writing is their lack of congruence with educational practices. Raimes (1990), for example, has criticized ETS' Test of Written English for its negative impact on ESL teaching and learning practices internationally. She questions the educational value of its brief writing tasks and simple rating scale, which have assumed a widespread authority in screening students for admissions to North American universities and colleges. Of major concern for educators is the manner in which the form and content of such tests are at odds with teachers' classroom assessment of students' writing. Teachers tend to have a more purely formative purpose and responsive manner, shaped by local contexts of teaching, learning, and individual endeavor (Leki, 1990; Zamel, 1985) which is difficult to account for in situations of normative, system-wide evaluation. Most current tests of second-language writing have been developed to function at the level of educational systems, rather than individual classrooms, learners or schools. But even within a system-perspective, many tests of second-language writing appear to be used more for entry or placement into programs than for determining achievement or certification (Cumming, 1995). This may be inevitable, given the limitations in the construct validation of such tests. Although leading figures in this area such as Hamp-Lyons (1991, pp. 261–263) have proposed the use of portfolio assessment for second-language writing, the idea has hardly caught on at a system level, seemingly because of the many difficulties outlined by Freedman (1991) in her review of recent efforts to use portfolio assessment in system-wide evaluations of mother-tongue writing. For example, Darling-Hammond, Ancess & Falk (1995) describe an innovative, collaborative approach to the assessment of the writing and other subject matter knowledge of minority English students in one high school in the U.S., but they acknowledge that the standards established in this situation would be difficult to extend beyond the local decision making of teachers and students in the particular school. (For more about portfolio assessment see Purves's review in this volume.)

FUTURE DIRECTIONS

The two concerns of construct validation and educational relevance are certain to occupy much future work in the testing of second-language writing. Testers in this area need fuller, more precise models of proficiency and achievement in second-language writing than presently exist before their tests can claim unambiguously to have the construct validity required to provide the basis of educational decisions. Efforts in this direction, however, are constrained by the sheer variety of situations and purposes for which people around the world learn to write in second languages, as well as by the related, intervening variables associated with these diverse circumstances (see Hornberger, 1989). Likewise, systematic inquiry is needed to understand how teachers, students, and others with key stakes in second-language education actually use tests of second-language writing and related forms of assessment (see Grierson, 1995). At present, a lack of description and theories of test utilization in this area limits not only what can be said about their operations in, and effects on, educational practices, but also what might be done to improve these.

A major future trend may be to address each of these concerns concurrently within single educational jurisdictions, such as ministries of education, school boards, or consortia of universities or colleges. One such example, on a very large scale, is the Council of Europe's (1996) recent draft of a comprehensive framework to guide language teaching and learning in European nations. This framework combines different approaches to profiling students' language development (e.g., through portfolios) using sets of standard scales (including ones for various types of writing). The Council of Europe hopes that researchers can validate the framework and scales empirically so that they can serve as a basis for more educationally relevant, coherent curricula and programs of self-study in diverse languages within Europe. Similarly, we can expect to see in coming years many applications of computer technology to the testing of second-language writing (see Gruba and Corbel's review in this volume). The use of word-processing, and the electronic transmission of texts will lead to efficiencies and economies in the students' production of written texts, and such advances will be enhanced by the potential for sophisticated text analyses and rater support.

Ontario Institute for Studies in Education
University of Toronto, Canada

REFERENCES

American Council on the Teaching of Foreign Languages (ACTFL): 1986, *ACTFL Proficiency Guidelines*, ACTFL, Hastings-on-Hudson, NY.

Bardovi-Harlig, K. & Bofman, T.: 1989, 'Attainment of syntactic and morphological accuracy by advanced language learners', *Studies in Second Language Acquisition* 11, 17–34.

Bridgeman, B. & Carlson, S.: 1983, *Survey of Academic Writing Tasks Required of Graduate and Undergraduate Foreign Students* (TOEFL Research Report No. 19), Educational Testing Service, Princeton NJ.

Canale, M.: 1981, 'Communication – how to evaluate it', *Bulletin of the Canadian Association of Applied Linguistics* 3, 77–94.

Carlisle, R.: 1989, 'The writing of Anglo and Hispanic Elementary School students in Bilingual, Submersion, and regular programs', *Studies in Second Language Acquisition* 11, 257–280.

Carroll, B.: 1980, *Testing Communicative Performance: An Interim Study*, Pergamon Press, Oxford.

Carroll, J.: 1975, *The Teaching of French as a Foreign Language in Eight Countries*, John Wiley & Sons, New York.

Carson, J., Carrell, P., Silberstein, S., Kroll, B., & Kuehn, P.: 1990, 'Reading-writing relationships in first and second language', *TESOL Quarterly*, 24, 245–266.

Connor-Linton, J.: 1995, 'Looking behind the curtain: What do L2 composition ratings really mean?', *TESOL Quarterly* 29, 762–765.

Council of Europe, Education Committee: 1996, *Common European Framework of Reference for Language Learning and Teaching, Draft 1, Language Learning for European Citizenship*, Strasbourg, France.

Cumming, A.: 1990, 'Expertise in evaluating second language compositions', *Language Testing* 7, 31–51.

Cumming, A.: 1995, 'Changing definitions of language proficiency: Functions of language assessment in educational programs for recent immigrant learners of English in Canada', *Journal of the Canadian Association of Applied Linguistics* 17, 35–48.

Cumming, A. & Mellow, D.: 1996, 'An investigation into the validity of written indicators of second language proficiency', in A. Cumming & R. Berwick (eds.), *Validation in Language Testing*, Multilingual Matters, Clevedon, England, 72–93.

Cushing-Weigle, S.: 1994, 'Effects of training on raters of ESL compositions', *Language Testing* 11, 197–223.

Darling-Hammond, L., Ancess, J. & Falk, B.: 1995, 'Collaborative learning and assessment at international high school', in L. Darling-Hammond, J. Ancess, & B. Falk (eds.), *Authentic Assessment in Action: Studies of Schools and Students at Work*, Teachers College Press, New York, 115–167.

Dickson, P., Boyce, C., Lee, B., Portal, M., Smith, M. & Kendall, L.: 1987, *Assessment of Performance Unit: Foreign Language Performance in Schools, Report on 1985 Survey of French*, National Foundation for Educational Research in England and Wales, Slough, England.

Educational Testing Service: 1992, *TOEFL Test of Written English* (third edition), Educational Testing Service, Princeton NJ.

Freedman, S.: 1991, *Evaluating Writing: Linking Large-scale Testing and Classroom Assessment*, Occasional Paper No. 27, Center for the Study of Writing, Berkeley CA.

Grabe, W. & Kaplan, R.B.: 1996, *Theory and Practice of Writing*, Longman, London

Grierson, J.: 1995, 'Classroom-based assessment in intensive English centres', in G. Brindley (ed.), *Language Assessment in Action*, National Centre for English Language Teaching and Research, Macquarie University, 195–237.

Hamp-Lyons, L.: 1990, 'Second language writing: Assessment issues', in B. Kroll (ed.), *Second Language Writing: Research Insights for the Classroom*, Cambridge University Press, Cambridge, 69–87.

Hamp-Lyons, L. (ed.): 1991, *Assessing Second Language Writing in Academic Contexts*, Ablex, Norwood NJ.

Hamp-Lyons, L. & Henning, G.: 1991, 'Communicative writing profiles: An investigation into the transferability of a multiple-trait scoring instrument across ESL writing contexts', *Language Learning* 41, 337–373.

Harley, B., Allen, P., Cummins, J. & Swain, M. (eds.): 1990, *The Development of Bilingual Proficiency*, Cambridge University Press, Cambridge.

Harris, D.: 1969, *Testing English as a Second Language*, McGraw-Hill, New York.

Henmon, V. (ed.): 1929, *Achievement Tests in the Modern Foreign Languages, Prepared for the Modern Foreign Language Study and the Canadian Committee on Modern Languages*, Macmillan, New York.

Henning, G.: 1991, 'Issues in evaluating and maintaining an ESL writing assessment program', in L. Hamp-Lyons (ed.), *Assessing Second Language Writing in Academic Contexts*, Ablex, Norwood NJ, 279–291.

Homburg, T.: 1984, 'Holistic evaluation of ESL compositions: Can it be validated objectively?', *TESOL Quarterly* 18, 87–106.

Hornberger, N.: 1989, 'Continua of biliteracy', *Review of Educational Research* 59, 271–296.

Huot, B.: 1990, 'The literature of direct writing assessment: Major concerns and prevailing trends', *Review of Educational Research* 60, 237–263.

Intaraprawat, P. & Steffensen, M.: 1995, 'The use of metadiscourse in good and poor ESL essays', *Journal of Second Language Writing* 4, 253–272.

Ishikawa, S.: 1995, 'Objective measurement of low-proficiency EFL narrative writing', *Journal of Second Language Writing* 4, 51–69.

Jacobs, H., Zinkgraf, S., Wormuth, D., Hartfiel, V. & Hughey, J.: 1981, *Testing ESL Composition: A Practical Approach*, Newbury House, Rowley MA.

Kaplan, R.: 1966, 'Cultural thought patterns in intercultural education', *Language Learning* 16, 1–20.

Kelly, L.: 1969, *25 Centuries of Language Teaching: 500 BC – 1969*, Newbury House, Rowley, MA.

Kern, R. & Schultz, J.: 1992, 'The effects of composition instruction on intermediate level French students' writing performance: Some preliminary findings', *Modern Language Journal* 76, 1–13.

Kobayashi, H. & Rinnert, C.: 1996, 'Factors affecting composition evaluation in an EFL context: Cultural rhetorical pattern and readers' background', *Language Learning* 46, 397–437.

Kroll, B.: 1979, 'A survey of writing needs of foreign and American college freshmen', *English Language Teaching Journal* 33, 219–227.

Kroll, B. & Reid, J.: 1994, 'Guidelines for writing prompts: Clarifications, caveats, and cautions', *Journal of Second Language Writing* 3, 231–255.

Lado, R.: 1961, 'Writing a foreign language', in *Language Testing: The Construction and Use of Foreign Language Tests*, Longman, London, 248–260.

Laufer, B. & Nation, P.: 1995, 'Vocabulary size and use: Lexical richness in written production', *Applied Linguistics* 16, 307–322.

Leki, I.: 1990, 'Coaching from the margins: Issues in written response', in B. Kroll (ed.), *Second Language Writing: Research Insights for the Classroom*, Cambridge University Press, Cambridge, 57–68.

Lewis, E.G. & Massad, C.: 1975, *The Teaching of English as a Foreign Language in Ten Countries*, John Wiley & Sons, New York.

Morrow, K.: 1979, 'Communicative language testing: revolution or evolution?', in C. Brumfit & K. Johnson (eds.), *The Communicative Approach to Language Teaching*, Oxford University Press, 1975, 143–157.

Perkins, K.: 1980, 'Using objective methods of attained writing proficiency to discriminate among holistic evaluations', *TESOL Quarterly* 14, 61–69.

Polio, C.: 1997, 'Measures of linguistic accuracy in research on second language writing', *Language Learning* 47, 101–143.

Raimes, A.: 1990, 'The TOEFL test of written English: Causes for concern', *TESOL Quarterly* 24, 427–442.

Royal Society of Arts (RSA): 1980, *Examinations in the Communicative Use of English as a Foreign Language, Specifications and Specimen Papers*, London, Royal Society of Arts.

Rifkin, B. & Roberts, F.: 1995, 'Error gravity: A critical review of research design', *Language Learning* 45, 511–537.

Sasaki, M. & Hirose, K.: 1996, 'Explanatory variables for EFL students' expository writing', *Language Learning* 46, 137–174.

Shohamy, E., Gordon, C. & Kraemer, R.: 1992, 'The effect of raters' background and training on the reliability of direct writing tests', *Modern Language Journal* 76, 27–33.

Silva, T.: 1993, 'Toward an understanding of the distinct nature of L2 writing: The ESL research and its implications', *TESOL Quarterly* 27, 657–677.

Song, B. & Caruso, I.: 1996, 'Do English and ESL faculty differ in evaluating the essays of native English-speaking and ESL students?', *Journal of Second Language Writing* 5, 163–182.

Spolsky, B.: 1995. *Measured Words: The Development of Objective Language Testing*, Oxford University Press, Oxford.

Stansfield, C. & Ross, J.: 1988, 'A long-term research agenda for the test of written English', *Language Testing* 5, 160–186.

Tarone, E., Downing, B., Cohen, A., Gillette, S., Murie, R. & Dailey, B.: 1993, 'The writing of southeast Asian-American students in secondary school and university', *Journal of Second Language Writing* 2, 149–172.

Tedick, D. & Mathison, M.: 1995, 'Holistic scoring in ESL writing assessment: What does an analysis of rhetorical features reveal?' in D. Belcher & G. Braine (eds.), *Academic Writing in a Second Language: Essays on Research and Pedagogy*, Ablex, Norwood, NJ, 205–230.

Tyndall, B. & Mann Kenyon, D.: 1996, 'Validation of a new holistic rating scale using Rasch multi-faceted analysis', in A. Cumming & R. Berwick (eds.), *Validation in Language Testing*, Multilingual Matters, Clevedon, Avon, England, 39–57.

Valdes, G., Haro, P. & Echevarriarza, M.: 1992, 'The development of writing abilities in a foreign language: Contributions toward a general theory of L2 writing', *Modern Language Journal* 76, 333–352.

Vaughn, C.: 1991, 'Holistic assessment: What goes on in the raters minds?', in L. Hamp-Lyons (ed.), *Assessing second language writing in academic contexts*, Ablex, Norwood, NJ, 111–125.

Wall, D.: 1982, 'A study of the predictive validity of the Michigan Battery, with special reference to the composition component', in T. Culhane, C. Klein-Braley & D. Stevenson (eds.), *Practice and Problems in Language Testing*, University of Essex, Department of Language and Linguistics, 156–169.

Weir, C.: 1983, *Identifying the Language Problems of Overseas Students in Tertiary Education in the United Kingdom*, Unpublished doctoral dissertation, University of London.

Weir, C.: 1990, *Communicative Language Testing*, New York, Prentice Hall.

Wolf, R.: 1992, 'Performance assessment in IEA studies', *IEA Bulletin* 1(2) July, 1–2.

Zamel, V.: 1985, 'Responding to student writing', *TESOL Quarterly* 19, 79–101.

GARY BUCK

THE TESTING OF LISTENING IN A SECOND LANGUAGE

There is no widely-accepted, explicit theory of second language (L2) listening comprehension, nor is there a research tradition separate from other aspects of comprehension. Rather, thinking on L2 listening is influenced by work in a number of related fields: mainly reading comprehension, linguistics, psycholinguistics, and cognitive psychology. Currently, listening comprehension is seen as an interaction between a variety of knowledge types on the one hand, both linguistic (lexical, syntactic, semantic, discourse, etc.) and non-linguistic (situational, content-related, and general world knowledge, etc.), and on the other hand an inherently indeterminate acoustic signal. Listening comprehension is an inferential process in which the listener constructs meaning through this interaction; and the interpretation of the text is guided and influenced by the context of situation and the listener's purpose for listening. (Useful introductory texts on psycholinguistics are: Gernsbacher, 1994; and Taylor & Taylor, 1990. For more about the process of reading see the reviews by Thompson, and by Tunmer, both in Volume 2.)

Ideas on testing second language listening ability have generally reflected the major movements in second language testing: the discrete-point, integrative, and communicative paradigms. These are paradigms in the sense that they form a set of reasonably coherent ideas about the nature of language, and how it should be tested; but in practice they are not mutually exclusive, and listening tests often contain elements associated with different paradigms. Some of the ideas associated with each paradigm are explicitly stated, but others are implicit in the common practices associated with them.

Listening situations can be arranged on a continuum, based on the amount of interaction, or collaboration, between the listener and the speaker: from non-interactive monologue at one end to completely interactive discussion at the other. Virtually all second language listening tests use non-interactive tasks, that is tasks in which the listener cannot interact with the speaker; interactive listening is usually only assessed as part of a spoken interview (for more about testing spoken language see Fulcher's review in this volume). The emphasis too, is almost entirely on testing transactional language (whose function is to convey information), rather than interactional language (whose function is to maintain social relationships; see Brown & Yule, 1983 for a discussion). While it is fair to say that processing transactional language in non-interactive (i.e.

C. Clapham and D. Corson (eds), Encyclopedia of Language and Education,
Volume 7: Language Testing and Assessment, 65–74.
© *1997 Kluwer Academic Publishers. Printed in the Netherlands.*

non-participatory) situations is at the core of what most second language educators mean by listening comprehension, it is important to note that this emphasis often misses important aspects of successful listening. (Useful sources relevant to testing L2 listening comprehension are: Buck, 1991; 1992; 1994; Dunkel, 1991a; 1991b; Dunkel, Henning & Chaudron, 1993; Hale & Courtney, 1994; Hanson & Jensen, 1994; Jensen & Hanson, 1995; McNamara, 1991; Scott, 1996; Shohamy & Inbar, 1991.)

PROBLEMS AND DIFFICULTIES

There are three characteristics of spoken language which the listening-test maker needs to be aware off. Firstly, the input into the listening process is an acoustic signal, which is often unclear and indeterminate, and hence text processing requires a knowledge of the sound system of the language, and the phonological modification that takes place in fast informal speech (see John Oakeshott-Taylor, 1977; 1980; and Brown, 1990). Secondly, linguistically, spoken texts are very different from written texts. Generally, they do not consist of well-formed grammatical sentences, but rather short, clause-like idea units: each about seven words long, of about two seconds duration, consisting of a single coherent intonation contour; these are usually strung together, or joined by a series of coordinating conjunctions. Spoken language tends to have more non-standard features, such as dialect, slang, and up to date colloquialisms; and it also contains many disfluencies, such as fillers and hesitations (e.g. *well, er, anyway*, or *OK let me see*), false starts, self corrections, afterthoughts, and so forth (see Chafe, 1985). Thirdly, spoken texts occur in real-time: they are fast and fleeting. Thus, processing has to be automatic and efficient, and linguistic knowledge has to be immediately available for use (probably the most common problem with second language listening is not lack of knowledge of the language *per se*, but the inability to apply that knowledge quickly enough to fast, real-time texts). Furthermore, after listening there is no text to refer back to. All the listener has is a memory trace, which in L2 listening, may represent a partial, or very incomplete understanding of what was said.

There are two problems relevant to all attempts to test listening comprehension. Firstly, comprehension takes place in the mind, and there is no observable product. It is always necessary to provide some task which is dependent on successful comprehension (e.g. answering questions, filling-in a chart, summarizing a text, etc.) and to infer from performance on that task whether the listener understood or not. Hence testing listening is an indirect process, and listening scores will always be influenced by other skills required for task completion (e.g. reading questions, understanding charts, writing summaries, etc.). Secondly, listeners have different listening purposes, different interests, and different background knowledge, and their interpretation of the text, and the situation in which it takes place, will be greatly influenced by these. Thus, for all but the most simple information-style texts, such as announcements, there may be a variety of different, but reasonable interpretations, and the test-maker's interpretation will be only one of these. (Useful overall reviews of listening comprehension are: Brown & Yule, 1983; Dirven & Oakeshott-Taylor, 1984; 1985; Rost, 1990; and Flowerdew, 1994.)

EARLY DEVELOPMENTS

The first tests of second language listening comprehension with a clearly identifiable theoretic basis were the discrete-point tests of the structuralist/ audio-lingual period. In the discrete-point paradigm, language is characterized as consisting of individual discrete 'bits', and language proficiency as knowing these individual bits. Testing language is seen as a process of sampling from these bits of knowledge, and testing whether the L2 user knows them (Lado, 1961).

The basic technique for testing listening comprehension is to present a short oral utterance in the target language, and check whether the test-taker has grasped some crucial part of it. The parts targeted usually include segmental phonemes, stress patterns, intonation, vocabulary, morphology, and syntax. In the most extreme discrete-point tests, it is only necessary for the test-taker to understand the actual bit of information being targeted. However, this idea is not always followed so strictly (e.g., in order to test knowledge of the correct form of the past tense, it may be necessary for the test-taker to understand enough of the utterance to grasp the fact that it ought to be in the past tense). But the emphasis is on one small part of the utterance, and context is not generally considered important except to resolve ambiguity in the point being tested. Selected responses are most common, as this technique was first developed during the great age of multiple choice testing, although true/false questions are also very popular. It is rather rare to ask listeners to construct responses, and if they are, these are usually very short.

To over-simplify somewhat, generally such tests characterize listening as a process of decoding an acoustic signal into the words encoded in the signal; with very little emphasis on processing at the semantic level of understanding the meaning of the words and phrases. This is a knowledge-based approach, and examination of the tasks used suggests that this is declarative knowledge (i.e. knowledge of facts) rather than procedural knowledge (i.e. knowledge as ability to do something).

MAJOR CONTRIBUTIONS

In the early 1970's scholars began arguing for what came to be called *integrative* tests, based on what Oller called a 'pragmatic expectancy grammar'

(Oller, 1979). The basic argument is that during language processing, it is not only necessary to know the individual bits of language, but because there are regular and rule-governed connections and inter-relations between the various bits, it is also necessary to know how they relate to each other. In other words, Oller was claiming that the whole is greater than the sum of its parts, and thus in discrete-point testing, crucial aspects of linguistic knowledge are ignored. Language is highly redundant, and much important information is given in more than one form, and if we know a language well, we will be continually generating predictions about what will follow (Cohen, 1977). Thus, language processing consists of an 'expectancy generating system', and Oller further argued that this ability to make predictions is the ideal measure of general proficiency in the language. From this he developed tests of reduced redundancy: the two most common of which are the cloze test and dictation.

Although cloze tests have been very popular as reading tests (although see Weir's review in this volume), or tests of general language proficiency, despite numerous attempts (Templeton, 1977; Henning, Gary & Gary, 1983) they have not been widely adopted to test listening skills. The most used, and most useful, integrative test of listening has been the dictation (Oller, 1979; Angela Oakeshott-Taylor, 1977). The basic procedure is that test-takers hear a spoken passage twice; the first time all the way through, the second time divided into sections, interspersed with pauses, during which they write down what they have heard. The rationale is that the more listeners understand the language the better they can process it, chunk it into meaningful units, and hold it in memory. And while they may forget some of the actual words, the redundancy helps them to reconstruct the text. Dictations have been very popular, especially among teachers and test makers with limited resources, as they are relatively easy to construct, and often make excellent tests. There are a number of variants of the dictation, including noise tests, which are similar to dictation but with white noise added to reduce redundancy, and elicited repetition tasks, which are like dictation but rather than writing down what they have heard, the test-takers repeat it back, usually into a tape recorder. (For more about integrative tests, see the review by Read in this volume.)

The theoretical notions of listening comprehension associated with tests of reduced redundancy are clearly broader than those found in discrete-point testing. Linguistic knowledge is regarded as procedural knowledge, and application of that knowledge must be reasonably automatic. The emphasis is on processing the language, rather than just having individual bits of knowledge about the language. Listening comprehension is characterized as a process of decoding the meaning of the words, by means of an inference-based process of hypothesis generation and testing.

The basic psycholinguistic theories about language processing which underlie integrative testing have never been seriously challenged. Rather the problem is that integrative tests measure a narrow range of linguistic skills. In dictation, for example, it is only necessary to understand the literal meaning of the words; and it is not necessary to make pragmatic interpretations, or relate the meaning to any broader communicative purpose. Further, although context plays an important role in the interpretation of speech in most real-world situations, the only context that is provided in dictation is a small amount of surrounding text. There is usually little or no necessity to take into account the communicative situation in which the language is being used.

WORK IN PROGRESS

At the same time as Oller was arguing for integrative tests, Carroll (1972), was arguing that comprehension of a message is adequate, or satisfactory if the listener:

i) apprehends the linguistic information in the text, and
ii) is also able to relate that to the wider communicative context.

This is a broader conceptualization of listening than that found in the integrative-testing paradigm, in that the listener must not only understand literally what the words mean, but must also interpret what is meant by them. The main thrust for 'communicative' testing came about primarily in response to the 'communicative' language teaching movement. The basic idea is that language is used for the purpose of communication, in a particular situation and for a particular purpose, and that what is important is whether users can actually use the language to fulfill that communicative purpose. Language proficiency is thus seen as *communicative competence*. (See the reviews by Shirai and by Crandall, both in Volume 4.)

Since the notion of communicative ability, rather than knowledge of the language, has become the focus of much second language education, test-developers have often been under pressure to construct tests which would be judged as 'communicative' tests. However, current theoretical conceptualizations of communicative competence (see the review by Swain in Volume 5) are not very helpful. They tend to provide a descriptive taxonomy rather than a testable theoretical model: that is, they state what the components are, and provide some descriptions of them, but they do not specify how they should be operationalized, nor their relative importance in language proficiency. Since theories of communicative competence provide no clear guidelines for communicative test construction, nor criteria for communicative test validation, test developers have generally been left to decide for themselves what a communicative test is, and this has led to considerable dependence on the notion of *authenticity*. The reason is simple: given that there is doubt about exactly what knowledge, skills and abilities need to be included in a communicative test, one way to ensure that all the vital aspects are included is to replicate 'real-world' communication.

There has been extensive discussion of this notion of authenticity (for example, Messick, 1995; Bachman & Palmer, 1996; and Lewkowicz, 1996), but there are considerable problems with relying on the notion of authenticity in test design. Lewkowicz (1996) claims, for example, that authenticity is not a necessary quality of good tests and furthermore it is only partially attainable. A test is not an authentic communicative situation, it is a test, and is very unlikely to have the same characteristics as the target communicative situation. Furthermore, it is not always possible to identify those critical aspects of the target use situation which need to be replicated to make the test authentic. This is particularly difficult in listening comprehension situations, where critical aspects of the comprehension process take place within the mind of the listener (see the review by Lewkowicz in this volume).

Although there are no generally accepted criteria to determine whether a listening test is a communicative test, there appears to be considerable implicit agreement that in a communicative listening test:

(i) *texts should be as realistic as possible*: with the characteristics of natural 'real world' spoken language, and should be suitable to the purpose for which they are being used;

(ii) *tasks should also be as realistic as possible:* and replicate tasks the language users are likely to encounter in the 'real' world;

(iii) *tasks should motivate the language activity;* in the sense that the task should indicate to the test-takers the purpose for listening, and what they need to get from the text.

There are two serious issues which need to be confronted in making communicative listening tests: firstly, the small number of tasks which can be included in most tests, and secondly the fact that there is no one correct interpretation of many spoken texts. Regarding the first, it is obvious that most tests cannot include all possible tasks, but can only sample from a domain: performance on that small sample of tasks is intended to indicate ability to perform in the whole domain. However, within a broad performance domain, there are many communicative situations and contexts, and a large variety of topics and discourse domains, and it is only possible to sample a very small number of these. Unfortunately, successful performance on one complex communicative task does not always indicate the ability to perform well on another. Furthermore, because of the necessity of providing context, communicative test-tasks tend to take more time than other tasks, so the sample of tasks tends to be smaller. In other words, communicative tests often have fewer tasks, with lower generalizability. The second problem, that there is often more than one reasonable interpretation of many texts, has already been discussed. This is especially problematic when attempting to include wider communicative skills such as making pragmatic inferences about a speaker's implicit meaning, or the sociolinguistic appropriacy of a particular response. In 'real-world' communicative situations, the interpretation is often, at least to some extent, a matter of opinion. (For more about this problem see Weir's review in this volume.)

SOME PRACTICAL ADVICE

The most important thing to remember when designing and constructing tests of listening comprehension is that there is no one way that is suitable for all situations. In some cases it might be sufficient to know whether a test-taker can process correct, formal language presented quite slowly and deliberately; in another situation it might be necessary to know whether the test-taker can process fast, colloquial speech: clearly a test developed for the first purpose may not be useful for the second. In some cases it may not matter if test-takers need to read in the L2 in order to understand the questions, or be able to write well enough to produce a summary, whereas in other situations such requirements might unfairly disadvantage some test-takers. In some situations the focus may need to be on academic listening, in others on listening in a business context, and in yet others listening in social situations. When designing tests, everything depends on the purpose of the test, and the decisions that need to be made regarding the test-takers' ability. There will be advantages and disadvantages with any design, and compromises will usually be necessary.

However, some general advice seems appropriate. The basic idea of most listening tests is to assess the ability to use knowledge of the language for the purpose of understanding spoken texts. Thus, the listener must be able to apprehend the linguistic information in the text and understand the literal meaning of what has been said; and so test tasks must require fast, automatic, on-line processing of texts which have the typical linguistic characteristics of spoken language – especially the phonological characteristics. Furthermore, non-interactive listening tasks using transactional language are probably most useful and certainly easier to construct. This covers the basic core of second language listening ability, which is the strongest determiner of successful comprehension in all situations. Only after ensuring that this is covered does it make sense to think about testing listening ability in any wider communicative sense. Of course, if we know the target situation to which test performance should generalize – the tasks, texts, topics, or situations – then it makes sense to include as many of the characteristics of those as is reasonably possible. Beyond that, attempts to test broader communicative listening skills are commendable, but should not jeopardize assessment of the basic core, namely the automatic, on-line processing of realistic, spoken language. (Handbooks with useful practical advice on constructing listening tests are: Valette, 1977; Heaton, 1988).

FUTURE DIRECTIONS

Clearly new technology will influence the testing of listening comprehension. We are now in the age of computer-based testing, and a number of test-makers are putting listening tests on computers (see Dunkel, 1991a). (For more about computer-based testing see the review by Gruba and Corbel in this volume.) This raises the issue of multi-media. In most 'real-world' listening situations there is considerable visual information available to aid the comprehension process, but traditionally testers have not been interested in visual media for the presentation of listening texts. This is changing and test-makers have to decide what visual information should be presented along with the spoken text. Obvious alternatives are, for example: nothing of relevance to the text, still photographs of the context, or a full motion video of the participants. Researchers are now beginning to address the issues of how visual information affects listening comprehension, and how that in turn affects test performance (see Gruba, 1997).

Taking a longer perspective, we need to know more about the listening construct. At present, listening comprehension is not sufficiently well understood, and there are two main areas in which a greatly improved understanding of the construct would radically improve assessment. Firstly, we need to know which knowledge, skills and abilities are involved in processing listening texts, and how these relate to performance on individual listening tasks. This would enable diagnostic assessment of second-language listening abilities. Secondly, we need clearly defined criteria to describe levels of listening attainment (either in terms of general abilities, or performance on specific tasks). This would enable the development of criterion-referenced tests of listening comprehension. (For more about criterion referenced testing see the review by Lynch and Davidson in this volume.) The results of such diagnostic and criterion-referenced assessments would then be able to feed directly into second language pedagogy and inform teaching practice, and tests could then become truly useful to teachers and language-learners alike.

Educational Testing Service, Princeton
New Jersey, USA

REFERENCES

Bachman, L.F. & Palmer, A.: 1996, *Language Testing in Practice*, Oxford University Press, Oxford.
Brown, G.: 1990, *Listening to Spoken English* (second edition), Longman, London.
Brown, G. & Yule, G.: 1983, *Teaching the Spoken Language*, Cambridge University Press, Cambridge.

Buck, G.: 1991, 'The testing of listening comprehension: An introspective study', *Language Testing* 8, 67–91.

Buck, G.: 1992, 'Listening comprehension: Construct validity and trait characteristics', *Language Learning* 42, 313–357.

Buck, G:. 1994, 'The appropriacy of psychometric measurement models for testing second language listening comprehension', *Language Testing* 11, 145–170.

Carroll, J.B.: 1972, 'Defining language comprehension', in R.O. Freedle & J.B. Carroll (eds.), *Language Comprehension and the Acquisition of Knowledge*, John Wiley and Sons, New York, 1995.

Chafe, W.L.: 1985, 'Linguistic differences produced by differences between speaking and writing', in D.R. Olsen, N. Torrance & A. Hilyard (eds.), *Literacy, Language and Learning: the Nature and Consequences of Reading and Writing*, Cambridge University Press, Cambridge.

Cohen, A.: 1977, 'Redundancy as a tool in measuring listening comprehension', in R. Dirven (ed.), *Horverstandnis im Fremdsprachenunterricht. Listening Comprehension in Foreign Language Teaching*, Scriptor, Kronberg/Ts.

Dirven, R. & Oakeshott-Taylor, J.: 1984, 'Listening comprehension (Part I)', *Language Teaching* 17, 326–342.

Dirven, R. & Oakeshott-Taylor, J.: 1985, 'Listening comprehension (Part II)', *Language Teaching* 18, 2–20.

Dunkel, P.: 1991a, 'Computerized testing of non-participatory L2 listening comprehension proficiency: An ESL prototype development effort', *Modern Language Journal* 75, 64–73.

Dunkel, P.: 1991b, 'Listening in the native and second/foreign language: Towards an integration of research and practice', *TESOL Quarterly* 26, 431–457.

Dunkel, P., Henning, G., & Chaudron, C.: 1993, 'The assessment of an L2 listening comprehension construct: Tentative model for test specification and development', *The Modern Language Journal* 77, 180–191.

Flowerdew, J. (ed.): 1994, *Academic Listening: Research Perspectives*, Cambridge University Press, Cambridge.

Gernsbacher, M.A. (ed.): 1994, *Handbook of Psycholinguistics*, Academic Press, San Diego, CA.

Gruba, P.: 1997, 'The role of video media in listening assessment', *System* 25, Volume 3 (in press).

Hale, G.A. & Courtney, R: 1994, 'The effects of note-taking on listening comprehension in the Test of English as a Foreign Language', *Language Testing* 11, 29–48.

Hanson, C. & Jensen, C.: 1994, 'Evaluating lecture comprehension', in J. Flowerdew (ed.), *Academic Listening: Research Perspectives*, Cambridge University Press, Cambridge.

Heaton, J.B.: 1988, *Writing English Language Tests*, Longman, London.

Henning, G., Gary, N., & Gary, J.: 1983, 'Listening recall: A listening comprehension test for low proficiency learners', *System* 11, 287–293.

Jensen, C. & Hanson C.: 1995, 'The effect of prior knowledge on EAP listening performance', *Language Testing* 12, 99–119.

Lado, R.: 1961, *Language Testing: The Construction and Use of Foreign Language Tests*, Longman, London.

Lewkowicz, J.A.: 1996, *Investigating Authenticity in Language Testing*, unpublished Ph.D. dissertation, University of Lancaster, Lancaster, England.

McNamara, T.F.: 1991, 'Test dimensionality: IRT analysis of an ESP listening test', *Language Testing* 8, 139–159.

Messick, S.: 1995, 'The interplay of evidence and consequences in the validation of performance assessment', *Educational Researcher* 23(2), 13–23.

Oakeshott-Taylor, Angela: 1977, 'Dictation as a test of listening comprehension', in R.

Dirven (ed.), *Horverstandnis im Fremdsprachenunterricht. Listening Comprehension in Foreign Language Teaching*, Scriptor, Kronberg/Ts.

Oakeshott-Taylor, John: 1977, 'Information redundancy, and listening comprehension', in R. Dirven (ed.), *Horverstandnis im Fremdsprachenunterricht. Listening Comprehension in Foreign Language Teaching*, Scriptor, Kronberg/Ts.

Oakeshott-Taylor, J.: 1980, *Acoustic Variability and its Perception*, Peter Lang, Frankfurt.

Oller, J.W. Jr.: 1979, *Language Tests at School*, Longman, London.

Rost, M.: 1990, *Listening in Language Learning*, Longman, London.

Scott, M. L.: 1996, 'Examining validity in a performance test: The Listening Summary Translation Exam (LSTE) – Spanish version', *Language Testing* 13, 83–109.

Shohamy, E. & Inbar, O.: 1991, 'Validation of listening comprehension tests: The effect of text and question types', *Language Testing* 8, 23–40.

Taylor, I. & Taylor, M.M.: 1990, *Psycholinguistics: Learning and Using Language*, Prentice-Hall, Englewood Cliffs, NJ.

Templeton, H.: 1977, 'A new technique for measuring listening comprehension', *ELT Journal* 31, 292–299.

Valette, R.M.: 1977, *Modern Language Testing* (second edition), Harcourt Brace Jovanovich, New York.

THE TESTING OF SPEAKING IN A SECOND LANGUAGE

Although the viva has been used for centuries as a means of assessment, it is only since the Second World War that research has been conducted into the use of interviews for tests of speaking, rather than subject knowledge, and it is only in the last twenty years that most of the research on rating scales, task types, elicitation techniques, reliability and validity has been conducted. The criteria by which a good test of speaking can be judged are those which can be applied to all language tests: reliability, validity and practicality. In the testing of speaking, however, the problems in examining these qualities are heightened by the nature of speech itself. Eliciting a large enough language sample for adequate assessment is time consuming and expensive, while scoring will for the foreseeable future depend on the use of expert human judges. Issues such as sources of measurement error, generalisability and score interpretation, are more critical in the testing of speaking than in any other type of language test.

THE IMPETUS TO TEST SPEAKING: MILITARY ORIGINS

The modern interest in the testing of L2 speaking can be traced to the Second World War, when it was realised that many American service personnel and diplomats did not have the linguistic skills to carry out their duties effectively (Kramsch, 1986, p. 366). From the very beginning, the emphasis in the testing of speaking was upon developing tests which would be capable of providing information about a person which could be used to predict success in communication in some future real-life situation. Kaulfers (1944, p. 137) wrote:

> 'The nature of the individual test items should be such as to provide specific, recognisable evidence of the examinee's readiness to perform in a life-situation, where lack of ability to understand and speak extemporaneously might be a serious handicap to safety and comfort, or to the effective execution of military responsibilities.'

Kaulfers recommended the use of a performance rating scale in what is essentially a Languages for Specific Purposes (LSP) situation, and in this pioneering work he laid down the foundations on which the Foreign Service Institute (FSI) would build fourteen years later (Spolsky, 1995, pp. 103–106). (For more about LSP testing see Douglas's review in this volume.)

C. Clapham and D. Corson (eds), Encyclopedia of Language and Education,
Volume 7: Language Testing and Assessment, 75–85.
© *1997 Kluwer Academic Publishers. Printed in the Netherlands.*

The FSI was given the role of improving the speaking skills which would be needed by diplomats and other civil servants in overseas postings, but it was not until 1952 that testing was pushed to the fore as an issue, when the Civil Service Commission decided to create a register of personnel documenting their familiarity with foreign languages and cultures. A committee was established to produce the first oral rating scale; this consisted of six bands, Band 1 representing no ability in a language and Band 6 native speaker ability. A band score of 4 was required for overseas posting (Sollenberger, 1978). No rationale was provided for these decisions, but the use of a holistic rating scale with weak band descriptors linked to the notion of the 'native speaker', established the framework for debate which continues today. (For an explanation of holistic and analytic marking scales, see Cumming's review in this volume.)

FROM THE MILITARY TO THE CIVILIAN ARENA

The first modern speaking test was being trialled by 1956, and research into the early uses of the FSI speaking test showed that scores were affected by the rank and age of the officers being tested (Sollenberger, 1978). The first instance of potential bias had been identified.

By 1958 the first analytic rating scale had been developed by the FSI; it consisted of the following criteria: accent, comprehension, fluency, grammar and vocabulary. Its purpose was to act as a check on the single holistic mark by ensuring that raters paid attention to each of the factors listed. It was not intended that raters should actually use the scale for rating. Although each level in the new scale was only weakly described, the introduction of such a scale was something of a revolution. Until this time all rating scales (they were used mainly in the field of work evaluation) had consisted of nothing more than Likert-type scales with no verbal description, but with boxes for respondents to tick. Other speaking tests using prose descriptors which were at least in principle 'behavioural anchors' (that is, verbal descriptors which attempted to describe what learners could actually do) were not created until the late 1970s and early 1980s.

Confidence in the new FSI testing system was extremely high because of the reported accuracy of measurement, even though it was acknowledged that a test score was only a predictor of effective communication, and not a direct measure of the ability to speak (Sollenberger, 1978, pp. 7–8). During the 1960s this confidence led to the FSI system being adopted (and adapted) by the Defense Language Institute, the Central Intelligence Agency (CIA) and the Peace Corps. It was in the CIA test that for the first time the averaging of scores from multiple raters was used as a means of increasing test reliability (Quinones, no date). In 1968 these diverse agencies came together to produce a standardised version of the testing system, now known as the Interagency Language Roundtable (ILR) (Wilds, 1975).

These early developments in the testing of speaking generated interest in holistic versus analytical or componential rating, bands and their descriptors, bias, the difference between linguistic and communicative criteria for rating, and reliability. All of these issues remain high on the agenda of researchers today.

Use of the FSI system by the Peace Corps soon led to its use outside the U.S. government, and in the 1970s it was adopted by many universities and states for the purpose of bilingual teacher certification. This process began with the development of testing kits and workshops, initially for Spanish and French (Adams and Frith, 1979). The use of the oral proficiency interview (OPI) was popular, for a number of reasons. Firstly, as a direct test of speaking ability, the OPI was seen to have high face validity. Secondly, inter-rater reliability indices of .84+ had been constantly reported. Thirdly, by the late 1970s there was an increasing interest in notional/functional approaches in teaching, and many regarded the OPI as a natural adjunct of these new approaches (Barnwell, 1987, p. 36).

In 1979, there was a resurgence of interest in a paper published over ten years earlier by J. B. Carroll (1967), in which he had demonstrated that college majors in languages were frequently unable to score above the 2/2+ level on the FSI rating scale (which goes from 1 to 6). Now that the FSI system was rapidly spreading through universities, colleges and schools, it was realised that it would be necessary to make it more able to discriminate below this level. It would be unreasonable to subject students to many years of language study which could not be measured on the existing scale. Also in 1979, the President's Commission on Foreign Language and International Studies presented President Carter with its report 'Strength through Wisdom: A Critique of U.S. Capability'. Amongst its recommendations was the setting up of a national criteria and assessment programme to develop language tests and assess language learning in the U.S. The task of increasing discrimination and establishing the national programme was given to the American Council on the Teaching of Foreign Languages (ACTFL), originally founded as the pedagogical arm of the Modern Language Association in 1967. ACTFL approached the task of increasing discrimination by adding a number of bands (or levels) at the lower end of the scale. It published provisional Guidelines (which contain the scale) in 1982, and the final Guidelines in 1986 (ACTFL, 1986).

CURRENT CONCERNS

It may seem that in this review there is an overemphasis on work in the United States. This is unavoidable, as most work on the testing of speaking has been done in the U.S., and most developments in other countries are

based on the American OPI and on rating scales whose ancestor was the
FSI. One example of this is the Australian Second Language Proficiency
Ratings (ASLPR) (Ingram and Wylie, 1985; Ingram, 1990), which mirrors
much of the language and philosophy of the ACTFL scale. However, the
FSI also exists in many other forms throughout Europe (Spolsky, 1995,
p. 350), as can be seen from even a cursory glance at some of the rating
scales and test formats which are currently in use (North, 1994). The FSI
remains the generic ancestor of today's generation of oral tests.

Rating scales

From the recent beginnings of testing speaking, there has been a distinct
concern with the development of rating scales. Unsurprisingly, reliability
in their use was the first requirement, and once reasonable degrees of
reliability could be reported (despite the fact that Barnwell (1989) has since
demonstrated that high reliability coefficients are achieved only through
rater training), attention turned to the validity and meaning of the rating
scale band or level – or rather the lack of it. Lantolf & Frawley (1985, 1988)
and Pienemann, Johnson & Brindley (1988) observed that no rating scales
developed in the 1980s, including the ACTFL scales, had any empirical
underpinning; even Lowe (1987) admits that there have been few validity
studies conducted into the use of these scales, for their value is seen to lie
in their history, and the experience of those who have worked with them
for 40 years. Little has changed in this respect since Valdman (1988, p.
121) wrote that:

> '... it is fair to say that although the OPI may be experientially
> based, its theoretical underpinnings are shaky and its empirical
> support scanty.'

However, investigation into rating scale construction and the validity of
scores on rating scales has recently emerged as an area of key importance
in the testing of speaking.

Fulcher (1993; 1996b) has conducted research into the construction
of rating scales, demonstrating that it is possible to use insights from discourse analysis to provide an empirical basis for deciding how many bands
a rating scale should have, and for providing the descriptors for each band.
Fulcher recorded students taking speaking tests and attempted to describe
the features of speech which were perceived to be contributing to fluency.
These features were then used to compile the prose descriptors of rating
scales which could then be trialled on a new sample of students. Using
Rasch partial credit techniques, reliability for this scale was estimated at
.94, and from a generalisability study, at .90. (For introductions to Rasch
analysis and generalisabilty theory, see the reviews in this volume by Pollitt
and Bachman respectively.) Validity was investigated using the multitrait-
multimethod approach (Campbell & Fiske, 1959), and Rasch partial credit

techniques (McNamara, 1996). Discriminant validity could not be established against a rating scale of accuracy, but a Rasch partial credit analysis demonstrated that the scale had what Fulcher (1996b) refers to as 'coherence', in that expected scores on the scale did not differ enormously across (untrained) raters or tasks.

Upshur and Turner (1995) also describe an empirically based approach to scale construction which they term 'empirically derived binary-choice, boundary-definition scales'. This approach to rating speaking is different from rating scales in the FSI tradition in that there are a number of yes/no choices at each level of a decision tree, leading to a final score. However, like Fulcher's work, "a description of levels emerges from examination of a sample of actual task performances" (Upshur & Turner, 1995, p. 6). Upshur and Turner report reliability coefficients of between .81 and .87 for the rating scales, although post-hoc validity studies have yet to be carried out.

Whilst current research is focused on understanding the meaning of the rating scale in terms of what students can be seen to do, North (1995a, 1995b) is conducting a rating scale meta-analysis, which began with a thorough description of existing rating scales. The procedure being followed by North is to place as many bands from these scales as possible onto a 'super-scale', created using the Rasch partial credit model. The aim of this research is to create a framework for language proficiency certification within Europe. Spolsky (1995, pp. 349–335) has termed this type of research the 'search for the holy scale', and says that it misrepresents language proficiency as a linear, universal, phenomenon. This judgement is perhaps somewhat premature, although the onus must remain on the scale constructors to demonstrate that such a scale is capable of acting as a reliable and valid measurement instrument not only across tasks and raters, but also across languages.

Whatever the outcome of such meta-analyses, the examples provided here represent opposite ends of what is essentially a cline. At the one end is an attempt to construct a database upon which descriptions and explanations of performance can be modelled (and *may* be context bound in the sense of being relevant only to particular tasks or test takers), and at the other end, is a universal scale which is abstract and bears little relation to any context. At the moment, there is no way to judge which is the most likely approach to generate the most usable testing instrument for any given purpose.

Tasks in testing speaking

It has been increasingly observed that task type has a systematic effect on speaking test scores. Recommendations are frequently made for the use of multiple tasks (wider sampling) and even for the use of different rating scales for different tests and groups of test takers (Chalhoub-Deville, 1995). Yet, neither the nature nor the degree of the effect of tasks on scores from tests of speaking are well understood, and much useful research is being conducted into this aspect of test method facets.

Chalhoub-Deville (1995) relates the use of the rating scale to the issue of score generalisability across tasks. It does seem appropriate for tests that are specific to a particular communication situation to have their own rating scales. In other cases it is necessary to generalise from the results of a speaking test to other tasks and situations, and researchers like Bachman and Savignon (1986) have convincingly argued that the confusion of test method facet (references to specific tasks) and trait in rating scales for more general tests makes it impossible to carry out validity studies. Indeed, if generalisability from one task to another is not possible, then neither is generalisability from test task to non-test communication. Testing speaking then becomes a futile activity. Bachman, Lynch & Mason (1995) have shown that it is possible to achieve the kinds of generalisability which are necessary for speaking tests to be useful, and Fulcher (1996a) has shown that generalisability can be achieved if the rating scale descriptors do not refer to task-specific language performance.

The role of the effect of scores from sources such as the task is part of the investigation of the effect of test method facets (Bachman, 1990), and continued research in this area will allow us to see the extent to which we are able to minimise error in the measurement of speaking.

Other aspects of tasks, such as the number required to obtain an adequate sample, and the different types of discourse elicited by a range of tasks (such as role plays, discussions, reports and simulations) have received only passing attention (Shohamy, Reves and Bejarano, 1986), whilst some research has been conducted on affective factors and task type (Fulcher, 1986a). A related field is the study of discourse produced by a variety of task types and modes of interaction between the test taker and the interlocutor/assessor. Perrett (1990) and Lazaraton (1992) both claim to have isolated a test genre associated with the OPI, while Young and Milanovic (1992) also relate discourse outcomes to factors such as topic and examiner gender in addition to task type and interlocutor dominance. It is clear that there is further research to be done here (see Shohamy's review in Volume 4).

Models of communicative language ability

Since the pioneering work of Canale and Swain (1980), much work in the testing of speaking has been more theoretically driven than it had been previously. Bachman and Palmer (1983) were the first to call for the construct validation of FSI type tests; they used the multitrait-multimethod approach to analyse two traits and three methods, and concluded that compared to translation and self rating methods, the oral interview 'maximises the effect of trait while minimising the effect of test method' (Bachman & Palmer, 1983, p. 169). A similar approach has been used by Dandonoli and Henning (1990) to claim construct validity for the ACTFL rating scale, although the findings of this study have been challenged.

Bachman's (1990) reformulation of the model of communicative competence, specifically introducing descriptions of test method facets associated with measurement error has led to a great deal of on-going research in fields like the effect of tasks on scores (see above), the comparability of language tests, and test-taker characteristics. Understanding the role of test method facets in testing speaking will occupy researchers for many years to come.

Test discourse and simulated tests of speaking

In recent years there has been much research into the difference between 'test discourse' and 'natural' discourse (see Fulcher, 1996a, pp. 26–29). This problem is of great interest to those involved in developing simulated oral proficiency interviews (SOPIs, tests which are delivered by tape, with the test takers responding on tape for later scoring), for if there is a 'speaking test genre', its effect is likely to be heightened with a simulated OPI. Many simulated speaking tests have been developed for what are unflatteringly called the 'lesser taught languages', because the expense of an OPI cannot be justified.

Shohamy (1994) represents the current state-of-the-art thinking in this field, which is essentially that although high correlations can be achieved between SOPIs and OPIs (one can therefore predict the OPI score from the SOPI score), the OPI has more conversational features (in terms of discourse and strategy, for example) than the SOPI. This is not surprising, and for the moment it appears that users of SOPIs must accept that some features of natural conversation will not be elicited. But does this matter? All tests are predictive instruments. If scores on the SOPI predict scores on the OPI, then they may also predict non-test performance. How SOPIs are used and for what purposes, in relation to the language they elicit, and how that language is scored, is the focus of much continuing research. (For more about Shohamy's research, see Banerjee and Luoma's review in this volume.)

GORDIAN KNOTS

Conducting research into the testing of speaking is hard because of the difficulty of giving enough tests to a large enough sample of subjects to get an appropriate dataset, and it is labour intensive because of the need to make transcriptions and to perform data analyses. For this research, funding at a level rarely available in educational grants is required. Important research can, however, be undertaken by examination boards. In most cases this is not done (Alderson, Clapham & Wall, 1995), and when it is, it is often classified as proprietary information and not made available to researchers outside the examination board. Lack of funding and an unwillingness to share is hampering progress in the field.

An issue which will continue to plague research in the field is that of generalisability. This is related to the nature of the rating scale and the effect of the task (and other test method facets) on test scores. We still need to conduct research to unravel the problems of databased and universal scales, as described above. This is essentially a generalisability issue, but generalisability is also related to issues in second language acquisition. Theories which stress the context-specific nature of communication and question the notion of communicative competence, remove the possibility of generalisability. According to these theories, Kaulfer's (1944) aim of predicting from test to future non-test performance, still the main purpose of speaking tests, is impossible to achieve. Speaking is clearly related to context, but the relative importance of context and competence requires further investigation.

It is here that models of communicative competence, or language ability, are most relevant. It is possible, within the parameters of a model, to investigate which aspects of competence are measured in any given test. Yet, there are few studies which look at the components of a test within a particular 'skill', and none which provide even tentative indications of skill structure. 'Speaking' may be made up of any number of sub-skills, and applied linguists (Bygate, 1987) have attempted to describe them, but there is no evidence of divergent or convergent validity for these descriptions. Most research, such as it is, remains at the level of theoretical description.

FUTURE DIRECTIONS

The next ten years should see continuing work on the development of rating procedures for speaking tests, whether these be with traditional prose-based band descriptors, or other systems like those proposed by Upshur and Turner (1995). However, these efforts must be linked to more thorough empirical studies into what it means to be able to speak. It is highly likely that components of a skill are highly intercorrelated, and methods of investigating construct validity which do not rely on strict proof of convergent and divergent validity may have to be developed. Of particular value may be studies which involve the use of confirmatory factor analysis or structural equation modelling (see Crocker & Algina, 1986, p. 304). It is clear that rater training cannot be used if these investigations are to rely on scores awarded by judges. Training can only be implemented as a result of discovering acceptable validity evidence, or all issues are prejudged. Rater training is designed to change an individual's perception of the world so that he or she conforms to an institutional standard of rating; this is the definition of rater reliability, but does not make the institutional standard valid by definition. That is, training raters to rate samples of speech consistently does not ensure that they are actually rating whatever constructs the test was designed to measure.

When new speaking tests are produced, it will not be enough for the developers to say that they wish to 'test speaking'. If test development is to add anything to our understanding of speaking, and testing, then the test specifications must draw on insights from applied linguistics, discourse analysis, speech act theory, sociolinguistics, second language acquisition, and models of communicative language ability. Testing procedures and specifications, rubrics and rating systems, should be the subject of extensive validity studies. Some of these tests will require test users to generalise from test score to non-test situation. Evidence of validity should support the appropriateness of any such generalisation. Some tests, especially those which are designed as 'mirrors' of some real-life specific target situation, may be designed with context-specific rating scales. Here generalisability is not required, merely a sample of some known behaviour. Yet, we still need to know whether the genre-specific rating scale is a better predictor of its own domain than the non-genre-specific rating scale.

These directions amount to amassing evidence for (or against) the construct validity of any test of speaking, and, in the process, learning more about what it means to speak, which components of communicative language ability contribute to an ability to speak, and to what degree they do so. All these questions remain unanswered today.

University of Surrey, England

REFERENCES

ACTFL.: 1986, *ACTFL Proficiency Guidelines*, American Council on the Teaching of Foreign Languages, Hastings-on-Hudson, NY.

Adams, M.L. & Frith, J.R.: 1979, *Testing Kit: French and Spanish*, Department of State, Foreign Services Institute, Washington D.C.

Alderson, J.C., Clapham, C. & Wall, D.: 1995, *Language Test Construction and Evaluation*, Cambridge University Press, Cambridge.

Bachman, L.F.: 1990, *Fundamental Considerations in Language Testing*, Oxford University Press, Oxford.

Bachman, L.F., Lynch, B.K., & Mason, M.: 1995, 'Investigating variability in tasks and rater judgements in a performance test of foreign language speaking', *Language Testing* 12(2), 238–257.

Bachman, L.F. & Palmer, A.S.: 1983, 'The construct validation of the FSI Oral Interview', In J.W. Oller (ed), *Issues in Language Testing Research*, Newbury House, Rowley, MA, 154–169.

Bachman, L.F. & Savignon, S.J.: 1986, 'The evaluation of communicative language proficiency: A critique of the ACTFL Oral Interview', *Modern Language Journal* 70(4), 380–390.

Barnwell, D.: 1987, 'Oral proficiency testing in the United States', *British Journal of Language Teaching* 25(1), 35–42.

Barnwell, D.: 1989, 'Naive native speakers and judgements of oral proficiency in Spanish', *Language Testing* 6(2), 152–163.

Bygate, M.: 1987, *Speaking*, Oxford University Press, Oxford.

Campbell, D.T. & Fiske, D.W.: 1959, 'Convergent and discriminant validation by the multitrait-multimethod matrix', *Psychological Bulletin* 56(2), 81–105.

Canale, M. & Swain, M.: 1980, 'Theoretical bases of communicative approaches to second language teaching and testing', *Applied Linguistics* 1(1), 3–47.

Carroll, J.B.: 1967, 'The foreign language attainments of language majors in the senior year: A survey conducted in U.S. colleges and universities', *Foreign Language Annals* 1(2), 131–151.

Chalhoub-Deville, M.: 1995, 'Deriving oral assessment scales across different tests and rater groups', *Language Testing* 12(1), 16–33.

Crocker, L. & Algina, J.: 1986, *Introduction to Modern and Classical Test Theory*, Holt, Rinehart, Winston, Florida.

Dandonoli, P. & Henning, G.: 1990, 'An investigation of the construct validity of the ACTFL proficiency guidelines and oral interview procedure', *Foreign Language Annals* 23(1), 11–22.

Fulcher, G.: 1993, *The Construct Validation of Rating Scales for Oral Tests in English as a Foreign Language*, unpublished PhD thesis, University of Lancaster, U.K.

Fulcher, G. 1996a, 'Testing tasks: Issues in task design and the group oral', *Language Testing* 13(1), 23–51.

Fulcher, G.: 1996b, 'Does thick description lead to smart tests? A data-based approach to rating scale construction', *Language Testing* 13, 208–238.

Ingram, D.: 1990, 'The Australian second language proficiency ratings', in H.A.L. de Jong (ed), *Standardization in Language Testing*, AILA Review 7, Free University Press, Amsterdam, 46–61.

Ingram, D. & Wylie, E.: 1985, *Australian Second Language Proficiency Ratings*, Australian Government Publishing Service, Canberra.

Kaulfers, W.V.: 1944, 'War-time developments in modern language achievement tests', *Modern Language Journal* 28, 136–150.

Kramsch, C.J.: 1986, 'From language proficiency to interactional competence', *Modern Language Journal* 70(4), 366–372.

Lantolf, J.P. & Frawley, W.: 1985, 'Oral proficiency testing: A critical analysis', *Modern Language Journal* 69(4), 337–345.

Lantolf, J.P. & Frawley, W.: 1988, 'Proficiency: Understanding the construct', *Studies in Second Language Acquisition* 10(2), 181–195.

Lazaraton, A.: 1992, 'The structural organization of a language interview: A conversation analytic perspective', *System* 20, 373–386.

Lowe, P.: 1987 'Interagency language roundtable proficiency interview', in J.C. Alderson, K.J. Krahnke, & C. Stansfield (eds.), *Reviews of English Language Proficiency Tests*, TESOL Publications, Washington D.C., 43–47.

McNamara, T.: 1996, *Measuring Second Language Performance*, Longman, London.

North, B.: 1994, *Scales of Language Proficiency: A Survey of Some Existing Systems*, Council of Europe CC-LANG (94), Strasbourg, France, 24.

North, B.: 1995a, 'The development of a common framework scale of descriptors of language proficiency based on a theory of measurement', *System* 23(4), 445–465.

North, B.: 1995b, *The Development of a Common Framework Scale of Language*

Proficiency based on a Theory of Measurement, Unpublished PhD thesis, Thames Valley University, UK.

Perrett, G.: 1990, 'The language testing interview: A reappraisal', in J. de Jong & D.K. Stevenson eds.), *Individualizing the Assessment of Language Abilities*, Multilingual Matters, Philadephia, PA, 225–238.

Pienemann, M., Johnson, M., & Brindley, G.: 1988, 'Constructing an acquisition-based procedure for second language assessment', *Studies in Second Language Acquisition* 10, 217–234.

Quinones, J.: no date, *Independent Rating in Oral Proficiency Interviews*, Central Intelligence Agency, Washington, D.C.

Shohamy, E.: 1994, 'The validity of direct versus semi-direct oral tests', *Language Testing* 11(2), 99–124.

Shohamy, E., Reves, T. & Bejarano, Y.: 1986, 'Introducing a new comprehensive test of oral proficiency', *English Language Teaching Journal* 40(3), 212–220.

Sollenberger, H.E.: 1978, 'Development and current use of the FSI oral interview test', in J.L.D. Clark (ed.), *Direct Testing of Speaking Proficiency: Theory and Application*, Educational Testing Service, Princeton, N.J., 1–12.

Spolsky, B.: 1995, *Measured Words*, Oxford: Oxford University Press.

Upshur, J.A. & Turner, C.E.: 1995, 'Constructing rating scales for second language tests', *English Language Teaching Journal* 49(1), 3–12.

Valdman, A.: 1988, 'The assessment of foreign language oral proficiency: Introduction', *Studies in Second Language Acquisition* 10(2), 221–128.

Wilds, C.: 1975, 'The oral interview test' In R.L. Jones & B. Spolsky, (eds), *Testing Language Proficiency*, Center for Applied Linguistics, Arlington, VA, 29–44.

Young, R. & Milanovic, M.: 1992, 'Discourse variation in oral proficiency interviews', *Second Language Acquisition* 14, 403–424.

PAULINE REA-DICKINS

THE TESTING OF GRAMMAR IN A SECOND LANGUAGE

The testing of grammar continues to feature as a component of many school examinations and commercially available proficiency tests, as well as being the focus of class-based assessments. The construct of grammar itself carries different meanings but is still considered by many to be an important aspect in the measurement of an individual's overall performance in a language. This review surveys some main influences from linguistic theory on the testing of grammar, and examines the treatment of grammar in testing handbooks, as well as the place of grammar in some of the better known English language proficiency examinations. It also reviews relevant research in relation to construct validity and grammatical competence. Finally it identifies some of the main issues for the future testing of grammatical abilities.

EARLY DEVELOPMENTS

In the late 1950s and early 1960s (but see the historical account of foreign language testing from the 1870s in Spolsky, 1995), the major influences on the testing of grammatical competence are traceable to work in contrastive analysis and structural linguistics. The work of both Lado (1961) and Carroll (1961) has had a significant impact on the testing of grammar, albeit from different perspectives. Lado's work resulted in what Carroll (1961) called the 'discrete-point' approach to testing. As Spolsky summarises (1986, p. 148) "we set out to discover the atoms, as it were, of language proficiency: to list the individual linguistic items that make up knowing a language and then test each one, or, more practically, test a selected or random sample of them." Beyond the field of linguistics, the demands for rigorous test analysis in the form of classical test theory exerted a further important influence on test development. This period of development within language testing and educational measurement is well documented and coincided with the practical need for wide scale foreign language testing (Davies, 1978). A significant milestone in the measurement of language proficiency of this period is the Test of English as a Foreign Language (TOEFL), established on the basis of Carroll's work. This incorporates both discrete and integrative assessment of language aspects and skills, with structure assessed via decontextualised single sentence multiple choice items. Similar examples at around this time appear in a number of proficiency examinations both in the US (e.g. the

C. Clapham and D. Corson (eds), Encyclopedia of Language and Education,
Volume 7: Language Testing and Assessment, 87–97.
© 1997 Kluwer Academic Publishers. Printed in the Netherlands.

Comprehensive English Language Test for Speakers of English as a Second Language (CELT), Harris & Palmer 1970) and the UK (e.g. the English Proficiency Test Battery (EPTB), Davies, 1964).

One of the earliest reported construct validation studies was undertaken in order to examine the constructs underlying the different sections of the TOEFL (Pike, 1979). The TOEFL was first administered in 1964, and until 1976 consisted of 5 sections. These were reduced to 3 after the Pike report, with knowledge of structure and written expression being one of these. Other early construct evidence is cited by Stansfield (1986, p. 224), also in connection with TOEFL, where he notes that "performance on the structure and written expression items correlates highly with scores on direct measures of writing ability". Later research, however, suggests quite the reverse: i.e. that there is "little relationship between knowledge of correct written expression, as indicated by multiple-choice tests, and actual writing skills" (Angelis, 1982, cited in Stansfield, 1986). Two points emerge here. The first raises questions regarding the construct relationships between grammar tests and performance on more skills oriented tests. The second has to do with 'client' dissatisfaction with an indirect approach to testing via multiple choice test formats. Both concerns are reflected in subsequent research and views about the testing of grammar.

MAJOR CONTRIBUTIONS

The testing of language as structure in the 1960s and 70s achieved both stability and respectability, the former reflected in the reporting of high reliabilities, and appropriate item statistics; the latter through increased use in language proficiency examinations (e.g. TOEFL, EPTB and ELBA (the English Language Test Battery)) and published guidance to test construction in manuals such as Harris (1969).

The failure of structural linguistics to provide an adequate explanation of natural language led to a broader construct base for language. In terms of linguistic explanation, we perceive a changed perspective on the nature of grammar which moved from a traditional view reflected in the question: "What do these forms mean?" to a structural view: "Is this the correct form of the past tense?" to one in which the question is: "How are these meanings expressed?" (Halliday, 1985, p. xiv). In this way language 'forms' or 'structures' become a means to an end, rather than an end in themselves. Overall, the elaboration of communicative competence has had considerable impact on language testing generally but, ironically, the now accepted "immensely broad and diverse phenomenon" (Batstone 1994, p. 5) of grammar appears relatively little changed in the practice of grammar testing.

Construct Validity

Bachman (1990) has been particularly influential in stimulating research in the area of *construct validity*. Numerous examples impinge in different ways on the trait of 'grammar'. Some of this research is linked to the debate on whether there is a single underlying factor of 'language proficiency' or a number of underlying constructs, i.e. the unitary vs. divisible view of general language proficiency (see Oller, 1980); some represent direct attempts to validate different hypothesised components of communicative competence, with grammatical competence as one element (e.g. Bachman & Palmer, 1982; Sang et al., 1986; Rea-Dickins, 1987); whilst others have been primarily pedagogically motivated, and concerned with measuring training effects in the development of linguistic and communicative competence (e.g. Savignon, 1972). Results have been inconclusive. The evidence provides for different interpretations suggesting, for example, a strong interrelatedness between grammatical competence and communicative competence (Palmer et al. eds., 1979); a close association between aspects of grammatical competence and pragmatic competence (Bachman & Palmer, 1982); and a differentiation in the degree of integration as an artefact of different levels of language proficiency represented in samples (Ramirez, 1984). However, most of the studies are not strictly comparable, as they were constructed for different purposes, using different test formats, samples, and statistical procedures. A further difference resides in the status of the research with some studies 'exploratory' (e.g. Hosley & Meredith, 1979) and others 'confirmatory' in approach (e.g. Bachman & Palmer, 1982; Rea-Dickins, 1987; Cushing Weigle & Lynch, 1995).

Interest in construct validation remains current. Alderson (1993) reports an investigation into the relationship between a test of grammar and reading. In the context of the ELTS (English Language Testing System) Revision Project a grammar (structure and lexis) component was developed which was explicitly differentiated from the reading tests at the level of test specification and test design. His results demonstrate a consistent overlap between grammar and the modular reading tests and a failure to "identify separate factors for reading and grammar" (p. 213). Further, overall reliability of the test battery was not significantly altered by either the retention or elimination of the grammar test (p. 215).

The new English as a Second Language Proficiency Examination (ESLPE) is designed to measure study-related English language skills, which contrasts with the earlier version focused on "formal knowledge of English grammar" (Cushing Weigle & Lynch, 1995). As part of a larger validation study, it was hypothesised that recently-arrived international graduate students would have had greater exposure to discrete-point grammar exams than immigrant undergraduate students and would therefore perform better on the old grammar test than on the new academic language skills test. However, this hypothesis was not supported in their data, for which one possible explanation is that more advanced learners tend to exhibit a more integrated language proficiency that statistically comes out as unifactorial (see Cushing Weigle & Lynch, 1995).

The above listing is by no means exhaustive; numerous other studies have empirically analysed the distinctiveness of constructs underlying communicative competence and provide insights into relationships between tests of grammatical competence and tests of other language competencies, e.g. Palmer et al. (eds. 1979), Verhoeven & de Jong (eds. 1992).

Test Manuals

Testing handbooks for teachers of the 1960s and 70s (e.g. Lado, 1961; Harris, 1969) generally mirror the view that "language is a linguistic phenomenon and that in order to test it, it must be broken down into its linguistic components" (Davies, 1978, p. 150). A change becomes apparent from the early 80s. Harrison (1983) contains no references to grammar in his index with most examples focused on the testing of language skills, exploiting features of spoken and written language. In the edited collection of Heaton (1982), the articles are wide ranging with several concerned with 'language as communication'. The article by Rea (1982) specifically addresses the testing of grammar within the communicative curriculum and the need to incorporate semantics and pragmatics in grammar test designs, and she investigated these issues further in her later construct validation study (Rea-Dickins, 1987).

The teacher's handbook by Hughes (1989) would seem to signal a definite wind of change in grammar testing. He opens the short chapter on 'testing grammar and vocabulary' with the question "Can one justify the separate testing of grammar?" and then points out that at one time:

> "this would have seemed a very odd question. Control of grammatical structures was seen as the very core of language ability and it would have been unthinkable not to test it. But times have changed" (p. 141).

Heaton (second edition, 1990) does not have a separate chapter on grammar testing and includes a few grammar and structure items within the chapter 'testing writing skills' with grammar as one of four categories in the marking of students' writing (p. 109). By the time we get to Weir (1993), we have lost any specific reference to grammar testing, save for its appearance in lists of marking criteria.

In summary, therefore, in test manuals over the last thirty years, the importance of explicit grammar testing has become much diminished, as evidenced by the number of pages devoted to the testing of this particular trait. And, although views about what grammar is, and the role of grammar in language use, have changed, scant attention has been given to 'novel' test designs for testing grammar within a communicative curriculum. Nonetheless, grammar still figures as a central criterion in the analysis of written and spoken language.

Articles that focus directly on grammar testing are rare (but see Rea-Dickins, 1991, and O'Shannessy, 1995) even in recent ELT teacher education books devoted specifically to 'grammar and the language teacher' (Mitchell, 1994 is an exception).

Proficiency Examinations

Grammar testing appears to have a less prominent position in a number of the better known proficiency examinations. The revised ESLPE does not include a grammar subtest (Cushing Weigle & Lynch, 1995). The decision not to have a grammar subtest in IELTS was made on the basis of research evidence (Alderson, 1993). There are also examinations that have never included the explicit testing of grammar, e.g. the oral/aural examinations set by the ARELS Examinations Trust (University of Oxford Delegacy of Local Examinations) and the Certificates in Communicative Skills in English (RSA/UCLES). On the other hand, the TOEFL still retains a structure section; it is unclear at this stage what the recommendations concerning the multiple choice testing of structure and written expression will be as a result of the TOEFL 2000 initiative. The University Entrance Test in English for Speakers of Other Languages (UETESOL) has a section, Editing Skills, which carries 25% of the total available marks, and "particular attention will be paid to accuracy in grammar and vocabulary" (Northern Examinations & Assessment Board (NEAB) 1996, p. 2). An analysis of the University of Cambridge Local Examinations Syndicate (UCLES) suite of international proficiency examinations also confirms the status of grammar in the measurement of language proficiency, with grammar an explicit focus of attention throughout their suite of examinations at 5 levels. What is not clear in much proficiency test documentation is what proportion of marks is allocated to 'grammar' overall in these examinations. Neither is it clear to what extent the grammar focus is driven by market forces or informed by research. Further, many proficiency tests developed for specific institutions and purposes include a grammar component, e.g. Stansfield et al., 1990.

Several other factors emerge about the construct of grammar as reflected in proficiency examinations. Firstly, accuracy of language use is a key criterion in the marking of written and spoken language with, in the case of UCLES, accuracy of language use linked to effectiveness of communication, where only inaccuracies of language which impede an understanding of the message are penalised. Secondly, test formats may vary to include modified cloze and gap filling passages, guided short answer and summary tasks but the popularity of decontextualised multiple choice grammar items is much in evidence. Thirdly, grammar is defined more broadly than 'syntax and morphology' to include textual competence such as cohesion and rhetorical organisation. In other words, returning to the earlier definition of grammar, there is some evidence of grammar being tested 'as a means to an end', with attention to meaning in messages rather than an exclusive emphasis on accuracy of form.

In summary, the 'communicative' orientation of language teaching has led in some quarters to a diminished role for grammar in teaching. In turn, this has been reflected in pedagogically focused test manuals which have placed a greater emphasis on the testing of language skills and, in some cases, has left unexplained the omission of 'grammar testing'.

RECENT WORK

Like much recent research in language testing, Brown and Iwashita's study (1996) is primarily related to statistical test analysis and the use of Item Response Theory in test development. (For more about Item Response Theory see Bachman and Eignor's review in this volume.) Drawing on early work in contrastive analysis, they found that levels of item difficulty on a Japanese grammar test vary according to the first language of the candidates.

Turner & Upshur (1995), working from a school based perspective, observe that "a strong or major focus on grammatical accuracy remains evident in many classrooms" (p. 19). In this study they examine the relationship between communicative effectiveness and grammatical accuracy across different types of speaking tasks. Also from an applied perspective, recent work has focused on grammar in relation to the testing of language abilities in languages other than English, e.g. Mitchell (1994) and Rogers (1996). Rogers, in her analysis of the treatment of grammar in the German Advanced Level GCE examination, found evidence of traditional views of grammar together with a behaviourist view of learning.

As part of an investigation into different grammar testing practices across a range of different contexts (Rea-Dickins, in progress), pre-sessional course directors in the UK were asked about entry tests used on their programmes. Of 42 returns, 67% indicated that they test grammar as a separate component. Of these, 66% use a multiple choice single sentence format, although a number of respondents indicated dissatisfaction with a non-discourse based approach to testing grammar. A further 17% said they integrated the assessment of grammar within their writing tests.

Finally, there are obvious links with second language acquisition research (SLA). Ellis (1991) for example, critically analyses grammaticality judgement tasks and Thomas (1994), albeit with a broader focus, reviews approaches to assessing L2 proficiency in SLA research including the use of standardised test scores. She notes the TOEFL as the most commonly used proficiency measure but cites others mentioned earlier in this review, namely CELT and ELBA. Tonkyn (1996) reports work in progress into student gains on a three month intensive language course, using criteria related to grammatical complexity in monitoring students' progress in speaking. Although the use of T Unit analysis as a measure of language development is "never going to be part of the normal language tester's armoury" (p. 128), his work points to the interrelatedness between language testing, course evaluation, and SLA, thus reinforcing the interdisciplinary nature of testing.

PROBLEMS AND DIFFICULTIES

Grammar testing appears not to have kept apace with developments in other areas of language description and language teaching. Part of the explanation for this must derive from the communicative movement which had the unplanned outcome of diminishing the role for grammar as a respectable focus of teaching and learning. In language teaching, this imbalance is being addressed (e.g. Bygate et al., 1994; Batstone 1994). However, what does the overwhelming absence of research and debate on a broader range of grammar testing issues, both academic and professional, mean?

One of the reasons why much grammar testing still reflects the best practice of the 1960s is that high reliabilities are appealing to educational decision makers. A second is that any move away from the objective decontextualised and decomposable approach to grammar testing raises certain difficulties. 'Communicative' testing (as indeed teaching) places greater demands on teachers, and challenges their competence in English. More open ended writing tasks, through which grammar may be tested, require a new set of skills for test design, format, and item writing, with implications for more explicit marking schemes, e.g. the appropriate design and application of different rating scales. The continued use of well tried methods may also be explained by uncertainties about how to test grammar (or communicative grammar) communicatively, or may arise from constraints imposed by a syllabus. Where a syllabus and/or textbook reflects an exclusive form focused approach to teaching grammar, it is no surprise that any grammar testing may be similarly restricted in focus and format.

On the other hand, an absence of specifically focused grammar subtests could reflect the conscious decision not to assess grammar explicitly on the grounds that it is automatically processed and used in responding to skill based tests such as reading and writing. Nonetheless, even if we knew, and we do not, that it is not necessary to test grammar as distinct from, say, reading and writing, this would raise concerns about potential negative washback on teaching and a further lack of respect for the teaching of grammar. At its most extreme, if grammar were eliminated from testing what effect would this have on teaching?

FUTURE DIRECTIONS

Grammar as Construct

Grammar is defined and operationalised in a number of different ways in educational contexts. Fuller information is needed about the construct of grammar, in particular about the relationship(s) between different aspects of grammar and the assessment of language skills. To what extent is grammar a generalised ability? Can distinct subtraits be usefully identified (see Rea-Dickins, 1987), such as a 'knowledge of the linguistic system' or 'an appropriate use of grammar in meaning focused tasks'? What is the relationship between performance on tasks constructed to reflect different dimensions of grammatical ability? Are some tasks and response formats better suited to the assessment of particular grammatical abilities? One of the challenges for the testing of grammar is to ensure it is an accurate reflection of the underlying construct, as defined by recent work in descriptive linguistics, informed by research in second language acquisition, and one that is not an outdated and normative view of language use.

Grammar in Educational Contexts

A better understanding of the construct of grammar is needed in order to improve on the ways in which grammar is tested. But what does grammar mean? Syntax? Morphology? Cohesion? Knowledge of the linguistic system? Language awareness? Rhetorical organisation? Ability to use syntax and lexis to express intended meanings? We know that "grammar is not simply a formal network, but a communicative device which is 'functionally motivated'" (Batstone, 1994, p. 11) and, as Carroll observes, "language performance is rarely a matter of fishing for a word, worrying about particular points of grammar, or anything like that; rather, it is a matter of responding to all aspects of a communicative situation in an integrated way" (1986, p. 124). How do we justify tests of grammar, both those that focus on punctuation, spelling and sentence level accuracy divorced from the contexts in which we listen, read and respond in speech or writing and those more integrated measures that tap grammatical abilities indirectly through, say, writing tests? When is it appropriate, and when inappropriate, to assess grammar explicitly and implicitly?

Social Consequences of Grammar Testing

Future investigations should also examine ethics and fairness in relation to the consequences of grammar testing. Recent work in descriptive linguistics has documented changes in spoken language and grammar (e.g. Hudson & Homes, 1995). One implication carries important social consequences in terms of test impact on achievement of certain groups of learners by the way in which grammar is defined and adjudicated in the National Curriculum in England. To what extent, for example, is the bilingual learner (i.e. the non-native speaker of English) disadvantaged by the apparent obsession with standard written English and accuracy in terms of punctuation, spelling and language forms? Is there an appropriate balance between message focused and system focused criteria? Additionally, as Alderson (1993) points out, test results are an artefact of an individual's performance as measured by language tests which does not necessarily correlate with how an individual processes different language tests. Is this processing different across learners from different language backgrounds? It would seem important to know more about this from the perspective not only of EFL learners but also those of learners of English as an additional language (EAL) in English medium schooling.

SUMMARY

In summary, the assessment of grammar has not been high on the language testing agenda in recent years, from either pedagogical or research perspectives. We have incomplete evidence about grammar testing practices and incomplete knowledge about the nature of the construct. Some data strongly suggest that influences from the 1960s still predominate, as exemplified by the familiar testing preferences of the 'psychometric-structuralist' period, or earlier. There is clearly a need for greater research activity, in particular on account of a widespread uptake of variants of the communicative approach to language teaching, for a closer integration between grammar testing and teaching and research in second language acquisition, as well as a monitoring of the social consequences of grammar testing practices.

University of Warwick, England

REFERENCES

Alderson, J.C.: 1993, 'The relationship between grammar and reading in an English for Academic Purposes test battery', in D. Douglas & C. Chapelle (eds.), *A New Decade of Language Testing Research*, TESOL, Inc., VA, 203–219.

Angelis, P.: 1982, *Language Skills in Academic Study*, Final Report submitted to the

TOEFL Research Committee, Educational Testing Service, Princeton, NJ. (Cited in Stansfield, C. 1986, p. 233.)

Bachman, L.F.: 1990, *Fundamental Considerations in Language Testing*, Oxford University Press, Oxford.

Bachman, L.F. & Palmer, A.S.: 1982, 'The construct validation of some components of communicative proficiency', *TESOL Quarterly* 16(4), 449–466.

Batstone, R.: 1994, *Grammar*, Oxford University Press, Oxford.

Brown, A. & Iwashita, N.: 1996, 'Language background and item difficulty: The development of a computer-adaptive test of Japanese', *System* 24(2), 199–206.

Bygate, M., Tonkyn, A., & Williams, E. (eds.): 1994, *Grammar and the Language Teacher*, Prentice Hall International (UK) Ltd, Hemel Hempstead, Hertfordshire.

Carroll, J.B.: 1961, 'Fundamental considerations in testing for English proficiency of foreign students', in *Testing the English Proficiency of Foreign Students*, Center for Applied Linguistics, Washington D.C., 31–40.

Carroll, J.B.: 1986, 'LT + 25, and beyond?', *Language Testing* 3(2), 123–129.

Cushing Weigle, S. & Lynch, B.: 1995, 'Hypothesis testing in construct validation', in A. Cumming & R. Berwick (eds.), *Validation in Language Testing*, Multilingual Matters Ltd., Clevedon, Avon, 58–71.

Davies, A.: 1964, *English Proficiency Test Battery*, The British Council, London.

Davies, A.: 1978, 'Language testing', Parts 1 & 2, in *Language Teaching and Linguistics Abstracts*, Cambridge University Press, Cambridge, 11(3), 145–159 & 11(4), 215–231.

Ellis, R.: 1991, 'Grammaticality judgments and second language acquisition', *Studies in Second Language Acquisition* 13, 161–186.

Halliday, M.A.K.: 1985, *An Introduction to Functional Grammar*, Edward Arnold, London.

Harris, D.P.: 1969, *Testing English as a Second Language*, McGraw-Hill Book Company, New York.

Harris, D.P. & Palmer, L.: 1970, *Comprehensive English Language Test for Speakers of English as a Second Language*, McGraw-Hill, New York.

Harrison, A.: 1983, *A Language Testing Handbook*, Macmillan Publishers Ltd., London & Basingstoke.

Heaton, J.B. (ed.).: 1982, *Language Testing*, Modern English Publications Limited, Hayes, Middx.

Heaton, J.B.: 1990, Second edition, *Writing English Language Tests*, Longman Group (UK) Limited, Harlow.

Hosley, D. & Meredith, K.: 1979, 'Inter- and intra-test correlates of the TOEFL', *TESOL Quarterly* 13(2), 209–217.

Hudson, R. & Homes, J.: 1995, *Children's Use of Spoken Language*, Discussion Paper 1, School Curriculum and Assessment Authority, London.

Hughes, A.: 1989, *Testing for Language Teachers*, Cambridge University Press, Cambridge.

Lado, R.: 1961, *Language Testing: The Construction and Use of Foreign Language Tests*, Longman, Green and Co. Ltd., London.

Mitchell, R.: 1994, 'Grammar, syllabuses and teachers' in M. Bygate et al. (eds.), 1994, 90–104.

Northern Examinations Board (NEAB).: 1996, *Syllabus for 1996: UETESOL*, Manchester.

Oller, J.W. Jr. & Perkins, K.: 1980, *Research in Language Testing*, Newbury House Publishers, Inc., Rowley, MA.

O'Shannessy, C.: 1995, 'Testing grammar', in *Guidelines: A Periodical for Classroom Language Teachers* 17(2), 32–42.

Palmer, A.S., Groot, P.J.M., & Trosper, G.A.: 1979, *The Construct Validation of Tests of Communicative Competence*, TESOL, Washington, D.C.

Pike, L.: 1979, *An Evaluation of Alternative Item Formats for Testing English as a Foreign*

Language, TOEFL Research Report 2, Educational Testing Service, Princeton, NJ.

Ramirez, A.G.: 1984, 'Pupil characteristics and performance on linguistic and communicative language measures', in C. Rivera (ed.), *Communicative Competence Approaches to Language Proficiency Assessment: Research and Application*, Multilingual Matters 9, Multilingual Matters Ltd., Clevedon, Avon, 83–106.

Rea, P.M.: 1982, 'An alternative approach to testing grammatical competence', in J.B. Heaton (ed.), 1982, 43–47.

Rea-Dickins, P.: 1987, *The Relationship Between Grammatical Abilities and Aspects of Communicative Competence: with Special Reference to the Testing of Grammar*. Unpublished PhD Thesis, University of Lancaster, UK.

Rea-Dickins, P.: 1991, 'What makes a grammar test communicative?' in J.C. Alderson & B. North (eds.), *Language Testing in the 1990's*, Macmillan Publishers Ltd., London & Basingstoke, 112–135.

Rogers, M.: 1996, 'Modern foreign languages and curriculum policy at 16+: Plus ça change', in H. Coleman & L. Cameron (eds.), *Change and Language*, British Studies in Applied Linguistics 10, British Association of Applied Linguistics in association with Multilingual Matters Ltd., Clevedon, Avon, 52–63.

Sang, F., Schmitz, B., Vollmer, H.J., Baumert, J. & Roeder, P.M.: 1986, 'Models of second language competence: A structural equation approach', *Language Testing* 3(1), 54–79.

Savignon, S.: 1972, *Communicative Competence: An Experiment in Foreign Language Teaching*, Center for Curriculum Development, Philadelphia, PA.

Spolsky, B.: 1986, 'A multiple choice for language testers', *Language Testing* 3(2), 147–158.

Spolsky, B.: 1995, *Measured Words*, Oxford University Press, Oxford.

Stansfield, C.: 1986, 'A history of the test of written English: The developmental year', *Language Testing* 3(2), 224–234.

Stansfield, C.W., Karl, J., & Mann Kenyon, D.: 1990, *The Guam Educators' Test of English Proficiency (GETEP)*, Final Project Report, Revised, Center for Applied Linguistics, Washington, D.C.

Thomas, M.: 1994, 'Assessment of L2 proficiency in second language acquisition research', *Language Learning* 44(2), 307–336.

Tonkyn, A.: 1996, 'The oral language development of instructed second language learners: The quest for a progress-sensitive proficiency measure', in H. Coleman & L. Cameron (eds.), *Change and Language*, British Studies in Applied Linguistics 10, British Association of Applied Linguistics in association with Multilingual Matters Ltd., Clevedon, Avon, 116–130.

Turner, C.E. & Upshur, J.A.: 1995, 'Some effects of task type on the relation between communicative effectiveness and grammatical accuracy in intensive ESL classes', *TESOL Canada Journal* 12(2), 18–31.

University of Oxford Delegacy of Local Examinations, 1994, *The Oxford-ARELS Examinations in English as a Foreign Language*, Ewert House, Ewert Place, Summertown, Oxford.

Verhoeven, L. & de Jong, J.H.A.L. (eds.): 1992, *The Construct of Language Proficiency: Applications of Psychological Models to Language Assessment*, John Benjamins Publishing Company, Amsterdam.

Weir, C.: 1993, *Understanding and Developing Language Tests*, Prentice Hall International (UK) Ltd., Hemel Hempstead, Hertfordshire.

JOHN READ

ASSESSING VOCABULARY IN A SECOND LANGUAGE

The assessment of second language vocabulary has been affected by changing perceptions of the importance of vocabulary in language acquisition. From one perspective it is self-evident that vocabulary knowledge and skills are indispensable for successful communication in a second language; in fact, many learners and lay people see linguistic competence in terms of the number of words that they know. However, in the recent history of language teaching and research, vocabulary has tended to be taken for granted, with the main focus being on the acquisition of grammatical competence and the development of functional communication skills. Although there is renewed interest at present in the teaching and learning of vocabulary, that has not yet led to a re-definition of the role of vocabulary within language testing or to the development of many innovative procedures for lexical assessment.

EARLY DEVELOPMENTS

In Britain and elsewhere in Western Europe, assessment of foreign language learning, like other areas of the curriculum, was predominantly conducted by means of traditional examinations until well into the twentieth century. Candidates were required to compose essays, translate prose passages and supply extended responses to oral and written questions – all of which were marked both subjectively and holistically by their teachers. Within this tradition, particular components of language, such as vocabulary, were not separately assessed. It was only in 1970, for example, that the University of Cambridge Local Examinations Syndicate (UCLES) first used objective test items to assess individual linguistic elements in one of their examinations in English as a foreign language (Spolsky, 1995, p. 213).

By contrast, from the 1920s until very recently, second language testing in the United States (like most educational measurement in that country) has been dominated by the standardised objective test composed of multiple-choice items (Spolsky, 1995). From the beginning, vocabulary items have been one of the most common components in objective language testing. Such items are quite easy to write and the resulting tests not only are very reliable but they correlate highly with reading comprehension tests. For example, in a study of the Test of English as a Foreign Language (TOEFL) conducted in the early 1970s, Pike (1979) found that,

C. Clapham and D. Corson (eds), Encyclopedia of Language and Education,
Volume 7: Language Testing and Assessment, 99–107.

from a psychometric viewpoint, the vocabulary subtest could be regarded as a more efficient substitute for the reading comprehension one. It ranked the test-takers in essentially the same order as the reading test did, and did so more economically because the examinees did not have to spend time reading whole texts.

This style of vocabulary testing, now known as the discrete-point approach, is associated with the work of Lado (1961) but numerous subsequent authors of books on language testing (e.g. Harris, 1969; Heaton, 1975; Madsen, 1983) adopted essentially the same strategy: the use of various types of objective test items to assess learner knowledge of the meaning of individual words, usually within a limited sentential context.

MAJOR CONTRIBUTIONS

In the 1970s, the field of language testing was dominated for a time by the integrative approach to language proficiency assessment, as exemplified by the widespread use of dictation and the cloze procedure as measures of overall proficiency. By definition, this approach was not primarily concerned with assessing the contribution of specific components of linguistic competence, such as lexical knowledge, to the learners' performance in the test. One exception in the case of dictation is a test developed in about 1974 by H.V. George and Ronald Fountain (as reported by Nation, 1990, pp. 86–87), for which the text was carefully constructed to incorporate a sample of 80 content words of progressively lower frequency from the beginning of the test to the end. Although the test-takers attempt to write the whole text, the test is scored on the basis of how many of the 80 target words are correctly reproduced. An analogous type of cloze test is the one illustrated by Harrison (1980, p. 60), where content words are selectively deleted from a written text and the test-takers have to choose each missing word from four options. These can be described as integrative tests with a strong lexical focus. (For more about dictation see Buck's review in this volume.)

Research on various forms of the cloze procedure has shed light on the extent to which it can be regarded as a vocabulary measure. For example, Jonz (1990) estimated that, in standard cloze tests (where the words are deleted according to a fixed ratio), about 42 percent of the items require responses that are sensitive to the lexical content of the text. In a comparison with seven other vocabulary test formats that varied according to the amount of contextualisation of the words, Henning (1991) concluded that a multiple-choice cloze similar to Harrison's (as noted above) was technically the best, in terms of reliability, criterion-related validity and mean item discriminability. Yet another variation on the cloze theme is the C-test, in which the second half of every second word in the text is deleted. Chapelle & Abraham (1990) found that C-test scores correlated more highly with a vocabulary test than with reading, writing or listening tests. Thus, although it is not a 'pure' vocabulary test, the research evidence indicates that the cloze can be tailored to function primarily as a measure of lexical competence.

As a result of the shift to integrative and – later – communicative test formats, mainstream language testing gave less emphasis to vocabulary assessment, but scholars with a particular interest in second language vocabulary continued to develop tests for their own purposes. One focus of research was the estimation of learners' vocabulary size. The basic idea was to test knowledge of a sample of high-frequency words, on the assumption that these were the ones most likely to be both known and needed by the learners in using the target language. A test of these words would yield information that was useful for such purposes as placing students in language classes or planning a vocabulary learning programme.

To obtain a reliable measure of vocabulary size, a considerable number of words need to be tested and that means using simple, discrete-point test items. Nation's Vocabulary Levels Test (Nation, 1990, pp. 261–272) requires the test-takers to match words with short definitions in the form of a synonym or short explanatory phrase. There is a sample of 36 words at each of five frequency levels from 2000 to 10,000 words. Read (1988) found a substantial degree of implicational scaling in the test-takers' scores across levels, meaning that the learners generally knew more of the higher frequency words than the lower frequency ones. Another format, used by Meara and his associates (e.g. Meara & Buxton, 1987; Meara, 1996), is the checklist, where the learners simply report whether they know each of a list of words sampled from a range of frequency levels. Obviously, one potential problem with this kind of measure is that it may produce an inflated estimate of vocabulary size if some learners claim knowledge of words that they do not actually know. To address this problem, the Meara et al. checklists contain a certain proportion of items that are not real words in the target language. Test-takers who claim to know a number of the non-words are assumed to be overrating their knowledge of the real words as well, and thus the estimate of their vocabulary size is adjusted downwards accordingly. Both pen-and-paper and computerised versions of the checklist have been produced.

These vocabulary size tests are rather crude measures of vocabulary knowledge, since they set such a minimal criterion for 'knowing' a word. Nevertheless, despite this and other limitations, Meara (1996) argues that up to a level of 5000–6000 words, vocabulary size is the only significant dimension of a learner's lexical competence and that the checklist format is a serviceable method of measuring it.

WORK IN PROGRESS

Current work on vocabulary assessment is exploring several other areas. Two in particular will be considered here: depth of knowledge of individual words and the overall state of the learner's lexicon.

Depth of Word Knowledge

Standard vocabulary test items, like the multiple-choice, matching and checklist types, require a single limited response to each word. However, in certain situations we are interested in *how well* particular words are known, especially high-frequency words that have a range of meanings and uses. The traditional method of investigating depth of children's vocabulary knowledge has been the individual interview to obtain explanations of the words that can then be rated and analysed according to the investigator's purpose. A contemporary example of such a study is the one by Verhallen & Schoonen (1993), in which a highly structured procedure was employed to elicit all possible aspects of the meaning of six Dutch words from both monolingual Dutch and bilingual Turkish immigrant children in Holland. The results showed that the monolingual children supplied more extensive and more varied meanings of the target words than the bilingual children did and this was interpreted as one manifestation of the educational disadvantage of the immigrant children in the Dutch school system.

The time-consuming nature of individual interviews tends to restrict both the amount of vocabulary and the number of learners that can be included; hence, some more practical alternatives are being explored. Paribakht and Wesche (1993) devised a written procedure called the Vocabulary Knowledge Scale that requires learners to assess their knowledge of particular words as being on one of five levels, from 'I don't remember having seen this word before' to 'I can use this word in a sentence: (the learner supplies the sentence)'. Thus, it combines self-assessment with the production of verifiable evidence of word knowledge. The authors used the scale to measure gains in vocabulary acquisition during a semester-long ESL programme at a Canadian university. Subsequently, Joe (1995) and Read (1995) have employed modified versions of the scale, not as a written procedure but as a means of streamlining the elicitation and analysis of learner explanations of words in an interview setting. It remains to be seen, though, whether the levels of the scale really represent increments of word knowledge or meaningful stages in the acquisition of L2 vocabulary.

A different approach is found in the word associates test developed by Read (1993, 1995) to assess the depth of knowledge of subtechnical vocabulary among learners in an English for Academic Purposes course.

The test items consist of a target word plus eight others, of which four are semantically related to the original word and four are not. The test-takers' task is to identify the four related words, or 'associates', which are selected to cover several aspects of the meaning and use of the target word. Validation studies have shown that, although the test is a good measure of knowledge of the target vocabulary as a whole, willingness to guess is a significant factor in test-taker performance and there is reason to doubt whether responses to individual items are a reliable indicator of how well that particular target word is known. Thus, other test formats – perhaps ones requiring supplied rather than selected responses – may ultimately prove to be better measures of depth of knowledge than this one.

The Overall State of the Learner's Lexicon

The second area of current activity involves efforts to assess the learners' vocabulary knowledge more globally. The tests of vocabulary size re-viewed in a previous section represent earlier work along these lines, focusing on receptive knowledge of words. Laufer & Nation (1995) have been working with two more productive measures. One is a version of Nation's Vocabulary Levels Test (referred to above), in which the target words are presented in short sentences in a truncated form and the test-takers supply the missing part of each word. The other measure is the Lexical Frequency Profile (LFP), which is derived from a computerised analysis of the words a learner has used in a written composition. The words in the composition are first classified into word families or 'lem-mas', which means for instance that *see*, *sees*, *seeing*, *seen* and *saw* are counted as forms of a single lemma *see*, rather than as five separate items. Then the LFP is obtained by calculating the percentages of the total num-ber of lemmas that fall into each of four frequency bands. According to the authors, the profile – and in particular the percentage of low-frequency words used – is a reliable measure of lexical richness, which may be of value in assessing the quality of learners' writing and in monitoring how their ability to use L2 vocabulary develops. Although the researchers have obtained evidence of its reliability and validity, further study is needed to establish how stable the profile really is for various groups of learners and what aspects of vocabulary ability it represents. Laufer & Nation's research in this area can be seen as building on earlier studies by scholars such as Arnaud (1984) and Linnarud (1986) into the lexical richness of L2 compositions.

Another more global view is found in the work of Meara (1996), who has been exploring for some time ways of characterising the state of the mental lexicon of L2 learners. He has proposed that a person's vocabulary knowledge should be conceptualised as a network of items with a multiplicity of associative links among them, and that native-speaker vocabularies are distinguished from those of learners by their richer and more highly structured associations. In one study (Meara, 1992), subjects were asked to write chains of associations between pairs of randomly selected words, like *cold* and *desire*, in both L1 and L2. Contrary to expectation, the L2 chains were shorter than the L1 ones. Thus, it remains to be seen whether valid associative measures can be devised for assessment purposes.

PROBLEMS AND DIFFICULTIES

Since the 1980s the communicative approach to second language proficiency testing has been very influential, especially in the British orbit. From this perspective, the primary focus is on the test-takers' ability to perform communicative tasks effectively, and vocabulary knowledge tends to be regarded as a lower-order enabling skill. At best, the range, correctness and appropriacy of vocabulary use may be one of the criteria that raters apply in assessing the test-takers' performance in a speaking or writing test. Thus, if vocabulary assessment is to have a place in contemporary language testing, the lexical contribution to test-taker performance has to be defined afresh within the communicative paradigm.

One current problem is to determine the scope of vocabulary for assessment purposes. Virtually all of the discussion so far has assumed that the items to be assessed are individual words, together perhaps with phrasal verbs, idioms and the like. However, scholars such as Nattinger & De-Carrico (1992) have demonstrated that everyday language includes large numbers of 'lexical phrases': groups of words that look like generative grammatical structures but are in fact memorised lexical units with a variety of functions in spoken and written discourse. If these are to be accepted as vocabulary items, the question is whether they can be assessed by conventional means, especially since their meaning is as much pragmatic as semantic.

This brings us to the most enduring issue in vocabulary testing: the role of context. Traditionally context has been given a narrow syntactic definition, generally as being a sentence in which the target word occurs. In the light of our developing understanding of the nature of lexis, a new conception is required that defines context in broader semantic and pragmatic terms. This suggests a need for assessment procedures that present or elicit lexical items in rich discourse contexts. However, there is a logical difficulty here in that the richer the context in which vocabulary items occur, the more factors other than lexical knowledge play a part in the test-takers' performance. In other words, we no longer have a pure measure of vocabulary and it may be difficult to assess the extent to which lexical ability has contributed to successful completion of the test task.

FUTURE DIRECTIONS

Numerous inventories of the components of vocabulary knowledge have been produced (e.g. Richards, 1976; Nation, 1990, p. 31), but what is needed for the future is a broader construct that includes the ability to draw on that vocabulary knowledge effectively for communicative purposes. Chapelle (1994; in press) has pointed the way with her proposal for a general model of vocabulary ability consisting of three components: 1) the context of vocabulary use; 2) vocabulary knowledge and fundamental processes; and 3) metacognitive strategies for vocabulary use. Most vocabulary assessment to date has focused on the second component of the model. Now it is necessary to explore more systematically the way that lexical items relate to the textual and sociolinguistic contexts in which they occur (the first component), and in addition to consider how learners – and language users generally – exploit their lexical resources to deal with communication problems as they arise (the third one).

There is also scope for more psycholinguistic measures of vocabulary of the kind that Meara (1992; 1996) has been investigating, as noted above. The challenge is to find suitable ways of assessing the properties of the learner's mental lexicon, as it develops beyond the point where vocabulary size tests are useful means of assessing it. So far word association has been the main concept underlying work in this area but others – such as ease, or 'automaticity', of access to items stored in the mental lexicon – should be studied as well.

In classroom teaching and learning of vocabulary, there is a continuing role for relatively discrete test items that show whether, and how well, learners know particular useful words in the target language. However, if vocabulary assessment is to have a place in language proficiency testing, it will be necessary to concentrate on vocabulary in use and to assess the learners' ability to cope with the lexical demands of a range of receptive and productive communication tasks. Currently, proficiency assessment relies a great deal on rating scales and other tools that produce global measures of the test-takers' performance. But what aspects of the performance influence the raters' judgements? A recent study by Engber (1995) found a substantial relationship between measures of lexical richness and holistic scores for a set of timed essays by ESL students. This suggests a function for vocabulary measures as reliable indices of quality to complement the subjective judgements of raters and to yield diagnostic information about specific strengths and weaknesses in the learners' performance of the task. Thus, in addition to tests that are designed just to assess aspects of vocabulary knowledge and ability, there is likely to be a range of lexical measures that are embedded within larger assessment tasks.

Victoria University of Wellington
New Zealand

REFERENCES

Arnaud, P.J.L.: 1984, 'The lexical richness of L2 written productions and the validity of vocabulary tests', in T. Culhane, C. Klein-Braley & D.K. Stevenson (eds.), *Practice and Problems in Language Testing*, University of Essex, Colchester, 14–28.

Chapelle, C.A.: 1994, 'Are c-tests valid measures for L2 vocabulary research?', *Second Language Research* 10, 157–187.

Chapelle, C.A.: in press, 'Construct definition and validity inquiry in SLA research', in L.F. Bachman & A.D. Cohen (eds.), *Language Testing – SLA Interfaces*, Cambridge University Press, Cambridge.

Chapelle, C.A. & Abraham, R.G.: 1990, 'Cloze method: What difference does it make?', *Language Testing* 7, 121–146.

Engber, C.A.: 1995, 'The relationship of lexical proficiency to the quality of ESL compositions', *Journal of Second Language Writing* 4, 139–155.

Harris, D.P.: 1969, *Testing English as a Second Language*, McGraw-Hill, New York.

Harrison, A.: 1980, *A Language Testing Handbook*, Macmillan, London.

Heaton, J.B.: 1975, *Writing English Language Tests*, Longman, London.

Henning, G.H.: 1991, *A Study of the Effects of Contextualization and Familiarization on Responses to the TOEFL Vocabulary Test Items*, TOEFL Research Reports, No. 35, Educational Testing Service, Princeton, NJ.

Joe, A.G.: 1995, 'Text-based tasks and incidental vocabulary learning', *Second Language Research* 11, 149–158.

Jonz, J.: 1990, 'Another turn in the conversation: What does cloze measure?', *TESOL Quarterly* 24, 61–83.

Lado, R.: 1961, *Language Testing*, Longman, London.

Laufer, B. & Nation, P.: 1995, 'Vocabulary size and use: lexical richness in L2 written production', *Applied Linguistics* 16, 307–322.

Linnarud, M.: 1986, *Lexis in Composition: A Performance Analysis of Swedish Learners' Written English*, CWK Gleerup, Malmö.

Madsen, H.S.: 1983, *Techniques in Testing*, Oxford University Press, New York.

Meara, P.: 1992, 'Network structures and vocabulary acquisition in a foreign language', in P.J.L. Arnaud & H. Béjoint (eds.), *Vocabulary and Applied Linguistics*, Macmillan, London, 62–70.

Meara, P.: 1996, 'The dimensions of lexical competence', in G. Brown, K. Malmkjaer & J. Williams (eds.), *Performance and Competence in Second Language Acquisition*, Cambridge University Press, Cambridge.

Meara, P. & Buxton, B.: 1987, 'An alternative to multiple choice vocabulary tests', *Language Testing* 4, 142–54.

Nation, I.S.P.: 1990, *Teaching and Learning Vocabulary*, Heinle and Heinle, New York.

Nattinger, J.R. & DeCarrico, J.S.: 1992, *Lexical Phrases and Language Teaching*, Oxford University Press, Oxford.

Paribakht, T.S. & Wesche, M.B.: 1993, 'Reading comprehension and second language development in a comprehension-based ESL program', *TESL Canada Journal* 11, 9–29.

Pike, L.W.: 1979, *An Evaluation of Alternative Item Formats for Testing English as a*

Foreign Language, TOEFL Research Reports, No. 2, Educational Testing Service, Princeton, NJ.

Read, J.: 1988, 'Measuring the vocabulary knowledge of second language learners', *RELC Journal* 19, 12–25.

Read, J.: 1993, 'The development of a new measure of L2 vocabulary knowledge', *Language Testing* 10, 355–371.

Read, J.: 1995, 'Refining the word associates format as a measure of depth of vocabulary knowledge', *New Zealand Studies in Applied Linguistics* 1, 1–17.

Richards, J.C.: 1976, 'The role of vocabulary teaching', *TESOL Quarterly* 10, 77–89.

Spolsky, B.: 1995, *Measured Words*, Oxford University Press, Oxford.

Verhallen, M. & Schoonen, R.: 1993, 'Lexical knowledge of monolingual and bilingual children', *Applied Linguistics* 14, 344–363.

Section 2

Methods of Testing and Assessment

DAN DOUGLAS

LANGUAGE FOR SPECIFIC PURPOSES TESTING

Testing language for specific purposes (LSP) refers to that branch of language testing in which the test content and test methods are derived from an analysis of a specific target language use situation such as *Spanish for business, Japanese for tour guides, Italian for language teachers*, or *English for air traffic control*. LSP tests are usually contrasted with 'general purpose' language tests, in which 'purpose' is more broadly defined, as in the *Test of English as a Foreign Language*. It is important to note that tests are not *either* general purpose *or* specific purpose; there is rather a continuum of specificity from very general to very specific, with a given test falling at any point on the continuum. Typically, however, LSP tests have been construed as those involving language for *academic purposes* and for *occupational* or *professional purposes* (Swales, 1985). LSP testing is related both theoretically and practically to 'communicative' language testing, based on a theoretical construct of contextualized communicative language ability (Bachman, 1990; Sajavaara, 1992). Two aspects of LSP testing, however, may be said to distinguish it from more general purpose language testing: *authenticity of task* and *the interaction between language knowledge and specific purpose content knowledge* (Douglas, 1998). *Authenticity* involves both the extent to which the test tasks share features of the target language use situation, and the extent to which a test taker's language knowledge, strategic knowledge, and world knowledge are engaged by the test task. The interaction between *language* knowledge and specific purpose *content* knowledge relates to the hypothesis that some test takers could be disadvantaged by taking a test based on content outside their own academic field. We will return to these and a number of other concerns in LSP testing later in this article.

EARLY DEVELOPMENTS

The development of LSP testing has followed closely the development of LSP courses and materials, and began in earnest in the mid-1970s with the development of the British General Medical Council's *Temporary Registration Assessment Board* (TRAB) test in 1976. The TRAB English language component was based on an analysis of the language used by doctors, nurses and patients in British hospitals (Clapham personal communication, June, 1996; Rea-Dickins, 1987). It was developed on the basis of an empirical analysis of the language of physicians, nurses,

C. Clapham and D. Corson (eds), Encyclopedia of Language and Education,
Volume 7: Language Testing and Assessment, 111–119.
© 1997 Kluwer Academic Publishers. Printed in the Netherlands.

and patients in British hospitals, and consisted of a taped listening test, a writing test, and an oral interview. A revised version of the TRAB was the better-known Professional and Linguistic Assessment Board (PLAB) Written English and Comprehension of Spoken English tests. However, they were phased out of the PLAB in January, 1997, and candidates are now required to obtain a passing score on the International English Language Testing System test (IELTS) before being admitted to the PLAB medical component. The new PLAB assessment, known as the *Objective Structured Clinical and Oral Examination* (OSCOE) contains a new test of the clinical skills of candidates, including the ability to communicate effectively with patients, relatives, colleagues and other health workers in the context of U.K. medical practice (GMC, 1995).

The British Council's *English Language Testing Service* (ELTS) test, introduced in 1978, was based on an analysis of the communicative needs of foreign students in various disciplines in British universities (Carroll, 1980), and contained 'general' listening and reading modules taken by all candidates, and writing, study skills and oral interview modules in one of five subject areas: life sciences, medicine, physical sciences, social sciences, or technology. This test has since been revised and will be discussed further in the next section. Another early example of an LSP test is the *Test of English for International Communication* (TOEIC), introduced by Educational Testing Service in 1979 to evaluate the English language skills of non-native speakers in business-related contexts (Woodford, 1982). The TOEIC is only moderately specific and test takers with good English abilities can do well on it even without much business-related background knowledge. Thus, it falls more toward the 'general' end of the test purpose continuum mentioned above. Other notable early examples of LSP tests are the *Certificado de Español Comercial* and the *Diploma de Español Comercial*, constructed in 1978 at the Instituto de Formacion Empresarial, Madrid, for the Madrid Chamber of Commerce.

MAJOR CONTRIBUTIONS

The major examples of LSP tests since the earliest work described above include tests of language for academic purposes (LAP) and language for occupational purposes (LOP). Perhaps the most well-known test of academic language is IELTS, which is, of course, a revised version of the original ELTS. The ELTS test has been revised twice, in fact, since its inception in 1978: a major revision begun in 1987 and concluded in 1989 with the launching of IELTS (Alderson & Clapham, 1992), and a more modest revision in April 1995. One effect of these revisions has been to make the test less and less specific purpose. For example, where the original ELTS test contained specific purpose modules in five subject areas, the 1989 IELTS contained three (life sciences, physical sciences, and arts and social sciences), while after the most recent revision of IELTS there is only a single academic module.

A second test of academic English of British origin is the *Test of English for Educational Purposes* (TEEP), originally introduced by the Associated Examination Board in 1984. The test content and format are based on an extensive analysis (Weir, 1983) of the language demands made on students in the disciplines most commonly studied by overseas students (arts/business/administrative/social studies and science/engineering studies). (For more about Weir's research see Lewkowicz's review in this volume.) A Canadian test of academic English for placement and diagnostic purposes is the *Ontario Test of English as a Second Language* (OTESL), which contains a science and technology module and a social sciences module, each presenting candidates with theme-related tasks based on two readings and an audio-taped lecture (Wesche, 1987). Read (1990) describes a writing test of English for academic purposes at the University of Victoria, New Zealand, also requiring the synthesis of information from readings and a lecture. Finally, another example of an academic English test which requires the integration of various language tasks is one produced at the English Language Institute of the University of Waikato, New Zealand, comprising reading, writing, listening and speaking components (Paltridge, 1992).

In the U.S., there are a number of tests of academic English, but none on so large a scale as the two British tests described above, because LSP tests in the U.S. have typically been developed at an institutional rather than at a national level. For example, there are a number of language performance tests aimed at assessing the ability of prospective 'international teaching assistants', a peculiarly American phenomenon. One of the earliest and most well-known of these, developed in 1985, is the *Taped Evaluation of Assistants' Classroom Performance* (TEACH), at Iowa State University, in which candidates prepare and present a five-minute lecture, explaining some aspect of an assigned topic in their field of study to an audience of three students and two or three raters, and then respond to three minutes of questions from the students (Abraham & Plakans, 1988). Other U.S. university tests of language for academic purposes include the *Language Ability Assessment System* (LAAS), a test of academic language ability for candidates for study abroad programs associated with the University of California, offered in Spanish and German; and the *Michigan Academic English Evaluation* (AEE) writing tests at the University of Michigan English Language Institute, which include an *Undergraduate Academic Writing Assessment*, comprising a synthesis task and an essay, and the *Graduate Tests of Academic Skills in English*, consisting of a report writing task and a commentary on some field-specific data.

In the area of tests of language for occupational/vocational purposes, perhaps the best-known is the *Occupational English Test* (OET) *for Health*

Professionals, introduced in its current form in 1991 by the National Languages and Literacy Institute of Australia, at the University of Melbourne. Eleven health professions use the results of the test, including physicians, dentists, nurses, physiotherapists, occupational therapists, speech pathologists, veterinarians, dietitians, radiographers, podiatrists, and pharmacists. The test comprises generic reading and listening components and eleven different profession specific writing and speaking components (McNamara, 1990; 1996).

An equally ambitious national vocational language testing project is the *Finnish Foreign Language Diploma for Professional Purposes* (FFLDPP), established to serve business sectors that require an ability to communicate in foreign languages. The first examinations for the FFLDPP were administered in 1989, in English and German, covering the areas of business and management and service and engineering. There are plans to develop tests in Swedish, French, and Russian, and to cover the fields of management and middle management, public administration, research and development plus technology, secretarial services, and service industries. Finally, another national vocational testing system is the *Diplomatic Service Language Allowance* (DSLA) Examinations. These are administered for the British Foreign and Commonwealth Office by Language Testing Associates to help determine whether a diplomatic service officer has attained the level of proficiency in a foreign language needed for a particular diplomatic service job (Cawood & Moore, 1994). The DSLA exams are given in a number of languages, including Arabic, Chinese, Czech, French, German, Greek, Hindi, Hungarian, Japanese, Malay, Norwegian, Persian, Spanish, and Thai, and reflect written and oral tasks that Diplomatic Service staff might be expected to carry out when serving outside the U.K.

Other occupational/vocational language tests include: the *English Language Skills Assessment* (ELSA), a qualifying test for overseas trained teachers, administered by the Adult Migrant English Service in Australia; the *Japanese Language Test for Tour Guides* and the *Proficiency Test for Language Teachers*, offered in Japanese, Italian, and Indonesian, both of which are produced and administered by the National Language and Literacy Institute of Australia, at the University of Melbourne; the *Midwives' English Proficiency Test* (MEPT), administered by the Ontario College of Midwives; the *Proficiency in English for Air Traffic Control* (PELA) test, administered by EUROCONTROL, the European Organization for the Safety of Air Navigation (Teasdale, 1993). Another such test is the *Listening Summary Translation Examination* (LSTE) – *Spanish*, developed recently for the Federal Bureau of Investigation (FBI). This is aimed at testing whether bilinguals' language skills are adequate for monitoring conversations in Spanish (when legally authorized to do so) between individuals suspected of illegal activities and for writing an English summary of the content. Further information about these and other tests can be found in Douglas (1998).

WORK IN PROGRESS

A 'textbook' example of an occupational LSP test development project is that being carried out by Second Language Testing, Inc. and the Center for Applied Linguistics on behalf of the FBI. They are constructing a test similar to the LSTE, but in English and Southern Min (a language of Eastern China and Taiwan), applying LSP test development principles: a concern for authenticity, both situational and interactional, based on an analysis of the target language use situation. The researchers first analyzed actual tape-recorded conversations of the type the candidate translators would deal with to determine general situational features such as frequent topics, tone, use of nicknames, colloquial expressions and code words. They then produced 'summary specifications' for the test, based on the analysis of the tapes, and also developed brief 'scenarios' outlining the gist of simulated conversations to be used in the test (Scott, Stansfield & Kenyon, 1996).

In the area of testing language for academic purposes, a development project being carried out by the Language Resource Program at UCLA involves the *Test of Oral Proficiency – Interview via Telephone* for an international Master of Business Administration program. The test has been developed using the Bachman-Palmer framework (Bachman & Palmer, 1996), involving an analysis of the language use of MBA students to determine situational and communicative features, which are then used to produce test tasks. The test is designed to be administered over the telephone to applicants to the MBA program.

Finally, an example of an ongoing test development project involving a large scale international test, is *TOEFL 2000,* at Educational Testing Service in the U.S. The project is aimed at producing a 'state of the art' test of English for academic purposes, considerably different from the current *Test of English as a Foreign Language* (TOEFL). The long-range plans involve incorporating both the techniques of LSP test development and the possibilities for test delivery and scoring offered by electronic technology. A number of LSP research projects are being pursued to inform the test development team, including the establishment of a database of 'course artifacts' – assignments given to students and materials produced by students in response to the assignments – interviews of faculty and students about specific academic demands, and research on the application of computer technology in language testing. The new test is scheduled for delivery early in the first decade of the new millennium.

PROBLEMS AND DIFFICULTIES

In the introduction to this review, it was suggested that two aspects of LSP testing distinguish it from more general purpose language testing: *authenticity of task* and *the interaction between language knowledge and specific purpose content knowledge*, and that both of these are sources of continuing concern in the field. Authenticity in LSP testing involves both *situational authenticity*, the extent to which the test tasks share features of the target language use situation, and *interactional authenticity*, the extent to which a test taker's language knowledge, strategic knowledge, and world knowledge are engaged by the test task (Bachman, 1991; Bachman & Palmer, 1996). Skehan (1984) and Douglas & Selinker (1985) have argued that LSP tests should consist of more than mere replication of the external features of context. Thus, mere replication of the features of the target language use situation is not sufficient to guarantee authenticity; the problem is how to make it more likely that the test takers' knowledge will be engaged in carrying out the test tasks.

A second continuing problem, also mentioned in the introduction, is that of the interaction between language knowledge and specific purpose background knowledge. Alderson & Urquhart (1985), in a number of studies, found some support for the hypothesis that some test takers could be disadvantaged by taking a test based on content outside their own academic field. Since then, research findings have been somewhat ambiguous, with Peretz & Shoham (1990) and Read (1990) finding little interaction between language knowledge and content knowledge, while Tedick (1990) and Tan (1990) found evidence *for* it. In perhaps the most extensive research into this area at the time, Clapham (1996) found that background knowledge made the greatest difference in LSP reading test performance when the text on which the test was based was highly specific, and when the test takers were at an *intermediate* level of language ability.

Another problem that has long vexed LSP testing practitioners, and continues to do so, is 'How specific is specific?' For example, Alderson (1981) suggested that 'the ultimate specification of a test situation must be that of one individual at one point in time; above that level, a claim of specificity must be invalid for some individual at some point in time' (p. 5). More recently, Sajavaara (1992) notes the theoretical specificity dilemma posed by LSP, but suggests that 'the problem of how specific LSP and LSP testing should be has no straightforward solution, because what is at issue here is the fundamental problem of how to categorize whatever there is in the world' (p. 124). It may not matter anyway, since Davies (1990) argues that "Tests of LSP/ESP are indeed possible, but they are distinguished from one another on non-theoretical terms. Their variation depends on practical and ad hoc distinctions that cannot be substantiated" (p. 62). On another level, this specificity dilemma raises the question of what the factors are that make an oral or written text more or less specific. Clapham (1996) found that it was not so much the amount of specific purpose vocabulary nor the source of the text that were related to degree of specificity, but rather the degree of contextualization (relative proportion of new information to information provided in the text) and the rhetorical function of the text (or portions of it) that made it more or less specific. Clearly, much more research is needed on the questions of how specific is specific, and why.

Finally, an ongoing problem for LSP testers lies in the development of a scoring scale that is, on the one hand, useable by raters who are not specialists in the field, and on the other, representative of the criteria that matter to those who *are* specialists in the specific purpose domain (Jacoby & McNamara, 1996). A recurring phenomenon in specific purpose testing has been that the linguistically-oriented criteria devised by applied linguists, even after an exhaustive study of the specific purpose language use situation, do not seem to reflect the features of communication that are deemed most desirable to practitioners in the target situation. Thus, test takers who succeed on the test may still exhibit communication problems from the point of view of their clients, peers and supervisors. A promising avenue of research into this problem is discussed in the next section.

FUTURE DIRECTIONS

It seems likely that LSP researchers and testers will continue to explore the analysis of target language use situations, particularly from the perspective of practitioners in the specific purpose fields themselves. Jacoby & McNamara (1996) have proposed a notion of 'indigenous assessment', which involves an analysis of the assessment criteria employed by subject specialists as they critique each other's communicative performances in, say, rehearsals of conference presentations or the review of draft papers for publication. Employing discourse analysis techniques, it appears to be possible to locate the assessment criteria used by professionals in authentic situational contexts and perhaps thereby to establish more authentic criteria for LSP assessment.

A second direction which may continue in the future is a possible tendency toward less and less specificity in LSP tests. For example, we have seen that the ELTS/IELTS has progressively become less specific in subsequent revisions. This phenomenon may be related to the questions discussed in the previous section concerning how specific is specific and how we can determine the degree of specificity of oral and written texts. Clapham's (1996) research has suggested that unless test content is highly specific, it may not make much practical difference whether test candidates take a test in their own or another field. However, it is only in very narrowly defined specific purpose domains, for instance that of air traffic control, that the use of very highly specific content can be justified. It may be, too, that test developers and researchers are less and less interested in what makes language use situations and texts different and more interested in what features they share. This trend is related to a concern for generalizability, the degree to which performance on a test can lead to inferences about performance in non-test situations.

Iowa State University, USA

REFERENCES

Abraham, R. & Plakans, B.: 1988, 'Evaluating a screening/training program for nonnative speaking teaching assistants', *TESOL Quarterly* 22, 505–508.
Alderson, J.C.: 1981, 'Report of the discussion on the testing of English for Specific Purposes', in J.C. Alderson & A. Hughes (eds.), *Issues in Language Testing*, ELT Documents No. 111, British Council, London, 1995, 123–134.
Alderson, J.C. & Clapham, C.: 1992, 'Applied linguistics and language testing: A case-study of the ELTS test', *Applied Linguistics* 13, 149–167.
Alderson, J.C. & Urquhart, A.: 1985, 'The effect of students' academic discipline on their performance on ESP reading tests', *Language Testing* 2, 192–204.
Bachman, L.: 1990, *Fundamental Considerations in Language Testing*, Oxford University Press, Oxford.
Bachman, L.: 1991, 'What does language testing have to offer?', *TESOL Quarterly* 25, 671–704.
Bachman, L. & Palmer, A.: 1996, *Language Testing in Practice*, Oxford University Press, Oxford.
Carroll, B.J.: 1980, *Testing Communicative Performance*, Pergamon Press, Oxford.
Cawood, G. & Moore, J.: 1994, 'Diplomatic Service Language Allowance (DSLA) examinations', *Language Testing Update* 15, 21–24.
Clapham, C.: 1996, *The Development of IELTS: A Study of the Effect of Background Knowledge on Reading Comprehension*, Cambridge University Press, Cambridge.
Davies, A.: 1990, *Principles of Language Testing*, Blackwell, Oxford.
Douglas, D.: 1998, *Testing Language for Specific Purposes*, Cambridge University Press, Cambridge.
Douglas, D. & Selinker, L.: 1985, 'Principles for language tests within the "discourse domains" theory of interlanguage', *Language Testing* 2, 205–226.
GMC: 1995, 'Changes to the PLAB test', unpublished paper, General Medical Council, London.
Jacoby, S. & McNamara, T.: 1996, 'Locating competence', paper presented at American Association for Applied Linguistics Annual Conference, Chicago, March.
McNamara, T.: 1990, *Assessing the Second Language Proficiency of Health Professionals*, Ph.D. dissertation, University of Melbourne.
McNamara, T.: 1996, *Measuring Second Language Performance*, Longman, London.
Paltridge, B.: 1992, ' EAP placement testing: An integrated approach', *English for Specific Purposes* 1, 243–268.
Peretz, A. & Shoham, M.: 1990, 'Testing reading comprehension in LSP: Does topic familiarity affect assessed difficulty and actual performance?', *Reading in a Foreign Language* 7, 447–455.
Read, J.: 1990, 'Providing relevant content in an EAP writing test', *English for Specific Purposes* 9, 109–122.
Rea-Dickins, P.: 1987, 'Testing doctors' written communicative competence: An ex-

perimental technique in English for specialist purposes', *Quantitative Linguistics* 34, 185–218.

Sajavaara, K.: 1992, 'Designing tests to match the needs of the workplace', in E. Shohamy & A.R. Walton (eds.), *Language Assessment for Feedback: Testing and Other Strategies*, Kendall/Hunt, Dubuque IA, 123–144.

Scott, M.L., Stansfield, C. & Kenyon, D.: 1996, 'Examining validity in a performance test: The listening summary translation exam (LSTE)', *Language Testing* 13, 83–109.

Skehan, P.: 1984, 'Issues in the testing of English for Specific Purposes'. *Language Testing* 1, 202–220.

Swales, J.: 1985, *Episodes in ESP*, Pergamon Institute of English, Oxford.

Tan, S.: 1990, 'The role of prior knowledge and language proficiency as predictors of reading comprehension among undergraduates', in J. de Jong & D. Stevenson (eds.), *Individualizing the Assessment of Language Abilities*, Multilingual Matters, Clevedon, UK, 214–224.

Teasdale, A.: 1993, 'Content validity in tests for well-defined LSP domains: An approach to defining what is to be tested', paper presented at the Language Testing Research Colloquium, Cambridge, UK and Arnhem, NL, August.

Tedick, D.: 1990, 'ESL writing assessment: Subject-matter knowledge and its impact on performance', *English for Specific Purposes* 9, 123–144.

Weir, C.: 1983, *Identifying the Language Needs of Overseas Students in Tertiary Education in the United Kingdom,* Ph.D. dissertation, University of London.

Wesche, M.: 1987, 'Second language performance testing: The Ontario test of ESL as an example', *Language Testing* 4, 28–47.

Woodford, P.: 1982, 'The Test of English for International Communication (TOEIC)', in C. Brumfit (ed.), *English for International Communication*, Pergamon Press, Oxford UK, 61–72.

JO A. LEWKOWICZ

THE INTEGRATED TESTING OF A SECOND LANGUAGE

When considering multi-skills testing it is useful to distinguish between *integrative* test tasks which may be viewed as falling at one end of a continuum, and *integrated* tests which fall at the other end of the continuum. To complete integrative tasks, test takers need simultaneously to employ more than one language skill. Such tasks include holistic measures of language proficiency such as cloze and dictation. As one moves along the continuum towards the integrated test, the test tasks increase in the degree of reality they attempt to replicate. The fully integrated test is performance-based. It is a test in which all the tasks are thematically linked and where the input that has been provided forms the basis for the response(s) to be generated by test takers. (For more about performance testing see McNamara's review in this volume.) An integrated test of this nature aims at assessing language proficiency directly in a context which, as far as possible, approximates real-life language use. An example would be a test of English for Academic Purposes (an EAP test) where test takers listen to and take notes on an extract of an academic lecture, read one or more extracts from academic papers on the same broad topic as the lecture and then use the spoken and written inputs to write an academic essay.

EARLY DEVELOPMENTS

Although integrative test tasks were commonly used during what is known as the pre-scientific or traditional period of testing (Spolsky, 1995), the term 'integrative test' was not introduced until 1961. John Carroll introduced the term to contrast an integrative approach to testing with the discrete-point approach that was in widespread use at the time. Carroll (1961) recognised that to predict how well learners would cope using language in the social situations they were likely to encounter, it was necessary to assess language performance holistically and in realistic situations. At the time, however, he was in favour not of replacing existing discrete-point tests, but of adding integrative tasks to the battery of performance indicators. Oller (1979) also advocated integrative testing, but for a different reason. He recognised the need to test language in context and under normal constraints of time. But he maintained that since language proficiency was indivisible, the single underlying factor to be assessed could equally well be tested using one task such as a cloze passage or dictation. He thus saw the integrative task

C. Clapham and D. Corson (eds), Encyclopedia of Language and Education,
Volume 7: Language Testing and Assessment, 121–130.
© 1997 Kluwer Academic Publishers. Printed in the Netherlands.

as replacing, not complementing, the discrete-point test (made up of its numerous subtests).

The strong form of Oller's hypothesis that there is a unitary factor underlying language proficiency (the Unitary Competence Hypothesis) was later rejected and the robustness of certain integrative measures such as cloze and dictation was also brought into question. Interest in testing 'language in use', however, did not wane. Instead, there was a shift along the integrative continuum towards more direct, performance-related measures of language proficiency.

MAJOR CONTRIBUTIONS

The shift in emphasis from the teaching of language structures to the teaching of language for communication, which was gaining momentum in the 1970s, resulted in a mismatch between teaching and testing practices. While language teaching was experiencing innovations in both approach and materials, language tests remained conservatively structural, and failed to evaluate what was being taught. Recognising this shortcoming, Morrow (1979) argued for the need to incorporate systematically into test tasks authentic language set within real communicative situations. He stressed the need to situate a test within a context that was appropriate for the test takers; to base the test on authentic stimulus material and to utilise tasks that simulated those the test takers would be expected to perform in the real-world. His views were put into effect in the development of the Royal Society of Arts (RSA) Communicative Use of English as a Foreign Language examination (renamed Certificates in the Communicative Skills in English (CCSE), under the aegis of the University of Cambridge Local Examinations Syndicate (UCLES)). This examination tests the four language skills, is based on authentic stimulus material, and achieves a level of skills integration beyond that evident in tests of the pre-communicative era. At the same time Morrow's views triggered the long standing debate on the nature of authenticity in language testing (Bachman, 1990, Bachman & Palmer, 1996) and the question of whether authenticity is an attainable or even desirable goal for a test (see, for example, Davies, 1978; Carroll, 1980; Alderson, 1981; Spolsky, 1985; Lewkowicz, 1997).

The 1970s saw two further developments which were to have an impact on test design and encourage greater integration. Munby's (1978) work on needs analysis led to the identification of the language requirements of specific groups of learners. This in turn was used as a basis for syllabus design and resulted in the second development, the growth in courses of English for Specific Purposes (ESP). Such courses, in addressing exclusively the needs of particular learners, were limited in content and focused only on those situations and activities identified as necessary. Tests were subsequently developed to reflect these changes, with systematic needs analysis being used to inform test specifications. In this way a link was forged between testing and the skills predicted to be prerequisite for future performance. (For more about the testing of ESP, see Douglas's review in this volume.)

In developing the Associated Examining Board's Test of English for Educational Purposes (TEEP), Weir (1983) carried out a very comprehensive needs analysis which went beyond the listing of skills and functions in Munby's (1978) terms. Weir looked at the activities which tertiary students are expected to perform and investigated the difficulties foreign students encounter in carrying out these tasks. The resultant test much more closely approximated the real-life language performance of tertiary students than any previous large-scale test. The test takers were required to process large texts and integrate information in order to produce their own response to an academic question. The empirical basis upon which this test was developed set the agenda for future test development in the field with tests such as the Ontario Test of English as a Second Language (OTESL) emulating the same systematic approach (Wesche, 1987).

The inclusion of content-based writing tasks in tests such as TEEP and OTESL was justified on two counts. The first was that providing test takers with texts on which to base their argument ensured they would have something to say and that they were not disadvantaged through lack of information (Read, 1990; Weir, 1993). The second was that by simulating the writing students are expected to undertake in their academic studies, the tasks enhanced the predictive validity of the tests (Wesche, 1987). Johns (1991) even went as far as to claim that there should be no test of academic writing that does not test reading ability as well. All these claims, however, have primarily been based on a priori content validation.

In a preliminary study comparing the validity and reliability of an integrated test with a more discrete point test, Emmings (1986) found that the integrated test offered a better means of assessing the underlying traits of language proficiency. Nonetheless, he advised against employing a purely integrated approach for two reasons, that of reduced test reliability and the difficulties associated with profiling candidates' performance.

A further reason for adopting caution in exclusively employing context-based writing tasks is suggested by Lewkowicz (1995; 1997) who compared the performance of students writing with access to source materials with those writing without such support. She found that although differences in writing were evident, when the essays were assessed by independent raters, there was no significant difference in the mean scores awarded across the two groups. In another study Lewkowicz (1997) compared students' perceptions of integrated and discrete-point tests and found that students do not necessarily perceive the integrated test as a better indicator of their academic skills.

WORK IN PROGRESS

A review of some of the major integrated tests that have been developed is necessary if the state of the art is to be appreciated. One reason for this is that work on integrated testing has gone largely unreported; it appears mainly in the form of tests and test syllabi. In addition, in cases where it has been reported, much of the literature is descriptive rather than empirically substantiated.

A number of EAP tests that have been developed are regarded as highly integrated. Among these are: the writing component of the Language Analysis Sessions (LAS) which, though no longer in use, was developed at the Language Centre of Hong Kong University to assess the academic writing skills of incoming first year students in the Faculty of Arts (for details see Low, 1982); the Carleton Academic English Language Assessment (CAEL) which is designed to determine students' eligibility for admission to a university programme at Carleton University, Ottawa (Fox, 1992); and another EAP Placement Test developed in New Zealand for admission purposes (Paltridge, 1992). What these tests have in common is that they were developed for in-house use and for a limited audience. The test developers, aware of the demands placed on the students within their institutions, were able to provide test takers with a relevant context as well as authentic input. They were also able to lead the test takers through a number of thematically linked tasks which replicated the tasks students are expected to perform in their studies.

The three tests, however, do not achieve the same degree of integration. Of these, CAEL appears to be the most highly integrated. In this test, not only are the listening and reading inputs genuine (using Widdowson's term, 1979) in that they are extracted from a first-year lecture and from academic articles, but according to the test designers, the tasks replicate those expected of students in their academic studies. The students take notes, write definitions, fill in flow charts and diagrams based on the input, and then use their notes and the readings from articles to write an academic essay. In contrast, the reading input for LAS was limited to part of an essay which students had to complete and some note cards which provided relevant information. As the candidates worked through the subtests, they performed various tasks including writing a paragraph based on some pictures, writing a paragraph based on the note cards, completing a discrete-point multiple-choice subtest assessing candidates' ability to recognise appropriate linking terms and connectives, and correcting the already provided introduction and conclusion to the essay. The five subtests were linked, and simulated the progression examinees should follow in completing an academic paper. They did not, however, simulate the actual performance expected of students in terms of reading, making judgements about which ideas to include in the writing, and joining these ideas together in written form. Even though there was continuity in the material, the tasks were independent of each other, and as Low (1986) himself pointed out, this was not compatible with having a strong line of development throughout a test. The EAP test described by Paltridge (1992), unlike the LAS test, culminates in the candidates writing a complete essay. Yet, before writing this essay, the test takers are led through a number of discrete-point subtests. These tasks assess the test takers' comprehension of the source material provided, but at the same time draw test takers' attention to those points the test setters consider important or testable.

The Language Ability Assessment System (LAAS) is a further example of a highly integrated language test developed for academic purposes. It was designed as a placement test in Spanish for students applying to the University of California Education Abroad Program. It was developed on a principled basis following a comprehensive needs analysis and utilising genuine lecture extracts and academic readings as input. Where this test differs from the EAP tests described above, is that it integrates the four macro skills, including speaking. It is also significant in being one of the first integrated tests to be researched in terms of reliability. Utilising modern measurement theory (G-theory and many-facet Rasch measurement), Bachman, Lynch and Mason (1995) investigated the reliability of rater judgements on the speaking subtest and demonstrated that the testing procedure, made up of complex tasks and involving multiple raters, afforded scores that were consistent across tasks as well as raters. (For more about Generalisability Theory and Rasch analysis, see the reviews in this volume by Bachman, Pollitt, and McNamara.)

A number of large-scale tests which fall within the broad category of testing academic study skills have also attempted a degree of integration. When the first draft of the International English Language Testing Service (IELTS) module for the Arts and Social Sciences was proposed, it was truly integrated. Initially there were no items testing reading, but since examinees had to receive marks for both reading and writing one or two token reading subtests were added. The main task was an essay which had to draw on six reading passages. These were extracts of academic papers consisting of a total of approximately 9,000 words. The task was intended to replicate the sort of tasks that students would have to do in their academic studies, and the amount of reading required was, therefore, intentionally heavy. In addition, one or two of the reading passages, although based on related subject matter, were not relevant to the task, so that among other skills, the test takers had to show their ability to discount unwanted material. The applied linguists who reviewed this draft module liked it better than the other, more traditional draft modules but, to the surprise of the test development team, most of the Arts and Social Science university teachers who commented on the draft were not happy with the amount of reading required for the task. They also felt that there should be two writing tasks, rather than one. It was therefore decided to make all three academic modules follow a more traditional, not so integrated design (for a more detailed account, see Coleman, 1989). The consequent integration turned out to be purely cosmetic with content remaining unassessed and candidates being able to complete the writing task without reference to the reading. This link between the reading and writing, therefore, has been dropped in the most recent, 1995 version of IELTS.

TEEP (Weir, 1983) and OTESL (Wesche, 1987) reflect more closely than IELTS the situation university students encounter. In both these tests the writing task is based on thematically integrated reading and listening input, but whereas for TEEP the input provides stimulus for the discrete testing of individual skills, the amount of linguistic manipulation required from candidates in the OTESL is kept to a minimum, with multiple choice questions, for example, being avoided. The question remains whether the revision of TEEP, currently being undertaken at the University of Reading, will move the test along the continuum towards greater integration, or whether research will focus on the need for greater task independence and more accurate reporting of language profiles.

One further test in this category deserves attention, namely, the Practical Skills for Work and Study (WASPS) developed by the Hong Kong Examination Authority and administered since 1989 as part of the Use of English Examination. The purpose of this test is to integrate reading and writing skills in tasks that require candidates to use their language skills fully (Bunton, 1995). The tasks, though not interdependent, are all thematically linked. In addition, all the content necessary to complete the tasks is provided, and candidates are assessed on their ability to select relevant material as well as to respond appropriately.

Integration has also been utilised with some degree of success in tests designed to assess the language proficiency of teachers. Brown and Lumley (1994) report on a test for Indonesian teachers made up of two subtests where the reading and writing tasks and the listening and speaking tasks are integrated. These integrated tasks are designed to be relevant for teachers in training and elicit the type of written and spoken language teachers are likely to use. A similar approach is also evident, though with a lesser degree of integration, in the Cambridge Examination in English for Language Teachers (CEELT).

The predominance of integrated tests for assessing students in academia and for assessing the language proficiency of teachers cannot be solely attributed to the homogeneity of the test population. It has been suggested that success in designing such integrated tests also depends on the testers' knowledge of the language used beyond the test situation (Milanovic, personal communication). Language teachers and testers know little about the real world of business, science and law, for example. Therefore, they are less able to design tasks that accurately reflect the day to day demands of real-life language in these fields. Language tests for business, commerce and trade such as those developed by UCLES and the London Chamber of Commerce and Industry (LCCI) consequently display a limited degree of integration. For example, in the UCLES Certificate in English for International Business and Trade and the LCCI English for Business and English for Commerce there is an absence of thematic development through the tests, and the tasks, though integrated, in many instances appear simulated and not taken from real-life language situations.

PROBLEMS AND DIFFICULTIES

One of the main problems of adopting integrated tests more widely is associated with their cost. They are by necessity only applicable to homogeneous test populations for whom future language use can be described. Hence, they are time consuming to develop and expensive to administer. Selecting themes of interest to test takers, but which introduce new information may, as Wesche (1987) has pointed out, be problematic. Furthermore, for test security reasons, relevant materials once identified have a limited lifespan and in some cases, like WASPS, are used only once. Tests of this nature, therefore, require a great deal of 'front-end' work (Wesche, 1987).

A second area of concern is associated with the problems of measurement. Task dependence which is characteristic of integrated tests gives rise to what Weir (1990) refers to as 'muddied measurement'. This occurs when performance on one test task affects that of another, for example, when the success in completing a writing task depends on understanding a reading or listening extract. In such circumstances it may be difficult to determine where the process has broken down and accurately to profile candidates' strengths and weaknesses. Moreover, in an integrated test the skills being assessed are likely to overlap across tasks, thus adding to the difficulty of reporting on students' performance.

Related to the question of profiling is the issue of generalisability: to what extent can valid generalisations about students' competence be made from the limited performance elicited during an integrated test? Judgements have to be made on two levels, in terms of what to test as well as how satisfactorily students have performed. The complexity of language is such that even where language needs are relatively restricted and well defined, it is difficult to ensure that the test will elicit a sufficient language sample. If judgements are to be valid, therefore, students need to be assessed on a range of tasks. However, by breaking down tasks and increasing their range, the authenticity of the test situation may be compromised as the task will no longer mirror real life. Integrated tests, in attempting to replicate a real life-situation contribute, on the one hand, to enhanced test validity, but at the same time they may limit the degree of abstraction that is possible from a student's performance.

FUTURE DIRECTIONS

Developments in integrated testing have been generally associated with Britain, Canada and Australasia. In the United States the strong psychometric tradition has led to concern with test reliability and a rejection of integration. However, there is evidence that this situation is changing: witness the adoption by the Educational Testing Service (ETS) of direct, more communicative tests of writing and speaking as part of the Test of English as a Foreign Language (TOEFL). These changes fall far short of requirements for fully integrated tests, but with developments in psychometrics, such as those adopted by Bachman, Lynch and Mason (1995) in establishing the reliability of the LAAS, it is probable that testing in the United States will experience a growth of interest in integration.

Successful integration depends on collaboration between subject specialists and language testers. This collaboration has usually taken the form of consultation, with subject specialists acting as informers, and advising on input, test tasks and what constitutes acceptable output. Tests, nevertheless, have remained predominantly focused on language, with test takers being aware of the fact that the test constitutes a simulation and that they have to demonstrate their language ability. In certain circumstances, however, there is no reason why such collaboration cannot be taken a step further with both the subject specialist and language tester acting as equal partners. This is the case at the Higher Colleges of Technology in the United Arab Emirates where final year Business Studies students are required to give an oral presentation and produce a written report which is co-assessed both for language and subject content (Howell, personal communication). The advantages of such an integrated approach to assessment include enhanced test validity as well as the streamlining of testing procedures with one test serving more than one purpose. They offer a potential benefit to all those engaged in the testing process. Hence, increased collaboration at least at the institutional level is likely to be one of the directions explored for future test development.

Perhaps the most important development will be in the more systematic reporting and dissemination of research and development in the field of integration arising from a growing professionalism in testing. At present, much of the work remains unpublished and unknown. There are, no doubt, integrated tests which have been developed on a principled basis, but these principles have not been promulgated through the literature, nor have the results of studies into the reliability and validity of integrated tests been made widely available. These are necessary if progress in integrated testing is to be achieved.

The University of Hong Kong, China

REFERENCES

Alderson, J.C.: 1981, 'Reaction to Morrow paper', in J.C. Alderson & A. Hughes (eds.), *Issues in Language Testing. ELT Documents 111*, The British Council, London, 45–54.

Bachman, L.F.: 1990, *Fundamental Considerations in Language Testing*, Oxford University Press, Oxford.

Bachman, L.F., Lynch, B.K. & Mason, M.: 1995, 'Investigating variability in tasks and rater judgements in a performance test of foreign language speaking', *Language Testing* 12, 238–257.

Bachman, L.F. & Palmer, A.S.: 1996, *Language Testing in Practice*, Oxford University Press, Oxford.

Brown, A. & Lumley, T.: 1994, 'How can an English proficiency test be made more culturally appropriate?: A case study', in S. Kaur Gill (ed.), *National and International Challenges and Responses. Proceedings of the International English Language Education Conference*, Language Centre, Universiti Kebangsaan, Kuala Lumpur, 122–128.

Bunton, D.: 1995, *Teaching for the 'Practical Skills' Exam*, Hong Kong Examinations Authority, Hong Kong.

Carroll, J.B.: 1961, 'Fundamental considerations in testing for English language proficiency of foreign students', in H.B. Allen (ed.), *Teaching English as a Second Language*, McGraw Hill, New York, 1965, 364–372.

Carroll, J.B.: 1980, *Testing Communicative Performance*, Pergamon Institute of English, London.

Coleman, H.: 1989, 'Testing "appropriate behaviour" in an academic context', in V. Bickley (ed.), *Language Teaching and Learning Styles within and across Cultures*, Institute of Language in Education, Hong Kong, 361–372.

Davies, A.: 1978, 'Language testing survey article Part 2', *Language Teaching and Linguistics Abstracts* II, 215–231.

Emmings, B.: 1986, *Integrated Testing: A Preliminary Investigation*. Unpublished M.A. Thesis, University of Lancaster, Lancaster.

Fox, J.: 1992, 'English proficiency tests in Canada', *Language Testing Update* 11, 6–9.

Johns, A.: 1991, 'Faculty assessment of ESL literacy skills: Implications for writing assessment' in L. Hamp-Lyons (ed.), *Assessing Second Language Writing in Academic Contexts*, Ablex Publishing Corp., NJ, 167–179.

Lewkowicz, J.: 1995, 'Authenticity of task vs. quality of written output' in M. Tickoo (ed.), *Reading and Writing: Theory into Practice*, SEAMEO: Singapore.

Lewkowicz, J.: 1997, *Investigating Authenticity in Language Testing*, Unpublished Ph.D. Thesis, University of Lancaster, Lancaster.

London Chamber of Commerce and Industry: 1995, *English Syllabuses*, London Chamber of Commerce and Industry Examination Board, London.

Low, G.D.: 1982, 'The direct testing of academic writing in a second language', *System* 10, 247–257.

Low, G.D.: 1986, 'Storylines and other developing contexts in use-of-language test design', *Indian Journal of Applied Linguistics*.

Morrow, K.: 1979, 'Communicative language testing: Revolution or evolution?' In C.J. Brumfit & K. Johnson (eds.), *The Communicative Approach to Language Teaching*, Oxford University Press, Oxford, 143–157.

Munby, J.: 1978, *Communicative Syllabus Design*, Cambridge University Press, Cambridge.

Oller, J.W.: 1979, *Language Tests at School: A Pragmatic Approach*, Longman, London.

Paltridge, B.: 1992, 'EAP placement testing: An integrated approach', *English for Specific Purposes* 11, 243–268.

Read, J.: 1990, 'Providing relevant content in an EAP writing test', *English for Specific Purposes* 9, 109–121.

Spolsky, B.: 1985, 'The limits of authenticity in language testing', *Language Testing* 2, 31–40.

Spolsky, B.: 1995, *Measured Words*, Oxford University Press, Oxford.

University of Cambridge Local Examinations Syndicate: 1996, *Cambridge Examination in English for Language Teachers Handbook*, UCLES, Cambridge.

University of Cambridge Local Examinations Syndicate, *Certificate in English for International Business and Trade Content and Administrative Information*, UCLES, Cambridge.

Weir, C.J: 1983, *Identifying the Language Needs of Overseas Students in Tertiary Education in the United Kingdom*. Unpublished Ph.D. Thesis, University of London Institute of Education, London.

Weir, C.J.: 1990: *Communicative Language Testing* (second edition), Prentice Hall, Hemel Hampstead.

Weir, C.J: 1993, *Understanding and Developing Language Tests*, Prentice Hall, London.

Wesche, B.: 1987, 'Second language performance testing: the Ontario test of ESL as an example', *Language Testing* 4, 28–47.

Widdowson, H.: 1979, *Explorations in Applied Linguistics*, Oxford University Press, Oxford.

TIM MCNAMARA

PERFORMANCE TESTING

A performance test is 'one in which some criterion situation is simulated
to a much greater degree than is represented by the usual paper-and-pencil
test' (Fitzpatrick and Morrison, 1971, p. 238). Haertel (1992, p. 984)
contrasts narrower and broader definitions of performance test, the latter including '... any test in which the stimuli presented or the response
elicited emulate some aspects of the nontest settings'. In this broader
sense, second language performance tests are characterized by a relatively
simple performance requirement, that is, that assessment will take place
when the candidate is engaged 'in an act of communication' (Savignon,
1972), that is, where the integrated use of linguistic and pragmatic skills
is required over a stretch of discourse. There are two traditions of performance assessment of languages: one (the *work sample* approach) focuses
on simulating closely the communicative demands of specific settings, for
example in academic or occupational contexts, the other, more *cognitive*,
on capturing the contextualized on-line processing required in all performance.

EARLY DEVELOPMENTS

Performance testing in second language contexts is not new; it has been
a consistent strand within second language testing for the last forty years,
although Spolsky (1995), who has recently redrawn the history of language testing, demonstrates that it has existed for over 100 years. In the
1950s, in the heyday of the introduction of 'scientific' approaches to language testing, with their focus on the careful assessment of knowledge of
discrete points of language, a complementary need was felt for practical
testing of productive language skills, particularly speaking: this resulted
in the introduction within the United States Government of the hugely influential Foreign Service Institute interview-based test of oral proficiency
(Oral Proficiency Interview, OPI) in a number of languages for personnel
being considered for postings abroad (Clark & Clifford, 1988). In the
1960s, the increase in the number of foreign students studying at British
and North American universities meant that there was a need for widespread testing of relevant language skills, and the resulting test batteries
contained a component of performance assessment. With the advent of the
communicative movement in language teaching in the 1970s, performance
assessment found a rationale in the theory of communicative competence.

C. Clapham and D. Corson (eds), Encyclopedia of Language and Education,
Volume 7: Language Testing and Assessment, 131–139.
© *1997 Kluwer Academic Publishers. Printed in the Netherlands.*

Since the 1970s, language performance tests have developed in response
to:

1. the practical need to respond to the requirements of public policy,
   for example, to develop selection procedures for foreign students
   wishing to study at English-medium universities, to control access
   to particular occupational roles requiring communicative skill in a
   second language, or to enhance the public accountability of language
   programmes through a greater focus on demonstrating measurable
   outcomes; and
2. the need to bring testing into line with developments in language
   teaching which resulted from the advent of theories of communicative
   competence.

More recently, in general education settings, particularly in North America, an interest in performance testing has been a feature of alternative
assessment, the move to base assessment not on multiple-choice format
tests but on actual instances of use by learners, in the form of performance
on written and spoken tasks.

MAJOR CONTRIBUTIONS

The two traditions of second language performance assessment are rather
separate, although there is considerable blurring of the lines: the *work
sample* tradition derives largely from work on performance assessment in
non-language settings, particularly in personnel selection; the more general
cognitive and psycholinguistic tradition focuses less on the verisimilitude
of the content of performances than on test process, and on what test
performances reveal about underlying ability and knowledge.

The work sample approach

This approach is clearly illustrated in language testing for academic and
specific occupational purposes, but it has also had an important influence on
general purpose performance testing, in particular the important traditions
of Oral Proficiency Interview testing now associated with the 'Proficiency
Movement' (see the discussion in Clark, 1972; see also Clark & Clifford,
1988). The key to this approach is the (more or less) realistic representation
of relevant real world tasks in the test setting. It is necessary to distinguish
between the *criterion* (relevant communicative behaviour in the target
situation; a series of performances subsequent to the test) and the *test* (a
performance or series of performances simulating, representing or sampled
from the criterion).

Because the criterion (the candidate's subsequent target language behaviour) is in principle unobservable, the test is used to make inferences
about it. One rationale for making the test as close as possible to the

criterion is that this will make the inferences as direct as possible (hence performance testing is sometimes called *direct testing*, although this term is potentially misleading, as all inferences about criterion behaviour are necessarily indirect).

In judging test performances, then, we are not interested in the observed performances for their own sake; if we were, and that is all we were interested in, the sample performance would not be a test. Instead, we are more interested in what the performance reveals of the potential for subsequent performances in the criterion situation; we seek in the test performance those qualities which are indicative of what is held to underlie it. For this we need a theory (implicit or explicit) of the relation between test performance and criterion behaviour. The relative lack of such a theoretical grounding of practice is a weakness in much performance testing, which tends to be resolutely atheoretical, with the result that the bases for inferences about test candidates remain unclear, and the threats to the validity of those inferences not open to investigation. The focus instead in work sample testing is on careful specification of the content of the test in terms of the criterion, and elaborate approaches to content validity (e.g. Weir, 1988) may be a feature of such methods. A job analysis of the target situation is carried out, often informed by a sociolinguistic framework for analysing aspects of the target language use setting. In this approach, the performance is the *target* of assessment (Messick, 1994). Considered from a theoretical point of view, this tradition can be characterized as behaviour-based and sociolinguistic in orientation. Clear examples include the British tradition of testing for English for Academic Purposes; public service testing in Canada (Hauptman et al., 1985); and Australian work on job-specific tests, for example the Occupational English Test (OET) (for health professionals) (McNamara, 1996), The Japanese Test for Tour Guides (Brown, 1995), and a series of language tests for teachers of science and mathematics on the one hand or a variety of modern languages on the other (see Hill, 1996 for a summary of these tests). (For more about LSP tests see the review by Douglas in this volume.)

Cognitive/psycholinguistic approaches

In the second, more general, cognitive and psycholinguistic tradition of performance testing, the performance task itself is of less interest than what the performance reveals of underlying ability. In the words of Messick (1994), the performance is the *vehicle* of assessment, rather than itself being the *target*. This second tradition represents the most common approach to general purpose performance assessment, and includes a wide range of 'communicative' tests of production (interviews, essays etc) and comprehension (listening and reading tests). In the 1970s, the rationale for this kind of test found expression in the work of Oller (1979), specifically his requirements for pragmatic tests (see the discussion of the relevance of this to performance testing in Wesche, 1985), as well as in testing with a more communicative orientation. Recently, this tradition has been revitalized in the work of Skehan (1995), who has used the characterization of the cognitive demands of test tasks as the basis for interpretations of test performance.

WORK IN PROGRESS

In both approaches, the validity of the inferences drawn about candidates must be established *empirically*. In order for this to be done there is a need for explicitness about the rationale for these inferences. The richness of the performance assessment setting (when compared with a multiple-choice format test) brings with it enormous complexity and potential variability, which can easily jeopardize the fairness and the generalizability of conclusions we may reach about individual candidates. For example, performance assessment typically involves judgements of quality against some rating scale. This introduces new features of the assessment setting such as the *raters* themselves, who will vary in the standards which they use and the consistency of their application of those standards; and the *rating procedures* which they are required to implement. The interaction of rater characteristics and the qualities of the rating scales they are using has a crucial influence on the ratings that are given, regardless of the quality of the performance. Similarly, *task choice* or *task processing conditions* and (in speaking tests) *interlocutor effects* may have an influence on test outcome, and we need to understand the effect of these factors. The rating finally given is thus a result of a host of factors interacting with each other; the process is like a piece of complicated machinery with a rating popping out at the end. This means that any idea that there is a transparent relation between the candidate's performance and the rating given is naive. Unfortunately, the belief that rating involves simply making a match between the qualities of the observed performance and characteristics outlined in rating scales is present in much of the rhetoric about direct testing from rating scales. It suggests that the work of the rater is merely to recognize the relevant objective signs, and categorize accordingly, rather like in chicken sexing. But Linacre (1989) has shown that allocation of instances to categories by judges is a probabilistic, not a deterministic phenomenon.

In order to have confidence in the rating procedures for which we may be responsible, or whose results we may be relying on, it is necessary to investigate and control for the effect of factors such as those discussed above. Happily, at the same time as the importance of performance assessment and a realization of its complexity have been growing, our power to conduct empirical research on performance assessment has been enormously expanded by recent developments in the field of measurement. These advances have enabled the investigation of the extent of the impact of particular variables and have suggested ways in which the variability may be constrained, in the interests of fairness. The most important of these are multifaceted Rasch measurement (Linacre, 1989; McNamara, 1996) and Generalizability theory (G-theory) (Brennan, 1983). In multi-faceted Rasch measurement, the impact of rater characteristics, task characteristics, or other variables of interest can be determined by analysis of data from appropriately designed test trials, and is expressed in terms of the difference these factors (*facets*) make to the chances of a candidate reaching some critical level, e.g. the level required for certification. The candidate's reported score is automatically adjusted in the light of what is discovered, to compensate for the particular conditions he/she faced. In addition to general patterns of harshness and difficulty, the effect of interactions between particular raters and particular tasks can be determined in a form of analysis known as *bias analysis*, and the impact of these distortions of the rating process can similarly be estimated and controlled for. Similar effects can be achieved through G-theory, although the procedures are somewhat less flexible and the data requirements for the analysis a little more rigid. (For more about Rasch analysis and Generalizability theory, see the reviews in this volume by Pollitt and Bachman respectively.)

The nature of the variability associated with interlocutor and task in oral assessment is also being investigated using more qualitative approaches, particularly from discourse analysis. Researchers since van Lier (1989) have examined the interaction between interlocutor and candidate, partly to capture the institutional character of the oral proficiency interview, and partly to assist with interlocutor training. Of particular interest is the line of work carried out within the tradition of Conversation Analysis (Lazaraton 1991; Young 1994; *inter alia*). Other work using discourse analytic methods has investigated task effects, for example in role plays (Lumley & Brown, 1995). (For more about qualitative methods see the review by Banerjee and Luoma in this volume.)

PROBLEMS AND DIFFICULTIES

At the heart of the construct validity of many performance assessments is a rating scale (used for assessment, or reporting, or both), as this offers an operational definition of the construct being measured, and is often the only place in which the test construct is defined. However, the genesis of such scales is rarely empirical (North, 1995); on the contrary, there is a tendency simply to reproduce wording from existing scales with minor modifications. Thus the influence of the FSI scale can be seen in scales such as the ACTFL scale (Clark & Clifford, 1988), for use in US schools and colleges, the Australian Second Language Proficiency Ratings (ASLPR), for use with adult immigrants in Australia, and the International English

Language Testing System (IELTS), for students wishing to study at British and Australian universities. Empirical research on this family of scales reveals assumptions about the nature of language and the relationship of second to first language speaker performance that betray the intellectual origins of the scales in the 1950s (Hamilton et al., 1993). The work of North (1995) is significant for its attempt to develop scale descriptors on a strictly empirical basis, although the problems in doing so have by no means been resolved (see also Fulcher's review in this volume); in the performance assessment of literacy skills in adult native speakers, scales have been developed on a fully empirical basis (e.g. Mosenthal & Kirsch, 1994), and this work is likely to prove significant in the second language field. There may however be constraints on the extent to which the empirical development and validation of scales is encouraged, as interpretative frameworks constituted in scales are frequently an instrument of government policy in relation to employment, education and vocational training (Brindley, 1995). Frequently, such frameworks are developed by policy committees and their 'validation' is a question of negotiating their political acceptability to interested stakeholders; the current 'validation' of the Council of Europe framework (Trim, 1996) is a recent example.

A more fundamental problem is that *interaction* in performance testing (for example, between candidate and interlocutor in speaking tests) has been inadequately conceptualized. Where the term interaction has featured in discussions of performance, as in the work of Bachman (1990), it has been used to refer to an internal cognitive interaction between the candidate and some feature of the context, or among various aspects of the candidate's underlying knowledge or skill, rather than as a social phenomenon. In other words, interaction has been understood as an intraindividual rather than an interindividual phenomenon, to use the terms of Halliday (1978). Challenges to this intraindividual view of interaction from more properly interindividual perspectives, for example those implicit in the work of Vygotsky, Halliday and the broad ethnomethodological tradition, lead to a view of joint responsibility for performance (for example, between candidate and interlocutor in speaking tests) which is problematic for assessment schemes which necessarily have to lead to judgements about individuals. The more broadly social nature of aspects of performance assessment, for example the way in which the construct is socially defined, or the intrinsically social character of rater judgements, have similarly been too little considered in discussions of performance testing (McNamara, 1997).

FUTURE DIRECTIONS

Developments in technology have not left performance assessment untouched. For example, attempts have been made, usually on the grounds of economy and feasibility, to deliver tests of speaking using a tape stimulus (as in simulated oral proficiency interviews or SOPIs) rather than a live interlocutor (as in the OPI). However, recent investigation of the equivalence of these two test formats using a combination of quantitative and qualitative methods by O'Loughlin (1997), following Shohamy (1994), has shown that the absence of interaction in the tape-stimulus format means that the two forms cannot be considered equivalent; they are assessing different things. Similarly, in the testing of reading, attempts to deliver test material by computer, particularly in a computer-adaptive test environment (Chalhoub-Deville, 1996), are promising, but problematic in the extent to which they can offer a true equivalent to performance-based tests of reading using a paper format. It may be, as with the SOPI/OPI question, that tests of different skills are involved, and that while a performance test of reading from a screen may be justified in its own right (replicating real world tasks in the age of the computer), it is not a substitute for a reading test delivered in a more conventional manner.

Crucial to the validity of performance tests are the criteria by which performances will be judged. Typically these criteria reflect *a priori* views of language and language use rather than being directly derived from empirical investigation of the criteria which apply in the context of use. Recent work on the application of *indigenous assessment* to specific purpose performance tests (Jacoby & McNamara, 1996) suggests that the study of interaction and discourse involving naturally occurring assessment and critique of practice in the target language use situation may have the potential to inform the development of more appropriate test criteria. This work will involve collaboration between discourse and interaction analysts and test developers, and represents one of many needed expansions of the overly narrow research base of much performance testing.

University of Melbourne
Australia

REFERENCES

Bachman, L.F.: 1990, *Fundamental Considerations in Language Testing*, Oxford University Press, Oxford.

Brennan, R.L.: 1983, *Elements of Generalizability Theory*, The American College Testing Program, Iowa City IA.

Brindley, G.: 1995, 'Assessment and reporting in language learning programs: Purposes, problems and pitfalls', Plenary Address at International Conference on Testing and Evaluation in Second Language Education, The Hong Kong University of Science and Technology, June.

Brown, A: 1995, 'The effect of rater variables in the development of an occupation-specific language performance test', *Language Testing* 12, 1–15.

Chalhoub-Deville, M.: 1996, 'Constructing an operational framework for a CAT of L2 reading proficiency', Paper presented at Seminar 'Issues in computer adaptive testing for assessing reading proficiency', University of Minnesota, Minneapolis MN, March.

Clark, J.L.D.: 1972, *Foreign Language Testing: Theory and Practice*, Center for Curriculum Development, Philadelphia PA.

Clark, J.L.D. & Clifford, R.T.: 1988, 'The FSI/ILR/ACTFL proficiency scales and testing techniques: Development, current status and needed research', *Studies in Second Language Acquisition* 10, 129–147.

Fitzpatrick, R. & Morrison, E.J.: 1971, 'Performance and product evaluation', in R.L. Thorndike (ed.), *Educational Measurement* (second edition), American Council on Education, Washington DC, 237–270, reprinted in F.L. Finch (ed.): 1991, *Educational Performance Assessment*, The Riverside Publishing Company, Chicago, 89–138.

Haertel, E.: 1992, 'Performance measurement', in M.C. Alkin (ed.) *Encyclopedia of Educational Research* (6th edition), 984–989.

Halliday, M.A.K.: 1978, *Language as Social Semiotic: The Social Interpretation of Language and Meaning*, Edward Arnold, London.

Hamilton, J., Lopes, M., McNamara, T.F. & Sheridan, E.: 1993, 'Rating scales and native speaker performance on a communicatively oriented EAP test', *Language Testing* 10, 337–353.

Hauptman, P.C., LeBlanc, R. & Wesche, M.B. (eds): 1985, *Second Language Performance Testing*, University of Ottawa Press, Ottawa.

Hill, K.: 1996, 'From job analysis to task design: Different approaches to simulating teacher language behaviour', Paper presented at the Symposium 'Bridging the gap between language and the professions: What do language testers need to know?', AILA Congress, Jyväskylä, Finland, August.

Jacoby, S. & McNamara, T.F.: 1996, 'Locating competence', Paper presented in the Symposium 'Discourse and the professions', Annual Conference of the American Association for Applied Linguistics, Chicago IL, March.

Lazaraton, A.: 1991, *A Conversation Analysis of Structure and Interaction in the Language Interview*, unpublished PhD dissertation, UCLA, Los Angeles CA.

Linacre, J.M.: 1989, *Many-Faceted Rasch Measurement*, MESA Press, Chicago, IL.

Lumley, T. & Brown, A.: 1995, 'An investigation of the authenticity of discourse in specific purpose language performance tests and its relevance to test validity', Paper presented at International Conference on Testing and Evaluation in Second Language Education, The Hong Kong University of Science and Technology, June.

McNamara, T.F.: 1996, *Measuring Second Language Performance*, Addison-Wesley Longman, London and New York.

McNamara, T.F.: 1997, 'Interaction in second language performance assessment: Whose performance?', *Applied Linguistics* 18, 446–466.

Messick, S.: 1994, 'The interplay of evidence and consequences in the validation of performance assessments', *Educational Researcher* 23, 13–23.

Mosenthal, P.B. & Kirsch, I.S.: 1994, 'Defining the proficiency standards of adult literacy in the U.S.: A profile approach', Paper presented at the National Reading Conference, San Diego, CA, Nov. 30–Dec. 4 [Eric Document ED 379 531].

North, B. 1995: 'The development of a common framework scale of descriptors of language proficiency based on a theory of measurement', *System* 23, 445–465.

Oller, J.W.: 1979, *Language Tests at School*, Longman, London.

O'Loughlin, K: 1997, *The Equivalence of Two Versions of an Oral Proficiency Test*, unpublished PhD thesis, University of Melbourne.

Savignon, S.J.: 1972, *Communicative Competence: An Experiment in Foreign Language Teaching*, The Center for Curriculum Development, Philadelphia PA.

Shohamy, E.: 1994, 'The validity of direct versus semi-direct oral tests', *Language Testing* 11, 99–123.

Skehan, P.: 1995, 'Task-based approaches to language testing', Plenary Address, International Conference on Testing and Evaluation in Second Language Education, The Hong Kong University of Science and Technology, June.

Spolsky, B.: 1995, *Measured Words*, Oxford University Press, Oxford.

Trim, J.L.M.: 1996, 'A common European framework of reference for language learning and teaching', Paper presented at Language Testing Research Colloquium, Tampere, Finland, July 31-August 3.

van Lier, L.: 1989, 'Reeling, writhing, drawling, stretching and fainting in coils: Oral proficiency interviews as conversation', *TESOL Quarterly* 23, 489–508.

Weir, C.J.: 1988, 'The specification, realization and validation of an English language proficiency test', in A. Hughes (ed.), *Testing English for University Study, ELT Documents 127*, Modern English Publications/The British Council, London, 45–110.

Wesche M.B.: 1985, 'Introduction', in P.C. Hauptman, R. Le Blanc & M.B. Wesche (eds.), *Second Language Performance Testing*, University of Ottawa Press, Ottawa, 1–12.

Young, R.E: 1994, 'Conversational styles in language proficiency interviews', *Language Learning* 45, 3–42.

PAUL GRUBA AND CHRIS CORBEL

COMPUTER-BASED TESTING

Within the broader use of technology to support language test development and management, the administration of language tests via computer is an area of particular interest. Computer-based tests have the potential to improve the accuracy, individualisation and efficiency of assessment instruments. However, there remain difficulties in the application of appropriate performance and statistical models, and concerns about test validity. So far, too, there seem to be only a limited range of possible item types.

One approach to computer-based testing essentially utilises technology to computerise conventional paper-and-pencil tests. Computers, used in this manner, can ease test scoring and management. In a review of these efforts, Alderson (1988) argued that much of the previous work done in computer-based English language testing (CBELT) had ignored opportunities for test innovation. Alderson thought that early CBELT developers, under the guise of technology, promoted the use of test methods that might have otherwise been questioned. To improve such non-adaptive instruments, Alderson developed a computer-based test which presented an innovative range of item types. In addition, Alderson proposed a comprehensive research agenda for this area.

Computer-based testing can also be used to assist human raters, as can be seen throughout the development of Exrater (Corbel, 1995). The application assists novice raters using the Australian Second Language Proficiency Ratings(ASLPR) proficiency scale by focusing rater attention on key aspects of language performance. The role of the computer is to enhance, rather than replace, the skills of the rater. A more complex manifestation of this approach, based on second language acquisition research, can be found in Rapid Profiler (Pienemann, 1990).

The bulk of research in computer-based testing, however, has centred on computer-adaptive tests (CATs). In this approach, the processing capabilities of the computer permit the development of examinations which go beyond the limits of conventional formats. Larson (1989) lists the attractions of CAT instruments. They include reduced administration time, decreased candidate frustration, self-paced tests, the production of immediate results, a need to have fewer test administrators, and improvements in test security.

Tung (1986) and Laurier (1991) describe how computer-adaptive tests work. In brief, examinees responding to an item correctly receive a progressively more difficult item; an incorrect answer causes an easier question

C. Clapham and D. Corson (eds), Encyclopedia of Language and Education,
Volume 7: Language Testing and Assessment, 141–149.
© 1997 Kluwer Academic Publishers. Printed in the Netherlands.

to be presented. Using a pre-calibrated bank of test items, the computer adjusts the test along a continuum of difficulty until a reliable estimate of ability is attained. At that point, the CAT finishes and is able to produce a score. The foundation of many CATs rests on Item Response Theory, of which Henning (1987) provides a description in the context of language testing. (For more about Item Response Theory see the reviews by Pollitt, and by Bachman and Eignor in this volume.) An extensive overview of CAT development is available in Wainer, Dorans, Flaugher, Green, Mislevy, Steinberg and Thissen (1990).

MAJOR CONTRIBUTIONS

Although CATs were first created in 1970 for use in mental and ability testing (Weiss, 1983), their implementation in foreign language assessment arose from research conducted at Brigham Young University in 1984 which led to the production of S-CAPE (Larson, 1989). Designed to assist in the placement of students in university Spanish language courses, S-CAPE utilised multiple-choice items to test grammar. In a related project, Madsen (1991) developed Computest ESL to assess tertiary reading and listening skills. When compared to paper-and-pencil tests, Madsen found that average candidates needed to answer only one-third as many items and responded positively to the computerised format.

A significant CAT research and development project under the auspices of the American Council for the Teaching of Foreign Languages (ACTFL) provided data to enable the organisation to refine proficiency scales (Kaya-Carton, Carton & Dandonoli, 1991). Specifically, the researchers used the guidelines as a basis for the development of a French reading proficiency CAT. In the process a definition of reading proficiency was established; desired characteristics of the test were determined; items were written on the basis of selected passages; and decisions regarding the appropriate model for item calibration and an application of test trials to the criterion referenced nature of the scales were made. In the final test, authentic comprehension passages, which could not be legibly reproduced on a monitor, had to be presented in a booklet rather than on the screen. After an initial 'level check' passage, test candidates were directed by the computer to further relevant passages in the booklet, depending on their responses to each passage.

Hill (1991) discusses the development of the Test of English Proficiency (ToPE), a CAT which presents cloze tests constructed out of short (150–250 word) reading passages. To develop an item bank, approximately 500 paper-and-pencil cloze examinations were first constructed. Subsequent trials of the test required the administration of two forms and an 'anchor test' to a minimum of 30 students each at various language schools throughout Britain. Using results from the common anchor test, items were calibrated along a nine point scale. Candidate scores from the final CAT correlated very highly with other measures of student ability.

Stages in the production of a prototype English as a Second Language (ESL) listening comprehension CAT are described by Dunkel (1992). Based on ACTFL guidelines and an extended taxonomy of listening skills, the researcher designed an application capable of being used for test design, candidate assessment and score analysis. The prototype required the development of voice, test, direction, question, graphic and database computer files. The files were combined to assess the ability of candidates to respond to spoken questions, recognise synonymous statements and comprehend dialogues or conversations. One outcome of the project was a call for more awareness of emerging technologies, better definitions of listening comprehension constructs and improved test validation. (For more about testing listening as a second language see Buck's review in this volume.) In light of the complexities of the project, Dunkel advocated the need to adopt an interdisciplinary team approach to CAT development.

WORK IN PROGRESS

Alderson and Windeatt (1995) report on the continuing development of the Lancaster University Computer-Based Assessment Systems (LUCAS). Utilizing a non-adaptive approach to computer-based testing, the researchers have added an authoring tool to their assessment system and directed greater attention to interface considerations.

Following on from earlier Brigham Young University projects, Strong-Krause (1995) reports that additional CATs have been developed for use in German, French and Russian proficiency. Currently, development of a three-part computer-adaptive exam for English as a Second Language (E-CAPE) is underway. The first part of E-CAPE is a grammar exam which uses multiple choice, fill-in-the-blank and multiple choice error recognition items. The reading comprehension section employs 100 word passages followed by up to four multiple choice items to examine the candidates' ability to find main ideas and make inferences. A third section of E-CAPE assesses listening proficiency by initially providing a focus statement, which is followed by a brief passage and a multiple choice item.

Several current CAT projects focus on the measurement of reading proficiency. Chalhoub-Deville (1996) reports on the development of French, German and Spanish reading proficiency CATs at the University of Michigan. There are three stages to the project: the construction of a CAT item bank, pilot testing and item calibration, and field testing. In the initial phase of the project, researchers directed their efforts to the construction of a viable CAT framework and identified critical points that require further attention. In the area of technology, for example, choices needed to be made about appropriate software, platform, screen design and test features. A second concern of the project is successfully to adapt an appropriate model of second language reading proficiency assessment, with consideration of specifications for text selection, factors contributing to item difficulty, and the determination of appropriate item types. A third challenge to the project focuses on issues related to CAT development itself, and includes decisions regarding statistical models, the use of testlets, algorithm control, principled scoring and on-going item bank development. (For more about testlets, see Bachman and Eignor's review in this volume.)

Dunkel (1996) reports on the continuing development of listening proficiency CATs for the assessment of ESL, Russian and Hausa. Multimedia productions, able to combine full-motion video and speech in a single hyper-text environment, are the basis for the current set of examinations. Work in one part of the CAT project is focused on establishing a content model and an item-writing framework. A second part of the project explores appropriate measurement models. In this part, item trials and calibration are needed to determine the fit of the data to the selected model. Error-controlled, decision point, step ladder or multi-stage CAT formats with possible differences in algorithms are being considered. In the later stages of the project, Dunkel will evaluate the utility of the CAT framework from a perspective of second language acquisition, aspects of validity and advances in psychometric theory.

Researchers working on the Test of English as a Foreign Language (TOEFL) have begun to create a computer-based version of their examination (Eignor, 1996; Taylor & Kirsch, 1996). As part of the TOEFL 2000 project, developers aim to create an internationally available computer-based test which incorporates current theories of communicative competence, supplies additional information to score users and allows for continuous improvement. The project is being conducted on a number of fronts and developed in a series of incremental stages.

Eignor (1996) details the development of a computer-based examination, *Enhanced TOEFL*, to be introduced in early 1998. Two stages of a three phase developmental study for the project have been completed. The aim of the first stage was to investigate the extent to which CAT candidate abilities can be estimated based on the paper and pencil version of the TOEFL. Using IRT procedures, investigators compared scores for two language groups (Japanese and Spanish) against a mixed language group sample of test takers. Results for the listening comprehension section of the *Enhanced TOEFL* were deemed acceptable, but the presence of native language candidate test scores in both the structure and written expression section and the reading comprehension section caused difficulties. Estimated scores from the Spanish group of examinees, for example, were found to have a higher error rate than those in the Japanese sample.

The second stage of the *Enhanced TOEFL* study (Eignor, 1996) sought to determine the effects of particular IRT procedures on item selection and ability estimation in the structure and written expression section of the exam. To do this, researchers created a simulated Spanish CAT. Results indicated that differences between a mixed language group sample and the Spanish test takers were less than expected. The purpose of phase three of the study is to judge whether or not to make a CAT for the reading section of the test. Depending on the outcomes, test developers will decide whether the examination will be further developed as a CAT or as a randomly parallel linear computer-based test. Eignor keeps open the possibility that certain sections of the TOEFL may be developed as CATs while other sections may be randomly linear computer-based versions. Extended writing task sections will not be administered adaptively.

Burstein, Frase, Ginther & Grant (1996) are investigating computer-based scoring procedures that are able to accommodate natural language responses. Such procedures are needed, for example, to assess short answer and essay responses. Human raters assign scores to responses that the computer is unable to assess. To save time and reduce costs, researchers are first evaluating the utility of currently available computer technologies and software packages, including off-the-shelf grammar checkers.

PROBLEMS AND DIFFICULTIES

Wainer et al. (1990) discuss four central issues that face CAT developers. Firstly, there are administrative concerns with regard to time constraints, inappropriate test behaviour and candidate omission of items. Secondly, there are psychometric issues which include a further elaboration of statistical and cognitive models, determination of constraints on item selection algorithms and investigations of better ways to address the possibility of multiple alternatives. In this context, Canale's (1986) widely cited criticisms of computer-adaptive testing are still relevant. Canale argued that if the statistical model on which a computer-adaptive test is based necessitates the assumption that the attribute being measured is unidimensional, such an assumption may not be in keeping with current models of language proficiency.

A third issue, according to Wainer, Dorans, Green, Mislevy, and Steinberg (1990) is test design, particularly in the use of item clusters, or 'testlets', as their usage raises problems related to context effects, item ordering and content balancing. A fourth area of concern to CAT developers concerns policy issues related to test equity, including making provision for handicapped candidates, creating equivalent versions of the 'same' CAT, and equating CATs to conventional paper-and-pencil examinations. Possible legal challenges in these areas, Wainer et al. (1990) note, may be raised in the future.

Validity concerns of computer-based tests remain a central issue. Green (1988) argues that construct validity of computerised tests will be difficult to achieve and may require the modification of construct definitions. According to Henning (1991), a number of factors may influence CAT validity including the mode of presentation of test items, differential candidate experience and attitudes regarding computers, the speededness of the test, the influence of item sequences, test length, warm-up effects, the appropriate fit of a model, and item bank dimensionality.

In specific reference to reading proficiency CATs, Grabe (1996) raises a number of issues. Particularly, the mode of presentation may affect reading behaviour: Grabe points to a need for a better understanding of computer-based reading strategies and how the use of digital text may influence a candidate's reading options. Grabe notes that the development of a reading CAT for a non-Roman language will present challenges. New item types will need to be created for computer-based tests of reading (Yoes, 1996).

The computer-based assessment of listening proficiency and writing skills creates a particular technological challenge to test developers (Burstein et al., 1996; Dunkel, 1996). Demands on computer processing speed and memory, the development of specialised applications and a need to integrate additional equipment each raise barriers to the completion of CAT instruments. Because of these problems, development in the computer-based tests of listening and writing has lagged behind advances in CAT reading and grammar assessment.

Brown and Iwashita (1996) raise further questions concerning CAT validity and development. In the process of developing a CAT grammar test to be used for student placement in a tertiary Japanese course, the researchers trialled 225 paper-and-pencil test items with 1400 learners of Japanese from Australia, China and Japan. Subsequent calculations revealed that item difficulty differed depending on variations in sample group characteristics.

There are broader issues relating to test developers and users. Alderson and Windeatt (1995) state that although testers are willing to administer computer-based tests, they are reluctant to commit resources to innovative development in the area. Corbel (1993) identifies three possible institutional constraints on test implementation; organisational readiness; appropriacy of hardware and software; and the beliefs and practices of teachers. All stakeholders in the assessment process, Corbel emphasises, should be consulted when computers are introduced to an organisation.

FUTURE DIRECTIONS

An expanding base of computer resources in educational settings coupled with the maturation of computer-assisted language learning practices will ensure the continuing development of computer-based tests. At present, there is a gap between learning a language through computer-assisted methodologies and assessment by conventional paper-and-pencil examinations (Chapelle, 1996). The conceptual differences in learning and assessment are being broken down, however, and future trends will continue to blur this distinction (Berberich, 1995). As part of this trend, computer applications which integrate teaching and assessment will be more widely produced.

The rapid pace of technological change, most importantly in the area of locally and globally networked computers, will significantly affect the development and administration of computerised tests. Language test administrators can already deliver computer-based tests from a central location to remote sites (Johnston, 1996), and this practice will expand as costs are lowered and competition among test products intensifies. Several examples of on-line tests are available via the World Wide Web (see, for example http://www.surrey.ac.uk/ELI/ltr.html). Additionally, advanced linguistic analysis tools (Burstein et al., 1996), handwriting recognition technologies, digital video media and voice responsive computers are set to become an integral part of assessment instruments. To meet both technical and theoretical demands of CAT development, large inter-disciplinary teams of specialists will be required (Dunkel, 1996).

Finally, language proficiency constructs will be expanded in response to CAT developments. Definitions of listening proficiency, for example, will begin to take into account factors related to digital video media as a mode of presentation. The concerns of CAT developers, for the most part, will continue to move from those of technology to those focusing on conceptual issues (Burstein et al., 1996).

University of Melbourne
Australia

REFERENCES

Alderson, J.C.: 1988, 'Innovations in language testing: Can the microcomputer help?' *Special Report No. 1, Language Testing Update*, University of Lancaster, Lancaster, UK.
Alderson, J.C. & Windeatt, S.: 1991, 'Computers and innovation in language testing' in J.C. Alderson & B. North (eds.), *Language Testing in the 1990s*, Macmillan, London, 226–236
Alderson, J.C. & Windeatt, S.: 1995, 'Is there an interest in innovative items?' *Language Testing Update* 17, 58–59.
Berberich, F.: 1995, 'Computer adaptive testing and its extension to a teaching model in CALL', *CAELL Journal* 6, 11–18.
Brown, A. & Iwashita, N.: (1996), 'Language background and item difficulty: The development of a computer-adaptive test of Japanese', *System* 24, 199–206.
Burstein, J., Frase, L., Ginther, A. & Grant, L.: 1996, 'Technologies for language assessment', *Annual Review of Applied Linguistics* 16, 240–260.

Canale, M.: 1986, 'The promise and threat of computerized adaptive assessment of reading comprehension', in C. Stansfield (ed.), *Technology in Language Testing*, TESOL, Washington, DC, 29–45.

Chalhoub-Deville, M.: 1996, 'Constructing an operational framework for a CAT of L2 reading proficiency', in M. Chalhoub-Deville (ed.), *Issues in Computer Adaptive Testing of Second Language Reading Proficiency Conference Seminar Papers*, University of Minnesota, Bloomington, MN, 1–3.

Chapelle, C.: 1996, 'CALL-English as a second language', *Annual Review of Applied Linguistics* 16, 139–157.

Corbel, C.: 1993, *Computer-Enhanced Language Assessment*, National Centre for English Language Testing and Research, Sydney.

Corbel, C.: 1995, 'Exrater: A knowledge-based system for language assessors' in G. Brindley (ed.), *Assessment in Action*, National Centre for English Language Testing and Research, Sydney, 93–112.

Dunkel, P.: 1992, 'The use of PC-Generated speech technology in the development of an L2 listening comprehension proficiency test: A prototype design effort', in M.C. Pennington & V. Stevens (eds.), *Computers in Applied Linguistics: An International Perspective*, Multilingual Matters, Clevedon, Avon, UK, 273–293.

Dunkel, P.: 1996, 'Checking the utility and appropriacy of the content and measurement models used to develop L2 listening comprehension CATS: Implications for further development of comprehensive CATs', in M. Chalhoub-Deville (ed.), *Issues in Computer Adaptive Testing of Second Language Reading Proficiency Conference Seminar Papers*, University of Minnesota, Bloomington, MN, 27–37.

Eignor, D.: 1996, 'Adaptive assessment of reading comprehension for TOEFL', in M. Chalhoub-Deville (ed.), *Issues in Computer Adaptive Testing of Second Language Reading Proficiency Conference Seminar Papers*, University of Minnesota, Bloomington, MN, 46–52.

Green, B. F.: 1988, 'Construct validity of computer-based tests', in H. Wainer & H.I. Braun (eds.), *Test Validity*, Lawrence Erlbaum, Hillsdale, NJ, 77 – 86.

Henning, G.: 1987, *A Guide to Language Testing: Development, Evaluation, Research*, Newbury House, New York.

Henning, G.: 1991, 'Validating an item bank in a computer-assisted or computer-adaptive test', in P. Dunkel (ed.), *Computer-Assisted Language Learning and Testing: Research Issues and Practice*, Newbury House, New York, 209–222.

Hill, R.A.: 1991 'ToPE: Test of proficiency in English: The development of an adaptive test', in J.C. Alderson & B. North (eds.), *Language Testing in the 1990s*, Macmillan, London, 237–246.

Johnston, C.: 1996, 'Computerized testing on a large network: Issues for today and tomorrow', in M. Chalhoub-Deville (ed.), *Issues in Computer Adaptive Testing of Second Language Reading Proficiency Conference Seminar Papers*, University of Minnesota, Bloomington, MN, 7–10.

Kaya-Carton, E., Carton, A.S. and Dandonoli, P.: 1991, 'Developing a computer-adaptive test of French reading proficiency' in P. Dunkel (ed.), *Computer-Assisted Language Learning and Testing: Research Issues and Practice*, Newbury House, New York, 259–284.

Larson, J.: 1989, 'S-CAPE: A Spanish computerized adaptive placement exam', in W.F. Smith (ed.), *Modern Technology in Language Education: Applications and Projects*, National Textbook Company, Lincolnwood, IL, 277–289.

Laurier, M.: 1991, 'What we can do with computerized adaptive testing . . . and what we cannot do!', in S. Anivan (ed.), *Current Developments in Language Testing*, SEAMEO Regional Language Centre, Singapore, 244–255.

Madsen, H.S.: 1991, 'Computer-adaptive testing of listening and reading comprehension', in P. Dunkel (ed.), *Computer-Assisted Language Learning and Testing: Research Issues and Practice*, Newbury House, New York, 237–257.

Pienemann, M.: 1990, *LARC Research Projects 1990*, Language Acquisition Research Centre, Sydney.

Strong-Krause, D.: 1995, 'Computer-adaptive placement exams', *Language Testing Update*, 18, 63.

Taylor, C. & Kirsch, I., 1996, 'TOEFL 2000 project update 1996', Poster presentation at the 16th Language Testing Research Colloquium, Tampere, Finland [available on-line http://www.surrey.ac.uk/ELI/ilta/posters2.html].

Tung, P.: 1986, 'Computerized adaptive testing: implications for language test developers', in C. Stansfield (ed.), *Technology in Language Testing*, TESOL, Washington, DC, 11–28.

Wainer, H., Dorans, N.J., Green, B.F., Mislevy, R.J., Steinberg, L.: 1990, 'Future challenges', in H. Wainer, N.J. Dorans, R. Flaugher, B.F. Green, R.J. Mislevy, L. Steinberg & D. Thissen, (eds.), *Computerized Adaptive Testing: A Primer*, Lawrence Erlbaum, Hillsdale, NJ, 233–271.

Wainer, H., Dorans, N.J., Flaugher, R., Green, B.F., Mislevy, R.J., Steinberg, L. & Thissen, D. (eds.): 1990, *Computerized Adaptive Testing: A Primer*, Lawrence Erlbaum, Hillsdale, NJ.

Weiss, D.J.: 1983, *New Horizons in Testing: Latent Trait Test Theory and Computerized Adaptive Testing*, Academic Press, New York.

Yoes, M.: 1996, 'Exploring new item-types for computerized testing: New possibilities and challenges', in M. Chalhoub-Deville (ed.), *Issues in Computer Adaptive Testing of Second Language Reading Proficiency Conference Seminar Papers*, University of Minnesota, Bloomington, MN, 11–16.

PAULINE REA-DICKINS AND SHELAGH RIXON

THE ASSESSMENT OF YOUNG LEARNERS OF ENGLISH AS A FOREIGN LANGUAGE

For the purposes of this review, young learners (henceforth YLs) are defined as children from the ages of 6 to about 11. They range from children who have recently entered the compulsory schooling system to those who are approaching a transition stage in their education, either a change of school, or a transfer to a more senior level in the same institution.

English learning by pupils whose first language is not English is customarily divided into English as a Foreign Language (EFL) and English as a Second Language (ESL). ESL contexts vary from those in which English is an important language for day to day transactions, administration or education in a multilingual country such as Namibia, to those in which the learner is in a country such as the UK or Australia where the national or majority language is English. Although this review focuses on FL assessment, many of the insights have been drawn from the latter type of ESL assessment.

In the last ten years there has been a notable increase in the teaching of foreign languages, and English in particular, in the primary levels of many state school systems (Rixon, 1992). Motives include a political desire to meet parents' ambitions, educators' views on the benefits of an 'early start' from a psycholinguistic perspective, or simply a desire to prolong exposure to foreign language teaching in the school system.

EARLY DEVELOPMENTS

Classroom assessment of L1 English in primary schools in England in the 1960s and 70s was predominantly concerned with standardised summative measures of learner achievement focused on 'reading' (and the related concept of 'reading age'), verbal reasoning and vocabulary. In the 80s, however, there was a considerable amount of formative focused assessment of ESL (e.g. Barrs et al., 1988), with more use of descriptive records of learner development in language and learning, which tracked language development along with other curricular abilities.

In the 1960s and 70s researchers evaluating teaching programmes were commonly expected to justify and defend their efforts in narrow summative terms. The assessment component of the evaluation of primary French teaching in England and Wales (e.g. Burstall et al., 1974) is a notable example. Because of the assessment methods used, and because the 'early

C. Clapham and D. Corson (eds), Encyclopedia of Language and Education,
Volume 7: Language Testing and Assessment, 151–161.
© 1997 Kluwer Academic Publishers. Printed in the Netherlands.

starters' assessed at ages 14 and 16 had already been in the secondary system for a number of years, the results, which showed that primary school learners of French did no better than those who started later, have been somewhat discredited. They are widely agreed not to be directly useful for interpreting the achievements or potential of 'early starters' during or at the end of the primary phase of French learning. For many years, the negative conclusions drawn from this research discouraged similar programmes in other countries.

In EFL, the assessment of YLs for Certification has only recently been considered to be important. Interestingly, none of the UK tests reviewed in Alderson, Krahnke & Stansfield (1987) concern school assessment, although over half the American entries review ESL proficiency tests for children: "a response to a US Supreme Court decision (Lau vs. Nichols 1974) ... that publicly funded schools must provide special instructional programs for non-English speaking ... students" (Stansfield, 1987, p. 1).

There was, though, one set of EFL tests which were mostly geared towards young beginners. This consisted of the lower levels of the UK based Trinity College examinations in EFL (available since 1937, with regular updating). These oral/aural EFL examinations were, and are, even after revisions in the 1990s, largely based on the individual coping with predictable and closely specified functions of language in a limited context in dialogue with an examiner, see Maddock and Lee (1981).

MAJOR CONTRIBUTIONS

Research in language testing has focused almost exclusively on the older foreign language learner. For example, in the more than ten years of its existence, the specialist journal, *Language Testing*, has had only two articles on the assessment of YLs. Van Gelderen (1994) reports on the validation of a rating scheme for assessing oral communication tasks at the end of primary education (11–12 years), and Carpenter, Fujii & Kataoka (1995) document the development of six tasks which form an oral interview procedure for learners of Japanese aged 5–10. They identify some specific problems in assessing YLs.

A survey of EYL textbooks and teachers' manuals gives further indications of how under-researched this area is. In teachers' manuals, classroom assessment is on the whole barely touched upon (e.g. Brumfit et al., 1991; Halliwell, 1992; Vale & Feunteun, 1995). This may reflect a belief amongst editors and authors, that formal assessment is not appropriate for EYL. It might also reflect a cautious recognition that different countries have their own traditions of subject assessment within the wider primary curriculum, and that a book of general YL advice could not capture and discuss these. However, Brumfit (1991) discusses how the National Curriculum (in England and Wales) Attainment Targets in L1 English may or may not form useful points of reference for EFL assessment. The Attainment Targets have since been revised, but the question remains. Machura (1991) examines how the expectations of achievement may differ between non-native teachers of EFL, and teachers of L1 English in British schools. The non-native EFL teachers seem to focus on detailed linguistic accuracy, rather than global discoursal competence, especially in the written mode.

Most of the internationally published EFL textbooks for YLs provide testing materials. These are usually linked to the work of a single unit or a block of units, and tend to be narrowly focused on language at the level of the single sentence. The commonest items consist of matching words and pictures, or gap-filling with a lexical or grammatical item. Tasks involving the processing of connected discourse are rare. The most developed set of textbook-based EFL assessment materials is in the Teacher's Book for *Fanfare* (McHugh & Occhipinti, 1993) where advice on the description of pupils' achievements and on observation and elicitation procedures owes much to National Curriculum practice and the *Primary Language Record Handbook* (Barrs et al., 1988). This is, therefore, an attempt to introduce wider assessment procedures to textbook users but, for the teacher untrained in these approaches, this advice may raise as many problems as it solves.

The International Association of Teachers of English as a Foreign Language (IATEFL), and its Young Learners' Special Interest Group, has given some attention to YL assessment. Smith (1996a, 1996b) reports on her work in Israel as a primary EFL teacher and trainer, and suggests that since traditional pencil and paper tests cannot reflect the range of activities within a primary foreign language classroom, alternative assessment methods should be introduced aimed at formative rather than summative assessment (1996). She stresses the importance of 'confidence building', the emphasis on validity, rather than merely on reliability, and gives some practical suggestions for classroom assessment.

Performance testing in L1 and ESL contexts, with its focus on the validity of assessment tasks, might also affect EFL asessment. Since 1988, the National Curriculum in England and Wales has brought considerable changes to assessment and these changes are closely mirrored by developments in New Zealand and Australia. In spite of broadening assessment practices in some respects (e.g. by officially including teacher assessment, coursework and records of achievement), the National Curriculum has also reintroduced and reinforced the role of standardised and quantitative learner assessment by introducing formal summative examinations, including English, at key stages in the curriculum (ages 7 and 11). This has largely been directed towards accountability, and is emphasised by the publication of national 'league tables' which compare schools. Increasing interest has been aroused by the National Curriculum Standard Attainment Tests, and by the controversy about the value of summative assessment in the early years, particularly at Key Stage 1 (age 7). This has resulted in a fast growing literature (e.g. Gipps & Stobart, 1993; Daugherty, 1995). Unlike other approaches (described below), the National Curriculum sets up statements of expected performance against which learners are matched.

A different approach to performance assessment is used in 'descriptive profiling', which is more closely allied to formative, pedagogically oriented assessment, with greater teacher involvement in the process. The research and development work here has made a major contribution to the field in terms of the purpose, the focus on development as opposed to mere attainment, the process of gathering data through observation, the nature of the records themselves, and the uses to which they are put. In ESL, the most notable profiles of learner *development* are those of Barrs and colleagues at the Centre for Language in Primary Education (e.g. Barrs et al., 1988; 1990; Hester, 1993). In mainstream primary education, PROCESS (Profiling, Recording, and Observing Competencies and Experiences), a qualitative description of learning, was devised by Stierer and colleagues (1993). Materials were developed to support observing, profiling, and monitoring learners from their nursery classes. Both sets of materials also provide baseline data for individual learners, and thus may be said to have summative as well as formative functions. (For more about performance testing see the review by McNamara in this volume.)

In the Canadian Language Benchmark Programme, teachers may work from examples of good performances which guide them to describe what learners can do rather than what they 'should' be able to do at a given stage in the curriculum. Larter & Donnelly (1993, p.24) note that "teachers do not administer benchmarks to students as they would conduct traditional standardised tests. Instead, they use them as reference materials, an approach that has resulted in a variety of centralised and school-based initiatives". "Unlike externally developed and scored tests, benchmarks allow teachers, students, and parents to collaborate and remain in control of learning and evaluation" (ibid., p. 24). Learners, too, can use the benchmarks "as models of excellent performances" (ibid., p. 24). As an extension of this work, Spielman (1993) describes ways in which the Canadian Language Benchmark Programme (designed for describing English performance) have been successfully implemented in French Immersion classes. Their use has helped teachers to understand the assessment process itself and to plan activities for their learners, and has also lead to significant professional dialogue within groups of colleagues.

In Australia, "teachers are being increasingly called upon to monitor and record individual learner progress and achievement in much more systematic ways" (Brindley, 1995, p. 1). The Monitoring Standards in Education (MSE) programme shares some characteristics of the National Curriculum in England and Wales, and has produced standards of attainment expected of learners in years 3, 7, and 10 (Masters, 1990, cited in Broadfoot, 1996,

p. 39). Equally, the Student Needs Assessment Procedures (SNAP) aims to provide information "at classroom, school and system level" and to describe procedures that are "explicit, criterion-referenced, standardised, relevant and task-based" (Mincham, 1995, pp. 87–88).

As far as evaluation goes, governments and ministries, in many countries, are now less likely to demand rigorous and narrow justifications for teaching practices, and are more inclined to accept YL language teaching as 'good in itself'. It has been suggested (e.g. Kubanek-German, 1996) that in some countries the role of researchers has become that of investigators about how the teaching might best be done, rather than of 'defenders' of doing it at all. However, the role of formal tests in performing a major evaluative function is still in evidence in, for example, the national testing planned as part of the evaluation of pilot foreign language learning programmes in Italy (unpublished data).

A further example of assessment for evaluation purposes is that of Edelenbos and Suhre (1994) who report on an evaluation of two different Primary English language programmes in Holland, one based on a structuralist view of grammar, the other on a more communicative approach. Since they believe that positive attitudes will be reflected in the quality of learning, they use motivation and attitude scales as well as tests. The need for primary language learning to foster positive attitudes for further language(s) study at secondary level is a related issue which is reflected in the evaluation of the pilot foreign language programme in French Primary schools (Ministère de l'Education Nationale, 1991).

Mitchell (1992) conducted an evaluation of bilingual primary language education in the Western Isles of Scotland. In this study observational methods are mixed with measures of attainment to provide a more comprehensive statement about language programme implementation. Assessment tasks were developed in parallel English and Gaelic versions centred around 'talking about self', 'talking about school work', and 'retelling a story'. An initial proposal to investigate learners' attitudes towards the language and the target culture (cf. Edelenbos & Suhre, 1994) was later dropped.

The recent Scottish national pilot project for the teaching of foreign languages (FL) in primary schools has now matured into the country-wide diffusion of FL teaching. In spite of the strong manifesto that its main aims were the *hard* ones of language achievement, rather than *soft* ones such as language awareness, the preliminary evaluation of this project (Low et al., 1993) provided more than an assessment of how well pupils had fared linguistically. The results also fed into future work in the primary and secondary schools in the same spirit of wide-ranging information gathering to inform decision-making, as is shown in Genesee (1994) and McKay (1995). The evaluation study used a range of instruments including internal school-designed assessment: teacher-conducted and evaluator-conducted tasks; observed lessons; paired interviews, which involved talk in the FL about topics used in courses; and a vocabulary retrieval task that involved saying words in the FL that were known by pupils under topic headings. This information was gathered from 'new entries' into secondary school (1st and 2nd years) at a stage when the effects of primary learning were still fresh, and was comparable with data from children who had only started the FL at the age of 11.

For a child, unlike an adult learner, the possession of a certificate from an international examining board can have no 'outside world' value in career or education terms. However, a number of international exams for YLs do exist, and are probably valued by parents and schools as evidence of progress and achievement. The YLs themselves may also find them motivating as a 'goal', but questions remain about how much of their true language achievement can be captured by a fixed-format exam. Whereas in the 1970s the only certification was provided by Trinity College, other examination boards have now introduced tests designed for the EYL market. These include the Associated Examination Board Junior English Tests (7–12 years), the Association of Recognised English Language Schools (ARELS) First Junior Preliminary Certificate Examination, and the Pitman Examinations in ESOL for YLs (9–13 years). The most recent additions are the Saxoncourt Tests for Young Learners of English (STYLE, 6–12 years), recently launched in 1996, and the University of Cambridge Local Examinations Syndicate (UCLES) Tests for YLs, launched in 1997. Both Saxoncourt and UCLES provide syllabuses which seem to reflect the 'core' content of main internationally used EFL textbooks. The UCLES initiative may be instrumental in discouraging parents and schools from entering YLs for other high-prestige UCLES examinations, such as the Key English Test (KET) and the Preliminary Test (PET), that also reflect a 'beginners' or 'post-beginners' level of language learning, but are not suitable conceptually, or in the topics treated, for the maturity level of most YLs.

WORK IN PROGRESS

Research specifically focused on school-based assessment in the EFL context is being undertaken by Rea-Dickins and Rixon at the University of Warwick. A questionnaire-based survey of a number of countries (e.g. Hungary, France, Greece, Indonesia) has been conducted to identify some of the key factors in YL assessment, as perceived by both primary English language teachers and teacher trainers. In the next phase of the research, YLs will be interviewed, in the L1, about their perceptions of the assessment process, and teachers will be interviewed about the relation of assessment to the language learning programme.

We again have to turn to the ESL domain for significant current developments in assessment within the curriculum. Genesee & Hamayan (1994) and McKay (1995) write as educators of ESL learners in mainstream schooling (Canada and Australia respectively). (See McKay's review in this volume.) They agree that it is appropriate to integrate ESL learners with their fellow pupils as much as possible for all curricular subjects, and that it is necessary for language specialists and teachers of curricular subjects to cooperate. They also propose that language assessment should be concerned with performance in tasks that are part of curricular learning, either realistically simulated or taking place as part of normal learning. Such assessment is used for decision-making about instruction rather than as a means of merely grading children. The development of diagnostic test materials for classroom purposes is being developed in similar initiatives in Sweden by the National Agency for Education, Language Teaching & Testing Research Unit, University of Göteborg (Nihlen, 1997), and in Norway at the University of Bergen (Hasselgren, 1997).

Genesee & Hamayan (1994) offer a rich repertoire of methods by which a classroom teacher may capture a child's abilities and needs: observation, conferences (private discussion between pupil and teacher on needs, attitudes, achievements and problems), student journals, tests, together with advice on record-keeping, the building of student portfolios, and the use of checklists for both teacher and pupil to assist in the information gathering process. They also stress the importance of monitoring language development in the social and affective areas and not only in academic-related fields. A number of other writers highlight the range of potential procedures for classroom assessment purposes (e.g. Smith, 1996a; 1996b; Sutton, 1995). In Amiens, France (unpublished data), teachers have devised self assessment procedures for use with YLs across the range of foreign languages taught at primary level.

PROBLEMS AND DIFFICULTIES

The EFL YL assessment culture appears to be at odds with that of mainstream education and of ESL assessment. The distinction between assessment for formative developmental purposes on the one hand and summative attainment purposes on the other is not really addressed. The rich repertoire of approaches and procedures mentioned above is not matched in the EFL context. There is a wide gulf between the current 'whole child' and 'whole curriculum' approaches of the ESL and L1 fields, and the generally more 'discrete language-item based' approaches found in many current EFL situations. The very marked development that has been seen, over the last 20 years, in ESL fields, from a 'discrete language item' concern towards a concern for the ability to *use* language for specific and valued purposes, suggests that the difference in approach is not so much a consequence of the difference between the learning contexts but a reflection of the fact that work in the EFL assessment field is lagging behind that in ESL.

Further difficulties lie in the little researched area of the nature of YLs as 'test takers' as distinct from the older school learner or adult. How different should EYL assessment practices be from those used with older learners? Is there a real, as opposed to a cosmetic, difference? Is the increased unreliability of YLs' results caused by stress or nervousness? Does this differ significantly from older age groups? It is clearly important that children should be motivated to learn another language and not discouraged by inappropriate assessment practices.

There is often a discontinuity between the rationale for introducing primary foreign language teaching and the assessment of children's learning. Programme aims vary but can include some of the following: the building of positive attitudes to language learning in general, the conceptual and general value of learning another language, the development of language awareness, the development of cross cultural awareness, and linguistic knowledge. However, the research findings of Rea-Dickins & Rixon (in progress) strongly suggest that it is linguistic knowledge that is the main focus of assessment, and that there is little attempt to address other dimensions such as language awareness. There are few procedures in EFL to monitor attitudes towards the target language or examine the development of cultural awareness, although in countries such as Germany (see Kubanek-German, 1996), and in French as an FL in the UK (Heighington, 1996), there is evidence of concern for appropriate monitoring in these areas.

There is often a major discrepancy between assessment and the underlying construct and content of YL language learning programmes. Much EFL primary practice emphasises the oracy skills of listening and speaking. Yet the findings of Rea-Dickins & Rixon suggest that formal pencil and paper tests predominate in the EFL classroom. Many rationales for EFL courses and syllabuses refer to the value of naturalistic acquisition of the language, but the nature of the proposed test items reflects a narrower view of language as discrete units of observable behaviour which the learner acquires linearly in terms of increasing complexity. Tests of this narrow content coverage and format, will give the 'wrong' message to both teacher and children about the nature of language learning.

YL assessment still has only a restricted role to play in programme evaluation. There are difficulties and limitations in administering national tests for evaluation purposes at the end of primary teaching in cases where there is no commonly agreed syllabus and no commonly agreed pattern of teaching. Government concerns with how well programmes are working are valuable but some evaluation approaches can lead to criticism from teachers (e.g. evidence from the National Curriculum in England and Wales).

With this concern for the validity of assessment instruments comes the need to ensure that there is also an acceptable degree of reliability. This, of course, is not confined to EYL assesment, but is a problem which besets all assessment in the communicative tradition.

FUTURE DIRECTIONS

Many future developments in EFL assessment may follow current ESL and L1 practice, but in the process of being adapted they may be distorted. Teaching cultures differ world-wide, and the concept of *classroom assessment* as a way of informing teaching rather than (only) classifying children for administrative or promotion purposes may not yet be acceptable to all countries.

The Canadian and Australian ESL interest in looking at performance on 'real' tasks, suitable to the learning context, is relevant in EFL countries. Already, there is some interest in the value of observation and narrative record-keeping, and/or the use of band scales. However, it is important to guard against using hastily-constructed and under-detailed instruments that do not fully respect the depth of research and experience that have informed ESL based instruments over the years.

Assessment results cause teachers to have certain expectations of their learners' potential; this affects the way they treat their pupils and tends to 'set' the pupils' level for ever (Bloor, personal communication). It is, therefore, extremely important to get the assessment of YLs right. It is also important that, rather than act as an unintended means of labelling certain learners or excluding them from future language learning experiences, it should promote an interest in language learning. It is important that assessment brings out the best in learners, whatever its purpose or context, and is not perceived by pupils or teachers to be an isolated activity and a 'special' and stressful experience.

University of Warwick, England

REFERENCES

Alderson, J.C., Krahnke, K.J. & Stansfield, C.W. (eds.): 1987, *Reviews of English Language Proficiency Tests*, TESOL, Washington, DC.
Barrs, M., Ellis, S., Hester, H. & Thomas, A.: 1988, *The Primary Language Record Handbook*, Centre for Language in Primary Education, London.
Barrs, M. et al.: 1990, *Patterns of Learning*, Centre for Language in Primary Education, London.
Brindley, G. (ed.): 1995, *Language Assessment in Action*, National Centre for Language Teaching and Research, Macquarie University, Sydney, New South Wales, Australia.
Broadfoot, P. & Osborn, M.: 1987, 'Teachers' conceptions of their professional responsibilities: Some international comparisons', *Comparative Education* 23(3), 287–301.

Broadfoot, P.: 1996, 'Performance assessment in perspective', in A. Craft (ed.), *Primary Education: Assessing and Planning Learning*, Routledge in association with the Open University, London, 35–65.

Brumfit, C.: 1991, 'Young learners: Young language', in C. Kennedy & J. Jarvis (eds.), *Ideas and Issues in Primary ELT*, Thomas Nelson & Sons Ltd., Walton on Thames, Surrey, 9–17.

Brumfit, C., Moon, J. & Tongue, R. (eds.): 1991, *Teaching English to Children: From Practice to Principle*, Harper Collins Publishers, London.

Burstall, C., Jamieson, M., Cohen, S., & Hargreaves, M.: 1974, *Primary French in the Balance*, NFER, Slough.

Carpenter, K., Fujii, N., & Kataoka, H.: 1995, 'An oral interview procedure for assessing second language abilities in children', *Language Testing* 12(2), 157–175.

Daugherty, R.: 1995, *National Curriculum Assessment: A Review of Policy 1987–1994*, The Falmer Press, London.

Edelenbos, P. & Suhre, C.J.M.: 1994, 'A comparison of courses for English in primary education', *Studies in Evaluation* 20, 513–534.

Edelenbos, P. & Johnstone, R. (eds.): 1996, *Researching Languages at Primary School: Some European Perspectives*, Centre for Information on Language Teaching and Research CILT, in collaboration with Scottish CILT and GION.

Genesee, F. (ed.): 1994. *Educating Second Language Children, The Whole Child, The Whole Curriculum, The Whole Community*, Cambridge University Press, Cambridge.

Genesee, F. & Hamayan, E.V.: 1994, 'Classroom-based assessment', in F. Genesee (ed.), 212–239.

Gipps, C.V. & Stobart, G.: 1993, *Assessment, A Teacher's Guide to the Issues*, Hodder and Stoughton Ltd, London.

Heighington, S.: 1996, 'Taking up the challenge', in A. Hurrell & P Satchwell (eds.), *Reflections on Modern Languages in Primary Education: Six UK Case Studies*, CILT, London, 55–61.

Halliwell, S.: 1992, *Teaching English in the Primary Classroom*, Longman, Harlow.

Hasselgren, A.: 1997, *Development of Diagnostic Test Material for the Norwegian Primary School*, Poster Presentation at the Euroconference on Evaluating Innovation & Establishing Research Priorities in the Teaching & Learning of Foreign Languages in European Primary Schools, University of Warwick, Coventry.

Hester, H.: 1993, *Guide to the Primary Learning Record*, Centre for Language in Education, London.

Kubanek-German, A.: 1996, 'Research into primary foreign-language learning in Germany: A trend towards qualitative studies', in P. Edelenbos & R. Johnstone (eds.), 3–15.

Larter, S. & J. Donnelly.: 1993, 'Demystifying the goals of education', *Orbit* 24(2), 22–24.

Low, L., Duffield, J., Brown, S. & Johnstone, R.: 1993, *Evaluating Foreign Languages in Primary Schools*, Scottish CILT, University of Stirling, Stirling.

Machura, L.: 1991, 'British school English and foreign learners' English: Two different worlds?', in C. Kennedy & J. Jarvis (eds.), *Ideas and Issues in Primary ELT*, Nelson, in association with the Centre for British Teachers, Walton-on Thames, Surrey, 32–42.

Maddock, V. & Lee, W.R.: 1981, *Getting Through Trinity College English*, Pergamon Press, Oxford.

McHugh, M. & Occhipinti, G.: 1993, *Fanfare*, Teacher's Book, Oxford University Press, Oxford.

McKay, P.: 1995, 'Developing ESL proficiency descriptions for the school context: The NLLIA ESL bandscales', in Brindley, G. (ed.), 31–63.

Mincham, L.: 1995, 'ESL student needs procedures: An approach to language assessment in primary and secondary school contexts', in Brindley, G. (ed.), 65–92.

Ministère de l'Education Nationale: 1991, *Evaluation de l'Extension de l'Enseignement des Langages Vivantes*, Inspection Genérale de l'Education, Paris.

Mitchell, R.: 1992, 'The "independent" evaluation of bilingual primary education: A narrative account'. In J.C. Alderson & A. Beretta (eds.), *Evaluating Second Language Education*, Cambridge University Press, Cambridge.

Nihlen, C.: 1997, *National Test of English for the 5th Year in Swedish Schools*, Paper presented at the Euroconference on Evaluating Innovation & Establishing Research Priorities in the Teaching & Learning of Foreign Languages in European Primary Schools, University of Warwick, Coventry.

Rixon, S.: 1992, 'English and other languages for younger children: practice and theory in a rapidly changing world', in *Language Teaching* 25(2), 73–93.

Smith, K.: 1996a, 'Assessing and testing young learners: Can we? Should we?', in Allan, D. (ed.), *Entry Points*, Papers from a Symposium of the Research, Testing and Young Learners Special Interest Groups, Cambridge, 17–18th March 1995, IATEFL, Whitstable, Kent.

Smith, K.: April 1996b, 'Action research on the use of portfolios for assessing foreign language learners', *Testing SIG Newsletter*, IATEFL, 17–24.

Spielman, S.J.: 1993, 'Adapting benchmarks to French immersion education', *Orbit* 24(2), 25–28.

Stansfield, C.W.: 1978, in J.C. Alderson, K.J. Krahnke, & C.W. Stansfield (eds.), *Reviews of English Language Proficiency Tests*, TESOL, Washington, DC.

Stierer, B., Devereux, J., Gifford, S., Laycock, E. and Yerbury, J.: 1993, *Profiling, Recording and Observing*, Teacher's Guide, Routledge, London.

Sutton, R.: 1995, *Assessment for Learning*, RS Publications, Salford.

Vale, D & Feunteun, A.: 1995, *Teaching Children English*, Cambridge University Press, Cambridge.

van Gelderen, A.: 1994, 'Prediction of global ratings of fluency and delivery in narrative discourse by linguistic and phonetic measures – oral performances of students aged 11–12 years', *Language Testing* 11(3), 291–319.

PENNY MCKAY

THE SECOND LANGUAGE ASSESSMENT OF MINORITY CHILDREN

For all education systems where the aim is for all students to meet their full potential, the development and assessment of minority school children's proficiency in the majority language is a central issue. This review deals with those students who are sometimes called *circumstantial bilinguals* (Valdés & Figueroa, 1994 p. 12), that is, those students who find that they must learn, and learn through, the majority language in order to participate economically and socially in the society of which they are a part. Past conquest, colonial occupation and immigration have resulted in unassimilated indigenous communities, generations of immigrant families maintaining their ethnic language in the community, and newly arrived immigrants or refugees settling into majority language communities. The United States, Canada, Australia, Mexico, Britain, Germany and Israel are some of the many countries with minority language learners in their schools. Assessment practices reflect social and political attitudes, but can also be a powerful instrument of change; and understandings of assumptions behind the language assessment of minority students are therefore crucial to excellence in education.

EARLY DEVELOPMENTS

The initial response to the education and assessment of minority children was essentially assimilationist, with *submersion* (inclusion into the mainstream classroom without specialist assistance or recognition of cultural or linguistic difference) the normal practice. Minority children's progress in this situation was generally assessed in terms of their achievement in the mainstream classroom (knowledge gains in specific subject matter areas) rather than in terms of their language proficiency. Children who had problems with their work were often considered to have learning difficulties when their problems were in fact caused by difficulties with language.

As a result many language minority children were wrongly diagnosed, and wrongly taught, resulting in loss of confidence and failure in school. Minority children have often been relegated to special education programs for mentally retarded children (Valdés & Figueroa, 1994, 123–129; Cummins, 1984a), with faulty educational and psychological assessment practices providing *false positive* (where a learning difficulty is diagnosed

C. Clapham and D. Corson (eds), Encyclopedia of Language and Education,
Volume 7: Language Testing and Assessment, 163–173.
© 1997 Kluwer Academic Publishers. Printed in the Netherlands.

where none is present) and *false negative* (where there is a failure to diagnose a learning difficulty) information to educators (Hall, 1995, p. 15).

Traditional forms of assessment were questioned at least from the early 1980s (e.g. Stansfield, 1981) as being inappropriate and inequitable for minority language children; research into the validity of current practices was carried out, and calls were made for more comprehensive and ethnographic approaches to assessment. Standardised tests normed on the mainstream population were found not to predict academic achievement or reveal the linguistic skills necessary for success at school (see various papers in Rivera, 1983 and later publications in the same series). However, in countries like Britain and Australia, standardized tests had not taken hold; classroom achievement-based assessment of minority language children was the norm (with second language assessment available only where ESL teachers were appointed) though still without training of mainstream classroom teachers or formal consistency in common reporting systems.

In the USA in the 1960s federal statutes (e.g. Lau v Nichols 414 U.S. 563) entitled children to learn in their first language if they were not proficient enough in English to do so effectively (see e.g., Valdés & Figueroa, 1994, for details of these political developments in North America). This decision involved assessment of both first language and English abilities, and spurred on a large amount of research and development into language assessment.

In the 1970s Cummins, responding to these developments, built on the work of Skutnabb-Kangas & Toukomaa (1976) to develop hypotheses on the nature of language proficiency (see below), which were designed to inform the education and assessment of these children.

MAJOR CONTRIBUTIONS

Cummins postulated a theoretical framework which sets out (amongst other ideas relevant to the cognitive and academic effect of different forms of bilingualism) a distinction between different aspects of learners' 'surface fluency' in their second language. This distinction between Basic Interpersonal Communication Skills (BICS) and Cognitive Academic Language Proficiency (CALP) aimed to account for the fact that bilingual students' abilities to converse appropriately in social, face-to-face situations often masked large gaps in academically-related aspects of language proficiency, both in their first and (consequently, according to Cummins) in their second language. This distinction was later refined (e.g., Cummins, 1984b) and presented as two interrelated continua: context-embedded to context-reduced language use, and cognitively undemanding to cognitively demanding language use. This framework has given educators a guide to understanding that different activities involved different degrees of reference to and support from the context, and were cognitively demanding to different degrees. The proposal was that second language learners found the context-reduced and cognitively demanding activities to be more difficult. The framework suggested, then, that any assessment of minority language learners should take account of these factors. Various practitioners have written about how to use Cummins' framework to select appropriate assessment activities (e.g. Hall, 1995; Robson, 1995).

A major conference took place in the United States in 1981 at which the work and ideas of Cummins and others were presented and discussed. Proceedings of the Language Proficiency Assessment Symposium (LPA) conference (Rivera, 1983 and later publications in the same series) present a range of high level discussions on issues in bilingual assessment, with emphasis on an enthnographic/sociolinguistic approach to proficiency assessment.

Cummins (e.g. Cummins, 1994) has more recently begun to turn his attention to the need to consider social as well as linguistic and instructional factors in any effort to understand the factors contributing to the success of bilingual programs. Explanations for failure at school go beyond linguistic considerations to cultural and political considerations, including the mismatch between white middle-class expectations and the bilingual child's pre-school language socialization experiences. Writers on bilingualism (Trueba, 1989; Baker, 1988; Skutnabb-Kangas & Cummins, 1988), whilst not working in the area of assessment in particular, contribute to the understanding of minority children's experiences at school, which in turn, inform assessment practices. "It is important to discuss the linkage between language and culture in order to understand the problems language minority children often face in adjusting to American schools and society" (Trueba, 1989, p. 32). Thus assessment procedures need to be understood by educators as being positioned in a political and cultural milieu which will strongly influence outcomcs.

Valdés & Figueroa (1994) review the issues and research in bilingualism and testing. The authors' major thesis is that educational policy makers must deal with the problems caused by standardized testing in the education of minority children in the United States. They suggest ways to overcome the problem and call for a moratorium on standardized tests for circumstantial bilinguals when such testing involves decision-making about individuals. They also recommend a gradual phasing in of new alternative assessment procedures, and a set of standards for testing bilingual individuals (Valdés & Figueroa, 1994, p. 181).

The move has continued towards alternative assessment. Law and Eckes (1995) have provided teachers with a handbook on the second language assessment of minority language learners. They condemn standardized tests though they believe that standardized assessment is 'here to stay', at least in North America. They give detailed guidance for teachers on alternative approaches to assessment, with samples of work from students to supplement understanding. Genesee and Hamayan (1994) also give guidance on alternative assessment for the classroom. They emphasise the need to collect 'overlapping' information from multiple sources to ensure reliable decision-making, including information about the students' background and L1 proficiency.

Alternative assessment is also emphasised in work in Australia and Britain. In Australia, McKay & Scarino (1991) have provided guidance for teachers by tying assessment of ESL learners to a map of language-related goals and objectives through from beginning to advanced learners of a second language within school contexts from kindergarten to Year 12. Assessment schemes made up of age-level appropriate classroom tasks guide teachers to place students in a *stage*. Having determined the stage of the learner, teachers are able to refer to the relevant *stage description* which guides them to select and teach the appropriate range and level of content needed for present and future success in the school context. The stages also assist teachers to report on progress. The National Languages and Literacy Institute of Australia (NLLIA) ESL Development: Language and Literacy in Schools project (NLLIA 1993) has developed curriculum-based age-level tasks (Lumley et al., 1993) set in teaching cycles, which enable teachers to observe performance, and place students on a set of common reference profiles or standards, the ESL Bandscales (see McKay, 1995). In Britain, the influential *Primary Language Record* (Barrs et al., 1988) approached assessment and reporting through teacher observation and record keeping, followed by a detailed profile report of student's progress. The profile report included details of the student's background (language, years of schooling in the first language etc.), important information for a valid assessment and report. This work in Britain, including a 5-point proficiency scale developed by Hester, has influenced the NLLIA development in Australia, which, in turn, is attracting attention from North America and other countries.

In addition, important developments have included the establishment of centres such as the National Clearinghouse for Bilingual Education and the National Clearinghouse for ESL Literacy Education, which are now accessible through the internet.

WORK IN PROGRESS

The most recent developments in assessment in schools have been in 'profiles' (staged descriptions of progress, stated in terms of behaviour and/or outcomes). Various types of profiles are being or have been developed in a number of countries, and are variously called standards, bandscales, scales and benchmarks. Australia has developed two ESL profiles (NLLIA, 1993; Australian Education Council, 1994) describing stages of progress for second language learners learning English in schools. The political tensions that develop from these developments have been documented by Moore (1996). Individual Australian States continue to work on their own adaptations of these profiles.

In England the Standard Assessment Tasks (SATs) of the national curriculum apply to all learners, regardless of language background or other differences (the argument being that all learners are entitled to the national curriculum), and therefore no separate ESL instruments are made available. However, work is going ahead on the development of ESL profile and assessment materials at the Thames Valley University, again with reference to the Australian and other profiles.

The TESOL Association has been given the task of producing ESL standards in the United States; these have been drafted after consultation with teachers, and are currently being trialled (TESOL, 1996). Principles for the teaching and assessment of ESL learners accompany the profiles, which in this case are staged descriptions of outcomes in English. The standards will also include assessment guidelines, currently under construction by appointed TESOL members (Gottlieb & Ewy, 1996).

The value and use of second language profiles such as these needs to be researched, and in Australia a Commonwealth government project is investigating how teachers use the available ESL profiles for assessment and reporting purposes. Brindley (1995) is investigating the validity, advantages and disadvantages of profiles, and he signals the need for caution about the tension that exists between system needs (administration, accountability) and teacher needs (teaching and learning) in the use of profiles. Advantages can be found in the fact that the profiles provide a common reference point for teachers, as well as explicit criteria, through which teachers can obtain diagnostic feedback. A disadvantage of profiles is that they are often developed and administered by education authorities for accountability purposes, with the result that they strongly influence teaching and become quasi-curriculum documents, a purpose for which they are not designed. A further disadvantage is that profiles are also often developed by education authorities without due attention to the validity of descriptors and levels. Systematic investigation is needed in this area (e.g. Leung & Teasdale, 1996).

Assessment projects are in progress in many parts of North America. The Illinois State Board of Education is developing a state-wide assessment system for language minority students based on both a standardised and local model of assessment. The Illinois Measure of Annual Growth in English (IMAGE) is a standardised test in reading and writing which provides an accountability system for students in bilingual programs during their three year exemption from the Illinois Goal Assessment Program (IGAP). In addition to the State-wide standardised IMAGE test, guidelines are provided for teachers to assess through content-based assessment tasks, that is, tasks which include and relate to the subject matter that their particular students are currently studying in the mainstream curriculum. This approach addresses the (at present, in North America) unavoidable requirements of the State for accountability through standardized assessment, and is at the same time promoting school-based and content-based assessment, guided by carefully designed sets of assessment criteria and exemplars based on principles of second language acquisition. A further example of an assessment project is found in Quinhagak, Alaska, where educators are creating a portfolio scoring guide for Yup'ik students in elementary and upper grades, based on the State language arts standards. Classroom teachers are contributing input, and developers are referring to the Australian NLLIA materials as a guide to the development of a proficiency continuum. With consultation occurring with Australian counterparts, it is fair to say that the latest important developments in the assessment of minority language learners include encouraging moves towards international collaboration.

The work of Bachman, and Bachman and Palmer (e.g., 1996) has informed the development of the Australian NLLIA Project, and is recognised as influential in publications in North America (e.g. Valdés & Figueroa, 1994, pp. 31–34). The framework of communicative language ability is providing the assessment field with a comprehensive and integrative map of the components of and influences on communicative language ability and use, which need to be tested and described (e.g. McKay, 1995; NLLIA, 1993; Australian Education Council, 1994; Valdés & Figueroa, 1994, pp. 31–34). The accompanying *test method facets* guide developers in relation to the factors which impinge on the validity of language assessment.

PROBLEMS AND DIFFICULTIES

Ultimately, many difficulties in the assessment of minority language learners relate to issues of educational policy. True multicultural policy encourages differential assessment for minority learners in order for each student's needs to be diagnosed and teaching to occur with which to meet these needs; yet a policy of entitlement for all, as in Britain, discourages differentiation in formal assessment, preferring rather to differentiate in teaching and in expectation of outcome in classroom-based assessment (Hall, 1995, p. 53). Broader government policy has both explicit and implicit consequences for the education of minority learners (Moore, 1996). Influential educational change is often carried out through changes in the formal assessment of learner progress (Shohamy, 1993), and therefore educators need to be active in alerting policy developers to the most appropriate assessment practices for minority language learners.

Assessment practices influence teachers' and administrators' perceptions of minority language learners in schools. There needs to be a strong message in all assessment practices that minority language learners are progressing along a continuum of second language growth (the principle of *emergence*), rather than simply performing badly in comparison to their native-speaking classmates. Separate ESL profiles (e.g. NLLIA, 1993, Australian Education Council, 1994) and ESL curriculum pathways (e.g. McKay & Scarino, 1991; TESOL, 1996) are valuable to all teachers because they set out explicitly the second language learning pathways that minority learners are taking and help to increase understanding of minority learner strengths and needs. The difficulty for ESL personnel is in counteracting the influence of assessment practices (tests, profiles and guidelines) designed for mother-tongue speakers and administered to all learners regardless of language background. These can quickly render minority learners and their second language learning needs invisible to teachers, and can result in inappropriate teaching, professional development and resource allocation.

The assessment of second language progress is complex, and even more so for teachers when assessment needs to be done in the context of schooling where factors to be considered include (a) the cognitive maturity of learner, (b) the learner's knowledge of the content under instruction, and (c) the variables in the testing context, often the mainstream classroom. Assessment of minority learners in schools needs to take account of these dynamic elements, all of which are not generally included in assessment frameworks (e.g., Canale & Swain, 1980; Bachman & Palmer, 1996). Cognitive maturity must be considered in assessment procedures for young children in the selection of the tasks and task content appropriate to the age group. Profiles of second language development need to build into their staged descriptions growing cognitive maturity alongside growing language proficiency. With immigrants entering at all levels of schooling, these two factors, cognitive maturity and language proficiency do not necessarily grow hand in hand, as, for example, older children will be beginning second language learning at a more mature stage of their development. Issues of content (e.g. subject area, degree of cognitive demand, background knowledge) and of context of assessment (e.g. degree of support from the teacher, degree of support in pre-task instruction, time allowed for task) are critical in school-based language assessment, but not always considered (McKay, 1995). The NLLIA materials (McKay, 1995) have attempted to take these factors into consideration and to map beginning to advanced second language development from kindergarten to Year 12. Collier's (1995) framework which integrates academic development, cognitive development, social and cultural processes with language development is a useful reference for content-based second language assessment, as is Bachman and Palmer's (1996) framework which includes Topical Knowledge amongst its components. (See Snow et al., 1989 and Mohan, 1986 for other valuable frameworks available to inform content-based assessment.) In practical terms, the lead of some school systems should be followed, where all content teachers have the responsibility to assess (and therefore some responsibility to teach) language development in their content area under the formal assessment procedures for that system (e.g., SSABSA, 1992).

From the work in Australia on profiles (NLLIA, 1993) a *plateau level* has been described, at which students tend to stabilise in their academic proficiency development. Those students who are assisted to overcome the plateau level are those who become successful in more decontextualised and cognitively demanding tasks (Collier has called this *deep academic proficiency* (Collier, 1995)), and are more likely to succeed at school. Research is needed to monitor learners' progress through particular success barriers, and provide badly needed insights into the development of academic language proficiency.

Valid and reliable assessment of minority children by teachers requires teachers and administrators to have a formidable knowledge base about the process of second language acquisition, an understanding of teaching, learning and assessment through content, and knowledge of the language proficiency required for success in content area study at various levels of schooling. Few educators can be said to have expertise in all these areas, and so more pre-service and professional development for teachers is always needed.

FUTURE DIRECTIONS

Future directions in terms of new assessment practices continue to be related to educational policy directions. Ideally, a move away from standardized assessment is required, so that teachers and students can be granted the power to negotiate instruction based on the individual needs of students. Places like Australia where standardized assessment has not taken hold need to maintain this privileged position for minority students, though further work in assessment materials designed to assess both language and content are needed. Alternative assessment practices which are carried out by teachers, who then report according to the common framework of a profile are promising, if the profiles are validly constructed. This latter issue needs a great deal more attention (is the description based on a language proficiency framework? are the descriptors consistent?) Where common assessment for all learners is used, there is a need to explore ways in which assessment practices can be modified to accommodate minority learners, for example, by providing extra time, administering tests orally, using an interpreter, and modifying the format of a test from narrative to short answer (in achievement tests). A further strategy is to provide an additional report to the standard report, giving an interpretation of or additional comment on the grade received (Law & Eckes, 1995, p. 235).

Since learning situations where assessment develops out of well-laid teaching plans are more effective than those which are assessment-driven, (assessment-driven teaching can, for example, lead to a narrowing of the curriculum (Barrs, 1990)), more attention needs to be focused on developing second language curriculum statements which teachers can integrate with current subject content, and vice versa. More work on profiles is needed so that an effective balance is achieved between the need to provide detail in descriptors for the sake of validity, and the need to avoid so much detail that the descriptors are too difficult for busy teachers to use and understand. In addition, research is needed on profiles for indigenous groups, where cultural differences become manifest in some behavioural differences which teachers need to observe and include in placement. This latter practice may be seen as too specific (we could do the same for each ethnic group) but assessment guidelines influence teachers' understandings of learning patterns and needs, and teachers' specific understandings are needed to cater for cultural and contextual differences in such learners. Some indigenous minorities learn their minority language as a second language, and profiling for assessment of progress needs investigation (see, for example, the current work of Daigle, Cumming, Burnaby and Corson at the Ontario Institute of Studies in Education on Ojibway as a second language for Ojibway First Nations students in Ontario schools).

Issues relating the place of and the development of critical literacy for minority language learners are tied to the wider issues of social change mentioned above. More attention should be given to addressing the assessment of critical literacy as an integral aspect of second language assessment. (For more about this see the review by Luke in Volume 2.)

In summary, as in all assessment practices work is continuing on the validity (in which cultural issues are strongly represented), reliability and practicality of assessment activities for minority children, whether in stan-dardised assessment, or in curriculum-based/alternative assessment prac-tices. Concern for consequential validity (Messick, 1989) must also be strong in language minority assessment, for the influence of assessment on the lives of children is the ultimate evaluation of educational practice.

Queensland University of Technology
Australia

REFERENCES

Australian Education Council: 1994, *ESL Scales*, Curriculum Corporation, Melbourne.
Bachman, L.F.: 1990, *Fundamental Considerations in Language Testing*, Oxford University Press, Oxford.
Bachman, L.F. & Palmer, A.S.: 1996, *Language Testing in Practice*, Oxford University Press, Oxford.

Baker, C.: 1988, *Key Issues in Bilingualism and Bilingual Education*, Multilingual Matters, Clevedon, Avon, England.

Barrs, M.: 1990, *Words not Numbers: Assessment in English*, National Association of Advisers in English, London.

Barrs, M., Ellis, S., Hester, H. & Thomas, A.: 1988, *The Primary Language Record: A Handbook for Teachers*, Centre for Language in Primary Education, London.

Brindley, G.: 1995, 'Assessment and reporting in language learning programs: Purposes, problems and pitfalls', *Plenary presentation at International Conference on Testing and Evaluation in Second Language Education*, Hong Kong University of Science and Technology, 21–24 June 1995.

Canale, M & Swain, M.: 1980, 'Theoretical bases of communicative approaches to second language teaching and testing', *Applied Linguistics* 1, 1–47.

Collier, V.P.: 1995, 'Acquiring a second language for school', *Directions in Language Education* 1(4).

Cummins, J.: 1984a, *Bilingualism and Special Education: Issues in Assessment and Pedagogy*, Multilingual Matters, Clevedon, England.

Cummins, J.: 1984b, 'Wanted: A theoretical framework for relating language proficiency to academic achievement among bilingual students', in C. Rivera (ed.), *Language Proficiency and Academic Achievement*, Multilingual Matters, Clevedon, England, 10.

Cummins, J.: 1994, 'Knowledge, power, and identity in teaching English as a second language', in F. Genesee (ed.), *Educating Second Language Children*, Cambridge University Press, Cambridge.

Genesee, F. & Hamayan, E.V.: 1994, 'Classroom-based assessment', in F. Genesee (ed.), *Educating Second Language Children*, Cambridge, Cambridge University Press.

Gottlieb, M. & Ewy, C.: 1996, 'Multi-level and multi-faceted: State and local assessment of linguistically and culturally diverse students', *Linguathon* 11(1), 3–4.

Hall, D.: 1995, *Assessing the Needs of Bilingual Pupils. Living in Two Languages*, David Fulton Publishers, London.

Law, B. & Eckes, M.: 1995, *Assessment and ESL*, Peguis, Winnipeg, Canada.

Leung, C. & Teasdale, A.: 1996, 'English as an additional language within the National Curriculum: A study of assessment practices', *Prospect* 12(2), 58–68.

Lumley, T., Raso E. & Mincham, L.: 1993, 'Exemplar assessment activities', in NLLIA (National Languages and Literacy Institute of Australia): *NLLIA ESL Development: Language and Literacy in Schools*, National Languages and Literacy Institute of Australia, Canberra.

McKay, P.: 1995, 'Developing ESL proficiency descriptions for the school context: The NLLIA bandscales', in G. Brindley (ed.), *Language Assessment in Action*, National Centre for English Language Teaching and Research, Sydney.

McKay, P. & Scarino, A.: 1991, *The ESL Framework of Stages*, Curriculum Corporation, Melbourne.

Messick, S.: 1989, 'Validity', in R.L. Linn (ed.), *Educational Measurement*, Macmillan, New York, 13–103.

Ministry of Education, New Zealand: 1996, *English in the New Zealand Curriculum*, Learning Media, Wellington, New Zealand.

Mohan, B.: 1986, *Language and Content*, Addison Wesley, Reading, M.A.

Moore, H.: 1996, 'Telling what is real: Competing views in assessing ESL development', *Linguistics and Education* 8(2), 189–228.

NLLIA (National Languages and Literacy Institute of Australia): 1993, *NLLIA ESL Development: Language and Literacy in Schools*, National Languages and Literacy Institute of Australia, Canberra.

Rivera, C. (ed.): 1983, *An Ethnographic/Sociolinguistic Approach to Language Proficiency Assessment*, Multilingual Matters, Clevedon, England.

Robson, A.: 1995. 'The assessment of bilingual children', in M.K. Verma, K.P. Corrigan

& S. Firth (eds.), *Working with Bilingual Children*, Multilingual Matters, Clevedon, England.

Skutnabb-Kangas, T. & Toukomaa, P.: 1977, *The Intensive Teaching of the Mother Tongue to Migrant Children of Pre-School Age and Children in the Lower Level of Comprehensive School*, The Finnish National Commission of Unesco, Helsinki.

Skutnabb-Kangas, T. & Cummins, J.: 1988, *Minority Education*, Multilingual Matters, Clevedon, England.

SSABSA (Senior Secondary Assessment Board of South Australia).: 1992, *English as a Second Language Studies. Stage 2. Detailed Syllabus Statement*, SSABSA, Adelaide, Australia.

Shohamy, E.: 1993, *The Power of Tests: The Impact of Language Tests in Teaching and Learning*, The National Foreign Language Centre Occasional Papers, Washington DC.

Snow, M.A., Met, M. & Genesee, F.: 1989, 'A conceptual framework for the integration of language and content in second/foreign language instruction', *TESOL Quarterly* 23, 201–217.

Stansfield, C.: 1981, 'The assessment of language proficiency in bilingual children: An analysis of theories and instrumentation', in R.V. Padilla (ed.), *Bilingual Education Technology*.

TESOL.: 1996, 'Promising futures: ESL standards for Pre-K-12 students', TESOL Professional Papers #1.

Trueba, H.T.: 1989, *Raising Silent Voices: Educating the Linguistic Minorities for the 21st Century*, Newbury House, New York.

Valdés, G. & Figueroa, R.A.: 1994, *Bilingualism and Testing. A Special Case of Bias*, Ablex Publishing, Norwood, NJ.

MATS OSCARSON

SELF-ASSESSMENT OF FOREIGN AND SECOND LANGUAGE PROFICIENCY

The field of self-assessment of language proficiency is concerned with questions of how, under what conditions, and with what effects learners and other users of a foreign or second language may judge their own ability in the language. Ability is used here in the broad sense of the term, i.e. with reference both to achievement ('course-related' ability, resulting from organized learning) and proficiency ('absolute' ability, irrespective of how it was attained). Techniques and materials used for the purpose of self-assessment include self-reports, self-testing, mutual peer-assessment, keeping of diaries, answering behaviourally anchored questionnaires, use of global proficiency rating scales, and responding to so-called 'can-do'-statements which request learners to state whether they are able to perform each of a number of specified language functions.

A number of other terms have been used in more or less free variation with the term 'self-assessment', for example, 'self-evaluation', 'self-appraisal', 'self-rating', and 'self-report', but the use of 'assessment' has been gaining ground and would seem to be the most appropriate. 'Self-rating' and 'self-evaluation' should probably be avoided because of their distinct connotation of 'making value judgements' rather than conveying the more neutral meaning of 'determining extent', or 'estimating level', which is what this kind of process really concerns.

The use of self-assessment as a technique for information-gathering in education is comparatively recent and has essentially grown out of the wider concern for more qualitatively oriented methods of research such as using interviews, participant observation and think-aloud records as primary bases for data collection and analysis. (For more about qualitative methods of data collection, see Banerjee and Luoma's review in this volume.) It also stems from the realization that effective and relevant learning is best achieved if the student is actively engaged in all phases of the learning process, as emphasized for instance by proponents of cognitive and constructivist theories of learning, according to which the learner's own reflection on and creative restructuring of already acquired concepts, understandings, and points of learning play a crucial role in the building of new knowledge (Gipps, 1995). This point of departure has led to the proposition that the assessment of learning too will benefit from learner participation. It has been argued, for instance, that learner self-assessment, based as it is on internal experience and not mere external observation and

C. Clapham and D. Corson (eds), Encyclopedia of Language and Education,
Volume 7: Language Testing and Assessment, 175–187.
© *1997 Kluwer Academic Publishers. Printed in the Netherlands.*

testing, is capable of providing unique supplemental information on that which is to be assessed (Shrauger & Osberg, 1981). Several other arguments in favour of self-assessment have been put forward. These relate, for instance, to learner autonomy and its possible positive effects on motivation and outcomes of learning, to the development of learners' study skills, and to aspects of co-operation and partnership between learners and teachers (Holec, 1988; Dickinson, 1987). Finally, the point can be made that self-regulated assessment is a necessary component of the concept of life-long learning, which now, in a fast changing society, requires learners to be able both to work independently and to assess their developing capabilities after having left formal education.

Needless to say, it has been widely recognized that the potential usefulness and relevance of data generated by self-assessment procedures is most obvious in general day-to-day teaching/learning contexts, typically involving mature learners who engage in it mainly for diagnostic monitoring of progress, whereas the use of self-assessment for grading, promotion, certification, or other 'high-stakes' purposes appears to be inappropriate.

RESEARCH AND DEVELOPMENT WORK

Although different modes of self-report have been used quite extensively in many fields of behavioural research, it was only during the 1980s that applied linguists began seriously to explore its potential in the context of foreign and second language assessment. In a comprehensive meta-analysis of studies comparing self- and teacher marks, Falchikov & Boud (1989) were only able to identify one set of studies out of 57 which dealt specifically with second language learning (see below). The relative scarcity of early self-assessment research in language education was also apparent in two previous surveys reported by Heidt (1979) and Oscarson (1984).

An early source of inspiration for the rather belated interest in self-assessment in the field of language learning was the concerted effort by the Council of Europe to devise a coherent and communicatively oriented system for adult FL learning, taking into account, among other things, possible ways of according the learner a more significant role in the teaching/learning process. This joint project, launched in the early 1970s (see, for instance, Council of Europe, 1981; Girard & Trim, 1988), resulted in a rich variety of activities, including a number of studies dealing with questions of learner autonomy and learner-centred procedures for evaluation (Holec, 1988; Oscarson, 1978; 1984; 1989).

AIMS OF STUDIES

The bulk of research conducted to date has had two main objectives: (a) the investigation of possible concrete ways of realizing the goal of learner participation in matters of assessment and evaluation, and (b) the investigation of the degree to which self-assessment instruments and procedures yield relevant and dependable results. The focus of interest has thus been on the development of methods and materials and on determining the validity of the approach.

Below are reviewed a number of studies which illustrate both past and recent research and developmental work. The emphasis is on validation studies, since the subjective nature of self-perceived attainment has been a matter of some concern among many experts on testing.

MATERIALS AND METHODS

In an early attempt at examining the usefulness of some basic experimental materials, Oscarson (1978) designed a number of simple self-assessment questionnaires using behavioural specifications as the general frame of reference. The materials proved to work well in pilot experiments (see below). A later review (Oscarson, 1984) presents further samples of tools including a proposed form for 'Continuous self-assessment' conceived of as a possible model for an instrument intended to be used on a regular recurrent basis.

Lewkowicz & Moon (1985) offer a practical and useful presentation of learner-centred evaluative materials and activities. They also give the timely reminder that while much interesting and promising development work has been undertaken, there also exist, in many contexts, considerable practical constraints – physical, social, cultural, etc. – which may hinder effective learner-centred methodology.

Strong-Krause (1997) conducted research aimed at determining the role of varying degrees of 'task specificity' in SA placement instruments and concluded that the predictive value increases the more specific the task is.

Much interest has further been devoted to the development and use of learner log books, diaries, journals and other 'introspective' materials, which are also used more generally as tools in language learning research focusing on the cognitive processes underlying human performance and ability.

VALIDATION STUDIES

Evidence of validity has predominantly been sought in terms of concurrent validity statistics obtained by means of correlating self-estimated ability data with various external measures of the same abilities. Test scores and independent expert ratings have been the external variables most commonly used for such purposes. Self-estimates have usually been elicited using different types of behavioural specifications, often in the form of descriptive multi-level rating scales and questionnaires.

Brief reference will first be made to two major meta-analyses. In a comprehensive comparative review of some 50 studies in psychological assessment (relating to academic and intellectual achievement, job performance etc.), Shrauger & Osberg (1981) studied the relative accuracy of self-assessments versus assessments by others. The validity of the former was judged, overall, to be at least comparable to that of other assessment methods against which self-assessment has been pitted. Summing up the research, the authors concluded that "at both the empirical and conceptual levels, there seems to be substantial support for the notion that self-assessors frequently have the appropriate information and motivation to make as effective judgements about their own behavior as can be made by any other means" (p. 347).

In a meta-analysis of 57 quantitative self-assessment studies (96 experimental conditions) in various subject areas comparing self- and teacher marks in higher education (e.g. medicine, educational psychology), Falchikov & Boud (1989) found clear overlap, but of varying degrees, between the two types of measure. The researchers attributed differences to the influence of variables such as level of learning (more accurate assessments at higher levels) and the broad area of study (with students in science courses appearing to produce more accurate assessments than students from other areas). The choice of statistic for the analysis of experimental effects and the quality of the design of the study were other significant factors (closer agreement between student and teacher marks was obtained in better designed studies), whereas the nature of the assessment task did not seem to be a salient variable.

A good deal of work has also been undertaken within the field of foreign and second language learning itself. Working on the hypothesis that most learners of a language have a certain capacity for determining their own language ability – provided they have at their disposal a measuring standard by which they may express their intuitions – Oscarson (1978) found that adult learners studying EFL were indeed able to make fairly accurate appraisals of their linguistic ability using a variety of scaled descriptions of performance as rating instruments. The criteria against which the self-assessments were validated were teacher ratings and written test scores. While the results thus suggested that self-assessment may be used to good effect, at least in adult education, the author also recognized the need for training in order for learners to be able to make reliable judgements on their performance.

In a later review of the literature, covering research reported by the beginning of the 1980s, the same author (1984) noted that the studies then surveyed disclose a pattern of agreement between learners' self-estimates and external criteria. Not infrequently, correlations were of about the same magnitude as those obtained between different sub-sections in a major language test battery. It was pointed out, however, that "a given self-assessed score may be affected by errors having to do with (the learner's) past academic record, career aspirations, peer-group or parental expectations, lack of training in self-study and self-management etc" (p. 31). Later studies have brought attention to yet other influential variables, e.g. that of cultural background (Strong-Krause, 1997).

In a pilot experiment preceding a large-scale survey of US college students' FL interest and proficiency, Clark (1981) compared self-assessment of speaking, listening, and reading with FSI (Foreign Service Institute) interview scores and listening and reading test scores. Most of the correlations between self-assessment data and the corresponding actual language skill test scores proved to be strong enough (close to .60) to warrant the use of the self-estimates in the survey of proficiency in designated foreign languages for U.S. college students.

In a series of experiments undertaken at the University of Ottawa, first-year students in undergraduate second language programs were asked to rate their language skills in listening and reading using a self-assessment questionnaire (LeBlanc and Painchaud, 1985). They were then tested by means of standardized proficiency tests. High correlations (in the order of .80) were obtained between the two kinds of measure. The experiments led to the use of self-assessment as a placement instrument in the university's second language programs (see below).

Bachman and Palmer (1989) investigated the construct validity of self-assessment tasks using a multitrait-multimethod design and confirmatory factor analysis. Basically the design chosen implies that, in this case, three language abilities or traits (grammatical, pragmatic, and sociolinguistic competence) were all tested by means of three different methods of self-assessment (relating to perceived ability, level of difficulty experienced, and ability to recognize the trait in input). The analyses of the results appeared to indicate, among other things, that language users are more aware of the areas in which they have difficulty than of the areas they find easy. The authors found evidence of validity in the methods employed and concluded that "self-ratings can be reliable and valid measures of communicative language abilities" (p. 22).

In a study focusing on speaking proficiency, Wilson (1996) sought to obtain empirical evidence of the validity of the Self Assessment (SA) approach using English, German, and French language SA adaptations of the well-known FSI/ILR (Foreign Service Institute/Interagency Language Roundtable) oral proficiency rating scale, in conjunction with an objective norm-referenced test. On the basis of the results obtained, Wilson was able to infer that Swiss educated native and non-native speakers of French and

German are capable of placing themselves "as they probably would have been placed, on the average, by professional raters using the (FSI-type) Language Proficiency Interview procedure" (p. 17). Intercorrelations between test scores and self-assessments for different subgroups were in the region of .70 throughout. Previous studies conducted by Educational Testing Service (ETS) staff and associates, e.g. Hilton et al. (1985), Wilson (1989), provide support for the conclusions drawn in this study.

Other researchers have come to less encouraging conclusions. In a Canadian study, Peirce, Swain & Hart (1993) found only weak relationships between self-assessments by French immersion students in Grade 8 and language test results. According to the authors, one of the possible reasons for this is the fact that "many French immersion students do not have an authentic native speaker peer standard with which to compare their proficiency in French". The lack of opportunity for native speaker comparison is of course shared by many other groups of language learners, so if this is found to be a critical feature, the self-assessment option may be open to doubt in a great many educational contexts. On the basis of the results of a study aimed at assessing key factors which influence individuals' orientation to self-assessment tasks – e.g. question interpretation, language learning background, and self-esteem – Moritz (1995) took the position "that it seems unreasonable to employ self-assessment as a measurement tool in any situation which entails a comparison of students' abilities". Blue (1994) obtained a poor match between teachers' and students' assessments of their English for Academic Purposes learning at university level.

MIGRANT STUDIES

Evidence of lack of validity in self-estimates has also been reported by Janssen-van Dieten (1992) who obtained only a moderate relationship between performance by adult immigrants on a test of Dutch as a second language and the same subjects' performance on a self-assessment version of the test (r = .26 to .64). Nor was any systematic relationship obtained between assessments and background variables such as age, length of stay, country of origin, and length of Dutch language training.

These findings seem to be at variance, however, with results obtained in some other studies of second language acquisition by migrants, for instance that reported by Latomaa (1996), whose data derive from a sociolinguistic research project comparing variability on background factors and self-assessed proficiency levels among adult immigrants in the Nordic countries. Furthermore, von Elek (1985), found strong agreement between adult immigrant students' assessments and assessments made by their Swedish teachers. Smith & Baldauf (1982) examined the concurrent validity of self- and trained interviewer ratings obtained for migrants to

Australia and found quite a close association between the two categories of data. The researchers concluded that the self-rating technique is valid for the collection of large-scale research data. Much the same experience was gained by Wylie (personal communication) working with large sociolinguistic surveys using self-assessment by both students and teachers.

Coombe (1992) studied Russian, Vietnamese, and Cambodian refugees learning ESL in the US and obtained results which showed a strong relationship between self-assessment ratings and functional literacy skills ($r = .83$). No statistically significant gender effects were detected.

RESEARCH ON RELATIONSHIPS

The degree to which self-perceived competence in a language may depend on variation in affective and other factors has been the object of much discussion, and also some research. MacIntyre et al. (1997), for instance, examined bias introduced by language anxiety and found that this variable was negatively correlated with perceived proficiency. Anxious students tended to underestimate their ability more than students who were more relaxed. Heilenman (1990) studied tendencies to respond to factors other than item content and concluded that they were strongest for less experienced learners. Erickson (1996) found that girls, more than boys, held what proved to be an unfounded pessimistic view of their possible success in a language test which they had taken before the self appraisal. Blanche (1990) failed to detect any systematic relationship between prior exposure to foreign languages and self-assessment 'error rates'. Investigation of the interaction between computer adaptive testing techniques and SA of oral ability is reported by Myles (1997). (For more about Computer Adaptive Testing see Gruba and Corbel's review in this volume.)

SELF-ASSESSMENT APPLIED

Self-assessment is quite often used for the purpose of placing students according to ability at the beginning of a language training program. The study by LeBlanc and Painchaud (1985) referred to above resulted in the substitution of self-assessment questionnaires for the previously used standardized proficiency tests. Heilenman (1991) describes steps that may be taken in the practical development of self-assessment placement materials. Hargan (1994) reports on a self-assessment procedure at university level which resulted in much the same level placements as indicated by a traditional multiple choice test. Krausert (1991) reports similar research findings. On the basis of earlier research of this kind, von Elek (1985) developed a self-diagnostic test of Swedish as a second language which was published and marketed for use in adult education.

Cram (1992) provides a practical illustration of self-assessment applied in the second language classroom. A sequence of activities is proposed which, it is argued, will lead to critical self-assessment of learning. Harris (1997) gives further examples and discusses the general role of self-assessment in formal settings. With reference to primary education, Towler & Broadfoot (1992) give concrete examples of ways in which even young children can assess their progress in the areas of oral expression and emergent writing.

The self-assessment approach has also been employed as a research tool in various empirical investigations and evaluations of language learning effects, for example in the large cross-national studies undertaken by the International Association for the Evaluation of Educational Achievement (IEA). Measures of students' own perception of their ability were obtained which allowed the researchers to make certain international comparisons. Countries which rated themselves highly also tended to compare favourably with other countries in terms of achievement test results (Lewis & Massad, 1975). Likewise, students generally rated their decoding (receptive) skills higher than their encoding (productive) skills, which of course makes good sense. Hilton et al (1985) validated, with convincing results, a self-rating questionnaire to be used in lieu of interviews in a US national survey of the oral language proficiency of secondary school French and Spanish teachers. The researchers concluded that self-assessment may be used in such surveys as a useful substitute for more costly and cumbersome means of measurement.

Self-assessment has furthermore been used as a technique for measuring degrees of bilingualism. Surveying the field, Skutnabb-Kangas (1981) drew the conclusion that the technique is fairly reliable but also made the point that informants tend to over-rate their skills in the language which has the higher status.

SUMMARY OF SOME SALIENT FEATURES OF RESEARCH FINDINGS

As previously indicated, self-assessment research relating to language education is of fairly recent date and it would of course be premature to draw far-reaching conclusions about findings at this stage. The following summary, therefore, is only tentative.

1. Although no consensus has been reached on the merits of the self-assessment approach, a clear majority of the studies surveyed report generally favourable results.

2. It seems to be fairly commonly agreed that the question of accuracy and appropriateness of self-estimates of proficiency depends, to a considerable degree, on features of context and on the intended purpose of the assessment in each individual case.

3. In accordance with general expectation, decoding skills (reading, listening) tend to be assessed higher than encoding skills (speaking, writing).

4. Self-assessments are more accurate when based on task content closely tied to students' situations as potential users of the language in question.

5. The evidence is that it is easier for learners to assess their ability in relation to concrete descriptions of more narrowly defined linguistic situations than in relation to descriptions of broad behavioural objectives and 'macro-skills'.

6. Self-assessments appear to be more accurate when subjects use assessment tools written in their respective native languages rather than in the target language.

7. There do not seem to be any clear-cut gender effects in self-assessment data (Shrauger & Osberg, 1981; Smith & Baldauf, 1982; Coombe, 1992; Strong-Krause, 1997).

PROBLEMS AND ISSUES

The emerging area of learner self-assessment of language competence has highlighted a number of more or less new problems in language pedagogy and evaluation, some of which are touched upon below.

1. Given the fact that assessment is a very forcible mechanism of educational control, a major problem facing the field is that of reconciling the natural need of learners to be in control of some aspects of the evaluation of their own learning with the conflicting demands of external imperatives.

2. Another problem area is the question of how to relate learners' tacit conceptions of goals of learning to externally specified goals and of how to translate such conceptions into more transparent categories and easily understood assessment criteria. In the case of an apparent mismatch between goals of learning as conceived by the learner on the one hand and the educationalist on the other, it will be necessary to find ways of negotiating specifications – or of negotiating the choice of criteria as, since this too may often be subject to learner-instructor deliberation.

3. In some cultures, the notion of learner autonomy may not be highly esteemed. In others, social etiquette requires modesty, which may affect the degree of accuracy in assessments. Circumstances such as these raise the question of how to deal with mixed populations of learners in which attitudes may differ considerably and in unpredictable ways. Further investigation of variable attitudes and divergent response effects due to differences related to cultural background is clearly needed.

4. The learner's need for practice in assessing his or her own performance tends to be a neglected consideration. Therefore the importance of learner guidance, particularly at the initial stages, needs to be stressed. There is also a need for greater attention to this aspect of evaluation in teacher training.

   In many cases it will be useful to view and discuss learners' need for practice in terms of stages of development. The learner may proceed through the following degrees of support:

   a. Dependent stage: Full dependence on external assessment
   The learner has no part in decisions concerning objectives or methods for assessment. What is to be assessed, as well as the forms for assessment, is determined by 'an outside agent', usually the learner's instructor. Ability is in most cases measured through continuous expert evaluation or by the use of formal tests.

   b. Co-operative stage: Collaborative self- and external assessment
   Instructor and learner use co-operation and discussion to negotiate the quality and anticipated level of achievement. This normally relates to established criteria such as formal test scores, end-of-course grades, and expert ratings.

   c. Independent stage: Full reliance on independent self-assessment
   Experiential data are viewed as significant and the learner's own assessment is the primary criterion by which learning is judged. External evidence may, depending on context, be perceived as complementary to self-assessment.

5. The question of how to view self-assessment data in relation to the concepts of formative and summative functions of assessment may need some clarification. Clearly, teacher assessments may serve both purposes. Externally administered tests will typically serve the latter function only. Self-assessment evidence will primarily serve the formative function, although a summative type of self-assessment has proved to be useful in certain contexts (e.g. for placement purposes in post-secondary education). Generally speaking, learner-centred assessment ought to be viewed as a process-oriented, integrative, and ongoing activity rather than as an incidental summative exercise.

POSSIBLE DIRECTIONS IN FUTURE RESEARCH

There are two broad fields of enquiry in which there is likely to be further research and development: firstly, a theoretical or conceptual area, relating to the study of psychological and other factors that govern the outcome of self-assessment procedures in various language learning settings; and secondly a procedural or didactic area, relating primarily to practice, i.e. to questions of materials and methods instrumental in the process of self-assessment.

The following tasks and questions seem particularly relevant. The more theoretical items are listed first.

1. Investigation of the relationship, in various contexts, between cultural and educational conditions on the one hand and feasibility, meaning-fulness, and accuracy of self-assessment procedures on the other. More focused attempts at characterizing the general conditions under which self-managed types of assessment are likely to prove useful and appropriate.

2. More penetrating investigation of the relationship between psycho-logical or developmental variables and prospects for meaningful and accurate assessment, taking into account, for instance, the learner's level of maturity, educational background, and range of language experience. A closer look at the effects of self-directed assessment procedures on motivation and goal-achievement would seem to be a priority.

3. Empirical study of the role of supportive environments, e.g. in terms of access to the language and encouragement from the instructor. To what degree do they further successful self-managed assessment? How can better self-reliance and self-esteem be fostered? Consider-ations such as these may be crucially important.

4. Further studies on the relationship between perceived and more objec-tively determined levels of performance, as well as on the incidence and possible causes of over- and under-estimation of ability. Inves-tigation of ways of achieving enhanced consistency and validity in various approaches to learners' assessments.

5. Attempts to determine the proper balance between self-managed and 'other-managed' assessment under various circumstances, including consideration of the role of teacher-learner collaborative assessment.

6. Experiments trying to determine the extent to which the ability to make sound assessments improves with practice.

7. Practically oriented development work trying to describe more pre-cisely in what different concrete ways the element of self-assessment can be incorporated into courses and individual study in order to provide continuous formative feedback.

The principles and activities discussed in this review by no means represent a complete coverage of the dimensions of self-managed language learning assessment. They reflect and exemplify, rather, some of the concerns and experiences that have been given increasing attention in foreign and second language education and evaluation over the last couple of decades.

There is every reason to believe that this area of research will continue to grow.

Göteborg University
Sweden

REFERENCES

Bachman, L. & Palmer, A.S.: 1989, 'The construct validation of self-ratings of communicative language ability', *Language Testing* 6, 14–25.

Blanche, P.: 1990, 'Using standardized achievement and oral proficiency tests for self-assessment purposes: The DLIFLC study', *Language Testing* 7(2), 202–229.

Blue, G.M.: 1994, 'Self-assessment of foreign language skills: Does it work?', *CLE Working Papers*, n. 3, ED396569. FL 023 929, University of Southampton, UK, 18–35.

Clark, J.L.D.: 1981, 'Language', in T.S. Barrows et al. (eds.), *College Students' Knowledge and Beliefs: A Survey of Global Understanding*, Change Magazine Press, New Rochelle, NY, 25–35.

Coombe, C.: 1992, *The Relationship between Self-Assessment Ratings of Functional Skills and Basic English Skills Test Results in Adult Refugee ESL Learners*, Ph.D. Dissertation, Graduate School, Ohio State University.

Council of Europe: 1981, *Modern Languages (1971–1981)*, Council for Cultural Co-Operation, Council of Europe, Strasbourg, France.

Cram, B.: 1992, 'Training learners for self-assessment', *TESOL in Context* 2(2), 30–33.

Dickinson, L.: 1987, *Self-Instruction in Language Learning*, Cambridge University Press, Cambridge.

Erickson, G.: 1996, *Lärare och elever tycker om standardprovet i engelska: Resultat av två enkätundersökningar* [Teachers and students reflect on the (Swedish) standardized test in English: Results from two questionnaire studies]. Report from The Language Education Unit, Department of Education, Göteborg University, Sweden.

Falchikov, N. & Boud, D.J.: 1989, 'Student self-assessment in higher education: A meta-analysis', *Review of Educational Research* 59(4), 395–430.

Gipps, C.: 1995, *Beyond Testing: Towards a Theory of Educational Assessment*, The Falmer Press, London.

Girard, D. & Trim, J.: 1988, *Project No. 12: Learning and Teaching Modern Languages for Communication*, Council of Europe, Council for Cultural Co-operation, Strasbourg, France.

Hargan, N.: 1994, 'Learner autonomy by remote control', *System* 22(4), 455–462.

Harris, M.: 1997, 'Self-assessment of language learning in formal settings', *English Language Teaching Journal* 51(1), 12–20.

Heidt, E.: 1979, 'Self-Evaluation in learning: A report on trends, experiences, and research findings', UNESCO, Division of Structures, Content, Methods, and Techniques of Education, Paris.

Heilenman, L.K.: 1990, 'Self-assessment of second language ability: The role of response effects', *Language Testing* 7(2), 174–201.

Heilenman, L.K.: 1991, 'Self-assessment and placement: A review of the issues', in R.V. Teschner (ed.), *Assessing Foreign Language Proficiency of Undergraduates*, Heinle & Heinle, Boston, MA, 93–114.

Hilton, T.L., Grandy, J., Kline, R.G., & Liskin-Gasparro, J.E.: 1985, *The Oral Language Proficiency of Teachers in the United States in the 1980's: An Empirical Study*, Educational Testing Service, Princeton, NJ.

Holec, H. (ed.): 1988, *Autonomy and Self-Directed Learning: Present Fields of Application*, Council of Europe, Council for Cultural Co-operation, Strasbourg, France.
Janssen-van Dieten, A.M.: 1992, *Zelfbeoordeling en tweede-taalleren* ("Self-Assessment in second language learning"), Ph.D. Dissertation, Katholieke Universiteit, Nijmegen, The Netherlands.
Krausert, S.R.: 1991, *Determining the Usefulness of Self-Assessment of Foreign Language Skills: Post-Secondary ESL Students' Placement Contribution*, Ph.D. Dissertation, University of Southern California.
Latomaa, S.: 1996, 'Self-reported second language proficiency among four immigrant groups in the Nordic countries', *Jyväskylä Cross Language Studies* 17, 169–78.
LeBlanc, R. & Painchaud, G.: 1985, 'Self-assessment as a second language placement instrument', *TESOL Quarterly* 19(4), 673–687.
Lewis, E.G. & Massad, C.E.: 1975, *The Teaching of English as a Foreign Language in Ten Countries*, Almqvist & Wiksell International, Stockholm.
Lewkowicz, J.A. & Moon, J.: 1985, 'Evaluation, a way of involving the learner', in J.C. Alderson (ed.), *Lancaster Practical Papers in English Language Education, Vol. 6: Evaluation*, Pergamon Press, Oxford, 45–80.
MacIntyre, P.D., Noels, K.A., & Clément, R.: 1997, 'Biases in self-ratings of second language proficiency: The role of language anxiety', *Language Learning* 47, 2.
Moritz, C.: 1995, *Self-Assessment of Foreign Language Proficiency: A Critical Analysis of Issues and a Study of Cognitive Orientations of French Learners*, Ph.D. Dissertation, Cornell University.
Myles, L.: 1997, 'The interaction between a computer adaptive test and self-assessment of second language ability', report on work in progress (Concordia University) at the 19th Annual Language Testing Research Colloquium, Orlando, Florida.
Oscarson, M.: 1978, [formerly spelt Oskarsson]. *Approaches to Self-Assessment in Foreign Language Learning*, Council of Europe, Council for Cultural Co-operation, Strasbourg, France.
Oscarson, M.: 1984, *Self-assessment of Foreign Language Skills: A Survey of Research and Development Work*, Council of Europe, Council for Cultural Co-operation, Strasbourg, France.
Oscarson, M.: 1989, 'Self-assessment of language proficiency: Rationale and applications', *Language Testing* 6, 1–13.
Peirce, B.N., Swain, M., & Hart, D.: 1993, 'Self-assessment, French immersion, and locus of control', *Applied Linguistics* 14, 25–42.
Shrauger, J.S. & Osberg, T.M.: 1981, 'The relative accuracy of self-predictions and judgments by others in psychological assessment', *Psychological Bulletin* 90(2), 322–351.
Skutnabb-Kangas, T.: 1981, *Tväspräkighet* [Bilingualism], Liber, Lund, Sweden.
Smith, K. & Baldauf, R.B.: 1982, 'The concurrent validity of self-rating with interviewer rating on the Australian Second Language Proficiency Scale', *Educational and Psychological Measurement* 42(4), 1117–1124.
Strong-Krause, D.: 1997, *How Effective is Self-Assessment for ESL Placement?* Paper presented at TESOL '97, Orlando, Florida, March 1997.
Towler, L. & Broadfoot, P.: 1992, 'Self-assessment in the primary school', *Educational Review* 44, 137–151.
von Elek, T.: 1985, 'A test of Swedish as a Second Language', in Y.P. Lee et al. (eds.), *New Directions in Language Testing* Pergamon Press, Oxford, 47–57.
Wilson, K.M.: 1989, *Enhancing the Interpretation of a Norm-Referenced Second-Language Test Through Criterion Referencing: A Research Assessment of Experience in the TOEIC testing contexts*, ETS RR-89-39, Educational Testing Service, Princeton, NJ.
Wilson, K.M.: 1996, *Validity of Global Self-Ratings of ESL Speaking Proficiency Based on an FSI/ILR-Referenced Scale: An Empirical Assessment*, in collaboration with R. Lindsay, Educational Testing Service, Princeton, NJ.

ANNIE PIOLAT

WRITERS' ASSESSMENT AND EVALUATION OF THEIR TEXTS

In this chapter, the term 'assessment' will refer to the writer's evaluation of his or her own text for purposes of revision and improvement. The concepts used for describing these phenomena come from the field of cognitive psychology.

From simple observation we know that adult writers keep returning to their text while they are writing or once they have finished writing in order either to re-read or transform it. In other words, they assess and rewrite their text more or less frequently during the process of writing. However, many writers are unable to detect text problems, and even if they are able to detect them, may not know how to correct them. Conversely, even if they have this knowledge, error detection is not guaranteed.

In terms of the processes and knowledge involved, it is possible to address the question of how writers assess their own text by comparing their evaluation processes as writers with those of a control group evaluating student writing (see, for example, Huot, 1990). In determining a grade, the evaluators elaborate a mental representation of the text they are reading and they compare this representation with the form and content criteria the text is supposed to meet. However, it is more relevant and closer to the real processes involved in assessment activities to describe the writer's competence in terms of cognitive models of the writing process (planning, sentence generation, and revising) and to consider research that precisely specifies when, why, and how reviewing (e.g. going back to the ongoing text) is used by writers of different levels of expertise. 'Reviewing' is a component of the revising process. 'Revision' means making any change at any point in the writing process. It is a cognitive problem-solving process in that it involves (a) the detection of mismatches between intended and instantiated texts, (b) decisions about how to make desired changes, and (c) the process of making these changes.

THE PROCEDURAL MODEL

Since the early eighties, a number of authors have claimed that experienced writers use reviewing in a conscious and voluntary way throughout the process of writing and not only, as has been commonly thought, at the end of the writing process (see for example, Beach & Eaton, 1984; Butler-Nalin, 1984; Hull, 1987; Kievra, 1983; McCutchen, Hull, & Smith, 1987;

C. Clapham and D. Corson (eds), Encyclopedia of Language and Education,
Volume 7: Language Testing and Assessment, 189–198.
© 1997 Kluwer Academic Publishers. Printed in the Netherlands.

Nold, 1981). In fact, the function of reviewing is not limited to one simple rereading during the final editing. Rather, writers re-read their text in order to isolate their ideas, to co-ordinate them with what they are about to write, and, if necessary, to control and revise the form (e.g., mechanics and grammar) and also the content (semantic coherence, ideas, etc.) of what they have already written or what they intend to write next. The subprocesses involved in reviewing are also called revising processes (for a review, see Fitzgerald, 1987) and mainly consist of evaluation processes.

Scardamalia and Bereiter (1985) have described text revising in terms of a set of mental operations, namely Compare, Diagnose, Operate, and say that this sequence of operations is repeatedly activated in order for the writer to control the text. During the course of composition, two kinds of representations are built: one concerns the text as it is written and one as it is intended. The "Compare" process matches these two representations. When a disagreement (or a dissonance; e.g. incongruities between intention and execution) is detected, the 'Diagnose' operation is initiated. This operation identifies the nature of the disagreement. In the case of a successful diagnosis, writers have two options: either they question the internal plan of the text or they transform it ('Operate') according to a strategy that reduces the dissonance. This assessment procedure may affect all possible linguistic levels, from orthography to global semantic coherence. As Witte (1985) points out, the writer's intended text is as important as the actual written text.

The procedural model identifies in more detail those processes which play a role during evaluative reading. It also integrates some of the possible outcomes of the evaluation, such as 'Don't do anything', or 'Change the plan', or 'Change the text'. Finally, it emphasises the cognitive complexity involved in finding a linguistic solution that resolves the dissonance (e.g. 'Choose a tactic' and 'Generate text change'). In fact, writers can encounter problems in producing a solution if both the tactic chosen and the text changes fail.

THE COGNITIVE MODEL

The cognitive model of the revision process proposed by Flower, Hayes, Carey, Schriver and Stratman (1986) describes the functioning of the writer-reviser in terms of the knowledge and processes involved. This model also specifies the reviser's possible strategic choices during each stage of the revision procedure. The authors identify three functional stages: 1. task definition; 2. evaluation leading to a problem representation; and 3. strategy selection that could possibly lead to a modification of the text or plan:

   1. The task definition stage allows the reviser to specify the goals (e.g., clarity), the characteristics of the text to be examined (e.g., local or

global aspects of the text), and the means to reach the goal. This activity is metacognitive (e.g., conscious and intentional).

2. Next, the reviser reads the text (or parts of it) for evaluation. The evaluation process, a constructive process based on reading for comprehension, turns reading into testing. While reading, the reviser can focus on different levels such as verification of information, syntax or spelling. Depending on the type of reading (reading for text comprehension or reading for text evaluation), the reviser more or less automatically identifies very different types of problems.

   When the writer-reviser identifies a problem, such as dissonance or the fact that the writing could be improved in terms of style and/or content, he or she builds a mental representation of the problem which can be more or less specific. An ill-defined representation simply results in the detection of the problem (e.g., without the writer being able to specify what it is). It contains little information concerning a possible solution for reducing the dissonance. A well-defined representation, which is the result of a diagnosis, identifies the precise reasons for the dissonance. It is associated with a strategy that allows the dissonance to be efficiently reduced. Note that the writers' capacity to detect or diagnose a problem depends not only on their expertise (see below) but also on the linguistic level of the dissonance. For example, it is more difficult to define a problem of style (which will be detected) than a violation of rules (e.g., syntax or spelling, which will be diagnosed).

3. Once the representation of the problem is analysed, the writer can choose one of five strategies: 'Ignore, Search, Delay, Rewrite, and Revise'. Three of them, which are exploitation strategies of the revision process, consist of returning to reading and evaluation processes. Writers can ignore problems that are too difficult to resolve or not important enough, or they can delay their resolution or search for more information either in memory or in the text. By choosing one of the two other strategies, which are text modification strategies, the writer can rewrite the text so that the ideas, but not the written text itself, are preserved. This strategy is often used to resolve poorly specified problems. The writer can also revise the text, for example by changing what needs to be changed and preserving what can be preserved. For this operation, the writer uses specific knowledge (knowledge that is also used in text evaluation) which has been described in forms of a 'means-ends table'. This knowledge is organised in problem-solution pairs. The 'ends' concern the communicative aims as well as the different linguistic levels of the text. The 'means' concern operations of insertion, replacement or deletion, all of which allow the writer to modify the text.

All in all, the cognitive model specifies the various processes involved in the assessment and transformation of written texts. Thus, novice writers can encounter difficulties with all of these different processes: (a) faulty task representation, (b) insufficient knowledge of the written language, (c) non-automatic procedures, and (d) absence of metacognitive strategies. This model, via its means-ends table, also emphasises the full scope of potential linguistic problems a writer can encounter during revision and assessment of his or her writing. In addition, the assessment of text frequently results in a large variety of concrete text transformations (Faigley & Witte, 1981). These transformations are categorised as a function of (a) the operation applied for changing the text (deletion, addition, replacement, substitution, rearrangement), (b) the linguistic level in question (punctuation, spelling, word, phrase, clause, sentence, style, text organisation), and (c) the moment at which the writer revises the text (rough outline, first draft, final examination of an almost complete text).

WORK IN PROGRESS

Increasing the capacity to control the text during writing is an essential feature in developing writing (Espéret & Piolat, 1990). In addition, it is important to analyse how writers with different levels of proficiency assess their texts. A number of empirical studies using different methods have shown that, regardless of the point in time at which the writing activity is analysed, novice or inexperienced writers rarely return to their text to reread, control, or possibly modify it. During revision, they only correct the most superficial aspects of the text by using a limited number of transforming operations. This is illustrated in the following studies.

Fabre (1990) analysed the spontaneous writing of 6–8-year old children by collecting their rough drafts from the classroom's trash cans. On the basis of an analysis of all correction marks (erasures, substitutions of linguistic elements, etc.), she states that these children most frequently used suppressions and substitutions to replace one element of the text by another without disrupting the text sequence. In contrast, the addition of letters and words was rare and their displacement was non-existent. Thus, the younger writers only assessed their text in order to exert a linguistic vigilance that helped them to adapt their text to the calligraphic and orthographic norms. They rarely attempted to improve their text by adding or shifting information.

This vigilance is exerted at the very moment of the writing activity and not during later re-reading (Piolat, 1988). In an experiment in which 6–12-year old children were asked to write a story, all interruptions associated with a revision were analysed and the modified word or element was recorded. Very few writers (including the 12-year olds) reread their work while writing. The younger writers mainly revised common spellings and French grammatical orthography at the very moment of writing a word.

While they were writing, therefore, novice writers only assessed, and corrected if necessary, the word or part of a sentence which they were actually engaged in writing.

Even if younger writers may only spontaneously focus on evaluating the most superficial aspects of the text, this does not mean that they are unable to diagnose problems concerning different aspects, such as global text organisation. To test this potential capacity, Piolat and Roussey (1991) asked 10-year old children to revise a descriptive or narrative text that contained local and global errors which affected the coherence of the text. Only those children who were judged by their teachers to be the 'most experienced' in text writing managed to improve the text. However, even they only managed to improve the narrative; they did not improve the description. In a different experiment, Boscolo (1989) first asked 8–12-year old children to write a story. Then, he instructed them to transform their text according to a modification of the major theme (a sunny day turned into a rainy day). Only the older writers managed to modify the text while preserving the semantic coherence: the 12-year old writers were able to focus their evaluation process on the global organisation of their text if they were required to do so, although they failed on some specific revisions; the youngest writers introduced or kept more anomalies in their text.

Assessment capacities are clearly better developed in adult writers, but there is considerable interindividual variation depending on their level of expertise. Hayes, Flower, Schriver, Stratman and Carey (1987) asked different writers (university students, teachers of rhetoric courses, and professional writers) to revise a long letter. This letter contained several errors. They had to resolve problems of adjustment to the recipient, genre, style, syntactic units, lexical units, punctuation, and spelling. The participants first revised the text by expressing aloud their thoughts concerning the revision, then, once the corrections had been made, they explained the reasons for their modifications. The writers differed with respect to the processes and the different types of knowledge involved:

1. Experts, compared to less experienced writers, elaborated a richer, more complex, and more flexible task definition in order to improve the form and content of the text.
2. During text evaluation, experts detected and, above all, diagnosed more problems than less experienced writers. Less experienced writers detected fewer problems concerning text organisation. As soon as they had registered the problems, expert writers had already anticipated ways of resolving them. They eliminated almost all of the detected errors while novice writers only eliminated two-thirds. Analysing think-aloud protocols, the authors show that, in contrast to detection, diagnosis constitutes an optimal assessment strategy although it requires more time, attention, and knowledge.

3. Expert and novice writers differ to a large extent in their respective
   ability to use the five strategies (ignore the problem, postpone its
   resolution, search for more information, rewrite or revise). As concerns the assessment of text, the first three strategies are more efficiently used by experts. They often rely on the search strategy in order
   to determine the place, the frequency, and the extent of both the problems they detect and the information that is missing or poorly specified. Therefore, the search strategy constitutes a 'discovery strategy'.
   Finally, as concerns the text modification strategies of rewrite and
   revise, less experienced writers paraphrase more often than expert
   writers in order to preserve the information aims that guide sentence generation. In addition, during rewriting, novice writers exhibit
   greater difficulties in choosing between the new and the old version
   of the text.

PROBLEMS AND DIFFICULTIES

The previous statements lead us to believe that the acquisition of control
and evaluation of a text can go on for ever. How can we explain the
slowness and difficulty that writers experience while assessing their own
text in order to assure its quality?

One suggestion is that writers are penalised by a cognitive overload
due to the multitude of the processes involved in writing. For novice
writers, word searches and spelling are not sufficiently automatic for them
to direct their assessment (McCutchen, 1996). At the same time, reflexive
procedures which direct their deliberated evaluation to different text levels
(e.g. coherence, grammar etc.) are not available.

A second interpretation is that during assessment, writers do not manage
to turn away from the representation of their own text in order more
fully to appreciate the texts of other writers (Bartlett, 1982; Monahan,
1984). Less experienced and novice writers do not manage to adapt a
point of view that deviates from their own: the one of the future reader.
Young writers in elementary school impose their interpretation on the text
while confounding it with the literal meaning of the text. In addition,
they overestimate the comprehensibility of the text, and they impose their
interpretation on the future reader (Beal, 1993). Although the results
of Levy, Di Persio & Hollingshead (1992) question this interpretation,
Daneman & Stainton (1993) find similar results with undergraduate writers.
These writers were better at evaluating the texts of others because this
activity mostly implies a bottom-up process and not, as for their own
writing, a top-down process. Moreover, the students were more efficient
with their own text when the correction was delayed by two weeks.

To help writers to evaluate their writing more successfully, several interventions have been proposed. What they all have in common is that they aim at increasing the writer's capacity to question and criticise what he or she has written:

- work on tasks that include series of questions that either direct reflection to different levels of the text or exercise particular text transformations (Scardamalia & Bereiter, 1985; Matsuhashi, 1987);
- collaborative writing in which dialogue, negotiations, and even play during a task's realisation, improve self-regulation procedures (Britton, Dusen, Gulgoz, & Glynn, 1989; Daiute, 1989; Paoletti & Pontecorvo, 1991; Roussey, Farioli & Piolat, 1992; Sitko, 1992);
- the use of word processors containing help functions (spelling checks, synonym dictionaries, etc.) that can support the diagnosis of problems (Owston, Murphy & Wideman, 1992; for reviews see Piolat & Blaye, 1991; Sharples, 1991; Snyder, 1993).

Such interventions have had varying amounts of success.

FUTURE DIRECTIONS IN RESEARCH AND PRACTICE

The identification of the processes involved in assessment and text transformation seems well advanced. Butterfield, Hacker and Alberston (1996) have provided a modernised version of the revision model of Flower et al. (1986). This version integrates in the working memory and in the long-term memory of the reviser different cognitive and metacognitive functions. This new model has been used to help categorise more than 100 research reports.

Little data is available concerning the cognitive and metacognitive ways writers learn to assess their text. Investigations should be undertaken to verify whether writers use several evaluation cycles to check all text levels and whether they are able to evaluate the final result of their corrections. Such studies could break new research ground because they might help us to understand the functional relations between evaluation processes (detection and diagnosis) and text transformation processes (rewriting and revising). In relation to this, Hacker, Plumb, Butterfield, Quathamer & Heineken (1994) carried out two particularly important studies with high school students (aged 16–19). In the first experiment, the detection of surface and content errors and the correction of those errors were delayed by one week. In the second experiment, one subgroup of the students was asked not only to detect errors but also to respond to some questions focusing on implicit and explicit meanings of the text. The results show that in order to increase their assessment and evaluation capacities, students need firstly to have specific linguistic knowledge (grammatical, lexical etc.) so that they can detect and correct errors, and secondly to be able to focus on how others will comprehend their texts.

In addition, most of the studies concerning the assessment of writing and text revision have used literary material to investigate the processes involved in writing (Beason, 1993). However, writing is clearly useful for transmitting information in other situations, and this is particularly true for students who have to write texts in all the scholastic disciplines and thus have to use a variety of types of knowledge. Data should be collected that traces the acquisition of the writers' assessment competence as they compose different types of texts (argumentation, demonstration, description, etc.) which are outside the literature course, but which could be really useful in their personal and professional life.

Centre de Recherche en Psychologie Cognitive
Aix-en-Provence, France

REFERENCES

Bartlett, E.: 1982, 'Learning to revise: Some component processes', in M. Nystrand (ed.), *What Writers Know: The Language Process and Structure of Written Discourse*, Academic Press, New York, 345–364.

Beach, R. & Eaton, S.: 1984, 'Factors influencing self-assessment and revising by college freshmen', in R. Beach & L. Bridwell (eds.), *New Directions in Composition Research*, Guilford Press, New York, 149–170.

Beal, C.R.: 1993, 'Contributions of developmental psychology to understanding revision: implications for consultation with classroom teachers', *School Psychology Review* 22(4), 643–655.

Beason, L.: 1993, 'Feedback and revision in writing across the curriculum classes', *Research in the Teaching of English* 27(4), 395–422.

Boscolo, P.: 1989, 'When revising is restructuring: Strategies of text changing in elementary school children', in P. Boscolo (ed.), *Writing: Trends in European research*, UPSEL Editore, Padova, 1–11.

Britton, B.K., Dusen, L.V., Gulgoz, S. & Glynn, S.M.: 1989, 'Instructional text rewritten by five expert teams: Revisions and retention improvements', *Journal of Experimental Psychology* 81, 226–239.

Butler-Nalin, K.: 1984, 'Revision patterns in students' writing', in A.N. Applebee (ed.), *Contexts for Learning to Write: Studies for Secondary School Instruction*, Ablex, Norwood NJ, 121–215.

Butterfield, E.C., Hacker, D.J., & Albertson, L.R.: 1996, 'Environmental, cognitive, and metacognitive influences on text revision: assessing the evidence', *Educational Psychology Review* 8(3), 239–297.

Daiute, C.: 1989, 'Play as thought: Thinking strategies of young writers', *Harvard Educational Review* 59, 1–23.

Daneman, M. & Stainton, M.: 1993, 'The generation effect in reading proof-reading. Is it easier or harder to detect errors in one's own writing?', *Reading and Writing: An Interdisciplinary Journal* 5, 297–313.

Englert, C.S., Hiebert, E.H. & Stewart, S.R.: 1988, 'Detecting and correcting inconsistencies in the monitoring of expository prose', *Journal of Educational Research* 81, 221–227.

Espéret, E. & Piolat, A.: 1990, 'Production: planning and control', in G. Denhière & J.P. Rossi (eds.), *Texts and Text Processing*, North-Holland Amsterdam, 317–333.

Fabre, Cl.: 1990, 'Les brouillons d'écoliers ou l'entrée dans l'écriture' Ceditel, Grenoble'.
Fitzgerald, J.: 1987, 'Research on revision in writing', *Review of Educational Research* 57, 481–506.
Flower, L., Hayes, J.R., Carey, L., Schriver, K. & Stratman, J.: 1986, 'Detection, diagnosis, and the Strategies of Revision', *College Composition and Communication* 37, 16–55.
Hacker, D.J., Plumb, C., Butterfield, E.C., Quathamer, D., & Heineken, E.: 1994, 'Text revision: Detection and correction of errors', *Journal of Educational Psychology* 86(1), 65–78.
Hull, G.: 1987, 'The editing process in writing: A performance study of more skilled and less skilled college writers', *Research in the Teaching of English* 21, 8–29.
Huot, B.: 1990, 'The literature of direct writing assessment: Major concerns and prevailing trends', *Review of Educational Research* 60(2), 237–263.
Kievra, K.A.: 1983, 'The process of review: A levels of processing approach', *Contemporary Educational Psychology* 8, 366–374.
Levy, B.A., Di Persio, R. & Hollingshead, A.: 1992, 'Fluent rereading: Repetition, automaticity, and discrepancy', *Journal of Experimental Psychology: Learning, Memory, and Cognition* 18, 957–971.
Matsuhashi, A.: 1987, 'Revising the Plan and Altering the Text', in A. Matsuhashi (ed.), *Writing in real time. Modelling production processes*, Ablex, Norwood NJ, 197–223.
McCutchen, D.: 1996, 'A capacity theory of writing: Working memory in composition', *Educational Psychology Review* 8, 299–325.
McCutchen, D., Hull, G.A. & Smith, W.L.: 1987, 'Editing strategies and error correction in basic writing', *Written Communication* 4, 139–154.
Monahan, B.D.: 1984, 'Revision strategies of basic and competent writers as they write for different audiences', *Research in the Teaching of English* 18(3), 288–304.
Nold, E.W.: 1981, 'Revising', in C.H. Frederiksen & J.F. Dominic (eds.), *Writing: Process, development and communication*, Erlbaum Hillsdale NJ, 67–69.
Owston, R.D., Murphy, S. & Wideman, H.H.: 1992, 'The effects of word processing on students writing quality and revision strategies', *Research in the Teaching of English* 26(3), 249–276.
Paoletti, G. & Pontecorvo, C.: 1991, 'Planning a story in a collaborative computer task', European *Journal of Psychology of Education* 6, 197–210.
Piolat, A.: 1988, 'Le retour sur le texte dans l'activité rédactionnelle précoce', *European Journal of Psychology of Education* 3(6), 449–459.
Piolat, A. & Blaye, A.: 1991, 'Effects of word processing and writing aids on revision processes', in M. Carretero, M. Pope, R. Simons & J.I. Pozo (eds.), *Learning and Instruction. European Research in an International Context*, Vol. III, Pergamon Press, Oxford, 379–399.
Piolat, A. & Roussey, J.Y.: 1991, 'Narrative and descriptive text revising strategies and procedures', *European Journal of Psychology of Education* 5, 155–163.
Roussey, J.-Y., Farioli, F. & Piolat, A.: 1992, 'Effects of social regulation and computer assistance on the monitoring of writing', *European Journal of Psychology of Education* 7(4), 295–309.
Scardamalia, M. & Bereiter, C.: 1985, 'Fostering the development of self-regulation in children's knowledge processing', in S.F., Chipman, J.W., Segal & R., Glaser (eds.), *Thinking and learning skills. Research and open questions*, L.E.A. Hillsdale NJ, 563–577.
Sharples, M. (ed.): 1992, *Computer and Writing. Issues and Implementation*, Kluwer Academic Publishers, Dordrecht.
Sitko, B.M.: 1992, 'Writers meet their readers in the classroom: Revising after feedback', in M. Secor & D. Charney (eds.), *Constructing Rhetorical Education*, Southern Illinois University Press Carbonale IL, 278–294.

Snyder, I.: 1993, 'Writing with word processors. A research overview', *Educational Research* 35(1), 49–68.

Witte, S.P.: 1985, 'Revising, composing theory, and research design', in S.W. Freedman (ed.), *The Acquisition of Written Language: Response and Revision*, Ablex, Norwood, NJ, 250–284.

EDUARDO C. CASCALLAR

THE ASSESSMENT OF LANGUAGE LEARNING APTITUDE

Language and language learning are ubiquitous phenomena in the human experience, and the acquisition of language can be considered a universal in humans. This universality argues for a shared *aptitude* to acquire language, while the biological constraints seem to indicate necessary minimal conditions. Already in 1924, Thorndike defined intelligence as the 'ability to learn,' and Tikhomirov (1988, p. 268) considers productive thinking "as the basis for the ability to learn". Thus, the measurement of learning potential is currently perceived as a central issue in education and psychology. In addition, with the trend to integrate the assessment of learning potential with the cognitive approach, new perspectives and methods have emerged to investigate second language learning aptitude (Hamers, Sijtsma & Ruijssenaars, 1993). These new perspectives improve our understanding of language aptitude, determining more precisely its relationships with other cognitive, motivational, and personality factors. The process of identifying those factors that contribute most to language-learning success will continue, and we shall come to understand their interactions in the prediction of success in second language learning under various circumstances and conditions.

EARLY DEVELOPMENTS

Some of the earliest language aptitude tests date back to the late 1920s. These early tests focused on two main approaches that are still evident today. Some had an analytical format, consisting of series of items assumed to correspond to hypothesized elementary cognitive abilities such as memory and vocabulary which are tapped and measured separately. Other instruments used a synthetic approach, which consisted of presenting the student with a brief lesson on an artificial or foreign language, observing their performance, and then generalizing results to real second language learning situations. Some of these early tests were developed by Stoddard & Vander Beke (1925), and Luria & Orleans (1928). In 1929, Henmon published a comprehensive review of the Modern Foreign Language Study and the Canadian Committee on Modern Languages, emphasizing the role of prognosis in language testing. Spolsky (1995a, b) describes these instruments and other early developments.

In 1932, Cheydleur studied students failing or dropping out of university language classes, and called for intelligence, placement, and progress tests

C. Clapham and D. Corson (eds), Encyclopedia of Language and Education,
Volume 7: Language Testing and Assessment, 199–210.
© *1997 Kluwer Academic Publishers. Printed in the Netherlands.*

to be used to manage student access to language classes, and to assess their advance. Although he recognised the value of such testing, several other researchers were soon either skeptical of the potential of aptitude assessment (for example, Kaulfers, 1939), or clearly pointed out the complexities and uncertainties inherent in aptitude assessment for predictive purposes. For example, Spoerl (1939) specified the need to take into account not only individual differences in aptitude, but also instructional and motivational factors. All of these considerations signaled the realization that the measurement of aptitude presented unique difficulties, conceptual and methodological, that needed to be addressed, and which could compromise the attainment of accurate and valid assessments.

After various unsuccessful efforts during World War II in the US, some more relevant and methodical research projects were embarked upon. Carroll (1962) examined language aptitude taking into consideration both the fairly specialized characteristics of foreign language learning, and the value of accurate predictions of high achievement in intensive foreign language courses. Most of this work was carried out during the 1950s and culminated in the development of the Modern Language Aptitude Test (MLAT) (Carroll & Sapon, 1959). The batteries tried out by Carroll included tests of verbal ability and phonetic discrimination, and included work-samples based on artificial language tests. Several moderately high correlations with learning outcomes were obtained using these tasks.

In 1966, Pimsleur reported the development of the Pimsleur Language Aptitude Battery (PLAB). This instrument, developed as an alternative to the MLAT, with the specific purpose of assessing the junior high school population, measures similar abilities to the MLAT, but Pimsleur also included motivation as an integral part of aptitude. A few years later, a major effort by the US Defense Department culminated in the development of the Defense Language Aptitude Battery (Petersen & Al-Haik, 1976), which addresses aptitude by measuring the ability of adults to learn an artificial language with visual and auditory inputs. The York Language Aptitude Test (Green, 1975), followed a different approach, and measured aptitude through the ability to apply analogical reasoning to produce items in another language. These developments provided the field of language aptitude assessment with several validated language aptitude instruments which could be used for further research.

MAJOR CONTRIBUTIONS

The role of aptitude and the participation of cognitive skills in measurements of intelligence and performance in various areas has been an ongoing theme in the learning literature. Several researchers have contributed with alternative views on the manner in which cognitive abilities participate and determine aptitude. The volume edited by Jenkins & Paterson

(1961) contained several classic papers that recommended that, in addition to cognitive abilities, personality characteristics – both conative and affective – should be included in the study of individual differences in learning. Oller (1981) proposed a single language factor, related to the concept of general intelligence, which could account for the variance in a wide range of language measures. Wesche, Edwards & Wells (1982), in a project that investigated the relationship between foreign language aptitude and intelligence, identified three second-order factors: first language verbal knowledge, abstract reasoning ability, and ability to learn new language elements and associations. In addition, a unitary third-order factor was identified. The authors interpreted the results as indicating that the conceptualization of language aptitude should subsume "specific abilities important for the language classroom under a more encompassing general ability, or general intelligence". Snow (1989) analyzed a series of cognitive-conative-learning interaction effects, and proposed a way of conceptualizing their relationships. Willerman (1979), on the other hand, examined individual differences in educational achievement and in aptitude and achievement testing by studying the role played by heritability on motivation, educational interventions, and other variables.

In an influential contribution using factor analysis, Carroll (1962, 1981) proposed a model, reflected in his work on the MLAT, which accounts for individual differences in foreign language learning. This model identified four components of language aptitude which had implications for assessment: phonemic coding ability, grammatical sensitivity, inductive language-learning ability, and and an ability to learn language by rote. It is noteworthy that this same author in another recent major work (Carroll, 1993) explored interesting connections that exist between some cognitive processes and the language abilities addressed in his work. He recognized the complexity of these relations, and suggested that since various factors of language ability are correlated, these relations could be controlled by complex genetic and environmental interactions, with some cognitive processes underlying the common effects found among those factors. Guthke, Heinrich & Caruso (1986) extended the application of Carroll's factors, by concentrating on inductive learning ability, for which, according to Carroll, no suitable tests had yet been developed. They developed a test using items which tapped recognition of structures, recognition of relations, and the ability to map recognized relations onto one another. Results suggested that this measure, together with a phonetic test, could be a valuable predictor of foreign language ability.

Kyllonen & Woltz (1989) worked on determinants of success in the acquisition of cognitive skills, and proposed a four-source model which presents learning success as a function of success in prior learning and of proficiency in four categories of general cognitive factors: (a) general and domain specific knowledge, (b) general and domain specific skills, (c) processing capacity (mainly working memory capacity), and (d) processing speed (retrieval speed, decision speed, etc.). These factors, based on the cognitive architecture suggested by Anderson (1983) in his ACT* theory, determine performance in the three proposed learning phases: knowledge acquisition, skill acquisition, and skill refinement. Some research in the area of language learning and acquisition followed this approach, and integrated concepts from the psycholinguistic and cognitive research areas with the problem of assessment of language aptitude and abilities, and with interactions with language proficiency testing. For example, Gathercole and Baddeley (1993) linked vocabulary acquisition, phonological working memory, the role of the central executive system in speech production, and language comprehension. Mulder, Wijers, Smid, Brookhuis & Mulder (1989) hypothesized that differences in cognitive abilities arise from three different sources: differences in elementary cognitive processes, and differences in strategic and knowledge aspects of thought. These authors also called for approaches emphasizing fast process research and electro-physiological measures. Similarly, Guttman (1986) studied fluctuations of learning capability, and found potential cortical shifts correlated with increased learning performance. Using some linguistic tasks, he suggested that it might be possible to induce 'a state of learning readiness'.

As a follow up to the Bristol Language Project (Skehan, 1989), an important set of studies examined the interrelations between first language development, foreign language aptitude, and achievement in a foreign language. Results suggested that in addition to a language ability factor, vocabulary, social class, and parents' level of education adequately predicted aptitude levels. Skehan (1989) pointed out that aptitude seems more strongly related to first language development than to achievement in the foreign language, because of the different learning situations that produce the latter. He also noted that the underlying language learning capacities of the student might not "be exploited in language teaching classrooms" (Skehan, 1989, p. 32), and noted that this effect might be due to the de-contextualized nature of foreign language learning. He went on to analyze and critique the current state of aptitude research, and suggested future investigations to determine the nature of the abilities that aptitude tests measure, and the nature of related variables, such as motivation, learning strategies, and aptitude-treatment interactions. In their review of foreign language research in Europe, van Els, de Bot & Weltens (1991) cautioned against not including teacher and instructional variables in the assessment of individual differences in learning outcomes. Parry & Stansfield (1990) reviewed several applications of the study of language aptitude, including the prediction of success in foreign language learning in intensive language programs for adult learners, the role of attitudes, motivation, and personality, and the role of learning styles and learning strategies.

Ellis (1994) extensively covers individual learner differences and summarizes the work on language aptitude assessment, noting that with few exceptions there have been almost no recent attempts to develop alternative language aptitude tests (Ellis, 1994, p. 499). He echoes Carroll's skepticism about the possibility of achieving better measures. Both Ellis (1994) and Skehan (1989) suggest that, in spite of the problems noted, and the many unanswered issues which still complicate this field of research, language aptitude is still the best single predictor of achievement in a foreign language.

WORK IN PROGRESS

Cascallar (1995) summarizes the goals of the 1994 International Language Aptitude Symposium, which addressed the concept of language learning potential from an expanded perspective, which included cognitive abilities, personality characteristics, motivational factors, and strategic components. Sternberg (1995) discusses the important role of styles of thinking (as "preferred modes of thinking, of using one's abilities"), and the importance of matching the style with the pattern of cognitive abilities to maximize performance and assessments. He introduces the theory of mental self-government, and stresses the need to take these constructs into account when improving language learning aptitude assessment.

McLaughlin (1995) and MacWhinney (1995) report their work in psycholinguistic research relevant to language aptitude and to the relationship between first and second language acquisition. McLaughlin supports the notion of a general language-processing ability much of which could be explained by the working memory construct, and suggests that this plays a significant role in the processing of a second language. In his view, this is not a fixed capacity, but rather one that can be modified as a result of learning and experience, within an individual's range of potential learning performance, as determined by pre-existing conditions. He defines individual differences in language learning aptitude as a function of "availability of knowledge about the target language and the speed and efficiency of working memory", and he sees this as resulting in the capacity to generate and restructure data as the processing stages progress. MacWhinney (1995) examines the low-level cognitive learning mechanisms that intervene in foreign language acquisition, and describes the participation of neural systems, motivational elements, and other strategic mechanisms necessary for this process. He proposes that different profiles of skills could interact differently with various languages which pose different demands on the declarative and strategic components of the cognitive system. While acknowledging that most of the individual differences in language aptitude could be explained by the overall cognitive ability of the learner and by the overall difficulty of the language (from the perspective of the native language of the learner), he sees a role for the study of lower-level interactions of component skills which might add further predictive value to the assessment of aptitude. Both authors call for the consideration of other factors such as instructional treatments, motivational variables, and personality characteristics.

An interesting point in terms of individual differences is explored by de Bot & Weltens (1991). In examining the phenomenon of attrition, they discuss evidence of regression patterns in the speech of foreign language learners after months of not using the newly acquired language. These patterns corresponded to incorrect patterns previously shown during acquisition. Interestingly, these authors state that "symmetry in the construction and dissolution of language may tell us more about the structure and storage of language" (de Bot & Weltens, 1991, p. 38). This view seems to bring together the same elementary cognitive constructs measured in language aptitude research, with the phenomenon of language loss, therefore, opening up the possibility of exploring the attrition in terms of some language aptitude cognitive variables.

Recent work by Kyllonen (1993), as part of the Learning Abilities Measurement Program (LAMP) at Armstrong Laboratory (US Air Force), examines aptitude testing from a formal information processing approach. Efforts like this could help take aptitude research beyond the "clustering and categorizing" of variables (Kyllonen 1993), and could connect it to advances in human learning and cognition. Several studies have shown that if variability in task-content-related performance is taken into account, the previously described four-source model of general cognitive factors (Kyllonen and Woltz, 1989) is a valid predictor of learning success. The methodology for this research included the use of the Cognitive Abilities Measurement (CAM) battery, which incorporates a wide variety of cognitive tasks.

Several additional research projects are currently being conducted that will contribute to the understanding of various aspects of language aptitude. An extension of the cognitive assessment work in the area of language aptitude is under way (Cascallar 1993). It involves the development of the Cognitive Assessment of Language Learning Ability (CALLA) battery, which adapts cognitive tasks appearing in the literature, and maximizes the language involvement in task performance. Current work investigates the relationship of these cognitive abilities to specific language learning conditions and language learner characteristics.

Another project (Sternberg, 1995) examines the processing of novel information as a predictor of language learning potential. Ehrman & Oxford (1995) explore the relationship of a large number of individual difference variables to proficiency ratings in two language skills (reading and speaking) upon completion of intensive training of adults in a variety of languages. Although their work again shows the preeminence of the cognitive aptitude construct in the prediction of outcomes, their work also provides very interesting information about a large number of other factors (learning strategies, learning styles, personality, anxiety, and motivation) and how they affect language training, particularly for learners at high levels of proficiency. This program of research is still continuing. Gardner (1991) carried out a vast program of research into the relationships between aptitude, motivation, attitudes, anxiety, and second language acquisition and loss. This research showed that aptitude exerts most of its influence on initial learning, while motivation also has an impact on later language use.

Results from several studies at the U.S. Defense Language Institute show the importance of cognitive abilities in the prediction of success in foreign language learning and of long-term proficiency, while other affective, motivational, and strategic variables provide useful information for instructional changes and student-specific adaptations (O'Mara, Lett & Alexander, 1994). For example, reading and listening skills were better predicted by these than were speaking proficiency ratings. Related work at the Federal Bureau of Investigation (Tabori & Cascallar, 1996) explores the impact of several background learner variables on the success rate of the selection of adult foreign language learners for intensive language training, with cognitive-related factors predicting learning outcomes most strongly.

Recent work in Europe has addressed questions with important implications for the understanding of language aptitude. Several papers (for example, de Jong 1990, de Jong & van Ginkel, 1992) address the interconnected problems of the determination of the components of language proficiency, their assessment, and the comprehensive modeling of proficiency. Many of the subskills identified at different levels of proficiency could be hypothesized to correspond to the impact of cognitive abilities which predominate at these various levels, such as declarative knowledge and channel capacity and control. Some of the distinctions made in these papers echo earlier studies in aptitude which, when discussing language knowledge and language use, distinguish between declarative and procedural knowledge.

PROBLEMS AND DIFFICULTIES

As interest in the assessment of language aptitude has increased, so has the awareness of some of the problems and limitations of the research. In part, some of these problems are of a methodological origin. In many instances, the sample of individuals on which data is collected is artificially homogeneous either because of self-selection of the sample, or because some prior criteria related (or even similar!) to aptitude has been used to select the participants in the study or the training program. The resulting restriction of range of the aptitude variable (and of any other variable equally affected in the study) has direct impact in the underestimation of the correlation of aptitude with other variables in the study, and could also affect the value of the reliability estimates of the instruments used. Another frequent problem found in the literature is that many of the studies have ambitious goals, and include too many variables for the number of subjects available for the project.

Also in the methodological arena, more longitudinal research is needed in order to test many of the hypothesized effects and interactions between the variables relating to the aptitude construct. In addition, the causal directionality of many of the proposed effects (i.e., motivation-anxiety) needs to be tested with models that disambiguate the potential sources of the effects under study. It is also important to include in the analyses those sources of variation that not all studies have taken into account. These factors include instructor characteristics, teaching modalities, testing method, and types of text and other materials, all with potentially high interaction effects with underlying learner aptitude, motivation, and affective components. In information processing models that have been reported in the literature, some of the problems have to do with the utilization of assessments made with insufficiently valid cognitive tasks, or are caused by biases in their selection. Models tested should either sufficiently and appropriately cover all hypothesized sources of effects, or should test very limited and specific hypotheses that address a given stage of processing or a certain factor within a given model.

As regards the research approach followed, the language aptitude field should move to a theory-driven paradigm, in which specific causal relationships can be hypothesized and rigorously tested. The requirement that scientific theories be falsifiable, which implies the need for specific hypothesis building, is at the center of the scientific method. Too much of the research available, although useful in that it has built a core of facts that will have to be accounted for in future model building, is not anchored in theoretical structures and causal modeling. An extraordinary amount of empirical data has been accumulated, with impressive inductive strategies for hypothesis building, but many of the current approaches have been remarkably weak in following a formal deductive approach for the causal analysis of the phenomena under study.

FUTURE DIRECTIONS

Aptitude research is likely to continue for both theory-driven and pragmatic reasons. These same factors will push for greater predictive power in the components under study. Some of the issues to be addressed will concern the achievement of a better understanding of the construct, including the elementary processes that jointly determine it, the range of modifiability in the operations of such processes, and the understanding of which factors and conditions can have an impact on those operations. As indicated before, the causal relationships will also have to be researched with appropriate methodologies. In turn, all these findings should inform teaching methodologies, instructional conditions, and student selection and advising. The cultural and social context of many of these effects will also have to be explored and their associations to individual differences explained. In general, the contexts of both the learning situation and the language performance have to be further explored.

The cognitive demands of tasks and learning conditions will have to be established in order to understand the processing load that they impose on the learner. The cognitive analysis of task demands and learner abilities should go hand in hand, and particular attention should be given to the interaction effects that result from the dyad task-learner (or language user). It is with attention to the individual differences in the profile of cognitive skills that their interactions with different languages, language skills, and learning and teaching conditions will be understood. The detailed analysis of all of these additional sources of variance, which could involve the development of more refined cognitive and language specific tests, will result in an improvement in the predictive power of the aptitude batteries. In addition, further analysis of the non-cognitive components will also extend the predictive power of our instruments, and explain the stage that each component influences. The result will be an increased theoretical understanding of learning and human cognitive processing, with specific reference to language, and to the cognitive, social, and individual affective and motivational variables that modulate language acquisition and performance.

A final thought is that perhaps we should no longer define *aptitude* as something that an individual *possesses* in some definable amount, or which results from an addition of components. It is perhaps time to view this construct as an *epiphenomenon* of the characteristics of the task or learning situation, as it *interacts* with the individual's elementary processing and affective components. It is possible then to conceptualize the individual characteristics of the resulting 'aptitude' construct as emerging from the persistent interaction between the individual and his or her environment – environment which, in the case of language, includes the related cognitive activity as well as the social milieu and interactions. These interactions generate the outcomes that in turn set the parameters for future interactions. The product is the overall ability to learn, or aptitude.

The City University of New York
USA

REFERENCES

Anderson, J.R.: 1983, *The Architecture of Cognition*, Harvard University Press, Cambridge MA.
Carroll, J.B.: 1962, 'The prediction of success in intensive foreign language training', in R. Glaser (ed.), *Training Research and Education*, University of Pittsburgh Press, Pittsburgh PA, 87–136.
Carroll, J.B.: 1981, 'Twenty-five years of research on foreign language aptitude', in K.C. Diller (ed.), *Individual Differences and Universals in Language Learning Aptitude*, Newbury House, Rowley MA.
Carroll, J.B.: 1993, *Human Cognitive Abilities*, Cambridge University Press, Cambridge.
Carroll, J.B. & Sapon, S.: 1959, *Modern Languages Aptitude Test – Form A*, The Psychological Corporation, New York.
Cascallar, E.C.: 1993, *A New Cognitive Approach for the Assessment of Language Aptitude*, 15th Language Testing Research Colloquium (August 5–7), Arnhem, The Netherlands.
Cascallar, E.C.: 1995, 'Introduction', in E. Cascallar (guest ed.), *Special Issue on Language Aptitude, Language Testing* 12, 259–263.
Cheydleur, F.D.: 1932, 'Mortality of modern languages students: Its causes and prevention, *Modern Language Journal* 17, 104–136.
de Bot, K. & Weltens, B.: 1991, 'Recapitulation, regression, and language loss', in H. Seliger & R. Vago (eds.), *First Language Attrition*, Cambridge University Press, Cambridge, 31–51.
de Jong, J.H.A.L.: 1990, 'Response to masters: Linguistic theory and psychometric models', in J.H.A.L. De Jong & D.K. Stevenson (eds.), *Individualizing the Assessment of Language Abilities*, Multilingual Matters Ltd., Clevedon UK, 71–80.
de Jong, J.H.A.L. & van Ginkel, L.W.: 1992, 'Dimensions in oral foreign language proficiency', in L. Verhoeven & J.H.A.L. de Jong (eds.), *The Construct of Language Proficiency: Applications of Psychological Models to Language Assessment*, John Benjamins Publishing Co., Amsterdam, 187–205.
Ehrman, M.E. & Oxford, R.L.: 1995, 'Cognition plus: Correlates of language learning success', *Modern Language Journal* 79, 67–89.
Ellis, R.: 1994, *The Study of Second Language Acquisition*, Oxford University Press, Oxford.
Gardner, R.C.: 1991, 'Second language learning in adults: Correlates of proficiency', *Applied Language Learning* 2, 1–28.
Gathercole, S.E. & Baddeley, A.D.: 1993, *Working Memory and Language*, Lawrence Erlbaum Associates, Hillsdale NJ.
Green, P.S.: 1975, *The Language Laboratory in School: The York Study*, Oliver & Boyd, Edinburgh.
Guthke, J., Heinrich, A. & Caruso, M.: 1986, 'The diagnostic program of "syntactical rule and vocabulary acquisition": A contribution to the psychodiagnosis of foreign language learning ability', in F. Klix & H. Hagendorf (eds.), *Human Memory and Cognitive Capabilities: Mechanisms and Performances – Part B*, Elsevier Science Publishers B.V., Amsterdam, 903–911.
Guttmann, G.: 1986, 'Fluctuations of learning capability', in F. Klix & H. Hagendorf (eds.), *Human Memory and Cognitive Capabilities: Mechanisms and Performances – Part B*, Elsevier Science Publishers B.V., Amsterdam, 639–648.
Hamers, J.H.M., Sijtsma, K. &Ruijssenaars, A.J.J.M. (eds.): 1993, *Learning Potential Assessment: Theoretical, Methodological and Practical Issues*, Swets & Zeitlinger B.V., Amsterdam.
Henmon, V.A.C.: 1929, *Achievement Tests in the Modern Foreign Languages, Prepared for the Modern Foreign Language Study and the Canadian Committee on Modern Languages*, Macmillan, New York.

Jenkins, J.J. & Paterson, D.G. (eds.): 1961, *Studies in Individual Differences*, Appleton-Century-Crofts, New York.

Kaulfers, W.V.: 1939, 'Prognosis and its alternatives in relation to the guidance of students', *German Quarterly* 12, 81–84.

Kyllonen, P.C.: 1993, 'Aptitude testing inspired by information processing: A test of the four-sources model', *The Journal of General Psychology* 120, 375-405.

Kyllonen, P.C. & Woltz, D.J.: 1989, 'Role of cognitive factors in the acquisition of cognitive skill', in R. Kanfer, P.L. Ackerman & R. Cudeck (eds.), *Abilities, Motivation, and Methodology: The Minnesota Symposium on Learning and Individual Differences*, Lawrence Erlbaum Associates, Hillsdale NJ, 239–280.

Luria, M.A. & Orleans, J.S.: 1928, *Luria-Orleans Modern Language Prognosis Test*, World Book Co., Yonkers NY.

MacWhinney, B.: 1995, 'Language-specific prediction in foreign language learning', in E. Cascallar (guest ed.), *Special Issue on Language Aptitude, Language Testing* 12(3), 292–320.

McLaughlin, B.: 1995, 'Aptitude from an information-processing perspective', in E. Cascallar (guest ed.), *Special Issue on Language Aptitude, Language Testing* 12, 370–387.

Mulder, G., Wijers, A., Smid, H., Brookhuis, K. & Mulder, L.: 1989, 'Individual differences in computational mechanisms: A psychophysiological analysis', in R. Kanfer, P.L. Ackerman & R. Cudeck (eds.), *Abilities, Motivation, and Methodology: The Minnesota Symposium on Learning and Individual Differences*, Lawrence Erlbaum Associates, Hillsdale NJ, 391–434.

Oller, J.W., Jr.: 1981, 'Language as intelligence?', *Language Learning* 31, 465–492.

O'Mara, F.E., Lett, J.A. & Alexander, E.E.: 1994, 'The prediction of language learning success at DLIFLC', in U.S. Department of Defense Report, *The Language Skill Change Project*, Defense Language Institute Foreign Language Center, Monterey CA, 1994, LSCP Report II.

Parry, T.S. & Stansfield, C.W. (eds.): 1990, *Language Aptitude Reconsidered*, Prentice Hall Regents, Englewood Cliffs NJ.

Petersen, C.R. & Al-Haik, A.: 1976, 'The development of the Defense Language Aptitude Battery (DLAB)', *Educational and Psychological Measurement* 36, 369–380.

Pimsleur, P.: 1966, *The Pimsleur Language Aptitude Battery*, Harcourt, Brace, Jovanovitch, New York.

Skehan, P.: 1989, *Individual Differences in Second-Language Learning*, Edward Arnold, London.

Snow, R.E.: 1989, 'Cognitive-conative aptitude interactions in learning', in R. Kanfer, P.L. Ackerman & R. Cudeck (eds.), *Abilities, Motivation, and Methodology: The Minnesota Symposium on Learning and Individual Differences*, Lawrence Erlbaum Associates, Hillsdale NJ, 435–474.

Spoerl, D.T.: 1939, 'A study of some of the possible factors involved in foreign language learning', *Modern Language Journal* 23, 428–431.

Spolsky, B.: 1995a, *Measured Words*, Oxford University Press, Oxford.

Spolsky, B.: 1995b, 'Prognostication and language aptitude testing, 1925–62', in E. Cascallar (guest ed.), *Special Issue on Language Aptitude, Language Testing* 12, 321–340.

Sternberg, R.J.: 1995, *Coping with the Unfamiliar*, Research proposal to the Center for the Advancement of Language Learning, Arlington, VA.

Sternberg, R.J.: 1995, 'Styles of thinking and learning', in E. Cascallar (guest ed.), *Special Issue on Language Aptitude, Language Testing* 12, 265–291.

Stoddard, G.D. & Vander Beke, G.E.: 1925, *Iowa Placement Examinations: Foreign Language Aptitude*, State University of Iowa Press, Iowa City IA.

Tabori, J.R. & Cascallar, M.I.: 1996, *Factors that Participate in the Prediction of Language Learning Success: Aptitude, Motivation, and Background*, Technical Report, Federal Bureau of Investigation, Washington DC.

Thorndike, E.L.: 1924, *An Introduction to the Theory of Mental and Social Measurement*, Wiley, New York.

Tikhomirov, O.: 1988, *The Psychology of Thinking*, Progress Publishers, Moscow.

van Els, T., de Bot, K. & Weltens, B.: 1991, 'Empirical foreign language research in Europe', in K. de Bot, R. Ginsberg & C. Kramsch (eds.), *Foreign Language Research in Cross-Cultural Perspective*, John Benjamins Publishing Co., Amsterdam, 21–32.

Wesche, M.B., Edwards, H. & Wells, W.: 1982, 'Foreign language aptitude and intelligence', *Applied Psycholinguistics* 3, 127–140.

Willerman, L.: 1979, *The Psychology of Individual and Group Differences*, W.H. Freeman, San Francisco CA.

ROSEMARY BAKER AND HELEN J. CHENERY

THE ASSESSMENT OF SPEECH AND LANGUAGE DISORDERS

This review encompasses the assessment of motor speech and language disorders. Motor speech disorders result from disturbances in the anatomy, physiology or neurology of the motor systems underlying speech production (Crystal, 1989). Language disorders, on the other hand, arise from disturbances to the neural and psycholinguistic processes involved in the perception, decoding, encoding and formulation of spoken language.

The discussion focuses on dysarthria, disorders of articulation and phonology, aphasia and developmental language disorders. Dysarthria, defined by Wertz (1991) as a group of speech disorders resulting from disturbances in muscular control, belongs within the motor speech category. Aphasia (language impairment following brain damage) and developmental language disorders belong within the language category. This traditional dichotomy cannot, however, be clearly maintained in the case of disorders of articulation and phonology.

The review does not deal with disorders of voice and fluency other than those relating to dysarthria and aphasia, or with apraxia, defined by Wertz (1991) as an articulatory disorder resulting from impairment (due to brain damage) in the capacity to program the positioning of speech muscles and the sequencing of muscle movements for the volitional production of speech.

Assessment of speech and language disorders is carried out both for clinical and research purposes. Such assessment falls principally within the domain of speech-language pathology. However, some aspects are also of importance to the fields of neurology, neurophysiology, psychology, neuropsychology, psychiatry, theoretical and clinical linguistics, neurolinguistics and psycholinguistics.

The aims of clinical assessments are: initial determination of the presence of a disorder; differential diagnosis (distinguishing one disorder from another); elucidation of the disorder; discrimination between speech/language deficits and associated problems (such as hearing or memory deficits); determination of a prognosis; selection of cases suitable for treatment; planning and monitoring progress of treatment; liaising with the client, family and other health professionals; and planning and auditing health services. Assessments may also be used for screening, for example to help detect remediable problems in young children. In research settings, applications of assessments focus mainly on the nature of the speech and

C. Clapham and D. Corson (eds), Encyclopedia of Language and Education,
Volume 7: Language Testing and Assessment, 211–223.
© 1997 Kluwer Academic Publishers. Printed in the Netherlands.

language disorders associated with particular conditions or diseases, the efficacy of different forms of therapy, and the testing of hypotheses deriving from theories of language processing or neurologic functioning.

EARLY DEVELOPMENTS AND MAJOR CONTRIBUTIONS

Dysarthria

Attention to assessment issues in motor speech disorders dates back only to the 1970s, to the emergence of two major themes in the literature. The first theme, emphasized by Darley, Aronson & Brown (1975), was that the various types of dysarthria resulted from impairment in the control or execution of the muscles used for speech production following some form of neurological damage. This neuropathological view heralded a major push for detailed physiological assessments that would test more directly the functional competence of the structures used for producing speech.

The second, but related, theme highlighted the importance of assessing the structural and functional integrity of certain anatomical sites where important speech activities occur. These so-called functional components of the speech production mechanism are structures (or sets of structures) that work to generate or valve the speech airstream, and include the abdominal muscles, diaphragm, rib cage, larynx, tongue, soft palate, jaw and lips (Netsell, Lotz & Barlow, 1989). An emergent literature then sought to clarify the effect of neuromuscular disturbances upon the speech processes, both individually and also collectively as an integrated functioning system.

Two general avenues in dysarthria assessment stem from these two themes: (1) the listener judgment-inferential approach and (2) the multiple component approach (Abbs & De Paul, 1989). These approaches have increasingly merged over the last ten years, and a comprehensive and theoretically sound assessment of dysarthria would draw upon both.

In the listener judgment-inferential approach, the clinician listens to and evaluates the patient's speech using various speech task manipulations, to identify the nature of the impairment in the speech production system, and the predominant components affected (e.g., respiratory, phonatory, articulatory). This perceptual analysis is supplemented by a routine examination of the motor speech apparatus (the oro-motor examination) and perhaps an articulation and/or intelligibility test. The assessment assists in the differential diagnostic process, and allows the clinician to infer the underlying pathophysiology of the patient's speech disorder by reference to parallel neurological studies describing the signs and symptoms associated with the various types of dysarthria.

The multiple-component approach has evolved from the traditional sequential model of speech production proposed by Netsell (1973). It involves detailed physiological analysis of individual speech motor sub-systems or functional components (e.g., lips, jaw, tongue, larynx etc.) to form an overall picture of how the neurological damage has affected the speech production mechanism. It is most often based on instrumental measures.

Disorders of Articulation and Phonology

The distinction between disorders of articulation and phonological disorders is an important theoretical one, yet remains somewhat imprecise. The older term 'articulation disorder' implies that the speaker, usually a child, has learned an inappropriate motor response (perhaps producing the sound [s] as [θ]), which occurs consistently in all contexts. A phonological disorder, on the other hand, implies that the child has learned an inappropriate phonological rule (Peterson & Marquardt, 1994), though some authors would argue that phonological disorders can also include persisting normal processes which remain in the child's pronunciation patterns long after the age at which they would normally have disappeared (Grunwell, 1995).

The testing of speech production, and the premises on which testing is based, have reflected changing theories over time (Peterson & Marquardt, 1994). The early literature emphasized an approach in which speech sounds were treated as minimal elements that were mastered sequentially as a function of age and motor skill (Templin, 1957). In the 1960s, the distinctive feature theorists viewed phonological development as entailing the mastery of a series of distinctive features during the course of maturation, i.e., as a rule-governed progression ordered with respect to a set of hierarchical relationships.

Subsequently, research has been dominated by further developments of rule-generated production theories, with speech errors described in terms of processes. Phonological processes are relational statements about the systematic correspondences between the speaker's pronunciation patterns and the target (or normal) patterns. They describe patterns such as substitutions, omissions, reductions, deletions and assimilations. Currently there are six widely known informal assessment procedures based on phonological process analysis (see Grunwell, 1995 for a review).

At present, then, speech production is usually assessed along four dimensions: the anatomical/physiological, the phonetic, the phonological and the developmental (Grunwell, 1993). The anatomical and physiological dimension is concerned firstly with determining the structural and functional integrity of the organs of speech production, by describing their size, shape and relationship. The phonetic dimension of speech assessment uses the techniques of articulatory phonetics to transcribe and classify the sounds produced. Assessment of the phonological dimension involves describing the person's pronunciation patterns and inferring from these the phonological rules which appear to underlie them. The developmental dimension draws upon developmental acquisition data to determine whether the child's pronunciation patterns are age-appropriate, or whether they are delayed or different from what might be expected (see Dodd, 1995 for a discussion of subgroups).

Developmental Language Disorders

Broadly defined, the term 'developmental language disorders' denotes a heterogeneous category of delays, deficits and disturbances in children's comprehension and/or expression of spoken language, compared with their normally-developing peers (Byers Brown & Edwards, 1989; Adams & Conti-Ramsden, 1995). Such disorders may occur either with or without a condition such as hearing impairment, intellectual impairment or autism, and may affect any or all linguistic levels.

The speech pathology literature of the 1940s and 1950s alluded to these disorders in discussions of 'delayed speech' and its possible causes. Lund & Duchan (1993) identify two main approaches to assessment which prevailed during the 1950s: a 'normative' approach, based on the performance of normal children of different ages on measures such as mean length of utterance in words, and parts of speech used; and a 'pathology' approach, which sought to identify the cause of the language disorder and other presenting symptoms, so that treatment could be directed at the underlying condition.

During the 1960s and 1970s, the fields of psychology, linguistics and child language acquisition brought major influences to bear on the conceptualisation, description and assessment of child language disorders, and provided the basis for numerous test instruments and profiling procedures. Bloom & Lahey (1978) list nearly 40 language-related instruments published during this period. Peterson & Marquardt (1994) review 20 tests published up to 1992, including the influential Illinois Test of Psycholinguistic Abilities (Kirk, McCarthy & Kirk, 1968).

Procedures for obtaining samples of children's spontaneous utterances, and for measuring their length and structural complexity, began to evolve from the mid-1920s (Peterson & Marquardt, 1994). A significant contribution dating from the 1970s was the application of descriptive techniques from linguistics to provide profiles of performance at the syntactic, phonological, prosodic and semantic levels (Crystal, Fletcher & Garman, 1989; Crystal, 1992).

Assessment in the 1980s and 1990s has been characterized by increased emphasis on pragmatic aspects of communication (see, for example, Prutting & Kirchner, 1983; Lund & Duchan, 1993), informed by sociolinguistic, discourse analytic and ethnographic approaches. Conti-Ramsden & McTear (1995) review several procedures for assessing pragmatic skills in conversational samples, and note also the recent introduction of a prag-matics perspective within a standardized testing format.

Aphasia

Aphasia is language impairment resulting from brain damage (e.g., from stroke, head injury, tumour, metabolic disorder, toxicity) which has destroyed neuronal cells in areas of the brain on which language seems to depend (Lesser & Milroy, 1993). Indeed, from the second half of the 19th century, exploration of language impairment was aimed at determining its anatomical correlates (Darley & Spriestersbach, 1978).

Kertesz (1979) offers a descriptive summary of 15 aphasia tests pub-lished between 1926 and 1971. Among those most widely used today are the Western Aphasia Battery (Kertesz, 1982) and the Boston Diagnostic Aphasia Examination (Goodglass & Kaplan, 1983). These meet Davis' (1983) criteria for comprehensive assessments of aphasia, in that they yield data on the person's perception and recognition in the receptive modalities, as well as both propositional and non-propositional uses of language in the expressive modalities, at word, sentence and discourse/paragraph levels in each case. These tests, which have their origins in the field of neurology but incorporate linguistic analysis, emphasize the classification of patients according to clinical aphasia syndromes (e.g., Broca's, Wernicke's, global, conduction).

Aphasia tests based on syndrome classification have been called into question in recent years for their inability to elucidate the underlying nature of the language disorder (Byng, Kay, Edmundson & Scott, 1990). An approach is evolving in which aphasic symptoms are investigated with reference to explicit models of language processing, as in Kay, Lesser & Coltheart's (1992) Psycholinguistic Assessments of Language Process-ing in Aphasia. This represents a hypothesis-testing approach to aphasia assessment, in which the investigator selects from a bank of 60 tasks to form a progressively more precise account of which components of the person's language processing system have become impaired. A more conventionally-structured test battery which shows the influence of theo-ries of underlying processing deficits (see, for example Caplan, 1992) is the Bilingual Aphasia Test (Paradis, 1987). This influence is particularly evident in the syntactic comprehension subtest.

A further strand in the development of approaches to assessment in aphasia has stemmed from the observation that performance on formal aphasia tests does not necessarily correspond with the ability to commu-nicate in naturalistic settings. Lesser & Milroy (1993) describe a range of procedures designed over the last 20 years to tap pragmatic aspects of language. Prominent among these has been Holland's (1980) standardized instrument for assessing communicative abilities in daily living.

CURRENT METHODS AND RESEARCH ISSUES

The assessment of speech and language disorders, whether for clinical or research purposes, comprises the collection of speech-language data from the speech therapy client or research subject(s), the application of scoring or analysis procedures to the data, and the presentation of the results in a form which promotes ease of interpretation. This section describes the main methods of assessment currently used, identifies their strengths and limitations, and discusses associated research issues.

Typically, clinical assessment includes a variety of data collection methods (both formal and informal), to sample a range of performance indicators from which to construct a representative profile. In research settings, more focused testing may be necessary. The selection of procedures in both cases is determined by the hypotheses the clinician or researcher aims to address.

Obtaining a Case History

Obtaining a comprehensive case history is a critical first step in the management of any client, whatever the nature of the disorder. Information from the case history is important in guiding the selection of assessment methods and in interpreting the results. This information can be gathered from a number of sources, including direct interview with the client or with others involved in their care or management, examination of the client's medical or educational files, and sometimes by the administration of topic-specific checklists or inventories of behaviours that can be completed either by the client or their family. This phase of the assessment is discussed by Darley & Spriestersbach (1978) and Chapey (1986). In research settings, the provision of sufficiently detailed case information is of great importance to the interpretation and generalizability of the results.

Test tasks

In clinical settings, tasks devised to assess various aspects of communication are administered in order to obtain a more comprehensive picture of the client's strengths and deficits than can be gained from interview alone. The tasks selected will usually reflect the investigator's theoretical perspective, either explicitly or implicitly. They may take the form of a published, standardized test, or they may be drawn from a variety of sources and grouped into an informal battery. In the former case, interpretations of scores will often be with reference to normative data supplied with the test. In research settings, the tasks will have been selected from published tests, or designed specifically by the investigator to elicit the type of data needed for the study.

Shipley & McAfee (1992) note that there are over 200 different formal tests for the assessment of speech and language disorders. They provide a list of publications which categorize and review substantial numbers of these. Thus there exists a vast array of individual tasks for assessing diverse aspects of speech/language performance, and the presumed underlying abilities. Lund & Duchan (1993) and Chapey (1986) survey the types of tasks found in tests designed for children and adults respectively. Tasks are at present almost all off-line, i.e. the response is made after language processing has taken place. However, the increased sophistication of personal computers has now made possible the development of on-line tasks, in which responses are made during processing.

The use of test batteries is subject to a number of limitations. In addition to time constraints, which are particularly stringent in clinical settings, further limitations may be imposed by client/subject characteristics such as distractibility, fatigue, and the presence of e.g. visual, motor or hearing problems. The interpretation of scores from norm-referenced tests raises the issue of the adequacy and appropriateness of the normative data provided. This is of particular concern in the use of tests across cultures because of the risk of bias and misdiagnosis. Enderby & Emerson (1995) cast doubt on the validity of precise characterizations of age-appropriate language use, and Peterson & Marquardt (1994) question the theoretical basis of some formal tests. These criticisms underline the importance of information from other sources against which to interpret performance on test tasks, and highlight the need for more rigorous research into testing procedures.

Spontaneous language samples

Methods for the collection of samples of spontaneous language have changed relatively little over the years, though the introduction of a discourse analytic approach has led to greater use of what Chapey (1986) terms "moderately structured spontaneous language observation", e.g., the elicitation of narratives, as distinct from the "unstructured observation" of communication in naturalistic contexts. Guidelines for collecting and recording samples are provided by Miller (1981). Recent research has focused on the outcome of different sampling procedures. Bain, Olswang & Johnson (1992) compared free-play with more structured sampling conditions, and found that the former yielded more types and tokens of the semantic relations under study. The usual practice of providing pictures and props for children to talk about is also called into question by Masterson & Kamhi (1991), who found with primary school children that the absence of these resulted in samples containing more complex sentences.

Methods of analysis of samples have been extended from simple counts, through profiling of performance at different linguistic levels (see Miller,

1981), to analysis of interactional aspects of language, e.g., conversational strategies used, and ways in which the interlocutor's communicative style influences these (Hansson & Nettelbladt, 1990). The depth of analysis possible in clinical settings is limited by time constraints, a point recognised by Crystal (1992, p. 2), whose linguistic profiles sought to provide "a compromise between the opposed demands of routine clinical practice and academic diagnostic research".

Instrumental measures

In recent years, instrumental methods have been used increasingly in the assessment of speech disorders. This has come about largely because of greater emphasis on a physiological interpretation of motor speech disorders and, at a more practical level, because of the easier access to sophisticated personal computers which facilitate the acquisition, analysis and storage of speech/language data.

The collection of physiological data on the structural and functional status of the various speech subsystems allows more direct evaluation of the underlying physiological support for speech than is possible using perceptual assessment alone. The advantage of instrumental approaches to assessment is that the clinician can more closely investigate the source of the speech problem and can quantify his/her observations in a highly detailed fashion. This in turn allows for more reliable and valid comparisons with normal performance (Peterson & Marquardt, 1994). In this way, instrumental assessment can address the limitations of perceptual assessment (i.e. its subjectivity and variability), by allowing the clinician to gather detailed information directly from the abnormal speech apparatus. In addition, collection of physiological data is useful for detecting possible interactions among the functional components of the speech production mechanism. A detailed, systematic, and preferably simultaneous, instrumental assessment of the multiple components of the speech production apparatus allows for more accurate diagnosis of the speech disorder, and for the development of specific and individual treatment plans (Higgins, Carney & Schulte, 1994).

Instrumental assessment is not without its limitations, however. There still exists only a limited physiological database from normal speakers with which to compare disordered performance. Further, the large variations that exist among normal speakers when instrumental measurements are taken of the structure and function of the motor speech production mechanism make diagnostic interpretations and decisions problematic when instrumental data alone are used. Best practice in assessment involves gathering data from a number of related sources (e.g., from instrumental assessments and perceptually-based test tasks) to give a comprehensive picture of the presenting disorder.

A major instrumental focus in the assessment of speech disorders has been on the assessment of the movements of the various speech structures (e.g., the respiratory muscles, larynx etc.) using strain-gauge, optical and electrical methods (such as electropalatography and electroglottography). As these structural movements induce volume changes and produce variations in air pressure and air flow, aerodynamic measurements of the speech stream are performed. Lastly, the emerging speech waveform is assessed instrumentally using acoustic analysis.

Structural movement

Strain-gauge transduction is used to monitor displacement of various speech structures, and operates on the principle that when a wire is stretched, it is reduced in diameter and increased in length, thus offering greater resistance to the flow of current. Strain-gauge transduction has been used in the assessment of the articulators (e.g., the jaw, soft palate and lips) and more recently, the muscles of respiration. Instrumental assessment using strain-gauge techniques has been shown to characterize more precisely the nature of the disturbed respiratory function in persons with Parkinson's disease than measures from a perceptually-based assessment. Specifically, patients rated with similar respiratory deficits on perceptual assessment were shown instrumentally to have quite different underlying respiratory disorders, which in turn had implications for the provision of appropriate and targeted treatment (Lethlean, Chenery & Murdoch, 1990).

Enhanced instrumental methods of assessment have also been shown to improve diagnostic accuracy. For example, the use of optical instruments such as videostrobolaryngoscopes that can view directly the structure and function of the vocal apparatus during speech was found to alter the diagnosis and treatment outcome by permitting the detection of subtle vocal fold pathology missed by conventional laryngoscopic techniques (Casiano, Zaveri & Lundy, 1992).

Air pressure/Air flow techniques

Various movements of the speech structures induce volume changes and produce variations in air pressure and air flow in the speech system. Of particular interest to the clinician are intraoral, intranasal, subglottic and atmospheric air pressure, and changes in flow across the glottis, the nasal cavity, and the oral cavity. Air flow measurements were compared with perceptual ratings of hypernasality in patients with dysarthria by Hoodin & Gilbert (1989). They found that the perceptual analyses were unable to differentiate between mildly and moderately hypernasal groups, even though instrumental assessment identified significantly different air flow rates between the two groups. Perceptually, the presence of hypernasality may have been masked by the disordered vocal characteristics of the dysarthric speakers. The instrumental assessment allowed a more direct measurement of velopharyngeal closure, without contamination from other disordered component systems.

Acoustic analysis

Acoustic analysis is a method of assessment that applies digital signal processing techniques to the analysis of the speech signal. Briefly, speech analysis systems convert an analog recording of speech into a digital waveform for purposes such as waveform capture and display, spectrogram generation, fundamental frequency analysis etc. (see Read, Buder & Kent, 1992 for a review and evaluation of seven current speech analysis systems).

Acoustic analysis, when used to assess the speech disorder in dysarthria, has been found to be more specific than perceptual assessment in identifying patterns of impairment associated with particular disorders. The perceptual assessment may be more useful for providing an overall indication of the severity of impairment, but detailed acoustic measures are able to highlight the differential patterns of impairment across dysarthria syndromes (Ludlow & Bassich, 1983, p. 141).

FUTURE DIRECTIONS

The field of speech and language disorders has in general been characterized by relatively little research into the assessment procedures themselves, the main exception to this being work concerned with the development of instrumental measures of motor speech functioning. As more fully articulated models of the functional architecture of the human speech/language processing system are proposed, however, methods of assessment are likely to become increasingly theory-driven. This has important implications for the management of people referred for speech therapy. It is widely accepted that the quality of clinical treatment is closely related both to the extent of theoretical knowledge and to the degree to which this can be used as the basis for reliable assessment procedures. Future developments in assessment methods are likely to focus on the use of profiles as distinct from global scores, the establishment of norms of speech/language variation, and the identification of reliable, sensitive and representative indices of speech/language impairment (Garman & Edwards, 1995).

The relationship between language and other cognitive domains, for example memory and attention, though more widely researched in recent times, remains unclear. This uncertainty affects our understanding of the relationship between developmental language impairment and cognitive development at one end of the age span, and of the effects on language abilities of generalized intellectual decline associated with age-related diseases at the other. Continued research into this assessment dilemma, using more sophisticated on-line and off-line methods, will help to separate out the influence of the various cognitive subsystems on language functioning.

Future progress will rest on the development of more precise, statistically-based assessments in which differential diagnosis and definitions of prognosis are founded on detailed analyses of the cognitive, linguistic and communicative patterns of large numbers of people with communication impairment. These advancements, combined with improved methods for capturing representative samples of naturalistic language, will provide a stronger foundation upon which the process of assessment can be based.

The University of Queensland, Australia

REFERENCES

Abbs, J.A. & De Paul, R.: 1989, 'Assessment of dysarthria: The critical prerequisite to treatment', in M.M. Leahy (ed.), *Disorders of Communication: The Science of Intervention*, Taylor & Francis, London, 206–277.

Adams, C. & Conti-Ramsden, G.: 1995, 'Developmental language disorders', in K. Grundy (ed.), *Linguistics in Clinical Practice*, Whurr Publishers, London, 313–328.

Bain, B.A., Olswang, L.B. & Johnson, G.A.: 1992, 'Language sampling for repeated measures with language-impaired preschoolers: Comparison of two procedures', *Topics in Language Disorders*, February 1992, 13–27.

Bloom, L. & Lahey, M.: 1978, *Language Development and Language Disorders*, John Wiley & Sons, New York.

Byers Brown, B. & Edwards, M.: 1989, *Developmental Disorders of Language*, Whurr Publishers, London.

Byng, S., Kay, J., Edmundson, A. & Scott, C.: 1990, 'Aphasia Tests Reconsidered', *Aphasiology* 4, 67–91.

Caplan, D.: 1992, *Language: Structure, Processing and Disorders*, MIT Press, Cambridge, MA.

Casiano, R.R., Zaveri, V. & Lundy, D.S.: 1992, 'Efficacy of videostroboscopy in the diagnosis of voice disorders', *Otolaryngology – Head and Neck Surgery* 107, 95-100.

Chapey, R.: 1986, 'The assessment of language disorders in adults', in R. Chapey (ed.), *Language Intervention Strategies in Adult Aphasia* (second edition), Williams & Wilkins, Baltimore, MD, 81–140.

Conti-Ramsden, G. & McTear, M.F.: 1995, 'Assessment of pragmatics', in K. Grundy (ed.), *Linguistics in Clinical Practice*, Whurr Publishers, London, 206–233.

Crystal, D.: 1989, *Introduction to Language Pathology* (second edition), Whurr Publishers, London.

Crystal, D.: 1992, *Profiling Linguistic Disability* (second edition), Whurr Publishers, London.

Crystal, D, Fletcher, P. & Garman, M.: 1989, *Grammatical Analysis of Language Disability: Studies in Disorders of Communication* (second edition), Cole and Whurr, London.

Darley, F.L., Aronson, A.R. & Brown, J.R.: 1975, *Motor Speech Disorders*, W.B. Saunders, PA.

Darley, F.L. & Spriestersbach, D.C.: 1978, *Diagnostic Methods in Speech Pathology* (second edition), Harper & Row, New York.

Davis, G.A.: 1983, *A Survey of Adult Aphasia*, Prentice-Hall, NJ.

Dodd, B.: 1995, 'Procedures for classification of subgroups of speech disorder', in B. Dodd (ed.), *Differential Diagnosis & Treatment of Children with Speech Disorder*, Whurr Publishers, London, 49–64.

Enderby, P. and Emerson, J.: 1995, *Does Speech and Language Therapy Work?: a Review of the Literature*, Whurr Publishers, London.

Garman, M. & Edwards, S.: 1995, 'Syntactic assessment of expressive language', in K. Grundy (ed.), *Linguistics in Clinical Practice* (second edition), Whurr Publishers, London, 134–166.

Goodglass, H. & Kaplan, E.: 1983, *Boston Diagnostic Aphasia Examination*, Lea & Febiger, PA.

Grunwell, P.: 1993, 'Assessment of articulation and phonology', in J.R. Beech, L. Harding & D. Hilton-Jones (eds.), *Assessment in Speech and Language Therapy*, Routledge, London, 49–67.

Grunwell, P.: 1995, 'Assessment of phonology', in K. Grundy (ed.), *Linguistics in Clinical Practice*, Whurr Publishers, London, 108–133.

Hansson, K. & Nettelbladt, U.: 1990, 'The verbal interaction of Swedish language-disordered pre-school children', *Clinical Linguistics and Phonetics* 4, 39–48.

Higgins, M.B., Carney, A.E. & Schulte, L.: 1994, 'Physiological assessment of speech and voice production of adults with hearing loss', *Journal of Speech and Hearing Research* 37, 510–521.

Holland, A.L.: 1980, *Communicative Abilities in Daily Living: A Test of Functional Communication for Aphasic Adults*, University Park Press, Baltimore, MD.

Hoodin, R.B. & Gilbert, H.R.: 1989, 'Parkinsonian dysarthria: An aerodynamic and perceptual description of velopharyngeal closure for speech', *Folia Phoniatrica* 41, 249–258.

Kay, J., Lesser, R. & Coltheart, M.: 1992, *Psycholinguistic Assessments of Language Processing in Aphasia (PALPA)*, Lawrence Erlbaum, Hove, East Sussex.

Kertesz, A.: 1979, *Aphasia and Associated Disorders: Taxonomy, Localization and Recovery*, Grune & Stratton, New York.

Kertesz, A.: 1982, *The Western Aphasia Battery*, Grune & Stratton, New York.

Kirk, S.A., McCarthy, J.J. & Kirk, W.D.: 1968, *Illinois Test of Psycholinguistic Abilities*, University of Illinois Press, Urbana, IL.

Lesser, R. & Milroy, L.: 1993, *Linguistics and Aphasia: Psycholinguistic and Pragmatic Aspects of Intervention*, Longman, London.

Lethlean, J.B., Chenery, H.J. & Murdoch, B.E.: 1990, 'Disturbed respiratory and prosodic function in Parkinson's Disease: A perceptual and instrumental analysis', *Australian Journal of Human Communication Disorders* 18, 83–98.

Ludlow, C.L. & Bassich, C.J.: 1983, 'The results of acoustic and perceptual assessment of two types of dysarthria', in W.R. Berry (ed.), *Clinical Dysarthria*, College-Hill Press, San Diego, CA, 121–154.

Lund, N.J. & Duchan, J.F.: 1993, *Assessing Children's Language in Naturalistic Contexts* (third edition), Prentice Hall, NJ.

Masterson, J.J. & Kamhi, A.G.: 1991, 'The effects of sampling conditions on sentence production in normal, reading-disabled, and language-learning-disabled children', *Journal of Speech and Hearing Research* 34, 549–558.

Miller, J.F.: 1981, *Assessing Language Production in Children: Experimental Procedures*, University Park Press, Baltimore, MD.

Netsell, R.: 1973, 'Speech physiology', in F.D. Minife, T.J. Hixon & F. Williams (eds.), *Normal Aspects of Speech, Hearing and Language*, Prentice Hall, NJ, 211–234.

Netsell, R., Lotz, W.K. & Barlow, S.M.: 1989, 'A speech physiology examination for individuals with dysarthria', in K.M. Yorkston & D.R. Beukelman (eds.), *Recent Advances in Dysarthria*, Little Brown & Co., Boston, MA, 3–37.

Paradis, M.: 1987, *The Assessment of Bilingual Aphasia*, Lawrence Erlbaum, Hillsdale, NJ.

Peterson, H.A. & Marquardt, T.P.: 1994, *Appraisal and Diagnosis of Speech and Language Disorders*, Prentice Hall, NJ.

Prutting, C.A. & Kirchner, D.M.: 1983, 'Applied pragmatics', in T.M. Gallagher & C.A. Prutting (eds.), *Pragmatic Assessment and Intervention Issues in Language*, College Hill Press, San Diego, CA, 29–64.

Read, C., Buder, E.H. & Kent, R.D.: 1992, 'Speech analysis systems: An evaluation', *Journal of Speech and Hearing Research* 35, 314–332.

Shipley, K.G. & McAfee, J.G.: 1992, *Assessment in Speech-Language Pathology: A Resource Manual*, Singular Publishing Group, San Diego, CA.

Templin, M.C.: 1957, *Certain Language Skills In Children*, Institute of Child Welfare Monograph Series No. 26, University of Minnesota Press, Minneapolis, MI.

Wertz, R.T.: 1991, 'Neuropathologies of speech and language: An introduction to patient management', in D.F. Johns (ed.), *Clinical Management of Neurogenic Communication Disorders* (second edition), Allyn and Bacon, Boston, MA, 1–96.

Section 3

The Quantitative and Qualitative Validation of Tests

LYLE F. BACHMAM AND DANIEL R. EIGNOR

RECENT ADVANCES IN QUANTITATIVE TEST ANALYSIS

A number of recent developments in the educational and language testing areas have brought about advances in quantitative test analysis, and three areas where these advances have taken place are discussed in this chapter. The first two of these areas have rich traditions, and the recent advances have involved refinements to these; the third area is new in nature and lacks the same solid tradition.

The first section of the chapter deals with recent advances in item response theory (IRT); these advances have been influenced by developments in the areas of performance assessment and computerized testing, particularly computerized adaptive testing (see the review by Gruber & Corbel in this volume). The second section, on advances in quantitative approaches to construct validation, can be viewed partly as a response to the call for a unified treatment of the concept of validity. This area has also been influenced by the movement to performance assessment. The final section deals with new advances in the development of ability descriptors, sometimes also called behavioral descriptors. This area has been influenced both by the performance assessment movement and by a growing dissatisfaction among test users about the level of information supplied by many current score scales.

RECENT ADVANCES IN ITEM RESPONSE THEORY APPLICATIONS

Early Developments

Item response theory (IRT), originally referred to as latent trait theory, was introduced in a unified format in the 1950s by Lord (1952, 1953), although a number of other researchers had previously worked on IRT-related issues. It was not until the 1970s, however, that IRT began to generate interest in the field of measurement. The summer 1977 special edition of the *Journal of Educational Measurement* on 'Applications of latent trait models' perhaps marked the beginning of this ascent to prominence. The late 1970s and the 1980s saw a proliferation of research studies on theoretical and applied IRT issues, and the beginnings of IRT-based research in the area of language testing.

C. Clapham and D. Corson (eds), Encyclopedia of Language and Education,
Volume 7: Language Testing and Assessment, 227–242.
© 1997 Kluwer Academic Publishers. Printed in the Netherlands.

Major Contributions

Hambleton (1989) provided a thorough review of the use of IRT in the field of education, and a number of language testing researchers (e.g., Henning 1987; Bachman 1990) have provided reviews of the use of IRT in the language area. Moreover, a variety of books can now be consulted for explicit development of the various IRT models and for discussions of related applications areas; noteworthy are books by Lord (1980), Hambleton & Swaminathan (1985), and Hambleton, Swaminathan & Rogers (1991). Most of the applications discussed in these books, however, are limited to the unidimensional IRT models for dichotomously (right/wrong) scored data. Examples of such models include the one parameter logistic (1-PL) or Rasch model and the more complicated two- and three-parameter logistic (2-PL, 3-PL) models. (See the review by Pollitt in this volume for a discussion of developments involving the Rasch one-parameter IRT model.) A number of computer programs for conducting 'standard' IRT analyses are now available, two of the most well-known of which are LOGIST (Wingersky, Barton & Lord, 1982) and BILOG (Mislevy & Bock, 1990).

Work in Progress

Recent developments in the area of computer-based testing, particularly computerized adaptive testing (CAT), and in the area of performance assessment have expanded or advanced the use of IRT models beyond straightforward implementations of the well known models for dichotomously scored data. General issues and developments in these two important areas of testing are discussed by Gruber & Corbel and by McNamara in this volume; this particular section will focus on the expanded IRT demands brought about by these developments.

Basic psychometrics for dealing with IRT-based CAT have existed in the literature since the 1980s (see Lord, 1980; Weiss, 1983). In these discussions, however, the role of test content in the CAT construction process has been given only minimal consideration. Test specifications were generally viewed as simple two-way grids or matrices of the underlying content by process dimensions, with the content subcategories typically listed along one axis and the process subcategories, such as the levels of Bloom's taxomony (see Bloom, 1956), listed on the other axis. The CAT procedure was then set up to work systematically through the cells of the grid in a cell by cell fashion, selecting a prespecified number of items from each of the cells subject to the additional stipulation that each item typically provide maximum IRT information at the current estimate of ability (see Kingsbury & Zara, 1989). Test specifications for many current tests are clearly not this simple (see Bachman & Palmer, 1996), thus necessitating a method for dealing with complex test specifications in the CAT construction process. A number of recent advances have applied linear programming techniques in the computer or automated assembly of paper-and-pencil forms (see Swanson & Stocking, 1993 and van der Linden 1987). A simple extension of these techniques allowed them to be applied in the construction of CATs (see Stocking & Swanson, 1993 and Eignor, Stocking, Way & Steffen, 1993). Typically, in the implementation of these procedures, content specifications are expressed as constraints, with specified upper and lower bounds on the number of necessary items in each CAT to satisfy each constraint. The statistical constraint on items, i.e., that they provide maximum information at the current ability estimate, can be expressed in a manner comparable to the other constraints. The algorithm for CAT item selection then attempts to minimize or maximize some function that explicitly incorporates these constraints. For example, the weighted deviations algorithm employed by Swanson and Stocking (1993) attempts to come as close as possible to meeting all specified constraints, including the constraint on IRT information, simultaneously. Other researchers have employed somewhat different approaches, with varying degrees of success.

What is new in these CAT construction procedures is not the application of new IRT models, but rather the explicit incorporation of other constraints besides statistical ones on the item selection process. Item selection is no longer 'optimal' in a statistical sense, but will now pattern what happens in reality with complex test specifications. These newly developed procedures have led to the implementation of CAT for a number of large-scale testing programs such as the Graduate Records Examination (GRE) General Test.

Unlike recent advances in the area of CAT, where well-known IRT models for dichotomously or right/wrong scored items are being used in new ways, the developments in the area of performance assessment have brought about implementations of certain IRT models not previously used to any great extent in the education and language testing areas. Typically, the extended constructed response items used in performance assessment tests, an example of which is the frequently used written essay, are polytomously scored, or scored in multiple ordered categories or levels from low to high, rather than simply right/wrong. Hence, with these items, the probability of an examinee reaching a specific score category or level needs to be described by an IRT model that is appropriate for such data, among which are the partial credit model (Masters, 1982) and its generalized version (Muraki, 1992), and the graded response model (Samejima, 1969; 1972). The generalized version of the partial credit model and the graded response model differ in the way the probability of reaching a particular score level is expressed in the model, while the generalized version of the partial credit model and the simpler partial credit model differ only in the number of item parameters used in determining the probability of reaching a particular score level. In addition, if the categories cannot be easily specified as being ordered, the nominal model (Bock, 1972) can be used. Hambleton (1989) and van der Linden & Hambleton (1996) provide greater detail on these models. Basically, these polytomous models are generalized from the dichotomous IRT models and reduce to the dichotomous models when there are only two response categories. This can most easily be seen with the partial credit and generalized partial credit models, which reduce to the Rasch model and two parameter logistic (2-PL) models, respectively, when there are two response categories (right or wrong). Linacre (1989) expanded the Rasch analog partial credit model for polytomously scored responses even further to deal with other effects or facets, such as, for instance, scorer or task effects. A computer program, FACETS (Linacre & Wright, 1992) is now available for performing these expanded sorts of analyses. These extensions to the partial credit model are covered in greater detail in the reviews by McNamara and Pollitt in this volume.

The polytomous IRT models have recently been successfully applied to data from a number of large-scale testing programs. For instance, the generalized partial credit model has been successfully used to calibrate complex exercises or tasks (i.e., estimate IRT parameters for the exercises) from the National Assessment of Educational Progress (NAEP, 1993). In addition, these models have been used in the concurrent calibration of both dichotomously scored and polytomously scored NAEP items, where the 3-PL model was used for the dichotomously scored items and the generalized partial credit model with the polytomously scored tasks. In such a concurrent calibration, the IRT parameters for both the dichotomously scored and polytomously scored items are estimated simultaneously in a single computer run. Tang and Eignor (1996) also successfully applied these models to concurrently calibrate combinations of items from the reading comprehension section of the Test of English as a Foreign Language (TOEFL) and the Test of Written English (TWE), and combinations of items from the TOEFL listening comprehension section and the Test of Spoken English (TSE). In both cases, the computer program PARSCALE (Muraki & Bock, 1993) was used, but other programs, such as MULTILOG (Thissen 1988), are also available for calibration purposes.

One notable feature of the Tang & Eignor (1996) study was the way in which the authors treated listening and reading passages and their associated items as 'testlets'. Wainer & Kiely (1987) were the first to propose the use of testlets, primarily to deal with item position and context effects in CAT. Wainer & Lewis (1990) expanded on Wainer & Kiely's initial work and discussed the use of a testlet approach for dealing with sets of items related to a single passage. In such a situation, the IRT assumption of local independence is likely to be violated if the individual item is considered to be the unit of analysis (see Yen, 1993). The assumption of local independence postulates that an examinee's responses to the items on a test are independent if the examinee's ability level is taken into account (see Hambleton, 1989). Of concern here is whether the responses of a specific examinee to a set of items based on a single passage can be viewed as independent. If the items are considered as a set, or testlet, and analysis done at that level, using one of the polytomous IRT models, then violations of local independence based on the structure of a passage item set can be avoided. Tang & Eignor (1996) used the generalized partial credit model to analyze the testlet data, although certain of the other models are also suitable.

Problems and Difficulties

As IRT is applied to more complex content domains, using models for either dichotomous or polytomous data, violations of the underlying uni-dimensionality assumption (i.e., that a single underlying ability or trait explains performance on a set of items) of the commonly used IRT models are bound to occur. This will necessitate either: 1) study of the robustness of the unidimensional models to violations of the unidimensionality assumption, so as to understand the consequences of employing the simple models with the more complex data; or 2) switching to existing multi-dimensional IRT (MIRT) models, where multiple underlying abilities are needed to explain performance on a set of items, or, more likely, developing new MIRT models. Van der Linden & Hambleton (1996) have provided a review of existing MIRT models and Tang (1995) has reviewed these models in the context of language performance tasks. The MIRT models have yet to be implemented to any great extent in the educational and language testing areas.

Likely Future Directions

Tests modeled on theories of communicative language ability (see Bachman 1990 and Bachman & Palmer 1996) are likely to employ test tasks that have characteristics corresponding to language use tasks that examinees normally perform in authentic or realistic situations, and such tests are likely to build in dependencies among tasks or exercises. For instance, an examinee might be asked to read a passage, answer some questions about the passage, and then use the content of the passage to write an essay. Clearly, the dependencies between the reading and writing tasks violate the underlying local independence assumption of all IRT models, as well as classical test theory models (see Yen, 1993). For instance, if an examinee receives a low essay score, it is impossible to determine whether the examinee has poor writing skills, poor reading skills, or is weak in both areas. Further, a multidimensional IRT model with underlying separate reading and writing dimensions or abilities will not account for this data. A new test theory will thus be needed to handle such dependencies. In the area of language testing, Mislevy (1995) has started the explication of such a theory, based on the use of Bayesian inference networks. Beland & Mislevy (1996) have initiated similar developments in the educational area. This approach, while still in its infancy, would appear to hold great promise for future language testing endeavors that will make use of linked performance tasks.

RECENT ADVANCES IN QUANTITATIVE APPROACHES TO CONSTRUCT VALIDATION

Overview

Construct validation (CV) is the process of building a case that supports a given interpretation or use of test scores, and involves examining both the evidence that supports a given interpretation and the ethical values that provide a basis or justification for that use (Messick 1989). CV thus involves both logical argumentation, and the collection of evidence, for which a variety of qualitative and quantitative approaches are typically used. (See the review by Banerjee and Luoma in this volume for a discussion of qualitative approaches.) The evidence that is relevant to CV is that which pertains to the various factors that affect test scores, and these include the construct we want to measure (e.g., language ability), other characteristics of individuals (e.g., cultural background, background knowledge) that may affect their test performance but which are not part of the construct we want to measure, and aspects of the measurement procedure or process itself (e.g., different items or tasks, different raters). (Procedures for dealing with aspects of the measurement process are discussed in the review of generalizability theory by Bachman in this volume.) To support a given score interpretation, we need to provide evidence that scores on our test are primarily a function of the ability we want to measure, and this takes the form of investigating *convergence*, or the degree to which our test scores agree with other indicators of the same construct. At the same time, we need to provide evidence that our test scores are relatively unaffected by factors other than the construct we want to measure, and this involves demonstrating *divergence*, or the degree to which indicators of other constructs tend not to agree with our test scores.

Within quantitative approaches to CV, one can identify a wide variety of specific designs and analytic techniques, ranging from experimental and quasi-experimental designs to *ex post facto* correlational designs. In recent years, with the view that language ability is a multicomponential construct, and with the increasing use of complex performance assessment tasks, the feasibility of employing experimental designs has decreased and researchers have moved more and more to the use of *ex post facto* correlational designs. The advantage of this approach is that it permits the researcher to investigate the relationships among a relatively large number of variables in a single study. Of the analytic procedures used with correlational designs, we will focus on two that have been widely used in recent years: factor analysis, both exploratory and confirmatory, and structural equation modeling, which includes as a subset the confirmatory factor analysis techniques. These procedures have been used to investigate the nature of the constructs measured, the effects on test scores of other factors, and the relationships among these factors and the constructs to be measured.

Methods for Investigating the Underlying Nature of the Constructs Measured

Work in this area has essentially taken place in two related, yet in some ways distinct, directions: 1) investigations involving the relationship between scores on a particular instrument or test and scores on other measures intended to measure the same construct or constructs and 2) investigations of the internal relationships among the items that constitute a particular instrument or test. For the first area, where test-level data are used, there is a well-established linear factor analytic tradition and an associated array of procedures for looking at relationships. For the second area, where item-level data are used, the tradition and array of procedures have been evolving over the past 40 years, and only recently have theoretically sound non-linear factor analytic procedures been put into place.

Factor Analysis of Scores from Several Different Tests

When working with test-level data, the relationships between the test scores being analyzed and the underlying traits are assumed to be linear, and any of a variety of established procedures for performing linear factor analysis are applicable. If little is known about the structure underlying the data, the factor analysis can be done in a purely exploratory fashion; this is usually referred to as exploratory factor analysis (EFA). Issues involved in the application of EFA include determining how many factors to specify in a given factor solution and how best to 'rotate' the resulting factor solution so that the results can best be interpreted. A wide variety of books of varying levels of technical sophistication can be consulted on EFA. In addition, a variety of procedures for performing EFA are offered in available statistical packages.

If somewhat more is known about the underlying structure of the data, perhaps by conducting one or more EFAs, then the linear factor analysis can conducted in a confirmatory fashion; this is referred to as confirmatory factor analysis (CFA). CFA procedures are, as mentioned above, a subset of structural equation modeling procedures. McDonald (1983; 1985) has provided a good explanation of the differences between EFA and CFA. Usually CFA is done by expressing the expected relationship among underlying variables or factors directly in a factor loading matrix, and then assessing the fit of the specified model to the data. Further details on fit can be found below in the section on structural equation modeling. A variety of computer programs for performing CFA and structural equation modeling are available; perhaps most noteworthy are LISREL (Jöreskog & Sörbom, 1993) and EQS (Bentler, 1992). For an example of factor analysis of test-level data in the language testing area, see Bachman, Davidson, Ryan & Choi (1994).

Item-level Factor Analysis

Working with dichotomously scored item-level data, as would be the case when investigating the underlying relationship or relationships among multiple-choice items on a test, is a bit more complex than working with test-level data, in that the relationship between the item scores and the underlying factors or traits will need to be modeled in a non-linear fashion. McDonald & Ahlawat (1974) have pointed out that a linear regression would be inappropriate for use with item/factor regressions because these regressions have to be non-linear given the bounded nature of the dichotomous or right/wrong data (which can range only between 0 and 1) and the unbounded metric for the underlying factor or factors. Indeed, it is for this very reason that the normal ogive or logistic curves of IRT (see Hambleton, 1989) have been used with item/factor regressions.

There is a long history of attempts to analyze dichotomously scored item-level data through the linear factor analysis of item phi or tetrachoric correlation matrices, and an equally long history of resulting artifactual or spurious, uninterpretable factors in the factor solution, due to item difficulty or guessing (see Cook, Dorans & Eignor, 1988; Mislevy, 1986; Carroll, 1983). Recently, more theoretically preferable approaches have been developed that attempt either to model the non-linear relationship between item score and underlying trait (or traits) directly in an IRT-like fashion, or model the relationships in a closely approximative fashion (i.e., fit curves/surfaces that have the same general shapes as IRT curves/surfaces, but are less complex mathematically). An example of the former is the IRT-based approach of Bock & Aitkin (1981), which has been operationalized for multiple dimensions in the computer program TESTFACT (Wilson, Wood, & Gibbons, 1984). Mislevy (1986) has provided a good review of this approach and the related approach attributable to Muthén (1978; 1984). An example of the latter approach can be found in the computer program NOHARM (Fraser, 1983; Fraser & McDonald, 1988) which makes use of harmonic analysis to approximate the modeling of multiple dimensions done by multidimensional IRT models. Frequently the non-linear approaches just discussed have been implemented in the CFA tradition. See Schedl, Gordon, Carey, & Tang (1996) for an example of a CFA application to reading comprehension data that makes use of NOHARM. Also, see Davidson (1988) for a more general application of factor analysis of item-level data in the language testing area.

For a variety of reasons, not the least of which is the need for a good deal of technical sophistication, researchers have encountered problems when working with these non-linear factor analysis procedures and programs. For instance, TESTFACT is not a particularly good procedure to use with either long tests or tests with a fairly large number of hypothesized factors (Mislevy, 1986). To simplify matters some researchers have been using 'linearization procedures' with the dichotomously scored item-level data. This involves the creation of testlets, with from 5–7 unique items in each testlet. Testlets thought to measure the same underlying dimension are grouped together, and then balanced to have the same level of average difficulty. This approach is based on the assumption that when the item scores are added together, or aggregated, to form testlet scores, a linear factor analytic model is again appropriate. Earlier work by Cattell (1974) provides some justification for the approach; an application of the approach in the context of CFA with LISREL can be found in Cook et al. (1988). This approach, while being very ad hoc in nature, has proved over a number of applications to be a reasonable procedure for use in the analysis of dichotomously scored item-level data from tests made up of substantial numbers of items.

Structural Equation Modeling

Structural equation modeling (SEM) is an analytic procedure that enables the researcher to simultaneously investigate relationships between observed variables (measures) and unobserved variables (factors) and relationships among factors, thus combining the advantages of multiple linear regression and factor analysis. Some measures and factors can be treated as dependent (endogenous) and some as independent (exogenous), so that in addition to enabling the researcher to investigate the factor structure that may underlie the measures in a given study, SEM also provides the means for specifying and investigating directional effects among the factors. In applying SEM, the researcher typically follows five steps: 1) model specification, 2) model identification, 3) parameter estimation, 4) testing model-data fit, and 5) respecifying the model (Bollen & Long 1993b).

The researcher begins by specifying, on the basis of substantive theory, a model in which hypothesized relationships among measures and factors are explicitly stated in terms of mathematical formulae. A structural equation model typically includes two types of components, the measurement component, consisting of one or more measurement models that specify the relationships between the measures and factors with which they are associated, and the structural model, which specifies the relationships among the factors. Any given model will include a number of parameters that will need to be estimated: 1) variances for the measures, factors and error terms in the model, 2) factor loadings and uniquenesses for the different measures, and 3) covariances (correlations or path coefficients) among the different factors in the model. Next, the researcher determines whether the model is identified, or whether unique estimates of the parameters in the specified model can be estimated. Appropriate indicators of the measures in this model are then collected, the covariances or correlations among them are computed, and the parameters of the model are estimated. Next, the hypothetical model is tested statistically to determine how well it explains or 'fits' the relationships among the observed measures in the study. The last step in applying SEM typically involves respecifying the model, on the basis of both substantive theory and fit statistics provided by the modeling program. This then leads to the iterative application of estimation, checking model fit and respecification, until at least one model that fits the sample data reasonably well and in which all the parameters are substantively meaningful and interpretable is obtained (Jöreskog 1993).

The estimation of model fit and the determination of what constitutes a 'reasonable' model fit has been at the same time one of the most controversial areas in SEM and one of the most productive, in terms of recent developments. While SEM was originally developed as an alternative to experimental designs for testing hypotheses about causal relationships among large numbers of variables, it is now much more commonly used as a means for generating and refining explanatory models (Jöreskog, 1993). Thus, in addition to single indicators of 'global' model fit, researchers now have access to a wide variety of statistical indicators for the fit of individual parameters in a given model. The recent proliferation of fit statistics has been valuable in that it has provided researchers with a variety of approaches to estimating model and parameter fit, and hence the potential for utilizing specific fit statistics that are appropriate to a given model. At the same time, few specific criteria for deciding whether or not a given model fits, or for choosing the 'best' fitting model from among several that may be acceptable on both substantive and statistical grounds, have been provided. As a result, the current 'state of the art' in model fit consists largely of 'rules of thumb' and analytic strategies; many of these are discussed in papers in a collection by Bollen & Long (1993a).

Structural equation modeling has seen a number of applications in the area of language assessment. Studies that have investigated relationships among various personal characteristics and performance on language tests include Fouly (1985), who investigated the differential effects of instrumental and integrative motivation on test performance, Sasaki (1993), who looked at the relationships among second language proficiency, language aptitude and intelligence, Kunnan (1995), who investigated the differential effects of type of exposure and monitoring on language test performance, and Purpura (1996), who investigated the effects of the use of cognitive and metacognitive strategies on language test performance.

Difficulties and Likely Future Directions

The quantitative approaches to construct validation discussed above require considerable technical expertise on the part of the researcher, generally involve the collection of a large number of measures for a large number of individuals, and hence may present problems with feasibility in some situations. At the same time, the potential of these approaches, particularly SEM, for expanding our understanding of the various factors – language ability, personal characteristics, characteristics of the test tasks and procedure – that affect test scores, as well as the different processes that are involved in test performance, make it one of the most promising tools in the construct validation arsenal. One area that is particularly promising is that of modeling the effects of the content characteristics of test tasks on test takers and their test performance. A number of studies utilizing less powerful statistical procedures have already provided valuable insights in this area, and these form the basis for the specification of structural models that could include data from both the content analysis of test tasks and self-reports by test takers. To date, a large number of factors and processes that may affect test performance and test scores have been investigated, but only on a piecemeal basis. With the application of SEM, it should be possible to investigate virtually all these major factors and processes in a single structural model. Given the current consensus in the field of language assessment that all of these factors and processes are interrelated, continued research using SEM would appear to be a clear future direction.

RECENT ADVANCES IN THE GENERATION OF ABILITY DESCRIPTORS

Different areas of language ability are frequently assessed through the use of a variety of task formats, ranging from multiple-choice and short completion items to free-response tasks, and composite scores are typically derived by simply aggregating the item and task scores. For example, with the Advanced Placement (AP) Language Examinations, composite scores are derived by aggregating combinations of multiple-choice item scores and free response section scores. With such aggregate scales, a frequently asked question has been how to characterize exactly an examinee's ability at a particular score level. For instance, it might be asked what verbal skills an examinee with a Scholastic Assessment Test (SAT) verbal score of 450 has or has not mastered.

A number of analytical procedures have been developed or are in the process of being developed for attempting to attach proficiency descriptors to scores on scales that were not specifically constructed to yield such interpretations. The first such approach to be implemented was an IRT-based scale anchoring approach with the scales for the National Assessment of Educational Progress (NAEP). This approach, which is described in detail by Beaton & Allen (1992), was designed specifically to be used for the group-based score interpretations provided by the NAEP approach. With this procedure, diagnostic descriptors are generated by 1) identifying subsets of test items that provide superior discrimination at successive points on the test's reported score scale; and 2) asking subject-area experts to review the items and provide descriptions of the specific skills that groups of examinees at the selected score points (called anchor points) would be expected to have mastered. Forsyth (1991) criticized this approach, arguing that descriptors of what students at the anchor points can do must be limited to content areas that are not broadly defined or are not multi-dimensional. This criticism is very similar to the concern expressed by Bachman & Palmer (1996) about attempts to use global scales of language ability, which often appear multidimensional in nature, in assessing language ability through writing or speaking tasks. The NAEP scale anchoring approach, with some modification, has subsequently been applied by Educational Testing Service (Kirsch, Jenkins, Jungeblut, & Kolstad, 1993) and the Organization for Economic Corporation and Development (1995) to scales for both the national-and international-based Adult Literacy studies. As with NAEP, the scales for these studies were designed to be used for group-based score interpretations.

Recently, work in providing proficiency descriptors has been applied to scales designed to foster individual-based score interpretations, such as the scales for the SAT. A number of different procedures are being looked at, such as the rule space methodology, originally developed by Tatsuoka (1983) for cognitive diagnosis and classification (see Tatsuoka, Birenbaum, Lewis, & Sheehan, 1993). Another approach being investigated is a tree-based regression approach described by Sheehan (1996). These procedures are being tried experimentally with data from a number of testing programs. While results appear promising, it may be some time before test developers are comfortable using the resulting proficiency descriptors to actually characterize individual examinees' levels of ability.

University of California
Los Angeles, USA

and

Educational Testing Service, Princeton
New Jersey, USA

REFERENCES

Bachman, L.F.: 1990, *Fundamental Considerations in Language Testing*, Oxford University Press, Oxford.

Bachman, L.F., Davidson, F., Ryan, K. & Choi, I-C.: 1994, *An Investigation into the Comparability of Two Tests of English as a Foreign Language: The Cambridge-TOEFL Comparability Study*, Cambridge University Press, Cambridge.

Bachman, L.F. & Palmer, A.: 1996, *Language Testing in Practice*, Oxford University Press, Oxford.

Beaton, A.E. & Allen, N.L.: 1992, 'Interpreting scales through scale anchoring', *Journal of Educational Statistics* 17, 191–204.

Beland, A. & Mislevy, R.J.: 1996, 'Probability-based inference in a domain of proportional reasoning tasks', *Journal of Educational Measurement* 33, 3–27.

Bentler, P.M.: 1992, *EQS Structural Equations Program Manual*, BMDP Statistical Software, Inc., Los Angeles, CA.

Bloom, B.D.: 1956, *Taxonomy of Educational Objectives: Handbook I, Cognitive Domain*, David McKay Company, Inc., New York.

Bock, R.D.: 1972, 'Estimating item parameters and latent ability when responses are scored in two or more nominal categories', *Psychometrika* 37, 29–51.

Bock, R.D. & Aitkin, M.: 1981: 'Marginal maximum likelihood estimation of item parameters: Application of an EM algorithm', *Psychometrika* 46, 443–459.

Bollen, K.A. & Long, J.S.: 1993a, *Testing Structural Equation Models*, Sage Publications, Newbury Park, CA.

Bollen, K.A. & Long, J.S.: 1993b, 'Introduction', in K.A. Bollen & J.S. Long (eds.), *Testing Structural Equation Models*, Sage Publications, Newbury Park, CA, 1–10.

Carroll, J.B.: 1983, 'The difficulty of a test and its factor composition revisited', in S. Messick and H. Wainer (eds.), *Principals of Modern Psychological Measurement*, Lawrence Erlbaum Assoc., Hillsdale, NJ, 257–282.

Cattell, R.B.: 1974, 'Radial parcel factoring versus item factoring in defining personality structure in questionnaires: Theory and experimental checks', *Australian Journal of Psychology* 26, 103–119.

Cook, L.L., Dorans, N.J. & Eignor, D.R.: 1988, 'An assessment of the dimensionality of three SAT-verbal test editions', *Journal of Educational Statistics* 13, 19–43.

Davidson, F.: 1988, *An Exploratory Modeling Survey of the Trait Structures of Some Existing Language Test Data Sets*, unpublished Ph.D. Dissertation, University of California, Los Angeles, Los Angeles, CA.

Eignor, D.R., Stocking, M.L., Way, W.D. & Steffen, M.: 1993, *Case Studies in Computer Adaptive Test Design Through Simulation*, Research Report 93-56, Educational Testing Service, Princeton, NJ.

Forsyth, R.A.: 1991, 'Do NAEP scales yield valid criterion-referenced interpretations?', *Educational Measurement: Issues and Practice* 10, 3–9, 16.

Fouly, K.: 1985, *A Confirmatory Multivariate Study of the Nature of Second Language Proficiency and its Relationships to Learner Variables*, unpublished Ph.D. dissertation, University of Illinois at Urbana-Champaign, Urbana, IL.

Fraser, C.: 1983, *NOHARM: An IBM PC Computer Program for Fitting Both Unidimensional and Multidimensional Normal Ogive Models of Latent Trait Theory*, The University of New England, Armidale, Australia.

Fraser, C. & McDonald, R.P.: 1988, 'NOHARM: Least squares item factor analysis', *Multivariate Behavioral Research* 23, 267–269.

Hambleton, R.K.: 1989, 'Principles and selected applications of item response theory', in R.L. Linn (ed.), *Educational Measurement*, 3rd Ed., American Council on Education and Macmillan Publishing, New York, 147–200.

Hambleton, R.K. & Swaminathan, H.: 1985, *Item Response Theory: Principles and Applications*, Kluwer Publishing, Boston, MA.

Hambleton, R.K., Swaminathan, H. & Rogers, H.J.: 1991, *Fundamentals of Item Response Theory*, Sage Publications, Newbury Park, CA.

Henning, G.: 1987, *A Guide to Language Testing: Development, Evaluation, Research*, Newbury House, New York.

Jöreskog, K.G.: 1993, 'Testing structural equation models', in K.A. Bollen & J.S. Long (eds.), *Testing Structural Equation Models*, Sage Publications, Newbury Park, CA, 294–316.

Jöreskog, K.G. & Sörbom D.: 1993, *LISREL 8: User's Reference Guide*, Scientific Software International, Chicago, IL.

Kingsbury, G.G. & Zara, A.R.: 1989, 'Procedures for selecting items for computerized adaptive tests', *Applied Measurement in Education* 2, 359–375.

Kirsch, I.S., Jenkins, L., Jungeblut, A. & Kolstad, A.: 1993, *Adult Literacy in America: A First Look at the Results of the National Adult Literacy Survey*, National Center for Educational Statistics, Washington, DC.

Kunnan, A.J.: 1995, *Test Taker Characteristics and Test Performance: A Structural Modeling Approach, Studies in Language Testing 2*, Cambridge University Press, Cambridge.

Linacre, J.M.: 1989, *Many-Faceted Rasch Measurement*, MESA, Chicago, IL.

Linacre, J.M. & Wright, B.D.: 1992, *A User's Guide to Facets: Rasch Measurement Computer Program*, MESA, Chicago, IL.

Lord, F.M.: 1952, *A Theory of Test Scores*, Psychometric Monograph No. 7, Psychometric Society.

Lord, F.M.: 1953, 'The relation of test scores to the trait underlying the test', *Educational and Psychological Measurement* 13, 517–548.

Lord, F.M.: 1980, *Applications of Item Response Theory to Practical Testing Problems*, Lawrence Erlbaum Assoc., Hillsdale, NJ.

Masters, G.N.: 1982, 'A Rasch model for partial credit scoring', *Psychometrika* 47, 149–174.

McDonald, R.P.: 1983, 'Exploratory and confirmatory factor analysis', in S. Messick & H. Wainer (eds.), *Principals of Modern Psychological Measurement*, Lawrence Erlbaum Assoc., Hillsdale, NJ, 197–213.

McDonald, R.P.: 1985, *Factor Analysis and Related Methods*, Lawrence Erlbaum Assoc., Hillsdale, NJ.

McDonald, R.P. & Ahlawat, K.S.: 1974, 'Difficulty factors in binary data', *British Journal of Mathematical and Statistical Psychology* 27, 82–99.

Messick, S.: 1989, 'Validity', in R.L. Linn (ed.), *Educational Measurement*, 3rd Ed., American Council on Education and Macmillan Publishing Company, New York, 13–103.

Mislevy, R.J.: 1986, 'Recent development in the factor analysis of categorical variables', *Journal of Educational Statistics* 11, 3–31.

Mislevy, R.J.: 1995, 'Test theory and language-learning assessment', *Language Testing* 12, 341–369.

Mislevy, R.J. & Bock, R.D.: 1990, *BILOG 3: Item Analysis and Test Scoring with Binary Logistic Models*, Scientific Software, Mooresville, IN.

Muraki, E.: 1992, 'A generalized partial credit model: Application of an EM algorithm', *Applied Psychological Measurement* 16, 159–176.

Muraki, E. & Bock, R.D.: 1993, *PARSCALE: IRT Based Test Scoring and Item Analysis*, Scientific Software, Chicago, IL.

Muthén, B.: 1978, 'Contributions to factor analysis of dichotomous variables', *Psychometrika* 43, 551–560.

Muthén, B.: 1984, 'A general structural equation model with dichotomous, ordered categorical, and continuous latent variable indicators', *Psychometrika* 49, 115–132.

National Assessment of Educational Progress: 1993, *NAEP 1992 Technical Report*, Educational Testing Service, Princeton, NJ.

Organization for Economic Competition and Development: 1995, *Literacy, Economy, and Society: Results of the First International Adult Literacy Survey*, Author, Paris.

Purpura, J.E.: 1996, *Modeling the Relationships between Test Takers' Reported Cognitive and Metacognitive Strategy Use and Performance on Language Tests*, unpublished Ph.D. dissertation, University of California, Los Angeles, Los Angeles, CA.

Samejima, F.: 1969, *Estimation of Latent Ability Using a Response Pattern of Graded Scores*, Psychometric Monograph No. 17, Psychometric Society.

Samejima, F.: 1972, *A General Model for Free Response Data*, Psychometric Monograph No. 18, Psychometric Society.

Sasaki, M.: 1993, 'Relationships among second language proficiency, foreign language aptitude, and intelligence: A structural equation modeling approach', *Language Learning* 43, 313–344.

Schedl, M., Gordon, A., Carey, P.A. & Tang, K.L.: 1996, *An Analysis of the Dimensionality of TOEFL Reading Comprehension Items*, Research Report 95-27, Educational Testing Service, Princeton, NJ.

Sheehan, K.M.: 1996, *A Tree-Based Approach to Proficiency Scaling*, Educational Testing Service, Princeton, NJ.

Stocking, M.L. & Swanson, L.: 1993, 'A method for severely constrained item selection in adaptive testing', *Applied Psychological Measurement* 17, 277–292.

Swanson, L. & Stocking, M.L.: 1993, 'A model and heuristic for solving very large item selection problems', *Applied Psychological Measurement* 17, 151–166.

Tang, K.L.: 1995, *Multidimensional IRT Models and Their Potential Application to TOEFL 2000*, Report Prepared for TOEFL 2000 Project, Educational Testing Service, Princeton, NJ.

Tang, K.L. & Eignor, D.R.: 1996, *Concurrent Calibration of Dichotomously and Polytomously Scored TOEFL Items Using IRT Models*, Educational Testing Service, Princeton, NJ.

Tatsuoka, K.K.: 1983, 'Rule space: An approach for dealing with misconceptions based on item response theory', *Journal of Educational Measurement* 20, 345–354.

Tatsuoka, K.K., Birenbaum, M., Lewis, C. & Sheehan, K.M.: 1993, *Proficiency Scaling Based on Conditional Probability Functions for Attributes*, Research Report 93-50-ONR, Educational Testing Service, Princeton, NJ.

Thissen, D.: 1988, *MULTILOG*, Scientific Software, Mooresville, IN.

van der Linden, W.: 1987, *IRT-based Test Construction*, University of Twente, Enschede, The Netherlands.

van der Linden, W. & Hambleton, R.K.: 1996, *Handbook of Modern Item Response Theory*, Springer-Verlag, New York.

Wainer, H. & Kiely, G.L.: 1987, 'Item clusters and computerized adaptive testing: A case for testlets', *Journal of Educational Measurement* 24, 195–201.

Wainer, H. & Lewis, C.: 1990, 'Toward a psychometrics for testlets', *Journal of Educational Measurement* 27, 1–14.

Weiss, D.J.: 1983, *New Horizons in Testing: Latent Trait Theory and Computerized Adaptive Testing*, Academic Press, New York.

Wilson, D., Wood, R.L., & Gibbons, R.: 1984, *TESTFACT: Test Scoring and Item Factor Analysis*, Scientific Software, Chicago, IL.

Wingersky, M.S., Barton, M.A. Lord, F.M.: 1982, *LOGIST User's Guide*, Educational Testing Service, Princeton, NJ.

Yen, W.M.: 1993, 'Scaling performance assessments: Strategies for managing local item dependence', *Journal of Educational Measurement* 30, 187–213.

ALASTAIR POLLITT

RASCH MEASUREMENT IN LATENT TRAIT MODELS

Rasch models are the only class of statistical models that, rather than seeking to describe data, seek instead to implement the principles required by measurement theorists. In everyday measurement we can measure accurately enough for any normal purpose without difficulty, even if the *trait* in question is *latent*. An example would be temperature: we cannot see it directly, but we can 'observe' it by eliciting its effect on an enclosed volume of mercury. But the link between a latent mental trait like *ability* or *proficiency* and a student's performance is less exact, and the uncertainties involved force us to adopt statistical, or probabilistic, approaches. The methods pioneered by Georg Rasch try to maintain the logical rigour of scientific measurement in these problematic circumstances. (See van der Linden, 1994 for an excellent discussion of this issue).

This article considers the essential principles that distinguish Rasch models for mental measurement from other test models and will indicate the growing variety of Rasch models for different kinds of language testing data. It will not consider numerical problems in estimating model parameters, important though these are, as they are essentially general to all statistical modelling.

ORIGINS

In 1951 Rasch was invited to analyse a set of reading tests that had been used across an ability range too wide to be spanned by a single test – in other words to construct a scale for measuring reading ability that would be independent of any particular test that might be used. One test method involved counting the number of errors made by children reading aloud, and Rasch noticed that, within reasonable limits, the *ratios* of errors made on two texts were constant for all children. Thus if one child made half as many errors on Text A as another child did, then they made half as many on *any* text. As he described it (Rasch, 1960/1980), 'the test cancelled out', and it was tempting to say that the first child was twice as good a reader as the second, so generalising across all the texts, and to all other similar texts. This success with text based tests led Rasch to seek a model for the more common sorts of tests made up of many questions, hoping that the question could be cancelled out in a similar way, thus defining 'ability', and that the student could be cancelled out to define question 'difficulty'. In its simplest form, the model he constructed was:

C. Clapham and D. Corson (eds), *Encyclopedia of Language and Education,*
Volume 7: Language Testing and Assessment, 243–253.
© *1997 Kluwer Academic Publishers. Printed in the Netherlands.*

$$\text{odds} = \frac{\text{person ability}}{\text{question difficulty}} = \frac{B_n}{D_i}$$

The odds that person n will get question i correct are the ratio of n's ability to i's difficulty. For convenience this is generally transformed logarithmically:

$$\log \text{odds}_{ni} = \text{ability}_n - \text{difficulty}_i = b_n - d_i \qquad (1a)$$

Equation 1a is the fundamental statement of the simple Rasch model for *dichotomous* questions, i.e. questions that are marked either right or wrong, and are worth one mark each.

To see how the all important cancelling out happens, consider a second equation, that describes what may happen when a different person m tries the same question:

$$\log \text{odds}_{mi} = b_m - d_i \qquad (1b)$$

On the left hand sides of these two equations are probability statements, while on the right hand sides are the differences between parameters, the measurements we are seeking. Since the two sides of Equation 1b are equal, we can subtract them from the corresponding sides of Equation 1a, without disturbing the equality. This gives:

$$\begin{aligned} \log \text{odds}_{ni} - \log \text{odds}_{mi} &= b_n - d_i - (b_m - d_i) \\ &= b_n - d_i - b_m + d_i \\ &= b_n - b_m \end{aligned}$$

The difficulty parameters, d_i, cancel out and we are left with a direct comparison of two people's abilities *with no reference to* a particular question. From data provided by question i we get an estimate of the relative ability of the two people; this can be repeated with the other questions in the test, *and will give more or less the same answer.* This separability of the person and question parameters is the defining feature of Rasch models; it makes possible objective, or 'instrument free', measurement of person abilities.

During the same period, Lawley, Lord and others developed an alternative Item Response Theory (IRT), a strictly mathematical attempt to model in a sample free way the properties of items that test developers traditionally used (Lord & Novick, 1968). The simplest of their models is mathematically identical to the Rasch model in Equation 1a but this exclusive concern for *items* is so alien to Rasch's principle of *simultaneous* definition and measurement of ability and difficulty, or the essential symmetry of the facets, that it is inappropriate to include Rasch models under the term 'IRT'. Strictly the general class should be Latent Trait models, with two subsets, Rasch models and IRT models, which overlap only in the simplest case. Nevertheless, many authors do use 'IRT' as a name for the general class, and talk of Rasch and non-Rasch IRT models. (For more about IRT see the review by Bachman and Eignor in this volume.)

MAJOR CONTRIBUTIONS

The main credit for popularising Rasch's work is due to Benjamin Wright, through publications, computer programs and students who studied Rasch models with him. The dichotomous model of Equation 1a was described in Wright & Stone (1979), together with descriptions of estimation procedures and the BICAL program, and advice on item banking. In a second book, Wright & Masters (1982) described extensions of this model to polytomous data (questions worth more than one mark) – Andrich's Rating Scale model (Equation 2) and the Partial Credit model (Equation 3):

$$\textbf{log odds}_{nik} = \textbf{ability}_n - \textbf{difficulty}_i - \textbf{threshold}_k = b_n - d_i - t_k \quad (2)$$
$$\textbf{log odds}_{nik} = \textbf{ability}_n - \textbf{difficulty}_{ik} \qquad\qquad = b_n - d_{ik} \qquad (3)$$

Note that in these formulations both i and k refer to questions. In a dichotomous question there are two possible score categories, 0 and 1, and the question's difficulty parameter indicates how difficult it is to score 1 rather than 0. When a question has more than two possible scores it needs more than one difficulty parameter to separate them, and the set of parameters are called the *thresholds* between score categories. A question worth three marks has four possible scores, 0, 1, 2 and 3, and three thresholds will be needed to record the difficulty of scoring 1 rather than 0, the difficulty of scoring 2 rather than 1, and the difficulty of scoring 3 rather than 2.

In the Rating Scale model (Andrich, 1978a), a single set of threshold parameters is estimated for all questions, and questions are only allowed to differ in *overall* difficulty. This model was developed for attitude questionnaires, where categories like 'Strongly disagree', 'Disagree', and so on are used for every question, but it may fit well when, for example, multiple ratings are made of elements of speaking proficiency using a fixed common rating scale. Compared to this the Partial Credit model is slightly weaker, or less restrictive, since every item is allowed to have its own unique internal structure. This model will fit many data sets better than the Rating Scale one, and will probably be more appropriate if a test contains multiple mark questions that each have their own marking scheme, or when ratings are made of a piece of writing with different sets of descriptors for each scale. An example may be found in Pollitt & Hutchinson (1987), where three scales derived from Canale & Swain (1980) were used to assess performance in each of five writing tasks. Although similar rating scales were used in every case, the data did not fit the Rating Scale very well, and the Partial Credit model was used instead; the conclusion is that the raters perceived the common scale differently in different applications. These two models, and further elaborations of the Partial Credit model due to Glas & ver Helst (1991) and Linacre are currently implemented in several programs, including BIGSTEPS (Wright & Linacre, 1991).

Linacre (1989) extended the models further, to include sorts of data that these could not analyse, by introducing a third *facet* to the analysis, of great importance to language testers. Typically this facet recognises that a student's score in some tests depends on their ability, the tasks' difficulty or difficulties, *and* the relative severity of a rater. The model now is:

$$\log \text{odds}_{nik} = \text{ability}_n - \text{difficulty}_i - \text{threshold}_k$$
$$-\text{severity}_r = b_n - d_i - t_k - s_r \qquad (4)$$

for a Rating Scale, or a similarly extended version of Equation 3 for a Partial Credit scale. These models are implemented in the program FACETS. The many-facet model is the most widely applicable Rasch model currently in use (see, for example, McNamara, 1996); further facets can be added if appropriate to deal with many aspects of the data. For example, repeated measures can be analysed by adding an 'occasions' facet or, in a survey, subjects' membership of various sub-populations (sex, age, etc.) can be similarly modelled. Interactions between facets can be analysed, leading to studies of bias or 'differential item functioning'. In sum, FACETS can effectively carry out Rasch equivalents of many forms of the analysis of variance as used in experimental research.

In Europe, meanwhile, the mathematical bases of Rasch models were explored by several researchers. Of considerable importance was the proof by Andersen (1977) that Rasch models are the only latent trait models for which it is possible to use a simple summary of the data (such as the number of right answers) to estimate the ability or difficulty. In IRT models, for example, it is always necessary to use all of the data to estimate ability, because a student's ability estimate depends on which questions they get right and wrong, so that two students will get *different* ability estimates, even if they get the *same* score by different combinations of right and wrong answers. In technical terms, 'number right' (usually called raw score) is a sufficient statistic for estimating ability *only* in Rasch models. It is worth noting that this result thus implies that every time we use traditional test scores in reporting students' abilities, we are in effect assuming that the data fit a Rasch model.

Fischer & Kisser (1983) introduced a Rasch model for analysing 'time latency' or speed of response which is beginning to find applications in psycholinguistic research and is potentially applicable to measuring some kinds of language ability, such as vocabulary knowledge or listening proficiency.

In practice, important developments in Rasch testing have been closely bound up with the growth of *item banking*, an activity in which hundreds or thousands of questions are prepared in advance for test construction. Many workers have contributed here, but the important contributions in theory of Choppin (1978) and Masters (1984) and in practice of the North West Evaluation Association and Portland Public Schools should be noted.

The best comprehensive introduction to the principles of Rasch measurement is still Wright and Stone (1979). Readers who would like a briefer but very clear and simple introduction to the principles as applied to language testing might refer to Baker (1997).

WORK IN PROGRESS

New Rasch models continue to appear. In general, they extend one or other of those described above to new kinds of data, and are still being explored. Since it has been referred to already, we shall begin with the many-facet model.

Equation 4, or its Partial Credit equivalent, is increasingly being used in the development of speaking and writing tests. Traditionally, the subjective element in judgements has been considered only as a source of measurement error, and so as something to be minimised, in a vain attempt to achieve objective ratings of performance. When a test was administered there was no accurate way to control rater effects short of getting every rater to rate every student. In the many-facet model subjectivity is instead treated as a necessary element in the process, just like another source of difficulty; since some raters are more severe than others their severity is treated as another parameter to be estimated, one parameter for each rater. A student's score depends on their ability *and* the task's difficulties *and* the rater's severity. It is then the responsibility of the testing agency to decide what to do about raters who are too severe or too lenient. Several agencies are experimenting with the operational use of FACETS.

Rasch theory has also been applied to Thurstone paired comparison data. In this methodology, judges are required to choose between two objects (such as test performances) and to declare one of them as 'better' than the other (Thurstone, 1927). Thurstone showed that if judges make many such choices a scale can be constructed for measuring how 'good' each object is. Several authors have remarked on the similarities between the approaches of Rasch and Thurstone – the important point being that the forced choice 'cancels out' the judge (Andrich, 1978b). Thus even if a judge is unusually severe in all his or her ratings, this does not affect their judgement of which is the better of two performances, and the data can be used to construct a Rasch scale. Pollitt & Murray (1996) illustrate this method in studying the process of judging speaking proficiency. Linacre (1995) has described an extension of the procedure that allows the judge to say that two performances are equal. An important new application of this methodology is in *maintaining* standards between different forms of a test that involves subjective judgements (as in school examinations in England).

The standard Partial Credit model runs into trouble when there are more than about eight marks in a question. In order to estimate the full set of question difficulties there must be at least one student in every category, so that somebody scores 0, somebody 1, and so on up to at least one student scoring full marks. In language testing this often does not happen: raters do not often award 0 or full marks to a written essay. Andrich, Sheridan, & Lyne (1991) provide a solution with their program ASCORE; it uses a clever indirect way of estimating where all the thresholds will be (technically, it estimates the mean, standard deviation and other features of the distribution of the difficulties rather than the actual values themselves).

Verhelst, Glas & Verstralen (1994) offer the program OPLM which allows test developers to specify different discrimination parameters for different sets of items; although it is arguable whether this is true to the spirit of Rasch measurement, sufficient statistics certainly exist for ability and difficulty, and the ideal estimation procedures can be used. This model may prove useful in those cases where different types of items must, for linguistic or educational reasons, be included in a single test.

In practical testing, as opposed to research and test development, the major applications of Rasch are undoubtedly in item banking and computerised adaptive testing. Since the initial suggestions in Wright & Stone (1979), many groups have worked on developing Rasch based item banks. Basically, items are pre-tested, and then trialled in 'tests' that each contain some set of anchor items taken from the pre-existing bank. Rasch analysis constructs a unique scale within each test, and these are then adjusted so that the anchor items have the same difficulty on the new scale as on the old. The new items have then been *calibrated* on to the established bank scale. The scale is the essential feature of the bank, and it exists independently of any particular question or set of questions. Items may be deleted or added without, it is assumed, altering it significantly. This has several implications.

First, any set of questions can be selected to measure the latent trait, so that different tests may be given simultaneously, or on different occasions, to different groups of students, but the measurements made will all be expressed on a common scale. Where tests consist only of dichotomous items the design of ideal tests for different groups and purposes is very easy with Rasch calibration, though it becomes more complex if polytomous questions are used; Timminga & Adema (1994) provide solutions for designing ideal tests in this case, using the mathematical techniques of linear programming.

Second, for agencies running regular testing programmes, the test development cycle can be optimised, as questions are calibrated whenever convenient, instead of by fixed deadlines. The impact of this systematisation on work practices and on the quality of the resulting tests should not be underestimated.

Third, a Rasch calibrated bank provides an ideal resource for adaptive testing. A computer administers a test to a student, estimating his or her ability at each step and picking the most suitable next item; with Rasch again this choice is trivial, as the best item is the one whose difficulty is closest to the current ability estimate. This form of testing seems bound to become much more common soon. (For more about computerised adaptive testing, see Gruba and Corbel's review in this volume.)

A rather different kind of item bank has been developed by Griffin, Smith & Burrill (1995). Rather than test questions, the items are descriptors of behaviour that indicates a student's development in reading, writing, listening or speaking. The resulting scales are used by teachers; they score a student on the set of indicators, generating a diagnostic profile for monitoring students' progress. North (1996) is developing similar scales for use in second language learning in Switzerland. In these, descriptors are being translated across English, German and French, and the consistency with which teachers of the various L1/L2 combinations order them is being used to create equivalent scales for different contexts.

PROBLEMS AND DIFFICULTIES

Rasch models are *strong* statistical models; that is they use as few parameters as possible to explain the data to which they are applied. In the 1970s a common area of contention concerned data from multiple choice tests. The Rasch model of Equation 1a frequently fitted poorly, and analysis showed clearly that the misfit was concentrated amongst low ability candidates tackling high difficulty items. Opponents argued that this showed the need for a 'guessing' item parameter, while proponents retorted that only poorly designed tests would encourage random guessing. Some textbooks advise that when data and model do not fit, progressively weaker models (such as IRT-2, IRT-3 or IRT-4) should be tried until the fit is adequate. The Rasch approach, in contrast, argues that we are not free to abandon the logic of measurement to achieve model/data concordance, and that this kind of misfit indicates problems with the procedures used to gather data.

But it is often the most theoretically approved task types that cause the biggest misfit problems. For example, Taylor developed a reading test explicitly to reflect recent developments in psycholinguistic understanding of the language comprehension process. The resulting test was found to violate the local independence assumption essential to all test models: people seemed to become more able each time they got an answer right, and less able each time they got one wrong (Pollitt & Taylor, 1996). It seems that a good comprehension test is not just a set of items but, to some extent, an integrated activity, and therefore *must* misfit.

A partial solution to problems of this kind may be the use of the poly-tomous models referred to earlier (Masters, 1987), with associated items grouped into *testlets*, but estimation problems can become very difficult, and huge samples may be required, if the testlets have more than about 6 marks. (For more about testlets, see Bachman and Eignor's review in this volume.) The OPLM program (see above) may provide another an-swer. But it is clear that the wishes of language testers to utilise novel forms of assessment will continue to stretch the ingenuity of measurement researchers to develop suitable Rasch measurement forms of analysis.

In practice, the most difficult issues to deal with are often the extent to which the results can be generalised. Rasch's claim that estimates of difficulty and ability were *specifically objective*, draws attention to the fact that their sample-free properties only hold within a specified domain of similar tasks and people. *Objective* refers to the sample-free nature of estimates and derives from the 'cancelling out' property, but *specific* is meant to indicate that this only works within limits, and it is up to testers to check that objectivity holds when their tests are applied. For example, it is often difficult to know in advance whether pre-test estimates of question difficulty obtained from local second language learners are accurate enough for standardising tests to be used in other countries. We do know that some grammar items vary in difficulty for learners with different first languages (eg Ryan & Bachman, 1992), but for each application of Rasch calibration the limits of safe generalisability need to be determined by experience.

FUTURE DIRECTIONS

In application, it is clear that the use of Rasch models in item banking and computer-aided testing will dominate interest in coming years. Rasch measurement is intended to be a scientific activity of constructing scales whose value will increase as they are used more widely than in single tests; indeed Rasch analysis for an isolated test offers little that cannot be gleaned from sensitive application of traditional methods. Computer marking is being developed to include more complex item types, as in the parsing scheme of Jones (1994); with time these too will be added to item banks, and we can expect applied linguists to be more willing to use computer administered tests than they are at present.

Certain problems are evident, and research will continue to address issues of the generalisability of measures, and the stability of item calibrations across sub-populations and across contexts. One vexing issue is the difficulties that accompany vertical equating of tests, where two tests are designed to cover different ranges of ability but must be linked to each other – ironically the very problem that prompted Rasch to develop his first 'Rasch model'. Several researchers have noted distortions in the extremes of the scale when language proficiency tests of different levels are joined end to end.

Judging by the most recent conference presentations, the greatest interest is currently in exploring applications of the many-facet model. When such a general model is proposed and made easy to use through a convenient program, time is needed to understand its power and, no doubt, limitations. One obvious gap as far as language testers are concerned, is an extension to the many-faceted model that can handle the large essay scales that Andrich's two-facet model is designed for.

Construct Researchers investigating the nature of test constructs have begun to utilise regression techniques (Stenner et al, 1983) and a componential Rasch model (Fischer & Kisser, 1983; Scheiblechner, 1979), to investigate the underlying features that cause question difficulty. Research like this will lead to better understanding of the meaning of the measures we make. A good example in language testing is the work by de Jong & Glas (1987) in constructing a consistent scale for measuring second language listening proficiency.

New models will doubtless continue to be developed for other data types, and research will continue into the relationship of Rasch models to other statistical techniques. For example, in Schumacker (1996) there are four articles outlining a Rasch alternative to exploratory factor analysis.

Many researchers are developing the Rasch approach to scientific method. The emphasis on theory, philosophy, and the fundamentals of measurement mean that many Rasch practitioners are concerned with justifying their activities to an extent unparalleled in mental measurement research. Interested readers can keep up with developments by contacting the Rasch Measurement Special Interest Group of the American Educational Research Association via MESA Press, Chicago.

University of Cambridge
Local Examination Syndicate, UK

REFERENCES

Andersen, E.B.: 1977, 'Sufficient statistics and latent trait models', *Psychometrika* 42, 69–81.
Andrich, D.: 1978a, 'Scaling attitude items constructed in the Likert tradition', *Educational and Psychological Measurement* 238, 665–680.
Andrich, D.: 1978b, 'Relationships between the Thurstone and Rasch approaches to scaling', *Applied Psychological Measurement* 2, 449–460.

Andrich, D., Sheridan, B. & Lyne, A.: 1991, *ASCORE: Manual of Procedures*, Murdoch University, Perth WA.

Baker, R. (1997) *Classical Test Theory and Item Response Theory in Test Analysis*, Special Report 2, Language Testing Update, Department of Linguistics, Lancaster University, Lancaster, England.

Canale, M. & Swain, M.: 1980, 'Theoretical bases of communicative approaches to second language teaching and testing', *Applied Linguistics* 1, 1–47.

Choppin, B.H.: 1978, *Item banking and the monitoring of achievement*, National Foundation for Educational Research, Slough, England.

de Jong, J.H.A.L. & Glas, C.A.W.: 1987, 'Validation of listening comprehension tests', *Language Testing* 4, 170–194.

Fischer, G.H. & Kisser, R.: 1983, 'Notes on the exponential latency model and an empirical application', in H. Wainer & S. Messick (ed.), *Principles of Modern Psychological Measurement*, Lawrence Erlbaum Associates, Hillsdale NJ, 139–158.

Glas, C.A.W. & ver Helst, N.D.: 1991, *Using the Rasch Model for Dichotomous Data for Analysing Polytomous Responses*, Measurement & Research Department Report 91-3, CITO, Arnhem, The Netherlands.

Griffin, P., Smith, P.G. & Burrill, L.E.: 1995, *The American Literacy Profile Scales*, Heinemann, Portsmouth, NH.

Jones, N.: 1994, *An Item Bank for Testing English Language Proficiency*, Unpublished PhD thesis, University of Edinburgh.

Linacre, J.M.: 1989, *Many-facet Rasch Measurement*, MESA Press, Chicago, IL.

Linacre, J.M.: 1995, 'Paired comparisons with ties: Bradley-Terry and Rasch', *Rasch Measurement Transactions* 9, 425.

Lord, F.M. & Novick, M.R.: 1968, *Statistical Theories of Mental Test Scores*, Addison-Wesley, Reading, MA.

McNamara, T.: 1996, *Measuring Second Language Performance*, Longman, London.

Masters, G.N.: 1984, 'Constructing an item bank using partial credit scoring, *Journal of Educational Measurement* 21, 19–32.

Masters, G.N.: 1985, 'Common-person equating with the Rasch model, *Applied Psychological Measurement* 9, 73–82.

Masters, G.N. & Evans: 1987, 'Banking non-dichotomously scored items', *Applied Psychological Measurement* 10, 355–367.

North, B.: 1996, *The Development of a Common Framework Scale of Descriptors of Language Proficiency Based on a Theory of Measurement*, Unpublished PhD thesis, Thames Valley University, London.

Pollitt, A.B. & Hutchinson, C.J.: 1987, 'Calibrating graded assessments: Rasch partial credit analysis of performance in writing', *Language Testing* 4, 72–92.

Pollitt, A.B. & Murray: 1996, 'What raters really pay attention to', in M. Milanovic & N. Saville (eds), *Studies in Language Testing*, Cambridge University Press, Cambridge.

Pollitt, A.B. & Taylor, L.B.: 1996, 'The reading process and reading assessment', Paper presented at Language Testing Research Colloquium, Tampere, Finland.

Rasch, G.: 1960, *Probabilistic Models for some Intelligence and Attainment Tests*, The Danish Institute of Educational Research, Copenhagen. (Expanded edition, 1980, University of Chicago Press, Chicago IL.)

Ryan, K.E. & Bachman, L.F.: 1992, 'Differential item functioning on two tests of EFL proficiency', *Language Testing* 9, 12–29.

Scheiblechner, H.: 1979, 'Specifically objective stochastic latency mechanisms', *Journal of Mathematical Psychology* 19, 18–38.

Schumacker, R.E. (ed.): 1996, *Structural Equation Modelling* 3, 1.

Stenner, A.J., Smith, M. & Burdick, D.S.: 1983, 'Toward a theory of construct definition', *Journal of Educational Measurement* 20, 305–317.

Thurstone, L.L.: 1927. 'A law of comparative judgement', *Psychological Review* 34, 278–286.
Timminga, E. & Adema, J.J.: 1994, 'Test construction from item banks', in G.H. Fischer & I.W. Molenaar (eds), *Rasch Models: Foundations, Recent Developments, and Applications*, Springer-Verlag, New York.
van der Linden, W.J.: 1994, 'Fundamental measurement and the Fundamentals of Rasch Measurement', in M. Wilson, (ed.), *Objective Measurement: Theory into Practice: Volume 2*, Ablex, Norwood, NJ.
Verhelst, N.D., Glas, C.A.W. & Verstralen, H.H.F.M.: 1994, *OPLM: Computer Program and Manual*, CITO, Arnhem.
Wright, B.D. & Linacre, J.M.: 1991, *BIGSTEPS*, MESA Press, Chicago, IL.
Wright, B.D. & Masters, G.N.: 1982, *Rating Scale Analysis*, MESA Press, Chicago, IL.
Wright, B.D. & Stone, M.: 1979, *Best Test Design*, MESA Press, Chicago, IL.

LYLE F. BACHMAN

GENERALIZABILITY THEORY

One of the perennial problems in measurement is that of estimating the relative effects of different sources of variation on test scores. One approach to this problem is generalizability theory (G-theory), which was developed by Cronbach and his colleagues in the 1960s and 70s (Cronbach, Gleser, Nanda, & Rajaratnam, 1972), and which has since had a number of proponents both in educational measurement (e.g., Brennan, 1983; Shavelson & Webb, 1991) and in language testing (e.g., Bolus et al., 1982, Bachman, 1990). G-theory has found applications in a wide range of language assessment situations, such as tests consisting of heterogeneous subsets of items, ratings of different components of language ability based on written compositions and oral interviews, and ratings of the content characteristics of test items. (Shavelson & Webb (1991) provide an excellent discussion of G-theory that is at an introductory level whilst being both technically sound and complete. Their text includes numerous examples, with data sets and output from the BMDP 8V computer program.)

G-theory constitutes a theoretical framework and set of procedures for specifying and estimating the relative effects of different factors on test scores. The G-theory model conceptualizes a person's performance on an assessment task as a function of several different factors, or *facets*, which can include the components of language ability to be measured as well as the characteristics of the assessment procedure. In a test consisting of a number of different items, for example, the facet of the measurement procedure that is of interest would be that associated with differing levels of item difficulty. In a writing test that includes multiple prompts, or tasks, and multiple raters, the two facets of interest are those associated with tasks of varying difficulties, and raters of varying severity. G-theory thus enables test users to distinguish different sources of score variance – language ability, facets of the measurement procedure and random errors – and to estimate their relative effects on test scores. In addition, G-theory provides a means for estimating the reliability – referred to as generalizability or dependability in G-theory – of measures associated with different sets of facets, and for both norm-referenced (NR) and criterion-referenced (CR) decisions.

C. Clapham and D. Corson (eds), Encyclopedia of Language and Education,
Volume 7: Language Testing and Assessment, 255–262.
© 1997 Kluwer Academic Publishers. Printed in the Netherlands.

GENERAL CONCEPTS

In developing or selecting a set of assessment tasks, the test user will define the components of language ability about which she wants to make inferences. Furthermore, because the test developer will want these inferences to generalize to situations other than the test tasks themselves, she will identify and describe a specific domain of non-test language use to which she wants her inferences about language ability to generalize. The conditions in this target language use domain can be described in terms of sets of characteristics, and these, in turn, define the *universe of generalization* for a given assessment. In the writing test example above, the test developer will describe the two facets – prompts and raters – as sets of characteristics of tasks and raters, respectively. These characteristics can be used as a basis for developing assessment tasks and selecting raters whose characteristics, or conditions of measurement, correspond to language use tasks and readers in the target language use domain. These characteristics also provide the basis for defining the specific conditions of measurement for these assessment tasks, and define a *universe of admissible observations*, any of which the test user is willing to accept for purposes of making inferences or decisions. For the writing test example, the test developer may specify that for the prompt facet she is willing to accept any prompt taken from a large number of possible prompts, while for raters, she will accept only raters from a finite pool of trained raters. In this case, the facet for prompts is considered to be *random*, since it includes an indefinite number of conditions, while rater facet is *fixed*, since it includes a specific number of conditions.

If one could obtain scores for a given individual on all measures in the universe of admissible observations, and then calculate the mean of these, or the *universe score*, this would be considered the most generalizable indicator of that individual's language ability. In the real world, however, we can only obtain scores from a limited sample of measures, and so we need to be able to estimate the *dependability* of a given observed score as an estimate of the universe score. If the universe score can be taken as the best indicator of an individual's ability, then dependability pertains to the degree to which inferences from the observed score are generalizable to the universe of generalization specified by the test developer or user. Thus, although dependability is often considered to be the G-theory analogue of classical psychometric reliability, it is a very different kind of concept. Whereas classical reliability pertains essentially to the consistency of measures, or observed scores, dependability pertains more directly to the generalizability of the inferences we make on the basis of observed scores. The G-theory concept of dependability thus subsumes classical reliability and provides a mechanism for treating considerations of reliability directly within the framework of construct validity.

In the majority of assessment situations, the *object of measurement* is an individual. However, because of the symmetry among facets in G-theory, any facet can be specified as the object of measurement, depending on the purpose of the particular study (Cardinet, Tourneur & Allal, 1981). In a study to investigate the consistency of ratings of test content, for example, test items were considered the object of measurement and test takers and raters as the facets (Bachman, Davidson, Ryan & Choi, 1991; Bachman, Davidson & Milanovic, 1996). The principle of symmetry thus makes it possible to extend G-theory to the investigation of a wide range of assessment questions.

PROCEDURES

There are two stages in applying G-theory to test development. First, the developer conducts a generalizability study (G-study), whose purpose is to estimate the effects of the various facets in the measurement procedure. Considering the uses that will be made of the test scores, the test developer designs the G-study so that the conditions that define the universe of admissible observations are clearly specified and distinguishable. In the writing example, the prompt facet might be defined in terms of a specific set of characteristics, such as topic, purpose and intended audience, while the rater facet might be defined in terms of relevant education or training and prior experience in teaching writing or in rating writing samples. Sample data for estimating the relative effects of the different facets are then collected through pretesting. On the basis of a G-study, the developer can estimate the magnitude of the *variance components* associated with each facet in the G-study design as well as with the interactions among the facets. In a study to investigate variability in speaking tasks and in rater judgments, for example, Bachman, Lynch & Mason (1995) specified the following G-study variance components in their design: 1) persons (the object of measurement), 2) raters, 3) tasks, and 4) the two-way interactions between persons by raters, persons by tasks and raters by tasks. In addition to these, there is always a variance component that includes the interaction among all of the facets, along with random error. The magnitudes of variance components reflect different scales of measurement, so that only their *relative* magnitudes, expressed as percentages of the total variance, can be interpreted. In the above example, relatively large variance components could be interpreted as follows: *persons* (differences in individuals' speaking ability); *tasks* (differences in difficulty of tasks); *raters* (differences in severity among raters). A relatively large variance component for the task by rater interaction would indicate that different raters are rating the different tasks differently. A large variance component for the person by task interaction would indicate that some tasks are differentially difficult for different groups of test takers, and this may be a source of bias. Similarly, a relatively large variance component for the person by rater interaction would indicate that some raters score the performance of different groups of test takers differently, and this could be an indication of rater bias. On the basis of the G-study, the test developer may revise the assessment procedure so as to minimize the effects of the relevant sources of measurement error.

In the second stage, the test developer conducts a *decision study* (D-study), the purpose of which is to design an optimal measure for the interpretations or decisions that are to be made on the basis of test scores. In conducting a D-study, the test developer can either collect new data from a large representative sample of test takers or use the G-study variance components to estimate the population values for the different sources variation in the design. For the D-study, the test developer will need to specify the following: 1) universe of generalization, and 2) the type of interpretation or decision to be made, and 3) the minimum acceptable level of dependability. The universe of generalization will be specified in terms of the conditions that defined the G-study universe of admissible observations, and may include all or a limited set of these conditions. In the writing example above, the numbers of tasks and raters specified for the D-study may be the same as or smaller than the numbers included in the G-study. Thus, if five prompts and three raters were used in the G-study, the D-study could include any number of prompts from one through five and any number of raters from one through three. The decision to be made can be either relative or absolute, while the types of interpretations associated with these decision types are criterion-referenced and norm-referenced, respectively. In specifying the minimum acceptable level of dependability, the test developer will need to consider the importance of the decision to be made and the number of individuals likely to be affected by the decision, the complexity of the construct to be measured, and the degree of comparability, in terms of task characteristics, of the tasks included.

Several estimates of dependability can be obtained from the D-study. The *generalizability coefficient* (G coefficient) provides an estimate of the proportion of an individual's observed score that can be attributed to his universe score, taking into consideration the effects of the different conditions of measurement specified in the universe of generalization. While G coefficients are appropriate for NR interpretations or decisions, an analogous index, the phi coefficient, that is appropriate for CR uses, can also be obtained. Another indicator of dependability, the signal-noise ratio, developed by Brennan and Kane (1977), provides a direct comparison between the error variance and the universe score variance, and can be interpreted as an indicator of the relative precision of the measure (Brennan 1983). As with the G coefficient and the phi coefficient, signal-noise ratios can be obtained for both NR and CR uses. Although all of these coefficients can be calculated directly by hand, once the relevant variance components have been estimated, using a standard computer program for statistics (e.g., BMDP 8C, SAS VARCOMP, or SPSS ANOVA), the availability of a special-purpose computer program (GENOVA, Crick & Brennan, 1983) that provides estimates for variance components and several different estimates of dependability has led to the increased use of G-theory by language testing practitioners.

In designing a D-study for the above example, the test developer might specify that she would be willing to generalize over a range of two to five tasks and from two to three raters. In setting these ranges, the test developer will consider both the target level of dependability and the resources that are available, with the intention of selecting the combination of tasks and raters that optimizes dependability and costs. It might turn out that the same level of dependability could be achieved in one of two ways: either with two tasks and three raters or with four tasks and two raters. Depending on the relative costs associated with developing and administering multiple tasks as opposed to the costs of multiple ratings, the developer may find that one of these two combinations is more efficient than the other.

PROBLEMS AND SOLUTIONS

Some of the problems that have been associated with G-theory derive from the use of the analysis of variance (ANOVA) model to estimate variance components. One problem is that estimating variance components with ANOVA requires designs that are complete (i.e., all interactions specified) and that are balanced, or orthogonal, with respect to nesting. In a test of reading, for example, in which several reading passages are presented, and each has associated with it a number of test items, the facet for items is nested within the facet for passage. Similarly, in a writing test in which each of several raters scores several compositions, the facet for compositions would be nested within that for raters. In cases such as these, which are quite common in language testing, in order to use ANOVA to estimate the variance component for the passage or the rater facet, the numbers of items for each passage, or compositions for each rater, respectively, would need to the same. This often imposes an unreasonable limitation, since it may not always coincide with the test developer's design, and it prevents the inclusion of cases with missing data. A second problem is that ANOVA-based estimates of variance components are sometimes negative, which often indicates a misspecification of the design model, and which is problematic for interpretability. The use of restricted maximum likelihood estimation provides a solution to both of these problems (Marcoulides, 1987). A third problem is that because variance components are essentially indicators of group performance, G-theory has provided little information at the level of individuals. This is particularly problematic in the context of performance assessment, where the test developer is often interested in diagnosing problems with individual tasks or individual raters. A recent extension of G-theory developed by Marcoulides and Drezner (1996) overcomes this limitation by providing a means for estimating indices for individual conditions within a given facet (e.g., tasks or raters) and for plotting these as two-dimensional coordinates for ease of interpretation.

NEEDS AND FUTURE DIRECTIONS

In both educational assessment and language assessment, current thinking and practice have moved away from the view that the abilities we want to measure consist of relatively unidimensional traits, to a view of ability as sets of interrelated cognitive processes. Multivariate G-theory models are well-developed that can specify multiple abilities, and provide estimates of variance components associated with these, as well as with the interactions among these and facets of the measurement procedure. Marcoulides (1996) describes how estimates of these can be obtained using a covariance structure analysis approach with standard structural modeling programs such as LISREL (Jöreskog & Sörbom 1993) and EQS (Bentler 1992). However, as with the ANOVA approach to estimating variance components, multivariate G-theory is unlikely be widely used by practitioners until the development of computer programs that facilitate its application to practical test development issues.

Another potential of G-theory that has not been fully realized in practical applications in that of optimizing resources with respect to dependability. Quite often the information that is available for this, from a D-study and from a cost analysis of various facets in the measurement procedure, is used in a fairly unsystematic and imprecise way to arrive at a decision for optimal test design. Recent work in optimization, however, provides a means for much more systematic and precise estimates of optimization alternatives (e.g., Marcoulides, 1993).

Recent extensions of G-theory make it particularly applicable to current thinking and practice in performance assessment, in which the abilities to be measured are seen as complex and the assessment tasks used are multifaceted. (For more about performance testing see McNamara's review in this volume.) The capability of multivariate G-theory for handling multiple abilities and multiple facets of the assessment procedure make it particularly applicable to investigating multiple components of language ability and the interactions among these and facets of the assessment procedure. The development of a model and procedures for investigating sources of error at the level of individual conditions within the facets of measurement means that G-theory will be useful for investigating multiple sources of error in a given measure at two levels: 1) the group level, to provide information on the general effects of different facets, and 2) the individual level, to provide diagnostic information for refinements in the assessment procedure, such as revising individual tasks or retraining or replacing individual raters. Finally, given the increased resources typically required by performance assessment tasks, the use of optimization models and procedures based on G-theory is likely to become an increasingly critical step in the test development process.

University of California
Los Angeles, USA

REFERENCES

Bachman, L.F.: 1990, *Fundamental Considerations in Language Testing*, Oxford University Press, Oxford.

Bachman, L.F., Davidson, F. & Milanovic, M.: 1996, 'The use of test method characteristics in the content analysis and design of EFL proficiency tests', *Language Testing* 13, 125–150.

Bachman, L.F., Davidson, F., Ryan, K. & Choi, I-C.: 1991, *An Investigation into the Comparability of Two Tests of English as a Foreign Language: The Cambridge-TOEFL Comparability Study*, Cambridge University Press, Cambridge.

Bachman, L.F., Lynch, B.K. & Mason, M.: 1995, 'Investigating variability in tasks and rater judgements in a performance test of foreign language speaking', *Language Testing* 12, 238–257.

Bentler, P.M.: 1992, *EQS Structural Equations Program Manual*, BMDP Statistical Software, Inc., Los Angeles, CA.

Bolus, R.E., Hinofotis, F.B., & Bailey, K.M.: 1982, 'An introduction to generalizability theory in second language research', *Language Learning* 32, 245–258.

Brennan, R.L.: 1983, *Elements of Generalizability Theory*, The American College Testing Program, Iowa City, IA.

Brennan, R.L. & Kane, M.T.: 1977, 'Signal/noise ratios for domain-referenced tests', *Psychometrika* 42, 609–625.

Cardinet, J., Tourneur, Y., & Allal, L.: 1981, 'Extension of generalizability theory and its applications in educational measurement', *Journal of Educational Measurement* 18, 183–204.

Crick, J.E. & Brennan, R.L.: 1983, *Manual for GENOVA: A GENeralized Analysis Of VAriance System*, ACT Technical Bulletin No. 43, American College Testing Program, Iowa City, IA.

Cronbach, L.J., Gleser, G.C., Nanda, H. & Rajaratnam, N.: 1972, *The Dependability of Behavioral Measurements: Theory of Generalizability*, John Wiley, New York.

Jöreskog, K.G. & Sörbom D.: 1993, *LISREL 8: User's Reference Guide*, Scientific Software International, Chicago, IL.

Marcoulides, G.A.: 1987, *An Alternative Method for Variance Component Estimation: Applications to Generalizability Theory*, unpublished Ph.D. dissertation, University of California, Los Angeles, CA.

Marcoulides, G.A.: 1993, 'Maximizing power in generalizability studies under budget constraints', *Journal of Educational Statistics* 18, 102–109.

Marcoulides, G.A.: 1996, 'Estimating variance components in generalizability theory: The covariance structure analysis approach', *Structural Equation Modeling* 3, 290–299.

Marcoulides, G.A. & Drezner, Z.: 1996, 'A method for analyzing performance assessments', in M. Wilson, K. Draney & G. Engelhard (eds.), *Objective Measurement: Theory into Practice*, Ablex Publishing Co., Norwood, NJ.

Shavelson, R.J. & Webb, N.M.: 1991, *Generalizabiity Theory: A Primer*, Sage Publications, Newbury Park, CA.

BRIAN K. LYNCH AND FRED DAVIDSON

CRITERION REFERENCED TESTING

Criterion referenced testing (CRT) has been a topic of debate and research in educational measurement for the past three decades. Discussions on this topic have occurred under various labels: criterion referenced measurement, domain referenced measurement, mastery testing and minimum competency testing. The dimensions along which CRT is usually defined include the types of decisions and purposes for testing, approaches to test construction and statistical analysis, and philosophical issues regarding the relationship of testing to teaching.

Furthermore, CRT has always been defined in opposition to norm referenced testing (NRT). Essentially, CRT aims to relate individual test performance to a well defined skill, behavior, or area of knowledge; whereas NRT is concerned with relating individual test performance to other individuals taking the same test. This fundamental difference results in the two approaches being considered more or less appropriate for certain types of test decisions or purposes. It has also resulted in different approaches to the construction of tests, different statistical procedures for the analysis of test data, as well as a significant difference in the importance attached to certain statistical properties of tests. Finally, it has been argued that CRT and NRT are based on different philosophies of both measurement and education and, thus, maintain critically different roles in relation to classroom teaching and learning.

The historical development of CRT has tended to focus much of its research on comparative statistical procedures for the analysis of test items traditionally used in NRTs. This can give the false impression that CRT is only concerned with so-called 'objective testing', or paper-and-pencil tests with items that can be scored 'right' or 'wrong.' This type of testing is crucial to NRT, with its primary objective of rank ordering, whereas CRT is also amenable to alternative forms of assessment, such as those that involve rating scales or qualitative profiles of test taker performances.

EARLY DEVELOPMENTS

The distinction between CRT and NRT was first made in an article by Glaser and Klaus in 1962; however, it was the essay published by Glaser in the following year that is most often cited (Glaser, 1963). This paper was only three pages in length, but it generated a direction in educational measurement that is still active and relevant today. That direction was first

C. Clapham and D. Corson (eds), Encyclopedia of Language and Education,
Volume 7: Language Testing and Assessment, 263–273.
© *1997 Kluwer Academic Publishers. Printed in the Netherlands.*

established by Popham and Husek (1969), who outlined the advantages of CRT over NRT in the context of individualized instruction – that CRT would provide the level of detail needed to monitor student progress, would allow for the assessment of student performance in relation to instructional objectives, and would therefore also be useful in program evaluation. This was followed by the work of researchers such as Hambleton and Novick (1973), who focused on the measurement problems associated with CRT. They looked at the special requirements for constructing CRTs, including how to establish mastery levels, or cut scores. This concern with cut scores is often mistaken for the defining characteristic of CRTs. Hively and his associates (Hively et al., 1973) developed procedures for the specification of criteria and the sampling of items to represent those criteria. For example, they presented minutely defined specifications, or "formalized item forms" for test items designed to assess criteria such as the ability to compare the weights of two objects using mathematical symbols. This work has been referred to as *domain referenced measurement*, and there is some disagreement in the literature as to whether this is the same as or different from CRT (Popham, 1978; Linn, 1994; Millman, 1994). Other early research, in the field of applied linguistics, that took notice of the distinction between CRT and NRT was done by Cartier (1968), and by Ingram, who depicted CRTs as focused on a "pattern of success or failure" and the construction of "homogeneous blocks of items . . . to test mastery of a particular teaching objective" (Ingram, 1977, p. 28).

MAJOR CONTRIBUTIONS

Cziko (1982) extended the notion of CRT for the field of language testing by commenting on the difference between *psychometric* and *edumetric* purposes, indicating that different measurement properties would be required for each. The concern for measures that would be sensitive to instructional success, or edumetrics, was properly identified with CRT, and the traditional, psychometric concern for aptitude, selection and prediction problems was identified with NRT.

The potentially positive CRT link between teaching and assessment was taken up in an ESL achievement testing context by Hudson and Lynch (1984). Glaser's distinction between NRT and CRT, briefly sketched earlier, was elaborated around the concept of *absolute* decisions (i.e., a test taker's standing in relation to a well-defined skill or ability), which are associated with CRT, and *relative* decisions (i.e., a test taker's standing in relation to other test takers), which are associated with NRT. Their analysis included statistical techniques for examining items from a CRT perspective. Most importantly, the NRT notion of item discrimination was contrasted with the CRT ideal of items that discriminate between instructed and uninstructed students. The traditional, NRT-based concept of reliability was also contrasted with the CRT definition of *dependability*. Traditional reliability is the consistency of measurement, from one test occasion to another, from one test form to another, and is usually estimated by internal consistency, or how well the items on a test correlate with each other. CRT replaces this notion with a concern for the dependability of decisions made from the test results, and has developed statistical estimates based on *generalizability theory* (Brennan, 1980; Brown, 1990). (For more about generalizability theory, see Bachman's review in this volume.)

However, not all applied linguists shared this favorable view of CRT's potential for language testing. Skehan (1984) was pessimistic, arguing that the need for detailed specification of the criterion ability made the construction of CRTs for language impractical, if not impossible. For example, in order to have a proper CRT of academic listening ability, a detailed definition and sampling of all possible types of academic lectures would be required.

Acknowledging the problems pointed out by Skehan, Hughes (1986) still found CRT to be of value, specifically in the potential for washback from testing to instruction and increased face validity and interpretability of the tests. His solution to the requirement for detailed specification of the criterion was to focus on the selection of texts, arguing that if a lecture, or reading passage, was appropriate in style and content (i.e., was representative of the target language situation), then tasks making use of them would naturally entail the specific subskills that define the global ability, or criterion to be tested. It is important to note that the method used by Hughes to obtain appropriate texts was the traditional ESP needs analysis, perhaps signaling a link between ESP testing and CRT.

The measurement properties of CRTs versus NRTs were investigated in more detail by Hudson (1989; 1991). His research examined the properties of an EFL proficiency test battery, the General Tests of English Language Proficiency (GTELP), using NRT, CRT, and Item Response Theory (IRT). (For more about IRT, see the reviews by Pollitt, and Bachman and Eignor in this volume.) He found that selecting items on the basis of high discrimination, as estimated by NRT biserials alone, was problematic. Items discriminating well overall may not, in fact, be discriminating well at the ability levels of interest (e.g., at the cut score points defining the levels). The importance of discrimination at ability levels of interest also underscored another finding in Hudson's research. NRT internal consistency estimates were found to correlate closely with one CRT estimate of dependability, Brennan's Φ, suggesting NRT and CRT coefficients were providing similar information. However, it was found that Brennan's $\Phi(\lambda)$, the CRT dependability estimate that takes the cut-score or standard for mastery decisions into account, provided uniquely useful information (Hudson, 1989, p. 172).

Brown (1989, p. 73) illustrated the development of a placement exam where items were selected based on both NRT and CRT statistical characteristics. His analysis of results suggested that this fusion was successful, a finding that was confirmed by Cook (1992), who argued further that the differences between the NRT and CRT approaches were ultimately not helpful to advancing our understanding of language testing. Brown (1990), while remaining a proponent of CRT, provided evidence that further questioned the distinction between NRT and CRT statistical approaches with his 'short-cut' estimators for dependability indices, which demonstrated a relationship between the *Kuder Richardson 20* internal consistency estimate and both Brennan's Φ and Brennan's $\Phi(\lambda)$ CRT estimates.

The research of Hudson and Lynch, Hudson, and Brown represents the tendency, noted earlier, to focus the investigation of CRT on the statistical analysis of traditional item formats (e.g., multiple-choice). It can be argued that the important difference between CRT and NRT is not in how they handle statistical item analysis, but in the degree of importance attached to these statistics in the development of assessment procedures. CRT's emphasis on content and detailed definitions of what is being assessed can be seen as advancing our understanding of language testing by considering more qualitative procedures, rather than immediately dismissing them because of their inability to produce the requisite statistical characteristics, as would be the case with NRT.

The continuing focus on a traditional, psychometric definition of testing led Davies (1990) to argue that CRT should not in any case be seen as a different method of test construction. Given his definition of a test as an instrument whose primary function is the determination of differences between individual test takers, Davies sees CRTs as only "special uses of NRTs" (p. 19). These special uses, or activities carried out in the name of CRT, are exercises; whereas only NRTs can be considered tests.

Wood (1991, p. 84) echoed Davies' insistence that CRTs will always need NRT interpretations with his paraphrase of Angoff (1974) that all CRTs can be considered NRTs, if we allow for comparisons between individual test takers. Even the original Glaser text (1963, p. 520), where he portrayed the criterion, or ability to be tested, as a "continuum of achievement", can be interpreted in this way. If CRTs function to place individual test takers on a continuum of proficiency, the difference between this activity and the rank-ordering of individuals can become obscured. However, it is important to keep in mind that the difference remains one of focus and emphasis. NRTs place the emphasis on traditional psychometric statistics and reliability of the rank-ordering process. CRTs place the emphasis on the clarity with which the skill or ability continuum can be defined and the dependability of deciding an individual's relationship to that continuum. Although Davies would maintain that tests will always require the same "canons of item discreteness and discrimination" (1990,

p. 18), there has been considerable effort and some success at developing alternative techniques for evaluating CRT items, including the use of IRT.

IRT has been particularly useful in relation to analyzing the reliability and validity of rating scales. However, the relationship between CRT and rating scales can be confusing, especially in light of the criticisms made by Davies and Wood. The use of a rating scale in CRT is typically addressed by its detailed elaboration in the test specification, in the section that lays out the 'response attributes', or what the test taker is expected to produce and how that will be judged. To the extent that the rating scale has thoroughly detailed descriptors of the expected language behavior(s) associated with particular levels on the scale, it can be considered as an element of CRT. However, since these scale descriptors can be assigned numerical values, the subsequent 'ratings' can be analyzed statistically (e.g., with IRT) and the resulting scores can be used to rank order test takers. In addition, individual raters may use a subconscious rank ordering system, and relate a test taker's performance to that of previous students whom they have assessed (Clapham, personal communication). This then begins to resemble NRT. The difference will depend on the degree to which an individual's rating can be traced back to a clear description of the criterion behavior being measured (CRT), rather than being limited to a sense of how the individual compares with other test takers or previous students (NRT).

Another problem with the focus on traditional psychometric views of testing is that IRT and some CRT statistics may not be practical in many testing contexts. In any case, the evaluation of item statistics, whether originally developed for NRT or IRT, will be different when used to construct CRTs, as will the general importance attached to statistical analysis for the test development process. As Wood (1991) reminds us, it is still important to realize what CRT has brought to the field of language testing – a heightened concern for clear descriptions of what is being measured, for the specification of test content. Rather than being considered as opposites, CRT and NRT should probably be seen as poles on a continuum. NRTs will attend to content, and CRTs will attach importance to the statistical properties of items, to varying degrees. What CRT has fostered is test development where concerns for the specification of content are prioritized and this, in turn, makes it more amenable to considering innovations in testing procedures, including more qualitative approaches.

WORK IN PROGRESS

The 1993 annual meeting of the American Educational Research Association presented a symposium on CRT, commemorating the 30th anniversary of the influential Glaser article. This symposium set the tone for work in progress in this area, bringing together the luminaries of CRT (at least the North American variety) – Ronald Hambleton, Robert Linn, Jason Millman, James Popham and the originator himself, Robert Glaser – and was published as a special edition of *Educational Measurement: Issues and Practice* in 1994 (*13*, 4). These proponents of CRT remind us that its unique contributions have been a focus on test specifications and the clear referencing of test scores to content, and that these characteristics make CRT particularly relevant for the present emphasis on performance testing and authentic assessment. In order to fulfill it potential to make contributions to these alternative forms of assessment, CRT researchers need to re-examine the formats currently being used for test specifications and the larger process of test construction.

Davidson and Lynch (1993) and Lynch and Davidson (1994) have presented a generalized form for the CRT specification, patterned after Popham's (1978) Instructional Objectives Exchange format, as a central feature of *criterion-referenced language test development* (CRLTD). The approach is criterion-referenced because of its conscious focus on the test specification and item or task writing stages of test development as a means of clarifying the criterion being tested. This clarification is the result of the iterative nature of CRLTD: the experience from the item writing stage and the test piloting stage feeding back to the elaboration of the test specification. In this way, the test specification also provides a detailed record of evidence for judging how well the test items or tasks match what the test claims to be measuring; i.e., it becomes a useful source of evidence for test validity.

Graded assessment, such as the General Certificate of Secondary Education, continues to be used in the United Kingdom, making use of some of the basic principles of CRT (Wood, 1991). This work reflects ongoing efforts in the UK to produce better definitions of the behavioral expectations of educational performance, an initiative that has come to be known as the *Graded Objectives* movement. In Finland, the national exams for foreign languages are constructed using CRT (Finnish National Board of Education 1995). This examination system is based on a framework of level descriptions for language proficiency (English, French, German Russian, Spanish, and Swedish) and includes tasks that ask the test takers to construct written and spoken responses that are assessed with rating scales. The Australian Adult Migrant Education Program has been experimenting with a form of CRT referred to as 'criterion-based assessment' (Brindley, 1989; Gunn, 1995). This effort is significant in that it involves classroom-based test development, where teachers control the design, implementation and evaluation of assessment procedures.

A major work which should be published soon is a book by Brown and Hudson (submitted). The authors explore CRT from a number of perspectives – its history and relationship to theoretical issues in language testing, its potential for informing curriculum development through performance assessment and other alternative forms, item types and statistical analysis, and the issues of validity and standard setting. In addition to providing a much needed general reference in CRT for language testing, Brown and Hudson's work promises to elaborate the potential for this testing approach to inform the development of alternative assessment formats, such as portfolios. This work should also make a contribution to strengthening the link between testing and teaching, the ongoing promise of CRT.

Davidson and Lynch are currently working on a book that will develop and illustrate CRLTD with examples drawn from the authors' experience and the experience of the teachers and students with whom they have explored the process. A number of specifications will be presented in various stages of development, along with discussion concerning the nature of their evolution. Rather than tests being delivered to teachers by outside experts, this work emphasizes procedures for teachers to take an active role in the specification and construction of test instruments. Another key aspect being developed in this work is the notion of the *mandate*, or the contextual constraints on test design. Finally, this work seeks to further the investigation of CRT and teaching, highlighted by a consideration of current scholarly treatment of washback (Alderson & Wall, 1993; Wall & Alderson, 1993; Alderson & Hamp-Lyons, 1996; Shohamy, Donitsa-Schmidt & Ferman, 1996; Watanabe, 1996). (For more on washback, see Wall's review in this volume.)

PROBLEMS AND DIFFICULTIES

An ongoing problem for CRT is the degree of specificity needed to define the criterion. The early days of CRT were influenced by the dominant learning theory of the time – behaviorism. There was a focus on operationalizing the construct to be measured, and on a detailed specification of the behavioral domain from which items (and texts, tasks) were to be sampled. This activity can be associated with the 'pure form' of domain-referenced testing (DRT) which, in practice proved feasible only for lower level skills and narrow domains, such as the addition of single digit numbers, or the recognition of discrete point grammatical features. Linn has pointed out that this led "to absurd reductionism and away from the measurement of broader, fuzzier, but more interesting achievements" (1994, p. 13), and claims that CRT should be dissociated from such DRT, reminding us of Glaser's original 'criterion' example: the preparation of an experimental report. Theoretically, there is nothing that prevents CRTs and their specifications from testing integrative skills and communicative language ability.

Popham (1994) expressed this same problem with reference to what he judged as the failure of CRT specifications to fulfill their potential for enhancing instruction. In order for the specifications to do so, they needed to be accessible to teachers as well as item writers, as pointed out by Lynch and Davidson (1994). At the same time, the specifications needed to provide sufficient detail adequately to describe the criterion to be tested. This resulted in what Popham (1994, p. 16) has termed *single-definition* CRTs, where the criterion is represented, or operationalized, by only one task or item type. He concluded:

> Far too many teachers end up providing targeted instruction aimed *only* at the student's mastering the skill or knowledge domain as defined in the criterion-referenced test's specifications. Accordingly, many students fail to attain *generalizable* mastery of the skill or knowledge domain being measured. Not only are students unable to apply their nongeneralizable mastery to other kinds of test items, they are also unable to apply their nongeneralizable mastery to non-school, 'real life' situations requiring the tested skills or knowledge (Popham, 1994, pp. 16–17; original emphasis).

The implications of this conclusion for language teaching and testing are of crucial importance, given our concern for communicative competence and the kinds of language skills and knowledge that do not lend themselves to the reductionism of single-definition specifications and tests. How, then, do we achieve the promise of CRTs for increased clarity in what is being tested and taught, without falling into the reductionist trap? Popham (1994, pp. 17–18) has suggested a radical revision of his earlier CRT specification format, in which a "boiled-down general description of what's going on in the successful examinee's head be accompanied by a set of varied, *but not exhaustive*, illustrative items (emphasis ours)". This approach to specifications would provide sufficient clarity for both teachers and item writers without encouraging instruction to focus on a particular operationalization of the skill or knowledge to be tested. That is, it would discourage the negative version of 'teaching to the test', while taking advantage of the CRT potential to promote a positive, generalizable connection between teaching and the test.

FUTURE DIRECTIONS

The CRT literature has been characterized by a top-down development model. Test specifications are generally treated as set in stone, often inviolate. The scholarly work has often focused on the ability of a test development system to create items and tasks that adhere to the specifications, and contains studies on 'fit to specification' or 'item congruence' to specifications. In this work, the specifications themselves were seen as fixed, and the test items were seen as entities to match the specifications.

What is more, the process by which the specifications were developed is not described thoroughly in the CRT literature. It is not codified and formalized in any manner. Future work on CRT should be the product of many minds and involve a consensus of interested parties (including the active participation of test users not usually included in the process, such as classroom teachers). As a test specification evolves from its earliest conception to its later forms, if its authors come to agree, then the specification itself is documented evidence of content validity. Of course, this is only partial evidence for content validity. It must also be demonstrated that the test items or assessment procedures that come to be used represent the content that is called for in the specifications. This representativeness, or evidence of content coverage, will be stronger if it is the product of the same group-based consensual procedure advocated above.

In addition, as Glaser (1994, p. 29) has recently indicated, CRT specifications need to develop more clearly interpretable, 'transparent criteria of performance', drawing upon knowledge from current cognitive and learning theory. In language testing, this would argue for attention to SLA theory, as well as classroom practice.

In conclusion, there is a need to re-visit and re-define CRT in a manner not found in the thirty-plus years of literature on criterion-referencing. To date there is no call for empowerment and advocacy for input on the test specification development process by, in particular, teachers. There are, of course, testing contexts in which teachers are involved to varying degrees in the design and approval of national exams. In addition to the previously cited work by Brindley and colleagues in Australia, Alderson, Clapham, and Wall (1995) report on British exam boards that have practising teachers working on their test specifications. There is also evidence that teachers are guiding the national test development process in several Eastern European countries (see Wall, Kalnberzina, Mazuoliene & Truus, 1996). However, in most contexts, we see, again and again, a re-casting of the NRT authoritarian test development model: testing 'experts' write the specifications and train others to write items from the specifications. The tests come to teachers from the outside, from above. Where teachers have been included, there has not been enough research focusing on the degree to which they are involved, the resulting test development dynamic, and the outcomes of these efforts as compared to traditional, expert-driven testing. The approach to CRT that is needed in the future should seek to loosen the traditional, top-down model of test development. In language testing this would mean greater allowance for teachers to formulate the criteria, based on classroom knowledge and practice, and to move from those criteria to the indicated assessment procedures. The role of language testing 'experts' will be similar to that of the language teacher in relation to language learners – that of facilitator. The resulting assessment procedures should provide a closer link between innovations in the language classroom and test formats.

University of Melbourne, Australia

and

University of Illinois, Urbana-Champaign, USA

REFERENCES

Alderson, J.C. & Wall, D.: 1993, 'Does washback exist?', *Applied Linguistics* 14, 115–129.
Alderson, J.C. & Hamp-Lyons, L.: 1996, 'TOEFL preparation courses: a study of washback', *Language Testing* 13, 280–297.
Angoff, W.H.: 1974, 'Criterion-referencing, norm-referencing, and the SAT', *College Board Review* 92, 2–5.
Brennan, R.L.: 1980, 'Applications of generalizability theory', in R.A. Berk (ed.), *Criterion-Referenced Measurement: The State of the Art*, John Hopkins University Press, Baltimore, MD.
Brindley, G.: 1989, *Assessing Achievement in the Learner-Centred Curriculum*, National Centre for English Language Teaching and Research, Sydney.
Brown, J.D.: 1989, 'Improving ESL placement tests using two perspectives', *TESOL Quarterly*, 7, 239–260.
Brown, J.D.: 1990, 'Short-cut estimates of criterion-referenced test consistency', *Language Testing* 7, 77–97.
Brown, J.D. & Hudson, T.D. (submitted) *Criterion-Referenced Language Testing and Assessments: A Teacher's Guide*, unpublished manuscript. University of Hawaii at Manoa, Honolulu, HI.
Cartier, F.A.: 1968, 'Criterion-referenced testing of language skills', *TESOL Quarterly* 2, 27–32.
Cook, G.: 1992, 'The place of placement tests', Paper presented at the 26th Annual TESOL Convention, Vancouver, B.C.
Cziko, G.A.: 1982, 'Improving the psychometric, criterion-referenced and practical qualities of integrative language tests', *TESOL Quarterly* 16, 367–379.
Davidson, F. & Lynch, B.K.: 1993, 'Criterion-referenced language test development: A prolegomenon', in A. Huhta, K. Sajavaara, & S. Takala (eds.), *Language Testing: New Openings*, University of Jyväskylä, Institute for Educational Research, Jyväskylä, Finland.
Davies, A.: 1990, *Principles of Language Testing*, Basil Blackwell, Oxford.
Finnish National Board of Education: 1995, *The Framework of the Finnish National Foreign Language Certificate*, Syrinx Oy/Libris Oy, Helsinki, Finland.
Glaser, R. & Klaus, D.J.: 1962, 'Proficiency measurement: Assessing human performance', in R. Gagné (ed.), *Psychological Principles in System Development*, Holt, Rinehart, Winston, New York, 421–427.
Glaser, R.: 1963, 'Instructional technology and the measurement of learning outcomes: Some questions', *American Psychologist* 18, 519–521.
Glaser, R.: 1994, 'Criterion-referenced tests: Part I, origins; Part II, unfinished business', *Educational Measurement: Issues and Practice* 13, 9–11, 27–30.
Gunn, M.: 1995, 'Criterion-based assessment: A classroom teacher's perspective', in G. Brindley (ed.), *Language Assessment in Action*, Research Series 8, National Centre for English Language Teaching and Research, Sydney, 239–270.

Hambleton, R.K. & Novick, M.R.: 1973, 'Toward an integration of theory and method for criterion-referenced tests', *Journal of Educational Measurement* 10, 159–170.

Hively, W., Maxwell, G., Rabehl, G., Sension, D., & Lundin, S.: 1973, *Domain-Referenced Curriculum Evaluation: A Technical Handbook and a Case Study from the MIN-NEMAST Project*, Center for the Study of Evaluation, UCLA, Los Angeles, CA.

Hudson, T.D. & Lynch, B.K.: 1984, 'A criterion-referenced measurement approach to ESL achievement testing', *Language Testing* 1, 171–201.

Hudson, T.D.: 1989, *Measurement Approaches in the Development of Functional Ability Level Language Tests: Norm-Referenced, Criterion-Referenced, and Item Response Theory Decisions*, Doctoral Dissertation, UCLA, Los Angeles, CA.

Hudson, T.D.: 1991, 'Relationships among IRT item discrimination and item fit indices in criterion-referenced language testing', *Language Testing* 8, 160–181.

Hughes, A.: 1986, 'A pragmatic approach to criterion-referenced foreign language testing', in M. Portal (ed.), *Innovations in Language Testing: Proceedings of the IUS/NFER Conference April 1985*, NFER-Nelson, Windsor, Berkshire, 31–40.

Ingram, E.: 1977, 'Basic concepts in testing', in J. P. B. Allen & A. Davies (eds.), *The Edinburgh Course in Applied Linguistics, Volume Four: Testing and Experimental Methods*, Oxford University Press, London, 11–37.

Linn, R.L.: 1994, 'Criterion-referenced measurement: a valuable perspective clouded by surplus meaning', *Educational Measurement: Issues and Practice* 13, 12–14.

Lynch, B.K. & Davidson, F.D.: 1994, 'Criterion-referenced language test development: linking curricula, teachers, and tests', *TESOL Quarterly* 28, 727–743.

Millman, J.: 1994, 'Criterion-referenced testing 30 years later: Promise broken, promise kept', *Educational Measurement: Issues and Practice* 13, 19–20, 39.

Popham, W.J. & Husek, T.R.: 1969, 'Implications of criterion-referenced measurement', *Journal of Educational Measurement* 6, 1–9.

Popham, W.J.: 1978, *Criterion-Referenced Measurement*, Prentice-Hall, Englewood Cliffs, NJ.

Popham, W.J.: 1994, 'The instructional consequences of criterion-referenced clarity', *Educational Measurement: Issues and Practice* 13, 15–18, 30.

Shohamy, E., Donitsa-Schmidt, S., & Ferman, I.: 1996, 'Test impact revisited: washback effect over time', *Language Testing* 13, 298–317.

Skehan, P.: 1984, 'Issues in the testing of English for Specific Purposes', *Language Testing* 1, 202–220.

Wall, D. & Alderson, J.C.: 1993, 'Examining washback: The Sri Lankan impact study', *Language Testing* 10, 41–69.

Wall, D., Kalnberzina, V., Mazuoliene, Z. & Truus, K.: 1996. 'The Baltic States Year 12 examination project', *Language Testing Update*, Issue 19.

Watanabe, Y.: 1996, 'Does grammar translation come from the entrance examination? Preliminary findings from classroom-based research', *Language Testing* 13, 318–333.

Wood, R.: 1991, *Assessment and Testing: A Survey of Research Commissioned by the University of Cambridge Local Examinations Syndicate*, Cambridge University Press, Cambridge.

JAYANTI BANERJEE AND SARI LUOMA

QUALITATIVE APPROACHES TO TEST VALIDATION

Validity can be defined as the extent to which a test measures or tests what it claims to test (Alderson Clapham & Wall, 1995). In the 1985 Standards for Educational and Psychological testing, it is characterised as "the most important consideration in test evaluation . . . refer(ring) to the appropriateness, meaningfulness and usefulness of the specific inferences made from test scores" (American Psychological Association & others, 1985, p. 9). This definition focuses on score *meaning* for, as Messick explains, "the function of validation is to marshal evidence and arguments in support of, or counter to, proposed interpretations and uses of test scores" (1989, p. 32). Bachman (1990) embraces Messick's definition and says that the focus is not on the test *per se* nor the scores but on how they are used to say something about the test-takers in a particular population (1990, p. 238).

What is implicit in such claims, is that the character and extent of the interpretations and uses of scores depend on a *thorough understanding* of the test: the way in which it is constructed; how test-takers give their responses; how these responses are evaluated; and, how the scores are used in making decisions about the test-takers. Certainly, the emerging consensus on validation is broad not only in terms of scope but also in terms of time. As Anastasi (1986) and Angoff (1988) point out, validation begins early, even as early as the point at which it is decided that a test is to be written, and continues all through its life.

Most of the methods proposed for validation enquiry are quantitative, very often correlational (for details of recent advances in the field, see Bachman and Eignor's review in this volume) and until recently, qualitative inquiry in test validation has focused largely on the use of expert judgements. The emphasis on qualitative techniques other than judgement in language test validation is, therefore, a relatively new development, perhaps reflecting the introduction of the view of language as communication and the consequent rise of performance assessment; the increased importance of process in theories of learning and teaching; and more recently, the legitimacy of multiple perspectives and constructions.

It is, however, difficult to distinguish between quantitative and qualitative approaches. As Seliger & Shohamy (1989) point out, attempts to explain the differences between quantitative and qualitative approaches result in oversimplification. Nevertheless, some differences might be hazarded. Qualitative approaches to research (test validation included) can

C. Clapham and D. Corson (eds), Encyclopedia of Language and Education,
Volume 7: Language Testing and Assessment, 275–287.
© *1997 Kluwer Academic Publishers. Printed in the Netherlands.*

be characterised as beginning with the individual rather than the group (Seliger & Shohamy, 1989, p. 115). Such approaches use verbal rather than numerical data as their *starting* point for analysis and tend to focus on small N sizes (Seliger & Shohamy, 1989 offer a more detailed discussion of the differences between qualitative and quantitative approaches). For example, O'Loughlin's (see below) research included an in-depth study of two test-takers in which he observed the test-taking process and conducted interviews with them after they had taken the test. He also performed detailed linguistic analyses of the test-takers' performances.

RATIONALE AND EARLY DEVELOPMENTS

While quantitative techniques in test validation provide information on the psychometric properties of the test, qualitative validation techniques provide information on the content of the test, the properties of the test tasks, and the processes involved in test taking and assessing. The information gathered by qualitative methods clarifies the nature of the performance that the scores are based on, and the characteristics of the rating process. Qualitative techniques thus provide evidence other than the test developer's statements about what is being assessed in the test, and how. Such information is important in order for the scores of any test to be interpreted responsibly.

The most common qualitative way of providing data for score interpretations is expert judgement (Messick, 1989, p. 36; Alderson et al., 1995, pp. 173–176). In the case of test content and task focus in language assessment, 'expert' usually refers to linguists or teachers; in the case of acceptability or face validity, candidates and possibly other stakeholders may also be consulted.

Shepard (1993, pp. 412–415) suggests that content validation begins from the appraisal of the statement of measurement intent and proceeds through the early stages of test design. These include the appraisal of the theories drawn on to establish the domain of the test, an evaluation of the appropriateness of this analysis and the assessment of how well the domain has been sampled in the test. In order for this to be achieved, Shepard (1993) recommends repeated appraisals at each stage of test development.

An example of such an approach in language testing is Weir's work (1983; 1988). His needs analysis for developing an EAP test involved classroom observations, interviews with teachers and students, and the development of a questionnaire (based on the observations and interviews). The information he collected was then used for writing the test specifications. It was also used as basic empirical evidence against which the test could be compared.

TECHNIQUES CURRENTLY IN USE

The qualitative methods currently used in language test validation include: introspection and retrospection through the use of verbal protocols
(Cohen, 1984; 1994; Nevo, 1989; Alderson, 1990; Li, 1992; Cushing
Weigle, 1994); observations (O'Loughlin, in press); questionnaires (Clark,
1988; Bradshaw, 1990; Cohen, 1994); interviews (Milanovic & Saville,
1994; O'Loughlin in progress; Luoma in progress); text, conversation
and/or discourse analysis of assessment instruments and performances
(Ross & Berwick, 1992; Lazaraton, 1992; Shohamy, 1994; Douglas, 1995;
O'Loughlin, 1995; Young, 1995; Lazaraton, 1996; Ginther & Grant, 1997);
and analytical frameworks e.g. task characteristics (Bachman et al., 1995).
It is becoming increasingly common to conduct validation studies which
employ a combination of two or more qualitative methods in order to triangulate the information collected (Cohen, 1994; Milanovic & Saville, 1994;
Luoma in progress), one example of such research being O'Loughlin's (in
progress) ethnographic study of the development of two modes of an oral
proficiency test (see below). This research, O'Loughlin suggests, "reveals
the potential for using individual case studies in the testing context in explorations of test validity and reliability. ... Such a change in perspective
has the potential to yield powerful new insights into what our tests appear
to measure and how accurately they do so" (personal communication).

For ease of presentation, each of the approaches will be dealt with in
turn.

Verbal Report

This refers to a group of techniques where the informants report on what
they do to complete a task. It is often difficult to distinguish between
different categories of verbal report – introspection and retrospection –
but distinctions can be made according to differences in time between
processing and reporting or according to the kinds of data elicited. Cohen
(1984) describes four categories beginning with concurrent introspection
or 'think-aloud'. Similar to this is introspection with a time lapse of 10–20
seconds between the thought and the verbalisation. Longer time lapses
(minutes) between the thought and its verbalisation result in 'immediate
retrospection' and time lapses of an hour or more (perhaps days) result
in 'delayed retrospection'. For instance, if test-takers doing an hour-long
multiple choice test were to speak their thoughts aloud as they answered
each item on a test, this would be classified as 'think-aloud'. If, at the
end of the test, the same test-takers were then asked to go back over their
performance and discuss the decisions they had taken and things they had
done, this would be classed as a 'delayed retrospection' as the time lapse

between their answering the question and their discussion of it would be an hour or more.

In language testing, verbal report data has been used to explore the processes and strategies test takers use to complete a reading comprehension task. This data has been collected in oral form (Cohen, 1984; Grotjahn, 1986; Alderson, 1990; Cohen, 1994; Dollerup et al., 1994) or through written skills checklists (Nevo, 1989; Li, 1992). In addition to specifying the processes that test takers engage in, the results of these studies have been used: to refine the test instrument (Cohen, 1984); to refine feedback procedures (Dollerup et al., 1994); and to guide learner training in strategy use (Cohen, 1984). Alderson (1990) and Li (1992) extended their results to question claims that test constructors can design items which test specific skills (see also the review by Weir in this volume).

A recent development in the use of verbal report is a focus on assessor processing. Much of this work is based on the need for a deeper understanding of what raters pay attention to and why. For instance, Cushing Weigle (1994) has studied the rating processes of raters marking ESL compositions, looking particularly at the effects of rater training on those processes. Milanovic & Saville (1994) have also investigated raters' strategies as they mark writing, their focus being on how these affect rater consistency. Also working with assessments of writing, Lumley (in progress) is investigating the relationship between raters' assessment processes and their severity.

On the other hand, Luoma (in progress) is studying raters marking speaking from video tapes. She is considering features of each candidate's performance and other possible influences which might affect ratings. She intends to triangulate this analysis by comparing the features the raters pay attention to when rating with the occurrence of these features in the actual performances. This will be achieved by an analysis of candidate performances from transcripts.

Apart from exploring what raters pay attention to, test developers have also used verbal protocols to investigate the validity and usability of scoring rubrics. Cohen (1994), for example, used such research to show that raters interpret and use scoring criteria differently. In order to improve the reliability of scoring, he argues that scoring rubrics should be devised and agreed upon by the raters and that a checking procedure be set up to ensure that the rubrics are actually used.

Observation

As part of his ethnographic study of two test modes – a face to face version and a tape-mediated version of the *access:* speaking test, O'Loughlin (in progress) observed item editorial meetings, the test-taking process, and the rating of performances. His observation data on the test taking process was combined with post-test interviews with candidates while his observations of the rating process was complemented by follow-up interviews and questionnaires. He analysed this data using techniques suggested in Lynch (1996) and his results suggest the existence of rater bias in relation to individual candidates on both versions of the test.

Observations were also conducted by Wall & Alderson (1993) in their investigation of washback in the Sri Lankan Impact Study. Unlike the other research described in this review, this study looked at the effect a test has on the teaching and learning situation, arguably an important focus for test validation studies. Indeed, Morrow (1986) argued that the consequences of a test should be researched as part of any test validation exercise, coining the term 'washback validity'. (For a full discussion of impact and washback, see Wall's review in this volume.)

Questionnaires and Interviews

Questionnaires in language test validation have been used to capture test-takers' reactions to and opinions of individual items and whole tests, and assessors' opinions of tests and scoring rubrics. They can take the form of Likert scales, yes/no prompts, and/or open-ended questions.

The aim of studies using questionnaire feedback is often to improve the quality of test instruments (Clark, 1988; Bradshaw, 1990; Kenyon & Stansfield, 1993; Brown, 1993; Halvari & Tarnanen, 1997). Hence the technique is often employed in connection with pilot testing, though Clark (1988) explored test-takers' preference for a particular speaking test mode when two ostensibly 'equivalent' measures were available, and Cohen (1994) used his questionnaire results to argue for the benefits/advantages of the summary tasks in testing not only because "well-constructed summary tests may promote a richer, more interactive approach to reading than do comprehension tests that focus more on details" (1994, p. 203) but because his respondents reported finding the tasks "instructive in themselves and a good reflection of the work they had done in their EAP course" (1994, p. 204).

Milanovic and Saville (1994) investigated raters' marking strategies through verbal protocols, but they also administered a background questionnaire, which included a section on the raters' perceptions of the marking strategies they used. In doing so, they were able to triangulate their data from other qualitative procedures; this is a use to which questionnaires and interviews are particularly suited. Indeed, questionnaires and interviews are seldom employed alone in test validation. They can be used together as in the content validation of the IELTS (International English Language Testing System) test (Clapham, 1997). In this case, the revised test and specifications were sent out with a detailed survey instrument to different stakeholders. Follow-up interviews were then conducted though, as Clapham (1997) note, "In most cases respondents did not complete the questionnaire themselves, but were interviewed ... so that potentially interesting answers could be followed up in detail" (1997, p. 51). In fact, interviews have great potential for following-up interesting points and have been used in conjunction with verbal protocols (Milanovic & Saville, 1994; Luoma in progress) and observation (O'Loughlin, in progress).

Analysis of test language

Studies on language use in tests focus on the nature of the language sample on which the scores are based. The issues hitherto addressed in these studies relate to the nature of test discourse, differences in language use between different tests and tasks, the relationship between the nature of the language sample and the grade awarded, and variability in the test instrument.

The key question, at the moment, in studies of the nature of test discourse, where tests of speaking are concerned, is the comparability between the language used within and outside tests. Lazaraton (1992; 1996) and Ross (1992) analyse the turn by turn structure of the test interaction, concentrating on the role of the interlocutor in particular. The studies provide evidence of some similarities and some differences, the latter most clearly related to the differing power and roles of the participants (the interviewer and the test-taker).

Research on variations in language use between different tasks (Shohamy et al., 1993; Pavlou, 1997) involves analysis of linguistic features of candidate performances such as register, turn-taking mechanisms, and backchanneling (the verbal signs e.g. 'yes' or 'go on' that an interlocutor gives to encourage the interaction). The studies by Shohamy et al. (1993) and Pavlou (1997) revealed that different tasks generated performances with different linguistic features. This raised the issue of how valid it would be to make inferences about communicative ability based on a single task. From this research, Shohamy et al. (1993) concluded that tests should employ multiple tasks.

The issue that different tasks yield different language was taken further in the research by Shohamy (1994) and O'Loughlin (1995) on linguistic differences between different test modes, in this case between face-to-face and tape-mediated speaking tests. Shohamy (1994) and O'Loughlin (1995), working on their respective tests, studied lexical density in particular. They raised the issue of the comparability between the two test modes and hence the desirability of various test forms as well as equity for candidates (see also the review by Fulcher in this volume).

Investigating the relationship between test discourse and the grade awarded, Berry (in progress) has focused on the personality of the test-taker (extroverts and introverts) and has analysed test performances for the effect of personality type on performances in paired interviews and group discussion tests. Ross & Berwick (1992), on the other hand, focused on the 'accommodation behaviour' of interlocutors (i.e. their tendency to adjust their own language and elicitation to the proficiency of the candidate) and found that such behaviour was closely related to the grade given. Young's (1995) focus was on candidate language, and results indicated that linguistic features of candidate performance such as rate of speech or amount of elaboration clearly distinguished between two proficiency levels, while discourse features such as the frequency of initiation of new topics or reactivity to topics did not. Unlike Ross & Berwick (1992), Young (1995) found that the interlocutors did *not* accommodate their elicitation to candidate proficiency. Douglas's (1994) main result from analysing candidate language and grades revealed that "similar quantitative scores . . . represent qualitatively different performances and . . . different scores do not reflect differing performances" (1994, pp. 133–134). However, Douglas (1994) recommends further research in order to understand "the bases of raters' judgements" better (1994, p. 136).

Brown & Lumley (1997) address the issue that Lazaraton (1996) raises: the variability in interlocutor conduct between test administrations and interlocutors. Confirming previous results, Brown and Lumley contend that variability exists, and detail features of interlocutor language which make role play tasks easier (factual questions, linguistic simplification, relinquishing control to candidate) and more difficult (sarcasm, interruption, repetition, lack of co-operation) for the candidate. The tester, as a part of the instrument, thus causes variation in the test instrument, which threatens test fairness (for a discussion of issues related to fairness see Hamp-Lyons' review in this volume). Brown and Lumley concur with Lazaraton (1996) in recommending interlocutor training to control for unwanted variability.

In writing assessment, the research has concentrated on the performances of test-takers of different proficiency levels, one example being research by Ginther & Grant (1997) (for more examples refer to Cumming's review in this volume). In their analysis of responses to writing prompts from the Test of Written English (TWE) Ginther & Grant (1997) *also* found that different topics elicit different language structures. In further research, they plan to "investigate the relationship between (the) structures produced and (the) rating assigned" (personal communication) because they argue that the nature of this relationship could have implications for test design.

Analytical Frameworks

Analytical frameworks consist of instruments which have been developed on the basis of theory and which are intended to assist qualitative investigation by guiding analysis or observation. An early example of a language-oriented framework is Munby's (1978) Communication Needs Processor, which guided Weir's (1983) development of an observation instrument for needs analysis. Analytical frameworks can be used as such, or, as in Weir's case, they can be used as a basis for developing a contextually adapted data collection instrument, such as an observation instrument, a survey instrument, or an interview structure.

A recent development in analytical frameworks is Bachman and Palmer's (1996) framework of Task Characteristics (TC). This framework assists the collection of expert judgements on features of task-related language use in great detail. The framework has proved useful for comparing two tests (Bachman et al., 1995) and Bachman and Palmer also propose its use for comparing differences between test tasks and target language use tasks. Indeed, TC are used in the design and content validation of each new version of the IELTS test. However, Clapham (1996) does warn that the framework is long and that the test method facets (as the TC were formerly called) are not always self-explanatory (1996, p. 162). (For another use of TC see McKay's review in this volume.)

PROBLEMS AND CONSIDERATIONS

Because of its nature and methodology, qualitative research in general is affected by a number of validity considerations. Qualitative approaches to test validation are no exception. These considerations can be divided into three areas: data collection, analysis and interpretation, and instrument validation.

Beginning with data collection, a number of decisions need to be made about the type of respondent chosen and the way the data collection is structured. For instance, in the case of verbal reports, it is important to find informants who are capable of providing fruitful introspections and retrospections. Informants must be chosen carefully since they must not only have enough language proficiency to conduct a self-report (if it is to be conducted in a language other than their first language) but must be articulate (Alderson, 1990). This, given the small N size of qualitative studies, has repercussions for the representativeness of the respondents and can affect the strength of any conclusions (i.e. their generalisability) a researcher might want to report.

Yet, even with articulate respondents and training (in the form of a modelled self-report and a practice run), researchers continue to be concerned about the accessibility of language processing for introspection since so much of the former is automatic (Alderson et al., 1995). There is also concern about the effect of the data gathering on the test taking (Cohen, 1984; Alderson et al., 1995). Was the observed behaviour affected by the act of observation? There is also pressure to ensure that data that is collected is recorded so that it can be retrieved and re-analysed. This, however, can prove difficult since it might involve the use of audio (or audio-visual) equipment, which might be intrusive, and might, therefore, make the observation less representative (Seliger & Shohamy, 1989, p. 104).

Furthermore, the interviewer/observer must not wait too long to gather data as this might result in data loss. Observers/ interviewers also have to resolve the tension between probing for a more detailed report and risking 'leading' the informant (Li, 1992). As a corollary to this, Allan (1995) argues that the use of self-report checklists such as the one designed by Nevo (1989) could have a substantial instrument effect; he thus casts doubt on the validity of any data gathered by this means. Certainly, the researcher will begin to select/impose categories either at the data collection or analysis and interpretation stages and these will play a part in the creation of the results. Consequently, the analysis can have a high degree of subjectivity which can be used to call any conclusions into question (Seliger & Shohamy, 1989).

As Lynch explains, "Because the data are recorded, summarised and interpreted in the form of words and not numbers, they may be suspect in the eyes of certain audiences, often such data are referred to as anecdotal, or subjective, implying that they are not as meaningful or convincing as quantitative data" (1996, p. 107). What is important, therefore, is that the data collected is triangulated and that all data collection and analysis procedures are reported carefully (as suggested by Cohen, 1997 in his detailed guidelines for maximising the benefit from verbal reports).

Finally, (perhaps 'above all') it is important to ensure that all data collection instruments are validated and that this validation is reported. This goes beyond piloting, which is generally aimed at ironing out the 'kinks' in an instrument. In fact, instrument validation seeks to establish that the data being gathered can actually answer the researcher(s) questions before much time and effort (even money) is spent on gathering imperfect and unhelpful data (Alderson & Banerjee, 1997).

FUTURE DIRECTIONS

From the previous discussion, it is clear that, in recent years, there has been an explosion in the use of qualitative methods for test validation. There is, however, much scope for expansion both in the number of studies in which qualitative methods are used and in the skill areas for which they are used. For instance, as the study reported by Buck (1994) has shown, verbal protocol analysis is a viable approach (within reason) to studying test-takers' processes as they take a listening test.

In addition to using current methods more extensively, however, alternative qualitative approaches to test validation could be explored. For instance, in their investigation of teacher interpretations of the UK National Curriculum descriptors, Leung & Teasdale (1997) employed a multi-method approach which included an audio-tape diary of observations and thoughts that the respondents thought relevant. Diaries might augment the approaches already in use (see above). Certainly, there is scope for more multi-method work to counter charges of subjectivity.

The use of qualitative software analysis programs such as NUD•IST, The Ethnograph and ATLAS/ti (see, for instance, Weitzman & Miles, 1995) can also support the analysis and interpretation of the data gathered. Such programs, some of which can link to external video recordings or to quantitative data analysis programmes, contribute to the retrievability of the data and make it readily available for re-analysis.

What, perhaps, is also lacking in the qualitative research conducted so far, is attention to the interpretations and uses of test scores by teachers and administrators. Shohamy (1997) foregrounded this area when she demonstrated how language tests are not simply used to assess language but also to promote bureaucratic agendas (and for gate-keeping and classification). The latter are not intended by the test developers but, covertly or overtly, they cannot fail to cause damage for which the test is likely to be blamed. Here, we might want to draw on methodology used by Cumming (1996) in his research into how teachers, students and school administrators use Canadian language standards (weekly interviews with teachers over a period of months and classroom observation).

Finally, studies have yet to use qualitative methods to investigate and appraise the underlying theories of language that a test is based on. Indeed, it is not even known if this is possible. What is clear, however, is that it is important to explore as many means as possible for establishing that the tests we use are working in the ways that we intend. Therein lies the challenge.

Lancaster University, England

and

University of Jyväskylä, Finland

REFERENCES

Alderson, J.C.: 1990, 'Testing reading comprehension skills (Part Two) Getting students to talk about taking a reading test (a pilot study)', *Reading in a Foreign Language* 7(1), 465–503.

Alderson, J.C., Clapham, C. & Wall, D.: 1995, *Language Test Construction and Evaluation*, Cambridge University Press, Cambridge.

Alderson, J.C. & Banerjee, J.V.: 1997, 'Validation and impact studies', paper presented at the annual conference of the American Association of Applied Linguistics, Orlando, Florida, March 1997.

Allan, A.I.C.G.: 1995, 'Begging the questionnaire: instrument effect on readers' responses to a self-report checklist', *Language Testing* 12(2), 133–156.

American Psychological Association, American Educational Research Association, and National Council on Measurement in Education: 1985, *Standards for Educational and Psychological Testing*, American Psychological Association, Washington D.C.

Anastasi, A.: 1986, 'Evolving concepts of test validation', *Annual Reviews of Psychology* 37, 1–15.

Angoff, W.H.: 1988, 'Validity: An evolving concept', in H. Wainer & H.I. Braun (eds.), *Test Validity*, Lawrence Erlbaum Associates (Publishers), Hillsdale, N.J., 19–32.

Bachman, L.F.: 1990, *Fundamental Considerations in Language Testing*, Oxford University Press, Oxford.

Bachman, L.F., Davidson, F. Ryan, K. & Choi, I.: 1995, *An Investigation into the Comparability of Two Tests of English as a Foreign Language. The Cambridge-TOEFL Comparability Study*, Cambridge University Press, Cambridge.

Bachman, L.F. & Palmer, A.: 1996, *Language Testing in Practice*, Oxford University Press, Oxford.

Berry, V.: in progress, *An Investigation into how Individual Differences in Personality Affect the Complexity of Language Test Tasks*.

Bradshaw, J.: 1990, 'Test-takers' reactions to a placement test', *Language Testing* 7(1), 13–30.

Brown, A:. 1993, 'The role of test-taker feedback in the test development process: Test-takers' reactions to a tape-mediated test of proficiency in spoken Japanese', *Language Testing* 10, 277–303.

Brown, A. & Lumley, T.: 1997, 'Interviewer variability in specific-purpose language performance tests', in A. Huhta, V. Kohonen, L. Kurki-Suonio & S. Luoma (eds.), *Current Developments and Alternatives in Language Assessment*, Universities of Tampere and Jyväskylä, Tampere, Finland.

Buck, G.: 1994, 'The appropriacy of psychometric measurement models for testing second language listening comprehension', *Language Testing* 11(2), 145–170.

Clapham, C.: 1996, *The Development of IELTS: A Study of the Effect of Background Knowledge on Reading Comprehension*, Cambridge University Press, Cambridge.

Clapham, C.: 1997, 'The Academic Modules Reading', in C. Clapham and J. C. Alderson (eds.) IELTS Research Report 3, The British Council, the University of Cambridge Local Examinations Syndicate and the International Development Project for Australian Universities and Colleges, Cambridge.

Clark, J.L.D.: 1988, 'Validation of a tape-mediated ACTFL/ILR-scale based test of Chinese speaking proficiency', *Language Testing* 5(2), 187–232.

Cohen, A.: 1984, 'On taking language tests: What the students report', *Language Testing* 1(1), 70–81.

Cohen, A.: 1994, 'English for Academic Purposes in Brazil: The use of summary tasks', in C. Hill and K. Parry (eds.), *From Testing to Assessment: English as an International Language*, Longman, London, 174–204.

Cohen, A.: 1997, 'Towards enhancing verbal reports as a source of insights on test-taking strategies', in A. Huhta, V. Kohonen, L. Kurki-Suonio & S. Luoma (eds.), *Current Developments and Alternatives in Language Assessment*, Universities of Tampere and Jyväskylä, Tampere, Finland.

Cushing Weigle, S.: 1994, 'Effects of training on raters of ESL compositions', *Language Testing* 11(2), 197–223.

Cumming, A.: 1996, 'Grade 9 teachers' use of language standards', *Research in Ontario Secondary Schools* 3(2), http://www.oise.utoronto.ca/field/centres.htm#10.

Dollerup, C., Glahn, E. & Rosenberg Hansen, C.: 1994, ' "Sprogtest": A smart test (or how to develop a reliable and anonymous EFL reading test)', *Language Testing* 11(1), 65–81.

Douglas, D.: 1994, 'Quantity and quality in speaking test performance', *Language Testing* 11(2), 125–144.

Ginther, A. & Grant, L.: 1997, 'Effects of language proficiency and topic on L2 writing', Paper presented at the annual conference for Teachers of English to Speakers of Other Languages, Orlando, Florida, March 1997.

Grotjahn, R.: 1986, 'Test validation and cognitive psychology: Some methodological considerations', *Language Testing* 3(2), 159–185.

Halvari, A. & Tarnanen, M.: 1997, 'Some aspects of using qualitative procedures to ensure comparability across languages within a testing system', in A. Huhta, V. Kohonen, L. Kurki-Suonio & S. Luoma (eds.), *Current Developments and Alternatives in Language Assessment*, Universities of Tampere and Jyväskylä, Tampere, Finland.

Kenyon, D.M. & Stansfield, C.W.: 1993, 'A method for improving tasks on performance-based assessments through field-testing', in A. Huhta, K. Sajavaara & S. Takala (eds.) *Language Testing: New Openings*, Institute for Educational Research, Jyväskylä, Finland, 90–102.

Lazaraton, A.: 1992, 'The structural organization of a language interview: a conversation analytic perspective', *System* 20, 373–386.

Lazaraton, A.: 1996, 'Interlocutor support in oral proficiency interviews: The case of CASE', *Language Testing* 13(2), 151–172.

Leung, C. & Teasdale, A.: 1997, 'Raters' understanding of rating scales as abstracted concept and as instruments for decision making', Paper presented at the Language Testing Research Colloquium, Orlando, Florida, March 1997.

Li, W.: 1992, *What is a Test Testing? An Investigation of the Agreement between Students' Test Taking Processes and Test Constructors' Presumption*, Unpublished MA Thesis, Lancaster University, England.

Lumley, T.: in progress, *The Processes of Assessing Writing Performance: The Raters' Perspective*.

Luoma, S.: in progress, *What Do Oral Test Scores Stand for: Evidence from Performances and Raters*.

Lynch, B.: 1996, *Language Program Evaluation: Theory and Practice*, Cambridge University Press, Cambridge.

Messick, S.A.: 1988, 'The once and future issues of validity: assessing the meaning and consequences of measurement', in H. Wainer and H.I. Braun (eds.), *Test Validity*, Lawrence Erlbaum Associates (Publishers), Hillsdale, N.J., 33–45.

Messick, S.A.: 1989, 'Validity', in R.L. Linn (ed.) *Educational Measurement* (third edition), American Council on Education/Macmillan, New York, 13–103.

Milanovic, M. & Saville, N.: 1994, 'An investigation of marking strategies using verbal protocols', *Paper presented at the 1994 Language Testing Research Colloquium*, Washington, D.C., March 1994.

Morrow, K.: 1986, 'The evaluation of tests of communicative performance', in M. Portal (ed.), *Innovations in Language Testing*, NFER/Nelson, London, 1–13.

Munby, J.: 1978, *Communicative Syllabus Design*, Cambridge University Press, Cambridge.

Nevo, N.: 1989, 'Test-taking strategies on a multiple-choice test of reading comprehension', *Language Testing* 6(2), 199–215.

O'Loughlin, K.: 1995, 'Lexical density in candidate output', *Language Testing* 12(2), 217–237.

O'Loughlin, K.: in progress, *The Comparability of Direct and Semi-Direct Speaking Tests: A Case Study*.

Pavlou, P.: 1997, 'Do different speech interactions in an oral proficiency test yield different kinds of language?', in A. Huhta, V. Kohonen, L. Kurki-Suonio & S. Luoma (eds.), *Current Developments and Alternatives in Language Assessment*, Universities of Tampere and Jyväskylä, Tampere, Finland.

Ross, S.: 1992, 'Accommodative questions in oral proficiency interviews', *Language Testing* 9, 173–186.

Ross, S. & Berwick, R.: 1992, 'The discourse of accommodation in oral proficiency interviews', *Studies in Second Language Acquisition* 14, 159–176.

Seliger, H.W. & Shohamy, E.: 1989, *Second Language Research Methods*, Oxford University Press, Oxford.

Shepard, L.: 1993, 'Evaluating test validity', *Review of Research in Education* 19, 405–450.

Shohamy, E.: 1994, 'The validity of direct versus semi-direct oral tests', *Language Testing* 11(2), 99–123.

Shohamy, E.: 1997, 'Critical language testing and beyond', *Plenary Address given at the annual conference of the American Association of Applied Linguistics*, Orlando, Florida. March 1997.

Shohamy, E., Donitsa-Schmidt, S. & Waizer, R.: 1993, 'The effect of the elicitation mode on the language samples obtained on oral tests', Paper presented at the Language Testing Research Colloquium, Cambridge, England, August 1993.

Wall, D. & Alderson, J.C.: 1993, 'Examining washback: The Sri Lankan impact study', *Language Testing* 10(1), 41–69.

Weir, C.J.: 1983, 'The Associated Examining Board's Test in English for Academic Purposes: An exercise in content validation', in A. Hughes and D. Porter (eds.), *Current Developments in Language Testing*, Academic Press, London, 147–153.

Weir, C.J.: 1988, 'The specification, realization and validation of an English language proficiency test', in A. Hughes (ed.), *Testing English for University Study*, Modern English Publications, Oxford, 45–110.

Weitzman, E.A. & Miles, M.B.: 1995, *Computer Programs for Qualitative Data Analysis: A Software Sourcebook*, Sage Publications Inc., Thousand Oaks, CA.

Young, R. 1995: 'Conversational styles in language proficiency interviews', *Language Learning* 45(1), 3–42.

Section 4

The Ethics and Effects of Testing and Assessment

DIANNE WALL

IMPACT AND WASHBACK IN LANGUAGE TESTING

'Impact' refers to any of the effects that a test may have on individuals, policies or practices, within the classroom, the school, the educational system or society as a whole. It is generally accepted that 'high-stakes' tests (defined by Madaus, 1988, p.87 as "those whose results are seen – rightly or wrongly – by students, teachers, administrators, parents, or the general public, as being used to make important decisions that immediately and directly affect them") will influence the way that students and teachers behave as well as their perceptions of their own abilities and worth. They may influence the content and methodology of teaching programmes, attitudes towards the value of certain educational objectives and activities, the academic and employment options that are open to individuals, and, in the long term, they may "reduce the diversity of talent available to schools and society" (Ebel, 1966, quoted in Kirkland, 1971, p. 305). Given this potential power, they "can become targets for contending parties who seek to maintain or establish a particular vision of what education and society should be" (Eckstein and Noah, 1993, p. 191).

'Washback' (also known as 'backwash') is sometimes used as a synonym of 'impact', but it is more frequently used to refer to the effects of tests on teaching and learning. Although there are many claims about the power of tests to affect what goes on in the classroom, the literature in language education offers few descriptions of the types of tests that are said to have this power and little empirical work has been undertaken to investigate whether washback really exists or what forms it might take (Alderson & Wall, 1993).

EARLY DEVELOPMENTS

Concern has long been voiced about the impact of tests on education and society. Simon (1974, p. 86) reports complaints about the negative effects of tests from as far back as 1802, when the introduction of a new examination at Oxford meant that "the student's education became more narrow than before, since he was likely to concentrate only on examined subjects" (quoted in Mathews, 1985, p. 27). The general education literature contains numerous discussions about the effects of tests in different educational settings. Kirkland (1971) describes how testing affects students (self-concept, motivation, levels of aspiration, anxiety, study practices, coaching effects, opportunities for advancement), parents, teachers (con-

C. Clapham and D. Corson (eds), Encyclopedia of Language and Education,
Volume 7: Language Testing and Assessment, 291–302.
© *1997 Kluwer Academic Publishers. Printed in the Netherlands.*

tent, teaching methods, evaluation of teaching effectiveness), schools (curriculum and methods), and society (allocation of opportunities, expanded concept of ability, maximising individual potential). Popham (1987) introduces the term 'measurement-driven instruction' to refer to situations in which important tests can lead to educational improvement. He maintains that measurement-driven instruction can succeed if the knowledge and skills that are to be measured are well chosen, if there is a manageable number of such skills, if the tests are criterion-referenced and provide clear targets for teachers, and if adequate support is given to teachers to help them to teach. Madaus (1988) condemns measurement-driven instruction as "nothing more than psychometric imperialism". He presents a set of 'principles' which summarise his own views on the impact of testing: the power of tests is a perceptual phenomenon, the higher the stakes attached to a test the more it will distort the teaching process, past exam papers eventually become the teaching curriculum, teachers adjust their teaching to fit the form of exam questions, test results become the major goal of schooling, and the agencies which set or control examinations eventually assume control over the curriculum. Crooks (1988) discusses the influence of 'classroom evaluation activities' on students. He believes that testing can have a positive effect on learning if teachers stress the need for 'deep learning' rather than 'surface learning', use evaluation to assist students rather than to judge them, use feedback to focus students' attention on their progress, set high but attainable standards, and select evaluation tasks to suit the goals being assessed.

Early references to the impact of tests in language education include Davies (1968), Madsen (1976) and Wesdorp (1982). In a report to the West African Examination Council on the feasibility of introducing a new oral exam, Davies presented three demands which must be met by every good educational test: it should be simple, its syllabus should be teachable, and its effects should be beneficial. Davies hoped that a new oral exam would produce beneficial effects not only in secondary schools, but in teacher training colleges and, by extension, in primary education. He stressed, however, that the test would need to possess both content and predictive validity, and would have to overcome various practical constraints within the educational setting. Madsen recounts the introduction of a new English examination in another part of Africa, which was supposed to be accompanied by new developments in teacher training and which was meant to be revised frequently in order to reflect changes in the curriculum. These developments did not take place, which led to a 'petrification' of the examination and 'devastating' effects on teaching. Wesdorp describes a series of investigations which were carried out in The Netherlands in the late 1970s, to determine whether the introduction of multiple-choice tests in Dutch and foreign language education would have adverse effects on teaching and learning. Wesdorp could find no evidence that the new tests were having the negative effects that teachers feared they would have (including an 'impoverishment' of the curriculum, a decline in the use of certain teaching methods, and effects on students' study habits).

MAJOR CONTRIBUTIONS

The past decade has witnessed growing interest in the notion of language test impact or washback. References can generally be categorised in one of three ways: claims about the importance of washback and expressions of hope or worry concerning the washback of specific examinations; enquiries into the nature of washback and other types of impact; and accounts of research undertaken to determine whether washback has occurred and, if so, what form it has taken.

There are many claims about the effects of tests on teaching, ranging from the axiomatic ("If it is a good examination, it will have a useful effect on teaching; if bad, then it will have a damaging effect on teaching", Heaton, 1990, p. 16) to the provocative – Morrow's coining of the term 'washback validity' and his belief that "the first validity criterion (should be) a measure of how far the intended washback effect was actually being met in practice" (1986, p. 6). Despite the warnings of Madaus (1988) and other general educationalists about the negative effects of testing, some language educators see washback in a positive way. Swain (1985) recommends that testers 'work for washback', and describes a test which she and colleagues developed in Canada in order to promote beneficial effects in French immersion situations. Davies (1985, p. 7) states that change in language teaching is best achieved through the syllabus and the examination and the teacher working together, but

> If a choice has to be made among these in order to move quickly,
> then undoubtedly the test/examination is the most sensitive; it
> is the most controllable, it acts overall, it is most difficult ... to
> ignore, it has most certainty in terms of its goals.

Davies warns, however, that the test should not move so quickly that the syllabus and the teacher cannot catch up. Pearson (1988) refers to tests as 'levers for change', and discusses attempts in Sri Lanka to reinforce innovations in other parts of the curriculum by introducing tests which match these innovations. Similar hopes are expressed by Li (1990) concerning tests in China, Wesche (1987) concerning the Ontario Test of English as a Second Language, and Allen (1994) concerning a new test of English for the Zimbabwean Junior Certificate. Other language educators fear the harmful effects that influential tests may have: Raimes (1990) laments the "proliferation of coaching and test-specific instructional materials" for the Test of Written English, and Peirce (1992) is concerned that the TOEFL

Reading Test may encourage an approach to reading texts which may not match what test-takers need outside the testing situation.

Alderson & Wall's 1993 review, 'Does Washback Exist?', claims that little evidence has been presented, either in general education or language education, to support the argument that tests influence teaching. They analyse the concept of washback and propose a number of Washback Hypotheses that researchers could use to sort out what effects tests have on teaching and for whom. They then review a number of empirical studies to discover the types of washback that are said to have occurred in certain settings, how the washback was measured and the factors that contributed to the effects. This research includes studies by Kellaghan, Madaus & Airasian (1982) into the effects of standardised testing in Ireland; Smith (1991) into the effects of mandated testing in Arizona; Wesdorp (1982) into the use of multiple choice tests in The Netherlands; Hughes (1988) into the effects of a high-stakes EAP test in Turkey; Khaniyah (1990) into the possible effects of the School Leaving Certificate in Nepal; and Wall & Alderson (1993) into the washback of a new O-Level examination in Sri Lanka. They found that most such research is based on analyses of test results or teachers' and students' accounts of what takes place in the classroom; only the Wall and Alderson study included classroom observation amongst its research methods.

Further discussions about the nature of washback include Bailey (1996) and Messick (1996), which both appear in a special issue of *Language Testing* (13/3) devoted to washback. Bailey explores the nature of washback, how it works, how it can be promoted and how it can be investigated, and constructs a model which elaborates on Hughes' 1993 distinction between washback on the participants, the process and the product of teaching and learning. Messick argues against the notion of a separate 'washback validity' (see Morrow, 1986), stating that

> washback is only one form of testing consequence that needs
> to be weighed in evaluating validity, and testing consequences
> are only one aspect of construct validity needing to be addressed
> (p. 242).

Other 'consequential aspects' include issues of bias, fairness and distributive justice. (See the reviews by Norton and Hamp-Lyons in this volume.)

Recent accounts of research into washback include several studies from Hong Kong: Lam (1993) investigates 10 hypotheses related to the New Use of English Examination; Boyle and Suen (1994) discuss a new listening test for the Hong Kong Certificate of Education Examination in English (HKCEE); Andrews and Fullilove (1994) discuss the effects of the same listening test and impression-marking in the same examination. In Israel Shohamy (1993) investigates the effects of three national language tests and reports that while they all achieved 'instrumental impact' in their first years of existence it was not clear whether they would achieve 'conceptual impact'. Shohamy, Donitsa-Schmidt & Ferman (1996) report on the long-term effects of two of the same tests. They conclude that washback varies over time, and that the nature of the washback at any given time is a function of the purpose of the test, its format, and other factors.

Alderson and Hamp-Lyons (1996) present an investigation into the effects of the TOEFL examination in a language institute in the United States, analysing TOEFL preparation classes and 'normal' classes being taught by the same teachers. They found that there were differences between the TOEFL and non-TOEFL classes for each teacher, but that the differences between the teachers was at least as great as the differences between types of classes. This leads them to conclude that it is not the test alone which determines what will happen in the classroom, but rather a complex set of factors, including individual characteristics of the teachers.

Watanabe (1996) discusses whether there is any connection between university entrance examinations in Japan and the prevalence of grammar-translation teaching in that country. He analyses the teaching which takes place at a *yobiko* (examination preparation centre) in central Tokyo, comparing the lessons given by two different teachers to prepare their students for two different university entrance exams – one which emphasises grammar-translation and one which does not. Watanabe concludes that it is too simple to expect that examinations will affect all teachers in the same way: like Alderson and Hamp-Lyons (1986) he considers that the personal characteristics of the teachers (in this case, educational background and beliefs about teaching) and, possibly, the proximity of the exam in terms of time have an important role to play in how teachers conduct their lessons.

WORK IN PROGRESS

Work in progress includes attempts to identify and account for the washback and other types of impact in high-stakes examinations in specific areas of the world, an analysis by a major examining body of the implications of washback for its own organisation, and an attempt to gain insights from work in the field of educational innovation that will be helpful to those who wish to introduce change through testing.

Cheng (1997, and in progress) has attempted to trace the impact of the revised HKCEE in English since the first official announcement that the exam was to be revised. As with many Hong Kong Education Authority (HKEA) examinations, the revision of the HKCEE in English was a deliberate attempt to provoke changes in teaching and learning. The announcement concerning the changes was followed very quickly by training seminars all over the territory, given by the HKEA itself, tertiary institutions, and textbook publishers. The publishers' seminars, which included presentations of materials and demonstrations of many classroom activities, attracted the largest audiences. Cheng used questionnaires, interviews and observations during the first year after the changes were announced, and discovered that the new examination was having considerable influence on the types of materials that teachers were using and on the activities that they were presenting in the lessons. She suggests, however, that these changes were changes of 'form' rather than of 'substance', and that teachers were more influenced by publishers' understanding of the new HKCEE than by their own. Further investigations the next year (the year just before the first administration of the revised examination) revealed that although the exam (or the publishers' understanding of the exam) influenced lesson content and some aspects of teacher behaviour, "it has not changed (teachers') fundamental beliefs and attitudes about teaching and learning, the roles of teacher and students, and how teaching and learning should be carried out". It will be interesting to investigate whether the first administration of the examination (May 1996) has affected teachers in more profound ways, or, indeed, whether any examination can provoke changes in teachers' beliefs about how best to teach.

Further work is being carried out in Hong Kong by Andrews and Fullilove (personal communication), who are investigating the washback effect of the oral component of the Use of English (AS-level) examination upon students' spoken language performance. Their data include videotapes of three cohorts of students performing oral tests similar to the Use of English speaking component, and examiners' marks for these performances. The next phase of their work will involve detailed analysis of the content of students' oral presentations and contributions to group discussion.

Other work on the influence of high-stakes examinations in regional or national settings includes Burrows and Perrins (personal communications). Burrows is using interviews and classroom observation to investigate the effects of testing within the New South Wales Adult Migrant Education Program, while Perrins is studying the effects on teacher practice and student motivation of examination requirements at Government Language Centres in Germany.

Milanovic and Saville (in progress) describe the efforts taken by the University of Cambridge Local Examinations Syndicate (UCLES) "to create positive impact and to monitor and assess the nature of the impact Cambridge examinations inevitably have". UCLES EFL examinations, which include the Certificate of Proficiency in English (CPE), the First Certificate in English (FCE), and the International English Language Testing System (IELTS) amongst others, were taken by over 500,000 candidates in 150 countries in 1995. Milanovic and Saville explain four maxims which the examining body have adopted for achieving appropriate impact: planning (using a rational and explicit approach to test development), supporting stakeholders in the testing process (item writers, consultants and experts in the field, examiners, local administrators, teachers, candidates, parents, publishers, employers and receiving institutions), communicating (providing comprehensive, useful and transparent information), and monitoring and evaluating the tests themselves and their impact. Under this last heading they refer to a group of studies which are currently being carried out into the impact of the IELTS examination (IELTS is designed mainly to assess candidates' ability to pursue higher education in English-speaking countries). The studies focus on the content and teaching activities in IELTS preparation classes, the nature of IELTS teaching materials, the attitudes of various user groups towards the examination, and details of the IELTS population and how test results are used. This work may be extended to investigate in detail the impact of other UCLES examinations.

Wall (1996) argues that those who wish to use testing as a way of bringing about change in the curriculum should consider not only the guidelines given by language specialists on how to produce positive washback (e.g. Hughes, 1989, Shohamy, 1992, and Bailey, 1996), but also the insights of testing specialists in general education and, more importantly, those of researchers in educational innovation. The starting point for Wall's interest in innovation was an examination evaluation project that she worked on in the late 1980s and early 90s, which investigated whether an exam which was designed to reinforce other curricular innovations was having the intended washback effect. The research revealed that there were many factors which influenced what teachers taught and how they taught it, and this led to the conclusion that

> ... if an exam is to have the impact intended, educationalists and education managers need to consider a range of factors that affect how innovations succeed or fail and that influence teacher (and pupil) behaviours. The exam is only one of these factors. (Wall & Alderson, 1993, p. 68).

Wall refers to several researchers in the field of educational innovation (amongst them Fullan 1991, Markee 1993, and Smith 1989) and reviews a number of ideas which are relevant for those who wish to innovate through testing. These include the notions that there are different phases in the process of innovation and different questions that need to be asked at each phase, that there are many participants involved in any attempt to introduce change and that the wants and needs of all of them must be taken into consideration, and that it is important to consider the attributes of the innovation, the resources available, and the peculiarities of the context in which the innovation is meant to develop. Wall suggests that an adequate model of impact must include all of these factors, and a description of the complex relationships between them.

PROBLEMS

Despite increasing interest in washback and other types of impact, there is still not enough research taking place to inform testers of the kinds of influence that it is reasonable to expect given certain test characteristics and certain features of the educational context, nor is there a comprehensive enough model to help educators to avoid the negative effects that are often associated with high-stakes testing ('narrowing of the curriculum' (Madaus, 1988), 'test score pollution' (Haladyna, Nolan & Haas, 1991), de-skilling of the teacher (Smith, 1991), etc.). As mentioned earlier, there have been attempts by various specialists to offer guidelines for the creation of positive washback; however, none of this advice incorporates all we need to know about tests, the uses to which they are put, the importance of the context, the test users, and other factors that are important to innovation.

It should be noted though that even if we were in possession of such a model there would still be practical problems to contend with. Whilst we are not fully aware of all the components that make for positive washback, many would agree with Frederiksen's view:

> An important task for educators and psychologists is to develop instruments to better reflect the whole domain of educational goals and find ways to use them in improving the educational process (1984, p. 201).

This, unfortunately, is easier said than done, especially when it means finding (and funding) special equipment (to test the ability to listen to conversations or media broadcasts), and highly proficient judges (to test the ability to write complete texts or to engage in spoken interaction, and to provide flexible yet reliable judgements). This may be possible in some settings, but it is bound to be difficult in contexts where it is necessary to test many candidates at the same time, or where there is poor resourcing, or where there are many teachers who have not received adequate training in either language or methodology. The desire for positive impact is thus frustrated by demands for practicality and reliability.

FUTURE DIRECTIONS

There is a clear need for more research into the nature of test washback and other forms of impact, and for a model which will guide testers on how best to produce and introduce tests in order to influence teaching, education and society in a positive way. This model should incorporate not only the views of language specialists but also those of:

- specialists from other subject areas (e.g. Pennycuik and Murphy (1988), who describe the impact of the Graded Tests Movement in the UK on the teaching not only of languages but also mathematics, science, business studies, etc.)

- educators from the primary, secondary and tertiary sectors
- examining bodies in non-English-speaking countries. This may be possible through associations such as the Association of Language Testers in Europe (ALTE) or the International Language Testing Association (ILTA).
- international organisations, which have developed an understanding of many educational systems. (Specialists from the World Bank (amongst them Kellaghan & Greaney, 1992) have produced a number of important publications concerning examinations in developing countries, which respond in part to requests made by Akoha (1991) for more information about test development and validation in difficult circumstances.)

There is a also a need for a model of testing impact to incorporate more insights from innovation theory. This would be of great value for countries which have recently gained independence and wish to create their own examining systems, responding to new national needs. Work is now being carried out in the Baltic States to create new tests of English, and many insights from innovation theory are being used to try to ensure that the tests are not only valid, reliable and practical, but also welcomed as a positive influence on teaching (Wall, Kalnberzina, Mazuoliene & Truus, 1996). It is important that studies concerning test impact be written up for other countries to study and learn from.

Finally, there is clearly a need for international organisations such as ILTA to consider test impact when they construct their codes of practice (see the review by Davidson, Turner and Huhta in this volume), and for those who offer courses in language testing to devote some attention to the factors that need to be considered when innovating through testing.

For those who believe that high stakes testing can only be harmful (Madaus, 1988) the solution is to lobby to reduce the stakes, but this seems an idealistic situation for many educational systems, at least at present. An alternative view is offered by Eisemon:

> Examinations can be a powerful and positive instrument of educational policy if their impact on instruction and learning is better understood (1990, p. 69).

What is required is continuous, co-ordinated research into the effects, positive and negative, of high-stakes assessment, and co-operation amongst testers so that we can learn from the mistakes and successes of others.

Lancaster University, England

REFERENCES

Akoha, J.: 1991, 'Curriculum innovation and examination reform in Benin, West Africa', in C. Alderson & B. North (eds.), *Language Testing in the 1990s*, Macmillan Publishers Limited, London and Basingstoke, 198–208.

Alderson, J.C. & Hamp-Lyons, L.: 1996, 'TOEFL preparation courses: A study of washback', *Language Testing* 13(3), 280–297.

Alderson, J.C. & Wall, D.: 1993, 'Does washback exist?', *Applied Linguistics* 14(2), 115–129.

Allen, K.: 1994. 'English education in Zimbabwe: Testing communicative competence', in C. Hill, & K. Parry (eds), *From Testing to Assessment: English as an International Language*, Longman, Harlow, 149–173.

Andrews, S. & Fullilove, J.: 1994, 'Assessing spoken English in public examinations – Why and how?', in J. Boyle & P. Falvey (eds), *English Language Testing in Hong Kong*, The Chinese University Press, Hong Kong, 57–86.

Bailey, K.M.: 1996, 'Working for washback: A review of the washback concept in language testing', *Language Testing* 13(3), 257–279.

Boyle, J. & Suen, D.L.K.: 1994, 'Communicative considerations in a large-scale listening test', in J. Boyle & P. Falvey (eds), *English Language Testing in Hong Kong*, The Chinese University Press, Hong Kong, 31–56.

Cheng, L.: 1997, 'How does washback influence teaching? Implications for Hong Kong', *Language and Education 235* 11(1), 38–54.

Cheng, L.: in progress, 'Teachers' perspectives and actions toward a public examination change'.

Crooks, T.J.: 1988, 'The impact of classroom evaluation practices on students', *Review of Educational Research* 58(4), 438–481.

Davies, A. (ed.): 1968, *Language Testing Symposium*, Oxford University Press, London.

Davies, A: 1985, 'Follow my leader: Is that what language tests do?', in Y.P. Lee, A.C.Y. Fok, R. Lord, & G. Low (eds.), *New Directions in Language Testing*, Pergamon Press, Oxford, 3–13.

Eckstein, M. A. & Noah, H.J.: 1993, *Secondary School Examinations: International Perspectives on Policies and Practice*, Yale University Press, New Haven and London.

Eisemon, T.O.: 1990, 'Examinations policies to strengthen primary schooling in African countries', *International Journal of Educational Development* 10(1), 69–82.

Frederiksen, N.: 1984, 'The real test bias: Influences of testing on teaching and learning', *American Psychologist* 39(3), 193–202.

Fullan, M.G. with Stiegelbauer, S.: 1991, *The New Meaning of Educational Change* (2nd edition), Cassell, London.

Haladyna, T.M., Nolan, S.B. & Haas, N.S.: 1991, 'Raising standardized achievement test scores and the origins of test score pollution', *Educational Researcher* 20(5), 2–7.

Heaton, J.B.: 1990, *Classroom Testing*, Longman, Harlow.

Hughes, A.: 1988, 'Introducing a needs-based test of English language proficiency into an English-medium university in Turkey', in A. Hughes (ed.), *Testing English for University Study*, ELT Documents 127, Modern English Publications, London, 134–153.

Hughes, A.: 1989, *Testing for Language Teachers*, Cambridge University Press, Cambridge.

Hughes, A.: 1993, 'Backwash and TOEFL 2000', unpublished manuscript.

Kellaghan, T. & Greaney, V.: 1992, *Using Examinations to Improve Education: A Study of Fourteen African Countries*, World Bank, Washington D.C.

Kellaghan, T., Madaus, G.F. & Airasian, P.W.: 1982, *The Effects of Standardized Testing*, Kluwen, Nijholf Publishing, London.

Khaniyah, T.R.: 1990, *Examinations as Instrument for Educational Change: Investigating the Washback Effect of the Nepalese English Exams*, Unpublished PhD dissertation, University of Edinburgh, Scotland.

Kirkland, M.C.: 1971, 'The effect of tests on students and schools', *Review of Educational Research* 41(4), 303–350.

Lam, H.P.: 1993, *Washback – Can It Be Quantified?*, Unpublished MA thesis, University of Leeds, England.

Li, X.: 1990, 'How powerful can a language test be? The MET in China', *Journal of Multilingual and Multicultural Development* 11(5), 393–404.

Madaus, G.F.: 1988, 'The influence of testing on the curriculum', in L.N. Tanner (ed.), *Critical Issues in Curriculum: Eighty-seventh Yearbook of the National Society for the Study of Education*, University of Chicago Press, Chicago, IL, 83–121.

Madsen, H.: 1976, 'New alternatives in EFL exams or "how to avoid selling English short"', *English Language Teaching Journal* 30(2), 135–144.

Markee, N.: 1993, 'The diffusion of innovation in language teaching', *Annual Review of Applied Linguistics* 13, 229–243.

Mathews, J.C.: 1985, *Examinations: A Commentary*, George Allen & Unwin, London.

Messick, S.: 1996, 'Validity and washback in language testing', *Language Testing* 13(3), 241–256.

Milanovic, M. & Saville, N.: in progress, 'Considering the impact of Cambridge EFL Examinations'.

Morrow, K.: 1986, 'The evaluation of tests of communicative performance', in M. Portal (ed.), *Innovations in Language Testing*, NFER/Nelson, London, 1–13.

Pearson, I.:1988, 'Tests as levers for change', in D. Chamberlain & R. Baumgardner (eds.), *ESP in the Classroom: Practice and Evaluation*, ELT Documents 128, Modern English Publications, Hayes, Mddx, 98–107.

Peirce, B.N.: 1992, 'Demystifying the TOEFL reading test', *TESOL Quarterly* 26(4), 665–689.

Pennycuik, D. & Murphy, R.: 1988, *The Impact of Graded Tests*, The Falmer Press, London.

Popham, J.: 1987, 'The merits of measurement-driven instruction', *Phi Delta Kappa*, May, 679–682.

Raimes, A.: 1990, 'The TOEFL Test of Written English: causes for concern', *TESOL Quarterly* 24(3), 427–442.

Shohamy, E.: 1992, 'Beyond proficiency testing: A diagnostic feedback testing model for assessing foreign language learning', *The Modern Language Journal* 76(4), 513–521.

Shohamy, E.: 1993, 'The power of tests: The impact of language tests on teaching and learning', *NFLC Occasional Papers*, June. The National Foreign Language Center, Washington D.C.

Shohamy, E., Donitsa-Schmidt, S. & Ferman, I.: 1996, 'Test impact revisited: Washback effect over time', *Language Testing* 13(3), 298–317.

Simon, B.: 1974: *The Two Nations and Educational Structure 1780–1870*, Lawrence & Wishart, London.

Smith, H.J.: 1989, 'ELT project success and the management of innovation', unpublished manuscript, Centre for Applied Language Studies, University of Reading, England.

Smith, M.L.: 1991, 'Put to the test: The effects of external testing on teachers', *Educational Researcher* 20(5), 8–11.

Swain, M.: 1985, 'Large-scale communicative testing: A case study', in Y.P. Lee, C.Y.Y. Fok, R. Lord & G. Low (eds.), *New Directions in Language Testing*, Pergamon Press, Hong Kong, 35–46.

Wall, D.: 1996, 'Introducing new tests into traditional systems: Insights from general education and from innovation theory', *Language Testing* 13(3), 334–354.

Wall, D. & Alderson, J.C.: 1993, 'Examining washback: The Sri Lankan impact study', *Language Testing* 10(1), 41–69.

Wall, D., Kalnberzina, V., Mazuoliene, Z. & Truus, K.: 1996, 'The Baltic States Year 12 examination project', *Language Testing Update* 19, 15–28.

Watanabe, Y.: 1996, 'Does grammar-translation come from the entrance examination? Preliminary findings from classroom-based research', *Language Testing* 13(3), 319–333.

Wesche, M.: 1987. 'Second language performance testing: The Ontario test of ESL as an example'. *Language Testing* 4(1), 28–47.

Wesdorp, H.: 1982, 'Backwash effects of language testing in primary and secondary education', *Journal of Applied Language Study* 1(1), 40–55.

F. DAVIDSON, C.E. TURNER AND A. HUHTA

LANGUAGE TESTING STANDARDS

The word 'standard' typically has four different meanings when applied to education (in general) and language education (in particular):

1. A standard can refer to a guideline for good practice; for example, an important standard for educational tests is that their developers should demonstrate evidence of test validity. This meaning equates 'standards' (in the plural) with a code of professional practice or set of professional guidelines which could cover all stages of test development, from initial construction, through trialling, and on to operational use.

2. A standard can also refer to an expected performance. Firstly, it can refer to an expected level on a numerical scale at which some decision is made; for example, a score of 35 out of 50 on a written driver's licensing exam qualifies the applicant to take the behind-the-wheel portion of the test. Secondly, it can refer to descriptions of behavior at one or many levels of performance; for example: "At level two, examinees can perform simple spoken transactions in the foreign language, such as those typically involved in negotiation of daily shopping". (For suggestions on how to develop tests from such statements, see the review by Lynch and Davidson in this volume.)

3. A standard can refer to a widely-accepted test of a given skill; for example, one could claim that the Test of English as a Foreign Language (TOEFL) is a standard for the assessment of English as a second/foreign language. (For more information on the TOEFL, see Educational Testing Service, 1996.)

4. The term 'standard' can also refer to a language norm, either to a particular language or to a particular language construction. We see this as a use of 'standard' from the science of linguistics and not as one that is widely applied in educational measurement. There are interesting linguistic overtones, however, to our third definition of 'standard' given here. Perhaps the language features tested by a major exam like the TOEFL could define English (as a language) as well as the TOEFL (as a 'standard' test). This question needs further research (Davidson and Lowenberg, 1996).

Because of the importance of 'standard' test administration and control in many educational contexts, this article focuses on the first of these definitions. Such control is often seen as essential to the consistency of measurement, and the comparability of results across years, classes,

C. Clapham and D. Corson (eds), Encyclopedia of Language and Education,
Volume 7: Language Testing and Assessment, 303–311.
© *1997 Kluwer Academic Publishers. Printed in the Netherlands.*

and demographic cohorts. It is also a key component in debates about test bias and fairness. As will be shown, however, there is a competing tension. Standardization, control, and central guidelines all stand opposite the *realpolitik* of cultural variation in human assessment. The present challenge to the international language testing community is to balance this need for central control against the diversity of measurement beliefs and practices.

Recently, the *Report of the Task Force on Testing Standards (TFTS) to the International Language Testing Association (ILTA)* was published (TFTS, 1995). All three authors of this present review were members of the TFTS. Because of its current and international focus, extensive reference will be made to this report throughout this article. It is described more fully under 'Major Contributions' below. Information on how to obtain it is given in the list of References.

EARLY DEVELOPMENTS

Arguably, for as long as there have been organized tests, there have also been testing standards. Any test administration guideline given to a test proctor or administrator can be considered as such. Perhaps the earliest written evidence of such guidelines is the set of instructions drawn up by the Jesuits in the sixteenth century. DuBois (1970) notes that "the Jesuit Order, founded in 1540 by St. Ignatius of Loyola, were pioneers in the systematic use of written tests" for both placement and achievement (p. 8). He then goes on to list guidelines for the conduct of examinations which were compiled by the Jesuits in 1599 as part of the larger *Ratio Studiorum*. These guidelines were largely administrative. For example, two of their admonitions were:

- Care should be taken that no copying be done by bench mates; if two compositions are found to be exactly alike, both of them (the students) are to be suspected since it is impossible to discover which of the two did the copying.
- When a student brings his finished composition to the prefect, he should take his books with him and depart quietly. The students that remain should not change their places but finish their work at their own desks (taken from McGucken, 1932, quoted in DuBois, 1970, p. 9).

The *Ratio* has formed the historical basis of much of Jesuit education and has been cited as one of the major works in the history of education in a survey of such publications (Pieper, 1953).

Another example of centralized, standard control of testing occurred in China, where for many years there was an extensive system of civil service tests. DuBois (1970) and Popham (1981) both discuss this and re-print a famous photograph of tightly clustered exam booths (originally published by the *National Geographic* in 1927). China's civil service testing was governed by a set of controls of great complexity and severity:

> (In Peking) in the Examination Hall were ten thousand cells, in which the contestants, cribbed and confined, lived with their own food and bedding for three separate days, while they wrote essays or theses on subjects announced to them after their imprisonment (Durant, 1935, p. 801).

Modern, large-scale test development continues to value centralized control, because it is thought that such control helps guarantee test quality. This quality is often checked using statistics; these are seen as a crucial tool in test development. The last 150 years have seen the development of a statistical methodology which bases test results on the normal curve distribution, a device for large-group decision making and socio-educational gatekeeping (see Gould, 1981; Kevles, 1985; Hacking, 1990). Such testing – now called 'norm referencing' – yields test results which are directly interpretable because they show where candidates rank among their peers. As long as a test is administered under controlled conditions, statistical procedures can provide the test constructor with the means for creating a normally-distributed test. Guidelines for good practice help to ensure that control.

MAJOR CONTRIBUTIONS

In 1993, recognizing the influence of such standards (i.e., guidelines and principles for test development and administration), ILTA formed the TFTS and asked it to conduct an international survey of existing assessment standards. As noted in the *TFTS Report*:

> The purpose of this project was twofold: first, it provides a general resource for scholars of educational and language assessment standards, and second, it serves as a specific resource for later ILTA efforts to draft its own code of practice, in that ILTA can consult this report to obtain information about extant documents of that nature. This was accomplished by contact with colleagues in the educational assessment community, both language testing and the broader educational testing domain (TFTS, 1995: p. 8).

The project was informed and aided by previous survey work on testing standards done in the U.K. and reported in Alderson, Clapham and Wall (1995).

The major component of the *TFTS Report* was a bibliographic database of documents returned from a survey of such writings. It reveals that there is great variability in the interpretation of 'standard' along the lines of the first three definitions cited at the beginning of this review: only 53.7% of the 110 respondent agencies yielded documents (or series of documents) which focused on Definition 1. What is more, within that 53.7% of responses, great variability was evident in the number of guidelines offered, and the length, focus and topic of each one. To illustrate this variability, here are the summaries of four sample entries from the *TFTS Report* bibliography:

Example 1

One major, influential document is that produced jointly by the American Psychological Association, the American Educational Research Association, and the National (U.S.) Council on Measurement in Education (hereafter 'APA/AERA/NCME Standards'). Its Table of Contents, which is presented below, shows the wide reach of its testing guidelines. The chapter headings are annotated to show how many standards are presented in each chapter:

Part I: 'Technical Standards for Test Construction and Evaluation'
    Chapter 1: 'Validity' (25 Standards)
    Chapter 2: 'Reliability and Errors of Measurement'(12 Standards)
    Chapter 3: 'Test Development and Revision' (25 Standards)
    Chapter 4: 'Scaling, Norming, Score Comparability, and Equating'
        (9 Standards)
    Chapter 5: 'Test Publication: Technical Manuals and User's Guides.'
        (11 Standards)
Part II: 'Professional Standards for Test Use'
    Chapter 6: 'General Principles of Test Use' (13 Standards)
    Chapter 7: 'Clinical Testing' (6 Standards)
    Chapter 8: 'Educational Testing and Psychological Testing in the
        Schools' (12 Standards)
    Chapter 9: 'Test Use in Counseling' (9 Standards)
    Chapter 10: 'Employment Testing' (9 Standards)
    Chapter 11: 'Professional and Occupational Licensure and Certifica-
        tion' (5 Standards)
    Chapter 12: 'Program Evaluation' (8 Standards)
Part III: 'Standards for Particular Applications'
    Chapter 13: 'Testing Linguistic Minorities' (7 Standards)
    Chapter 14: 'Testing People Who Have Handicapping Conditions'
        (8 Standards)
Part IV: 'Standards for Administrative Procedures'
    Chapter 15: 'Test Administration, Scoring, and Reporting' (11 Stan-
        dards)
    Chapter 16: 'Protecting the Rights of Test Takers' (10 Standards)
(TFTS 1995, pp. 145–146).

Example 2

As another example, 'Standards for the Design and Operations in IEA Studies', produced by the International Association for the Evaluation of

Educational Achievement, offers some samples of educational measurement guidelines. The IEA is an organization which studies educational practice and achievement across countries and cultures. Its activities require that it establish permanent standards for the design and data collection of IEA studies, as noted in the *TFTS Report*:

> The document first argues that the changing needs require permanent standards for the IEA studies (results from different studies need to be linked, educational achievement needs to be measured over time). Also, the credibility of the studies requires that minimum standards are specified and applied. Standards can ensure, e.g. that
>
> - populations and entities of reporting are in fact comparable
> - definitions of variables and their operationalizations are valid and equivalent
> - measurement of variables is consistent over time and across countries
> - data collection and management are comparable
> - data analyses match the type and quality of data and the reporting requirements
> - various survey constraints have a similar impact in different systems (TFTS, 1995, p. 105).

Example 3

Some world testing standards documents received by the TFTS reflect an understanding of cultural variation in assessment practice. One of these is a document from the United Nations Educational, Scientific and Cultural Organization (UNESCO) entitled 'Monitoring Education-For-All Goals' which focuses on learning achievement. Countries participating in the project were asked to prepare their own instruments for evaluating achievement according to a common framework. The document said that international studies such as its own should

> ... avoid common problems of dependency and encourage a participatory approach by:
>
> 1. ensuring that all issues relating to the overall project design (i.e. target groups, instrument construction, sampling procedures, data collection, analysis and reporting) were initiated, discussed, pre-tested and fine-tuned by a core group of national experts, under the guidance of the national task force in each country;
> 2. recognizing the uniqueness of each country's sociocultural, linguistic, developmental and educational characteristics, thus facilitating the analysis of country-based data; and

3. ensuring that the measurement indicators were set, defined and reported by the countries themselves and that basic learning competencies were defined and standards for literacy, numeracy and life-skills set by the countries themselves (TFTS, 1995 p. 85).

Example 4

The TFTS found that the definition of 'standard' as a guideline for good practice in assessment must, itself, be rather broadly interpreted. The above three examples tend to emphasize reliability and validity in measurement – they read as technical quality controls, like those an industry would impose on itself to keep its product viable. There were also documents which had a consumer-oriented tone. One example is the *Principles for Fair Student Assessment Practices for Education in Canada* (Joint Advisory Committee, 1993), which sought to "provide a nation-wide consensus on a set of principles and related guidelines generally accepted by professional organizations as indicative of fair assessment practice within the Canadian educational context". (*TFTS Report*, 1995, p. 54). This document is organized into two parts: the first is directed at school assessment at the elementary and secondary level, and the second at standardized commercial testing developed outside the classroom. Each part "contains five sections (of guidelines): 1. Developing and choosing methods for assessment; 2. Collecting assessment information; 3. Judging and scoring student performance; 4. Summarizing and interpreting results; and 5. Reporting assessment findings" (TFTS, 1995, p. 55).

WORK IN PROGRESS

The Association of Language Testers in Europe (ALTE) has written a *Code of Practice*, a document which has an international (albeit European) focus (ALTE, 1995). This *Code* is referred to in the *TFTS Report* (pp. 74–75), and its history and structure are reviewed by Alderson, Clapham and Wall (1995, p. 245). ALTE continues to grow, and it will doubtless refine and review these guidelines in coming years. (For more about ALTE, see the review by Norton in this volume.)

ILTA itself has undertaken to write its own set of standards, to be called a 'Code of Practice'. Two groups have been formed: a small core group which will write the code, and a larger advisory panel which will review the product of the core group. Because of ILTA's international membership, its Code, when completed, must speak to many different "measurement cultures" (Davidson & Bachman, 1990) – many epistemologies and philosophies of human assessment. The survey contained in the *TFTS Report* provides the foundation for the complex task of writing a set of professional guidelines for language testers around the world.

PROBLEMS AND DIFFICULTIES

The four samples cited above represent the complex variety found in the TFTS survey. The APA/AERA/NCME document is extremely large and somewhat oriented toward a statistical, norm-referenced 'standardized' vision of testing. The IEA document portrays the complexity of problems in international comparative education. The UNESCO booklet emphasizes the uniqueness of test practice in different cultures. The example from Canada displays a social, consumer-oriented concern.

In addition to the diversity seen in world standards of educational assessment, it must be pointed out that some classroom testing exists without any written guidelines. Some educational systems assume that if one is a qualified language teacher, then one is also a qualified language tester. This assumption adds yet further diversity to the scope of standards in language assessment. Many of the documents collected by the TFTS are as relevant to the classroom teacher as they are to the professional test developer (on this point, see Davidson et al., 1995). Standards relate to high- or low-stakes testing, and sometimes to both. For example, issues of testing consequence (see Messick, 1989) certainly apply to all forms of educational assessment, but the consequences of a classroom quiz are rather different from those of a national exam.

Whether intended for testing agencies, classroom use, or both, any standards document is shaped by questions of influence and enforcement. What, precisely, is a standards document? Is it a 'seal of approval' – does its authoring agency purport to evaluate and rate tests? Is it law? (The APA/AERA/NCME Standards are cited in the legal statutes of at least one state in the USA, see TFTS, 1995, pp. 150–151). Is its impact actually a function of the social and political influence of its authoring agency? Do standards function as agents of reform – of washback (Alderson and Wall, 1993)? Are standards equally applicable to all stages of testing and all testing purposes (e.g. formative versus summative)?

These various issues seem to reflect a single powerful theme – a persistent challenge facing any group which sets out to write international language assessment standards. There is a constant tension between a desire to coordinate and control testing on the one hand and a need to recognize contextualized diversity on the other. How can one set of standards – one 'code' – speak evenhandedly for so many needs?

FUTURE DIRECTIONS

The history of the first TFTS example given above may indicate how this tension could be resolved. Before the APA/AERA/NCME Standards were published (the earliest version appeared in the 1950s) there existed only catalogs of standard, accepted tests; these related to Definition 3 above.   As time passed, that professional service came to be supplied by two publications begun by Oscar Buros at Rutgers University: *The Mental Measurement Yearbook* and *Tests in Print* (see Buros Institute, 1983; 1992). These publications are serials; they are updated regularly to serve as bibliographic guides for professionals wishing to select a test. The U.S. testing industry grew from a need to recommend standard measures (Definition 3) to a need to catalog measures and recommend practice (Definition 1).

Perhaps international language testing is in a similar situation. Perhaps it needs not only culturally or contextually situated codes of practice (such as the APA/AERA/NCME document itself) but also some new meta-document, some new genre of educational assessment guidebook that represents a common shared vision of reliable, valid and fair assessment in all countries and cultures. Active discussions in ILTA suggest that the format and organization of its forthcoming Code are not yet fixed, and it is possible that the Code will offer suggestions for central organization and control while at the same time allowing for diversity of cultural approaches to educational assessment.

University of Illinois, Urbana-Champaign, USA

and

McGill University, USA

and

University of Jyväskylä, Finland

REFERENCES

Alderson, J.C., Clapham, C. & Wall, D.: 1995, *Language Test Construction and Evaluation*, Cambridge University Press, Cambridge.
Alderson, J.C., & Wall, D.: 1993, 'Does washback exist?', *Applied Linguistics* 14, 115–129.
American Educational Research Association/American Psychological Association/National Council on Measurement in Education: 1985, *Standards for Educational and Psychological Testing*, American Psychological Association, Washington, DC.
Association of Language Testers in Europe (ALTE): 1995, *The ALTE Code of Practice*, ALTE, Cambridge. To obtain this document, write to ALTE, c/o EFL Division, UCLES, 1 Hills Road, Cambridge, CB1 2EU, UK.
Buros Institute: 1983, *Tests in Print*, Buros Institute of Mental Measurements, Lincoln, Nebraska.
Buros Institute: 1992, *Mental Measurement Yearbook*, Buros Institute of Mental Measurements, Lincoln, Nebraska.
Davidson, F. & Bachman, L.: 1990, 'The Cambridge-TOEFL comparability study: An example of the cross-national comparison of language tests', in John H.A.L. De Jong (ed.), *Standardization in Language Testing: AILA Review* 7, 24–45.

Davidson, F., Alderson, J.C., Douglas, D., Huhta, A., Turner, C. & Wylie, E.: 1995, 'An international survey of language assessment standards', *TESOL Journal* 5, 6–7.

Davidson, F. & Lowenberg, P.: 1996, *Language Testing and World Englishes: A Proposed Research Agenda*, Paper presented at the Third International Conference on World Englishes, Honolulu, Hawaii, December 19-21, 1996.

DuBois, P.H.: 1970, *A History of Psychological Testing*, Allyn and Bacon, Boston.

Durant, W.: 1935, *Our Oriental Heritage*, Simon and Schuster, New York.

Educational Testing Service (ETS): 1996, *1996–97 Bulletin of Information for TOEFL*, TWE and TSE, ETS, Princeton, NJ.

Gould, S.J.: 1981, *The Mismeasure of Man*, Norton, New York.

Hacking, I.: 1990, *The Taming of Chance*, Cambridge University Press, Cambridge.

International Association for the Evaluation of Educational Achievement (IEA): 1994, *Standards for the Design and Operations in IEA Studies*, IEA, The Hague.

Joint Advisory Committee: 1993, *Principles for Fair Student Assessment Practices for Education in Canada*, Joint Advisory Committee, Edmonton.

Kevles, D.J.: 1985, *In the Name of Eugenics: Genetics and the Uses of Human Heredity*, Knopf, New York.

McGucken, W.J.: 1932, *The Jesuits and Education: The Society's Teaching Principles and Practice*, Especially in Secondary Education in the United States, Bruce Publishing Co., New York.

Messick, S.: 1989, 'Validity', in R.L. Linn (ed.), *Educational Measurement*, 3rd. Edition, NCME/ACE – Macmillan, New York, 13–103.

Pieper, G.W.: 1953, 'The educational classics', *History of Education Journal* 4, 78–80.

Popham, W.J.: 1981, *Modern Educational Measurement*, Prentice Hall, Englewood Cliffs, NJ.

Task Force on Testing Standards (TFTS): 1995, *Report of the Task Force on Testing Standards (TFTS) to the International Language Testing Association (ILTA)*, ILTA, Melbourne. To obtain this document, contact: NLLIA Language Testing Research Centre, Department of Applied Linguistics and Language Studies, The University of Melbourne, Parkville, VIC 3052, Australia. Alternatively, the Report is available in the Educational Resources Information Clearinghouse (ERIC) Microfiche archive, record number ED390268 and on the World Wide Web via the ILTA home page: http://www.surrey.ac.uk/ELI/ilta/ilta.html

UNESCO: 1994, *Monitoring Education-For-All Goals: A Joint UNESCO-UNICEF Project*, UNESCO, Paris.

BONNY NORTON

ACCOUNTABILITY IN LANGUAGE ASSESSMENT

In many language assessment projects, stakeholders include test takers, teachers, test developers, administrators, community agencies, public officials, and researchers. Increasingly, calls for accountability in language assessment have focused on the consequences of assessment practices for test takers, who have hitherto been relatively powerless stakeholders in the field of language assessment. The recognition that language assessment practices should be accountable to test takers is indicative of the broader trend towards democratization of educational assessment in general. Such concerns are equally important in debates on ethics in language testing and language testing standards (see the reviews by Hamp-Lyons, and Davidson, Turner and Huhta in this volume.)

EARLY DEVELOPMENTS

In his article, 'The measurement of communicative competence', Canale (1988) argued that what he called 'the naturalistic-ethical approach' should complement the three trends in language testing outlined by Spolsky (1978). These trends were the traditional approach, focusing on language testing as an art; the psychometric-structuralist approach, focusing on language testing as a science; and the integrative-sociolinguistic approach, focusing on language testing as both art and science. Canale's main argument was that any information, once gathered, can be used unethically, and that language testers are to some extent accountable for ensuring that the information they gather is used for ethical purposes. Drawing on Messick (1981), he argued that language testers need to consider the social consequences that the use of a given test may have and that adequate training in testing and test use is required if language test developers and test users are to be professionally accountable.

In advocating a fourth approach to language assessment, Canale was subscribing to the views of those scholars who were arguing for greater accountability to test takers. These scholars included Cummins, Cohen, Deyhle, Fillmore, and Swain. Cummins (1984) argued that there was confusion in the language assessment of students in bilingual programmes because of the failure to develop an adequate theoretical framework for relating language proficiency to academic achievement. Cohen (1984) conducted research on second language test-taking strategies and concluded that there should be a better fit between the expectations of test developers

C. Clapham and D. Corson (eds), Encyclopedia of Language and Education,
Volume 7: Language Testing and Assessment, 313–322.
© 1997 Kluwer Academic Publishers. Printed in the Netherlands.

on the one hand and test takers on the other. Deyhle's (1986) research with Navajo students demonstrated that test taking itself is a cultural activity and that Navajo and Anglo students had very different conceptions of testing. Fillmore (1982) found that the texts used in reading comprehension tests for young children were highly problematic, requiring an "uncommon degree of tolerance and co-operation" (p. 251) on the part of the test taker. Swain (1985) argued that test developers should "bias for best" in the test development process in order to give test candidates the greatest opportunity to demonstrate their knowledge of the target language. All this research represents growing recognition that test takers come from heterogeneous, culturally diverse backgrounds that must be taken seriously in the assessment process.

MAJOR CONTRIBUTIONS

The drive towards greater accountability to test takers has been gathering momentum (see Kunnan, 1996). Language testers have shown increasing interest in the investments that test takers have in language tests and have raised concerns about the limitations of existing instruments. The practice and theory of accountability in language testing is being explored in different countries and with different populations of test takers. Sometimes, the focus of the work is on language testing per se; sometimes, language testing is integrated into broader initiatives for greater accountability in educational assessment.

Basing her research on Nigeria, Parry (1994) examines material from the English examination of the West African School Certificate (WASC). She demonstrates that there are subtle contradictions between what is stated in the reading passages and what is implied in the tasks. In Israel, Shohamy (1993a) conducted research on Arabic as a second language, English as a foreign language, and Hebrew as a first language, and concluded that the use of tests to solve educational problems is a simplistic approach to a complex problem. In the United States, research has illustrated the disjuncture between test taker identities and investments on the one hand, and large-scale standardized language tests on the other. Lowenberg's (1993) research on the Test of English for International Communication (TOEIC) calls into question the assumptions on which the test is based, arguing, in particular, that what constitutes standard English is open to international debate. Peirce's (1992) research on the Test of English as a Foreign Language (TOEFL) reading test highlights the unequal relationship between test makers and test takers and focuses on the need for greater accountability to test takers. Raimes (1990) raises concerns about the validity of the TOEFL Test of Written English and the washback effects the test will have (see Cumming's review in this volume). In Canada, Elson (1992) examines English as a Second Language (ESL) proficiency testing in the admissions process at Canadian universities. He argues that universities use language proficiency tests in such a way as to avoid taking responsibility for the educational needs of students from diverse backgrounds. With reference to South Africa, Peirce & Stein (1995) examine an alternative university admissions test and argue that there is a discrepancy between the test format and its purpose. In England, Alderson & Buck (1993) conducted a survey of British examination boards that offer English language tests and questioned whether they met high standards in educational measurement. Matthews (1990), likewise, has raised concerns about the assessment criteria of international examinations of English as a foreign language, particularly with respect to the assessment of productive skills.

Because concerns have been raised about the extent to which large-scale language assessment is accountable to test takers, there have been concerted efforts at more local levels to achieve greater accountability. Cohen (1994) describes his research on the innovative use of summary tasks to assess proficiency in reading English in a Brazilian university context. In Australia, the Bandscales project (McKay, 1995; Moore, 1996) places ESL development in the context of the school and its curriculum. By directing ESL programs and teachers to 'across the curriculum' concerns, the Bandscales developers seek to be accountable to language learners. (For more about this work, see McKay's review in this volume.) Kalantzis, Cope & Slade (1989), alternatively, argue that Halliday's systemic-functional linguistics can provide a comprehensive framework for assessment because it overcomes the competence/performance dichotomy that characterizes much linguistic theory. With reference to Zimbabwe, Allen (1994) describes the weakness of the Zimbabwe Junior Certificate exam and outlines principles on which a new test should be based. In Japan, Ingulsrud (1994) examines the reading assessment component of the Joint First Stage Achievement Test (JFSAT) that governs entrance into Japanese universities. He demonstrates how test developers are required to defend their practices in a public forum. In South Africa, Duncan (1995) draws on both quantitative and qualitative assessment to demonstrate the effectiveness of an innovative project to enhance both mother-tongue and English language proficiency, while Yeld & Haeck (1993) describe how assessment instruments can be used to promote the access of disadvantaged students to tertiary education.

In the United States, Lacelle-Peterson & Rivera (1994) argue that educational reform that serves anglophone students will not necessarily benefit English language learners; to address this problem, they provide a useful framework for the equitable assessment of English language learners. In an edited volume, Holland, Bloome & Solsken (1994) draw together a number of innovative assessment projects addressing the language and literacy skills of young school children. The articles represent three broad theoretical and disciplinary perspectives that are gaining wider acceptance in educational practice: anthropological, sociopsycholinguistic, and reader response. In Canada, Cumming (1994) reviews the functions of language assessment for recent immigrants to Canada and argues that assessment instruments should meet the important criterion of facilitating the participation of immigrants into Canadian society. Larter & Donnelly (1993) describe the development of the Toronto Benchmark Program, arguing that it provides a framework that is accountable to students, parents, and teachers. Wesche (1987) describes the potential of a performance-based assessment instrument to be used for post-secondary admission in Ontario. In the United Kingdom, Holland & Street (1994) describe the methods of assessing literacy skills developed by the Adult Literacy Basic Skills Unit, focusing in particular on the 'Progress Profile'. All of these initiatives represent innovative responses to the question of how test makers can be more accountable to test takers.

WORK IN PROGRESS

Currently there is much work in progress on the development of codes of practice and benchmark standards in language testing. Some of this work is informed by the development of the American Psychological Association (APA) Standards and the Code of Fair Testing Practices in Education (see Stansfield, 1993). The Association of Language Testers of Europe (ALTE) has developed a Code of Practice to make explicit the standards they aim to meet and the responsibilities they have undertaken (ALTE, 1994). ALTE represents language testing organizations in France, Spain, the Netherlands, Portugal, Denmark, Italy, Germany and the United Kingdom. The Code of Practice distinguishes between the interests of examination developers, examination users, and examination takers, and its central undertaking is "to safeguard the rights of examination takers" (ALTE, 1994, p. 4). In Canada, the federal government has sponsored the development of a document that provides a common framework for describing the language skills of adult clients across the country (Citizenship and Immigration Canada, 1996). This document addresses the needs of adult learners of ESL as well as adult literacy learners. Assessment instruments to be used for placement purposes have been developed in accordance with this document (Peirce & Stewart, 1997). In the international TESOL (Teachers of English to Speakers of Other Languages) organization, a working group has been established to review key issues in assessing the language development of English language learners. This development is an outgrowth of the ESL Standards Project (Katz & Short, 1996). Likewise, the International Language Testing Association (ILTA) is in the process of developing a Code of Practice for Language Testers internationally. (For more about such codes of practice, see the review by Davidson, Turner and Huhta in this volume.)

There are an increasing number of conferences that are focusing on accountability to test takers. In April 1992, a symposium on 'Testing English Across Cultures' was commissioned as part of the 'World Englishes Today' conference held in Urbana, Illinois, USA. As Davidson (1993, p. 114) notes, this conference raised questions about the variety of English that is promoted in international tests of English, and the "consequent irrelevance of the concept of 'native speaker' ''. In Turfloop, South Africa, in October 1994, the South African Association for Academic Development (SAAAD) held a conference with the theme, 'Accountability in Testing'. The central question addressed at the conference was as follows: How can tests be used innovatively to increase the access of historically disadvantaged English language learners to tertiary education in South Africa? At the second International Conference on Evaluation, held in Toronto, Canada, in October 1995, two plenary speakers, Linda Darling-Hammond and Caroline Gipps, addressed accountability in assessment. At the annual meeting of the Language Testing Research Colloquium (LTRC) in Long Beach, California, in March 1995, the theme of the conference was 'Validity and Equity Issues in Language Testing'. Only two years later, in 1997, the theme of this same conference, held in Orlando, Florida was 'Fairness in Language Testing'. (For more about other presentations at international conferences, see Hamp-Lyons' review in this volume.) It is anticipated that all this work in progress will generate further research and publications on accountability in language assessment.

PROBLEMS AND DIFFICULTIES

Even as interest in accountability towards individual test takers has increased, there has also been a growing concern in the field of both educational assessment and language assessment that assessment practices should address system-wide accountability. Schools, colleges and universities are under pressure to inform the public about what they are teaching and how effective they are (see Darling-Hammond, 1994; Earl, 1995; Froese, 1997; Gipps, 1994). (For more about accountability and league tables see the review by Rea-Dickins and Rixon in this volume.) In this climate, there is tension between formative and summative assessment – what Gipps (1994, p. 12) calls a "paradigm clash". As Brindley (1995) argues:

> Teachers thus are now finding themselves under pressure from two different directions. On the one hand, they need to carry out detailed individual assessments at the individual level for purposes of diagnosis and feedback to learners, a role they are prepared to embrace because of the obvious effects on instruction (Broadfoot, 1992). However, at the same time, they are

increasingly being called on to report learners' progress against
national standards in order to meet accountability requirements.

The tension between these orientations is exacerbated by the fact that,
while much research questions the validity of large-scale, system-wide
assessment (see the section on 'Major Contributions' above), there is little research to support the validity of more learner-oriented assessment,
such as performance assessment and portfolio assessment (Hamp-Lyons,
1996; Reardon, Scott & Verre, 1994). In the field of language assessment,
McNamara (1995) identifies a number of problematic features of performance assessment in the main models proposed in the second language
assessment context, particularly with regard to the interactional aspect of
performance. Hill & Parry (1994, p. 146) point to some of the problems with alternative forms of assessment, focusing on the extent to which
they meet reliability criteria. Furthermore, as Darling-Hammond (1994)
argues, alternative assessment methods, that appear more accountable to
learners, are not necessarily equitable. She indicates that assessment reform is sometimes used as a means for external control of schools and
stems from a distrust of teachers. She suggests that the equitable use of
alternative assessments depends not only on the design of the assessments
themselves, but also on the extent to which teachers are an integral part of
the reform process. However, as Gearhart & Herman (1995) demonstrate,
attempts to integrate learner-oriented, performance assessment in large-
scale, system-wide assessment pose many challenges for all stakeholders.

FUTURE DIRECTIONS

The challenges for the future must be understood in relation to the struggles
of the past and the possibilities of the present. Firstly, there is a need
to address the tension between accountability to individuals on the one
hand and accountability to systems on the other. In this regard, the work
of Fulcher & Bamford (1997) raises important questions. Fulcher and
Bamford examined standards in language testing in the context of the
legal framework of the United States of America (USA) and the United
Kingdom (UK). They argue that while the threat of litigation has generated
much research on the reliability and validity of educational assessment
instruments in the USA, the same does not apply to the UK. They conclude
that it may only be a question of time before test takers in the UK (and by
extension other nations) seek legal means to ensure that language testers are
accountable to test takers. Current debates in the USA on the 'opportunity
to learn' (Guiton & Oakes, 1995) may become central in the quest for
accountable language assessment. Over time, innovative language testing
theory and practice may engender a complementary rather than adversarial
relationship between disparate stakeholders in language testing practices.

Secondly, there may be increased research on the washback effects of testing on teaching and learning. Xiaoju's (1990) research on the Matriculation English Test (MET), a new English matriculation test in China, for example, indicates that language testing can encourage innovative teaching practices. Research on Alderson & Wall's (1993) 'washback hypotheses' will make an important contribution to debates on accountability. An interesting avenue for research will be an investigation of ways in which teaching can inform testing. In this spirit, as Lacelle-Peterson & Rivera (1994), Peirce (1992) and Shohamy (1993b) have argued, if language testers are to be accountable to test takers, it will be necessary for them to enter into a dialogue with a broad range of stakeholders so that teaching and learning can be enhanced. (For more about washback, see Wall's review in this volume.)

Thirdly, language testers may become increasingly interested in the possibilities of computer adaptive testing (CAT) in attempts to be more accountable to test takers (see Jones, 1994; Tung, 1986). As Tung (1986) argues, not only does CAT take less time to administer than many other forms of assessment, but it may produce desirable 'affective effects' on test takers, who will find that while the test items are always challenging for them, they will seldom be beyond their capability. (For more about CAT, see Gruba and Corbel's review in this volume.)

Whatever trends in language assessment emerge in the next millennium, accountability in language assessment will remain a central priority for all stakeholders.

University of British Columbia, Canada

REFERENCES

Alderson, J.C. & Buck, G.: 1993, 'Standards in testing: A study of the practice of UK examination boards in EFL/ESL testing', *Language Testing* 10(1), 1–26.
Alderson, J.C. & Wall, D.: 1993, 'Does washback exist?', *Applied Linguistics* 14(2), 115–129.
Allen, K.: 1994, 'English education in Zimbabwe: Testing communicative competence', in C. Hill & K. Parry (eds.), *From Testing to Assessment: English as an International Language*, Longman, London.
Association of Language Testers of Europe: 1994, *The ALTE Code of Practice: The Code of Practice for the Association of Language Testers in Europe*, Version 1, January, 1994.
Brindley, G.: 1995, *Assessment and Reporting in Language Learning Programs: Purposes, Problems, and Pitfalls*, Plenary given at the International conference on Testing and Evaluation in Second Language Education, Hong Kong University of Science and Technology, 21–24 June, 1995.
Broadfoot, P.: 1992, *A Question of Quality: The Changing Role of Assessment in Education*, ACSA Workshop Report No. 4, Australian Curriculum Studies Association, Canberra.
Canale, M.: 1988, 'The measurement of communicative competence', *Annual Review of Applied Linguistics* 1987, 8, 67–84.

320 BONNY NORTON

Citizenship and Immigration Canada: 1996, *Canadian Language Benchmarks: English as a Second Language for Adults/English as a Second Language for Literacy Learners*, Working Document, Minister of Supply and Services, Ottawa, Canada.

Cohen, A.: 1984, 'On taking language tests: What the students report', *Language Testing* 1(1), 70–81.

Cohen, A.: 1994, 'English for Academic Purposes in Brazil: The use of summary tasks', in C. Hill, & K. Parry (eds.), *From Testing to Assessment: English as an International Language*, Longman, London.

Cumming, A.: 1994, 'Does language assessment facilitate recent immigrants' participation in Canadian Society? *TESL Canada Journal* 2(2), 117–133.

Cummins, J.: 1984, 'Wanted: A theoretical framework for relating language proficiency to academic achievement among bilingual students', in C. Rivera (ed.), *Language Proficiency and Academic Achievement*, Multilingual Matters, Clevedon, Avon.

Darling-Hammond, L.: 1994, 'Performance-based assessment and educational equity', *Harvard Educational Review* 64, 1.

Davidson, F.: 1993, 'Testing English across cultures: Summary and comments', *World Englishes* 12(1), 113–125.

Deyhle, D.: 1986, 'Success and failure: A micro-ethnographic comparison of Navajo and Anglo students' perceptions of testing', *Curriculum Inquiry* 16(4), 365–389.

Duncan, K.: 1995, 'The role of testing in the evaluation of a primary education project: The case of Molteno', in P. Rea-Dickins & A.F.L. Lwaitama (eds), *Evaluation for Development in English Language Teaching*, ELT documents, Macmillan Publishers Limited, London and Basingstoke, 107–116.

Earl, L.M.: 1995, 'Assessment and accountability in education in Ontario', *Canadian Journal of Education* 20(1), 45–55.

Elson, N.: 1992, 'The failure of tests: Language tests and post-secondary admissions of ESL students', in B. Burnaby & A. Cumming (eds), *Socio-Political Aspects of ESL in Canada*, OISE Press, Toronto.

Fillmore, C.: 1982, 'Ideal readers and real readers', in D. Tannen (ed.), *Analyzing Discourse: Text and Talk. Georgetown University Round Table*, 1981. Georgetown University Press, Washington, DC.

Froese, V.: 1997, 'National assessment the Canadian way', *Reading Today*, February/March 1997, 26.

Fulcher, G. & Bamford, R.: 1997, 'I didn't get the grade I need. Where's my solicitor?', *System*, 437–448.

Gearhart, M. & Herman, J.: 1995, *Portfolio Assessment: Whose Work Is It? Issues in the Use of Classroom Assignments for Accountability*, UCLA Center for the Study of Evaluation, Los Angeles, CA.

Gipps, C.V.: 1994, *Beyond Testing: Towards a Theory of Educational Assessment*, Falmer Press, Washington, D.C.

Guiton, G. & Oakes, J.: 1995, 'Opportunity to learn and conceptions of educational equality', *Educational Evaluation and Policy Analysis* 17(3), 323–336.

Hamp-Lyons, L.: 1996, 'Applying ethical standards to portfolio assessment of writing in English as second language', in M. Milanovich & N. Saville (eds.), *Performance Testing, Cognition and Assessment: Selected Papers from the 15th Language Testing Research Colloquium*, Cambridge University Press, Cambridge.

Hill, C. & Parry, K. (eds.): 1994, *From Testing to Assessment: English as an International Language*, Longman, London.

Holland, K., Bloome, D. & Solsken, J.: 1994, *Alternative Perspectives in Assessing Children's Language and Literacy*, Ablex, Norwood, N.J.

Holland, D. & Street, B.: 1994, 'Assessing adult literacy in the United Kingdom: The progress profile', in C. Hill & K. Parry (eds.), *From Testing to Assessment: English as an International Language*, Longman, London.

Ingulsrud, J.E.: 1994, 'An entrance test to Japanese universities: Social and historical context', in C. Hill & K. Parry (eds.), *From Testing to Assessment: English as an International Language*, Longman, London.

Jones, N.: 1994, *Adaptive Testing and Adaptive Learning*, Paper given at the Language Testing Forum, Cambridge, England, December, 1994.

Kalantzis, M., Cope, B. & Slade, D.: 1989, *Minority Language and Dominant Culture: Issues of Education*, Assessment and Social Equity, Falmer Press, London.

Katz, A. & Short, D.: 1996, 'ESL standards and the TESOL assessment guidelines project', *TESOL Matters* 6(2), 1 and 14.

Kunnan, A.J.: 1996, *Connecting Fairness with Validation in Language Testing*. Paper presented at the 18th Language Testing Research Colloquium, Tampere, Finland, August, 1995.

Lacelle-Peterson, M.W. & Rivera, C.: 1994, 'Is it real for all kids? A framework for equitable assessment policies for English language learners', *Harvard Educational Review* 64, 1.

Larter, S. & Donnelly, J.: 1993, 'Demystifying the goals of education: Toronto's benchmark program', *Orbit* 24(2), 22–28.

Lowenberg, P.: 1993, 'Issues of validity in tests of English', *World Englishes* 12(1), 95–106.

Matthews, M.: 1990, 'The measurement of productive skills: Doubts concerning the assessment criteria of certain public examinations, *ELT Journal* 44(2), 117–121.

McKay, P.: 1995, 'Developing ESL proficiency descriptions for the school context: The NLLIA ESL bandscales', in G. Brindley (ed.), *Language Assessment in Action*, National Centre for English Language Teaching and Research, Macquarie University, Sydney.

McNamara, T.F.: 995, 'Modelling performance: Opening Pandora's box', *Applied Linguistics* 16(2), 159–179.

Messick, S.: 1981, 'Evidence and ethics in the evaluation of tests', *Educational Researcher* 10(9), 9–20.

Moore, H.: 1996, 'Telling what is real: Competing views in assessing ESL development', *Linguistics and Education* 8(2), 189–228.

Parry, K.: 1994, 'The test and the text: Readers in a Nigerian secondary school', in C. Hill & K. Parry (eds.), *From Testing to Assessment: English as an International Language*, Longman, London.

Peirce, B.N.: 1992, 'Demystifying the TOEFL reading test, *TESOL Quarterly* 26(4), 665–689.

Peirce, B.N. & Stein, P.: 1995, 'Why the monkeys passage bombed: Tests, genres and teaching', *Harvard Educational Review* 65(1), 50–65.

Peirce, B.N. & Stewart, G.: 1997, 'The development of the Canadian language benchmarks assessment', *TESL Canada Journal* (in press).

Raimes, A.: 1990, 'The TOEFL Test of Written English: Causes for concern', *TESOL Quarterly* 24, 427–442.

Reardon, S., Scott, K., & Verre, J.: 1994, 'Symposium: Equity in educational assessment', *Harvard Educational Review* 64(1), 1–4.

Shohamy, E.: 1993a, *The Power of Tests: The Impact of Language Tests on Teaching and Learning*, National Foreign Language Center Occasional Paper, Washington, D.C.

Shohamy, E.: 1993b, 'The exercise of power and control in the rhetorics of testing', in A. Huhta, K. Sajavaara & S. Takalo (eds.), *Language Testing: New Openings*, Institute for Educational Research, Jyväskylä, Finland.

Spolsky, B.: 1978, 'Introduction: Linguists and language testers', in B. Spolsky (ed.), *Advances in Language Testing Research: Approaches to Language Testing*, Volume 2, Center for Applied Linguistics, Washington, D.C.

Stansfield, C: 1993, 'Ethics, standards, and professionalism in language testing', *Issues in Applied Linguistics* 4(2), 189–206.

Swain, M.: 1985, 'Large-scale communicative language testing: A case study', in S. Savignon & M. Burns (eds.), *Initiatives in Communicative Language Teaching*, Addison-Wesley, Reading, MA.

Tung, P.: 1986, 'Computerized adaptive testing: Implications for language test developers', in C. Stansfield (ed.), *Technology and Language Testing*, TESOL, Washington, D.C.

Wesche, M.: 1987, 'Second language performance testing: The Ontario Test of ESL as an example', *Language Testing* 4(1), 28–47.

Xiaoju, L.: 1990, 'How powerful can a language test be? The MET in China', *Journal of Multilingual and Multicultural Development* 11(5), 393–404.

Yeld, N. & Haeck, W.: 1993, 'Educational histories and academic potential: Can tests deliver?', in S. Angelil-Carter (ed.), *Language in Academic Development at U.C.T.*, unpublished manuscript.

LIZ HAMP-LYONS

ETHICS IN LANGUAGE TESTING

In a plenary address at the 1992 meeting of the American Association for
Applied Linguistics, Braj Kachru argued that awareness and discussion of
ethical issues in applied linguistics generally is essential, but he noted that
formal discussion of this is sadly lacking. An ethical approach is surely
yet more vital for language testers: their work perhaps more than that of
any other group of applied linguists can affect the lives of large numbers
of people they may never see, and who will never call them to account.
In a paper which overviews ethical issues in language testing, Stansfield
(1993) suggests that language testers need to define ethics as a standard of
right professional practice, and as a set of moral obligations.

EARLY DEVELOPMENT

Ethical issues, at least under that name, have arrived only very recently
on the agenda of language testers. A review of key early language testing
books, including Valette (1967; 1977), Heaton (1975), Allen & Davies
1977, Cohen (1980), and Carroll (1980) revealed no reference to ethics or
accountability. Even more recent language testing books such as Brindley (1986), Henning (1987) and Weir (1993) make no mention of ethical
issues. The only early language testers to focus on issues of ethics in
language testing are Spolsky (1977; 1980) and Stevenson (1981). Spolsky
(1977) sees language testing at that time as having moved from the "elitist"
approach that for him characterized "prescientific" testing, to an approach
that required full justification of all statements based on tests, which he
saw as a "move towards social justice" (p. 21). Spolsky (1980) pointed out
the abuse which testing and tests are subject to, and argued that language
testers must be as concerned with the prevention of bad testing as with
developing new tests, and that they must be sensitive to the possible
educational, social and political consequences of testing. Stevenson (1981)
may have been the first overtly to argue for language test development to
adhere to the "internationally-accepted standards for all educational and
psychological measures" (p. 19), a view which has only recently been
officially upheld by the International Language Testing Association in its
report on testing standards (Task Force on Testing Standards, 1995). He
argued for an "expanded view" of language testing in which all participants in the language testing processes, from their commissioning to their
implementation and interpretation, should be held accountable for their

C. Clapham and D. Corson (eds), Encyclopedia of Language and Education,
Volume 7: Language Testing and Assessment, 323–333.
© *1997 Kluwer Academic Publishers. Printed in the Netherlands.*

practices and the consequences of them. Stevenson further pointed out that despite the widespread use of standardized tests, there is no qualification system for people who intend to select, administer and interpret these tests. He asked: "Who is accountable to the pupils affected by these testing practices?" (p. 27) He asserted: "we (language testers) are not only accountable to ourselves, but also to those who teach, and are tested" (p. 28).

MAJOR CONTRIBUTIONS

It is probably too early to begin assessing the major contributions to thinking about ethics in language testing. Spolsky's (1995) history of language testing makes no reference to ethics, suggesting that there is not yet a historical perspective on this topic. The fact is that the foundation upon which the shaping of an ethicality agenda in language testing is being built lies outside our own field of applied linguistics, in developments in educational measurement validity theory (e.g., Messick, 1994; Moss, 1994). This is unsurprising, given the positivist paradigm to which language testing has until recently subscribed (Hamp-Lyons & Lynch, 1995; and in press; Lynch & Hamp-Lyons, 1996). A positivist approach to language testing starts from the belief that the object of our inquiry really exists, that this reality is governed by natural and absolute laws that are independent of who is conducting the inquiry, for what purposes, at what point(s) in time and with what methodology. Language testing research in a true positivist paradigm would not concern itself with ethics, because an absolute reality raises no ethical issues: it would concern itself instead with the technical excellence of its tools, successively refining them to better capture that absolute reality. We can, however, see the emergence of a concern with ethical issues in this decade, and the most recent relevant work in language testing is reviewed in the next section. A concern with ethics is part of the motivation for, and made possible because of, the development of alternative paradigms in evaluation (Guba & Lincoln, 1989). Informed by post-modernists such as Bhaskar (1989) and Habermas (1985), and critical discourse analysts such as Fairclough (1992), applied linguistics as a whole is tentatively engaging in a flirtation with moral philosophy, which is leading applied linguists closer to the development of a framework of ethical principles (Corson, 1997). The three principles of ethics identified by Corson (1997) – the principle of equal treatment; the principle of respect for persons; and the principle of benefit maximization – encapsulate the ethical concerns which are being brought to center-stage by the language testers whose work is cited in this review. The inclusive epistemology Corson (1997) argues for echoes the call in Hamp-Lyons & Lynch (1995; and in press) for 'other voices' in language testing research, and places emphasis on the consequences of actions as well as on *a priori* obligations to stakeholders. Bachman (1990) has been one of the few language testers to talk explicitly about "consequential or ethical ... validity" (pp. 279ff.); Bachman closes his discussion by saying "... it is our responsibility to provide as complete evidence as possible that the tests that are used are valid indicators of the abilities of interest and that these abilities are appropriate to the intended use, and then to insist that this evidence be used in the determination of test use" (p. 285). Hamp-Lyons (1989a; 1989b) argues that language testing is a political act, and that language testing researchers "must always be aware of the potential consequences of what they do ... we cannot validate a test in isolation from its administration, scoring, score analysis and reporting, nor from the interpretation and use of the information from the test, nor from its short-term or long-term social, cultural, economic, educational/curricular effects ... every decision made by a language tester, at either the research or operational stages, cannot avoid being a political and an ethical decision" (p. 111). This argument has much in common with the theory of consequential validity which has been developed by Samuel Messick over the past fifteen years (1980; 1988; 1989; 1994), and associated with, for example, Cronbach (e.g., 1988), and Madaus (e.g., Haney & Madaus, 1988; Madaus, 1995), and with the advocacy for ethics in educational measurement associated with, for example, Darling-Hammond (1993; 1994). This group of 'validity theorists' (Moss, 1995) has proved very influential among the small but growing group of language testers who have taken on what Canale (1988) has called a "naturalistic-ethical approach" to language testing, an approach which focuses on language testing as "an art, a science, and very much an ethical issue" (p. 77).

There is some discussion of ethicality issues within the language testing community and literature which does not occur under the actual term *ethics/ethicality*. Accountability is such a term, and is fully covered by Norton (in her review in this volume). We will not, therefore, explore it here. Other such terms are fairness and equity. Fair Test, The National Center for Fair and Open Testing, is a fairly new organization which fronts the concept of *fairness* , and is dedicated to ending "the overuse and misuse of standardized, multiple-choice tests and promot(ing) methods of assessment which are educationally relevant" (Exec. Director's letter, n.d.). The *Code of Fair Testing Practices in Education* (National Council in Measurement in Education, 1988) commits NCME members to safeguarding the rights of test takers; they focus on issues affecting the proper use of tests, and are intended to be understood by the general public. Equity (the assurance that all students have access to the resources, curricula, and pedagogies they need to learn effectively) is increasingly a key issue in educational assessment, as evidenced by the 1994 special issue of the *Harvard Educational Review* (Vol. 64, No. 1) on 'Equity in Educational Assessment', and by the *Principles and Indicators for Student Assessment*

Systems of The National Forum on Assessment, which focus on equity, accountability, and relevance to instructional goals. UNESCO's 'Monitoring Education-For-All Goals' stresses the need for tests that are to be used internationally to include experts from each nation (where the test is to be used) at all stages of design and validation, and for indicators and targets to be set for and by each country. In language testing, we have heard much less about equity; most of the equity/fairness concerns have focused on test bias, which is a statistical property of a test and can be monitored and remedied statistically (Bachman, 1990; Duran, 1988). There must be questions about the appropriacy of ethical requirements such as those set by UNESCO when a test, such as the Test of English as a Foreign Language (TOEFL), is to be used as an entrance 'barrier' for people from a range of countries to enter the (usually tertiary) educational system of another. What is the principle against which the ethicality of the test is to be judged? A further problem the developers of very large-scale tests like the TOEFL (Educational Testing Service) and FCE (First Certificate in English: UCLES (University of Cambridge Local Examinations Syndicate)) face is that the test's scores are put to a host of different uses. We must ask how much responsibility a testing agency has for the uses made of the test scores it generates. The TOEFL program publishes clear statements about the meaningfulness of its scores, and cautions against using them for other purposes. Is this enough? And if it is not, what might its parent company, ETS, Educational Testing Service, do to monitor score use and prevent abuse? This is a very difficult ethical issue.

Two other important parallel terms are *impact* and *washback*, both of which are treated in Wall's review in this volume. Tests have impact on the lives of test takers, classrooms, school systems and even whole societies (as can be observed in a test-focused society such as Hong Kong, as reported by Cheng, 1997). When testers take account of impact, and work consciously in test development, administration, reporting, *and advertising* to avoid negative impact and maximize the possibility of positive washback, they are leaving behind the simplistic form of the positivist paradigm and entering a relativist world, a world where reality is dependent on, rather than independent of, our inquiry, a world where 'facts' cannot be established independent of values (Hamp-Lyons & Lynch, in press). In *this* world, ethical issues are central.

WORK IN PROGRESS

Happily, ethics seem at last to be coming onto the language testing agenda in earnest. The (March) 1995 Language Testing Research Colloquium had as its theme, 'Validity and Equity Issues in Language Testing', and was significant for choosing as its opening keynote speaker Eva Baker, not herself a language tester but an educational measurement specialist, Director of the Center for the Study of Evaluation at the University of California at Los Angeles (UCLA), California. Baker described five challenges facing educational assessment: clarifying the purposes of testing; balancing the need for new approaches with the need to maintain stability; balancing the demand for technical quality in tests with the goal of impacting for instructional improvement; deciding what is realistic in the development of quality assessments while moving in enriching directions; determining what will be politically acceptable as social and educational values shift. In her response to Baker, Hamp-Lyons commented that this was to her knowledge the first time the need for testers to be conscious of political agendas and shape their tests reactively had been an overt theme of a presentation in this forum. At the (August) 1996 Annual Language Testing Research Colloquium in Tampere, Finland papers included not only that by Lynch and Hamp-Lyons previously referred to, but a paper by Anthony Kunnan on 'Connecting fairness and validation in assessment'; by Bonny Peirce and Gail Stewart on 'Culturally fair task-based assessment: The challenge of diversity'; by Alan Davies on 'Migrant gatekeeping through English proficiency: Is efficiency replacing equity?'; by Liz Hamp-Lyons on 'Ethical test preparation practice: the case of the TOEFL'; by Liying Cheng on 'The impact of a public examination change on student learning', and by Vivien Berry on 'Ethical considerations when assessing oral proficiency in pairs'. Also in August 1996, a colloquium at the International Applied Linguistics Association meeting in Jyväskylä, Finland, the papers from which will be published as a special issue of *Language Testing* (1997, Vol. 14, No. 3), looked at 'Good conduct in language testing: ethical concerns'. In this colloquium Alan Davies argued that codes of professional good practice are necessary, but do not ensure ethicality; indeed they may subvert it because of the intrusive nature of language testing and the normative nature of language tests. Brian Lynch questioned the morality of assessment; defining morality in terms of ethical issues such as harm, consent, confidentiality of data, and fairness, he asked whether any test can be defended as moral, and proposed "more ethical ways of assessing" by reference to work by the Australian Council of State School Organisations and the Australian Parents' Council, and by Wilson (1995). Elana Shohamy looked at the issue of method effect on language tests, a variable that testers have long been aware of, and considered what procedures are available to enable language testers to determine which method is 'fairer'. Tom Lumley examined the tension between the competing needs to offer a fair test and to offer one which tests the right things in the perceptions of stakeholders. Bonny Peirce considered the extent to which poststructuralist theories of textual meaning can address unequal power relations between test makers and test takers. Liz Hamp-Lyons looked at the intended and unintended consequences of tests on teaching, teachers and learners. Finally, Bernard Spolsky looked historically at the ethics of gatekeeping, reminding us that concerns about test fairness have been raised ever since Macaulay proposed the introduction of the Civil Service examination in Britain in 1853. Spolsky says: "What we are starting to do, I am pleased to see, is accept the inevitable uncertainty (in test scores), and turn our attention to the way tests are used, insisting on multiple testing and alternative methods, and realizing that the results need cautious and careful interpretation ... we must make sure that gatekeeping processes are under human and not automatic control" (p. 6). The March 1997 Annual Language Testing Research Colloquium in Orlando, Florida had as its theme, 'Fairness in Language Testing'. The keynote panel had discussion papers by Lyle Bachman, Liz Hamp-Lyons, Elana Shohamy and Bonny Norton Peirce, and 'fairness' was a theme running through a number of the papers, for example, Cathie Elder's 'Is it fair to assess both NS and NNS on school 'foreign' language examinations?'; Noriko Iwashita's 'The validity of the paired interview in oral performance testing'; and Carol Moder and Gene Halleck's 'Balancing fairness and authenticity in performance tests: An alternative rating approach'. Peter Lowenberg's 'Non-native varieties and issues of fairness in testing standard English as a world language' critiqued high stakes international tests for their linguicentricism, while John de Jong and Fellyanka Stoyanova's 'The relation between reliability and validity: an issue of test fairness' and Gary Cook's 'Investigating bias over time' explored fairness from more traditional viewpoints, fitting data to theoretical models, and using statistical bias analysis. Reviewing these recent conferences, it can be seen that both the classical and post-modern perspectives on ethical issues are now accepted as central to the considerations language testers must encompass in their development and validation of tests. At the 1997 Annual TESOL Convention, also in Orlando, the theme of the Academic Session of the Research Interest Section was 'Research in Language Testing: Consequences and Ethical Issues'. Even the inclusion of an entry on this topic in this encyclopedia is a sign of changing perceptions in language testing: twenty or ten and perhaps even five years ago it would not have appeared.

PROBLEMS AND DIFFICULTIES

There are both philosophical and practical difficulties associated with a rise in ethical awareness in language testing. The practical problems are difficult, and some of them have been suggested by the titles of papers listed above: What is the effect of 'assisted performance' in performance tests such as portfolio assessments? How do testers account for degrees of assisted performance in scoring/designing scoring instruments for performance assessments? If we are able to detect bias, what can we do about it? If we detect unethical test preparation practices, what can we do about it? If we see test scores being used for inappropriate purposes, how can we change that? If we are aware of a conflict between face validity and construct validity, how can we convince a test-consuming public that the construct-valid test is actually 'fairer' than the face-valid one? If we see tests being introduced with damaging washback effects, who can we convince to make changes?

But the philosophical problems may be more difficult still: perhaps they all boil down to one – is it our responsibility? If our tests are being used for gatekeeping purposes that are unrelated to actual language proficiency, is it our responsibility? Is ETS responsible for the fact that TOEFL scores are almost universally used for decision-making in ways and for purposes that ETS expressly says it is not suitable for? Is ETS responsible for the many TOEFL test preparation classes and programs around the USA and the world, which take students' time – and money – away from communicative language improvement courses? Is UCLES responsible for the proliferation of cram schools in Greece preparing candidates for the Certificate of Proficiency in English and the First Certificate in English? Are the developers of Australia's *access:* test responsible for its role in keeping some would-be migrants out of the country, and others out of funded language improvement and/or vocational training programs? Are the developers of the original English Language Testing Service (ELTS) responsible for later revisions which have caused the revised test, the International English Language Testing System (IELTS) to undergo a progressive reduction in the number of its academic subject modules so that it now bears little resemblance to the original design? The list of contexts and philosophical/ethical questions goes on and on, in all countries and at all levels.

It is worth noting in this section that, while standards of test development have improved since Stevenson's critique in 1981, and standards of training for language performance judges and test raters have improved markedly, there are still no qualifications required or even available for those who intend to interpret and make decisions on test data. It is also still true that the majority of masters' programs in applied linguistics or TESOL (teaching English to speakers of other languages) do not contain a course in language testing, or if they do, it is rudimentary in nature (Bailey & Brown, 1995). Those who have had professional preparation in language testing are equipped to appreciate the ethical dilemmas faced by test developers, administrators and score users, and to make ethical decisions themselves as they take on those roles: those who do not, are not.

FUTURE DIRECTIONS

The growing interest in ethics reflects a post-modern concern with self evaluation and self-reflection. As Stansfield (1993) points out, a profession is in part identified by having a professional association, and language

testers have had their own international organization, the International
Language Testing Association (ILTA), only since 1992: as this book goes
to press we are five years old! Stansfield distinguishes *ethics*, a branch of
philosophy concerned with the moral choices an individual must make in
relation to others, from *ethics* applied to a profession, where it refers to
a set of principles governing the conduct of members of the profession.
Stansfield reserves the term *standards* for the procedures language testers
adopt in developing tests, operating test programs, or administering and
interpreting tests and test scores (pp. 190–191). This is the view of
standards taken by Davidson, Turner and Huhta in their review in this
volume. Stansfield gives a number of convincing reasons why language
testers need a set of formally adopted standards and ethics, and points out
that related fields such as the American Psychological Association (APA),
the American Educational Research Association, and the National Council
on Measurement in Education, already have their own Code of Ethics –
the *APA Standards* (1985, and under revision), and that these standards
have had a "profound effect on test publishing in the United States" (p.
192). We can expect ILTA to adopt its own Code of Ethics in the next five
years: it has already taken a major step in this direction through its Task
Force on Testing Standards (see Davidson, Turner & Huhta's review in this
volume). Schmeiser (1992) analyzes Codes of Ethics across a range of
professions and concludes that the *APA Standards* are not comprehensive
enough in scope, suggesting some useful directions in which standards
should be developed. ILTA's standards project is still narrower in scope,
and makes little reference to ethics or any of the related issues and terms
discussed in this chapter: our professional association could learn much
from her survey.

Beyond this major step for language testing, another likely future development is increased interest in the other participants in the testing process:
following the early work of Cohen (1984) into test takers' reactions to
tests and test methods, and his work into test taking strategies (1994), we
can expect (and hope) to see an increased consciousness of the *presence*
of other players in the game. Davidson (1993) points to the power of
dominance exerted by tests used internationally, setting the scene for work
placing the activity of language testing, particularly the development and
use of large-scale, high stakes language tests across countries and cultures,
within a post-colonialism frame, such as that referred to above by Kunnan
(1997). This work too asserts the need for attention to the voices of a much
wider range of stakeholders in testing contexts. As such work appears, it
will signal the paradigm shift in language testers' beliefs about what we
do, why we do it, and how we should do it discussed by Hamp-Lyons &
Lynch (in press). As the new paradigm takes its place alongside the traditional paradigm, we can expect increasing tensions among testers about the
nature of legitimate questions to be asked and legitimate methods for un-

covering answers to them. The greater role and 'voice' for 'stakeholders' in tests and assessments will add tensions and complexities to the work of the language tester, as our tests increasingly have to meet the sometimes conflicting expectations of multiple audiences. This will increase the demand for applied linguists to have some training in language testing, since few of them will avoid the use or interpretation of tests. As for those of us who call ourselves 'language testers', as our view of our field expands, we will need, and we can expect to see, a wider range of research methods being applied, a wider perspective on what constitutes validity and validation data, and a deeper sense of what we must expect of ourselves as testing professionals.

Hong Kong Polytechnic University
China

REFERENCES

Allen, J.P.B. & A. Davies (eds.): 1977, *Testing and Experimental Methods. The Edinburgh Course in Applied Linguistics*, Volume 4, Oxford University Press, Oxford.

Bachman, L.F.: 1990, *Fundamental Considerations in Language Testing*, Oxford University Press, Oxford.

Bailey, K. & J.D. Brown: 1995, 'Language testing courses: What are they?', in A. Cumming & R. Berwick (eds.), *Validation in Language Testing*, Multilingual Matters, Clevedon, UK, 236–256.

Bhaskar, R.: 1989, *Reclaiming Reality: A Critical Introduction to Contemporary Philosophy*, Verso, London.

Brindley, G.: 1986, *The Assessment of Second Language Proficiency: Issues and Approaches*, National Curriculum Resource Center, Adult Migrant Education Program, Adelaide, Australia.

Canale, M.: 1988, 'The measurement of communicative competence', *Annual Review of Applied Linguistics* 8, 67–84.

Carroll, B.J.: 1980, *Testing Communicative Performance*, Pergamon Press, Oxford.

Cheng, L-y.: 1997, 'How does washback influence teaching? Implications for Hong Kong', *Language in Education* 11(1), 38–54.

Cohen, A.: 1980, *Testing Language Ability in the Classroom*, Newbury House, Rowley, MA.

Cohen, A.: 1984, 'On taking tests: What the students report', *Language Testing* 1(1), 70–81.

Cohen, A.: 1994, 'English for Academic Purposes in Brazil: The use of summary tasks', in C. Hill & K. Parry (eds.), *From Testing to Assessment: English as an International Language*, Longman, London, 174–204.

Corson, D.: 1997, 'Critical realism: An emancipatory philosophy for applied linguistics?', *Applied Linguistics* 18(2), 166–188.

Cronbach, L.J.: 1988, 'Five perspectives on validation argument', in H. Wainer & H. Braun (eds.), *Test Validity*, Lawrence Erlbaum, Hillsdale, NJ, 3–17.

Darling-Hammond, L.: 1993, *Creating Learner-Centered Accountability*, ERIC ED364592.

Darling-Hammond, L.: 1994, 'Performance-based assessment and educational equity', *Harvard Educational Review* 64(1), 5–30.

Davidson, F.: 1993, 'Testing English across cultures; summary and comments', *World Englishes* 21(1), 113–125.

Davidson, F., Alderson, J.C., Douglas, D., Huhta, A., Turner C. & Wylie, E.: 1995, *Report of the Task Force on Testing Standards to the International Language Testing Association*, ILTA (ERIC ED390268), Melbourne, Australia.

Duran, R.P.: 1988, 'Testing linguistic minorities', in R.L. Linn (ed.), *Educational Measurement* (third edition), American Council on Education/Macmillan, New York.

Fairclough, N. (ed.): 1992, *Critical Language Awareness*, Longman, London.

Guba, E.G. & Lincoln, Y.S.: 1989, *Fourth Generation Evaluation*, Sage, Newbury Park, CA.

Habermas, J.: 1985, *The Theory of Communicative Action: Volume 1, Reasoning and the Rationalisation of Society*, Heinemann, New York.

Hamp-Lyons, L.: 1989a, 'Applying the partial credit method of Rasch analysis: Language testing and accountability', *Language Testing* 6(1), 109–118.

Hamp-Lyons, L.: 1989b, 'Language testing and ethics', *Prospect: A Journal of Australian TESOL* 5(1), 7–15.

Hamp-Lyons, L. & B. Lynch: 1995, *Perspectives on Validity: A Historical Analysis of the LTRC*, Paper presented at the 17th Annual Language Testing Research Colloquium, Long Beach, CA, March.

Hamp-Lyons, & Lynch B.: In press, 'Perspectives on validity: A historical analysis of language testing conference abstracts', in A.J. Kunnan (ed.), *Issues in Language Testing Research: Conventional Valdity and Beyond*, Lawrence Erlbaum Associates, Inc., Mahwah, NJ.

Haney, W. & Madaus, G.: 1988, 'The evaluation of ethical and technical standards for testing', in R.K. Hambleton & J. Zaal (eds.), *Handbook of Testing*, North Holland Press, Amsterdam, 101–134.

Heaton, J.B.: 1975, *Writing English Language Tests*, Longman, London.

Henning, G.: 1987, *A Guide to Language Testing*, Newbury House, Rowley, MA.

Kachru, B.: 1992, *Why Applied Linguistics Leaks*, Plenary address at the conference of the American Association of Applied Linguistics, Seattle, Washington, Feb/March.

Kachru, B.: 1993, 'Ethical issues for applying linguistics, afterword', *Issues in Applied Linguistics* 4(2), 283–294.

Lynch, B. & L. Hamp-Lyons: 1996, *Positivist versus Alternative Perspectives on Validity within the LTRC*, Paper presented at the Annual Language Testing Research Colloquium, Tampere, Finland, August

Madaus, G.: 1995, 'A technological and historical consideration of equity issues associated with proposals to change our nation's testing policy', in M.T. Nettles & A.L. Nettles (eds.), *Equity and Excellence in Educational Testing and Assessment*, Kluwer Educational Publishers, Norwell, MA, 229–247.

Messick, S.: 1980, 'Test validity and the ethics of assessment', *American Psychologist* 35, 1012–1027.

Messick, S.: 1981, 'Evidence and ethics in the evaluation of tests', *Educational Researcher* 10(9), 9–20.

Messick, S.: 1988, 'The once and future issues of validity: Assessing the meaning and consequences of measurement', in H. Wainer & H.I. Braun (eds.), *Test Validity*, Erlbaum, Hillsdale, NJ, 33–45.

Messick, S.: 1989, 'Meaning and values in test validation: The science and ethics of assessment', *Educational Researcher* 18, 5–11.

Messick, S.: 1994, 'The interplay of evidence and consequences in the validation of performance Assessments, *Educational Researcher* 23(2), 13–25.

Moss, P.: 1994, 'Can there be validity without reliability?', *Educational Researcher* 23(2), 5–12.

Moss, P.A.: 1995, 'Themes and variations in validity theory', *Educational Measurement: Issues and Practice* 14(2), 5–13.

National Council of Measurement in Education: 1988, *Code of Fair Testing Practices in Education*, NCME, Washington, DC.

Schmeiser, C.B.: 1992, 'Ethical codes in the professions', *Educational Measurement: Issues and Practice* 11(3), 5–11.

Spolsky, B.: 1977, 'Language testing: Art or science?' in *Proceedings of the Fourth International Congress of Applied Linguistics*, Hochschulverlag, Stuttgart, 7–28.

Spolsky, B.: 1980, 'Some ethical questions about language testing', in C. Klein-Braley & D.K. Stevenson (eds.), *Practice and Problems in Language Testing 1: Proceedings of the First International Language Testing Symposium*, Verlag Peter Lang, Bern and Cirencester.

Spolsky, B.: 1995, *Measured Words: The Development of Objective Language Testing*, Oxford University Press, Oxford.

Spolsky, B.: 1996, *The Ethics of Gatekeeping Tests: What Have We Learned in a Hundred Years?*, Paper presented in the Symposium on the Ethics of Language Testing, AILA, Jyväskylä, August 1996.

Stevenson, D.K.: 1981, 'Language testing and academic accountability: On redefining the role of language testing in language teaching', *International Review of Applied Linguistics* 19, 15–30.

Stansfield, C.W.: 1993, 'Ethics, standards, and professionalism in language testing', *Issues in Applied Linguistics* 4(2), 189–206.

Task Force on Testing Standards (TFTS): 1995, *Report of the Task Force on Testing Standards (TFTS) to the International Language Testing Association (ILTA)*, ILTA, Melbourne. (For the address, see Davidson, Turner and Huhta's review in this volume.)

Valette, R.M.: 1977, *Modern Language Testing* (second edition), Harcourt, Brace, Jovanovich, New York.

Weir, C.: 1993, *Understanding and Developing Language Tests*, Prentice Hall International, Hemel Hempstead.

Wilson, L.: 1995, 'Principles for evaluating language development', *NLLIA Network News* 8, 3.

SUBJECT INDEX

NAME INDEX

Abbott 9
Abbs, J.A. 212
Abraham, R.G. 101, 113
Adams, C. 214
Adams, M.L. 77
Adema, J.J. 249
Ahlawat, K.S. 234
Airasian, P.W. 294
Aitken, M. 234
Akoha, J. 299
Albertson, L.R. 195
Alderson, J.C. 32, 41, 42, 44, 45, 82, 89,
    91, 95, 112, 116, 122, 141, 143,
    146, 152, 269, 271, 275–279, 282,
    283, 291, 294, 295, 297, 305, 308,
    309, 315, 319
Alexander, E.E. 205
Alexander, E.R. 23, 34
Algina, J. 82
Al-Haik, A. 200
Allal, L. 257
Allan, A.I.C.G. 283
Allen, J.P.B. 323
Allen, K. 293, 315
Allen, N.L. 238
Allen, P. 57
Ambady, N. 33
Anastasi, A. 275
Ancess, J. 59
Andersen, E.B. 246
Anderson, J.R. 202
Andrews, S. 294, 296
Andrich, D. 245, 247, 248
Angelis, P. 88
Angoff, W.H. 266, 275
Arnaud, P.J.L. 103
Arneson, P. 35
Arnold, H. 2
Aronson, A.R. 212
Aschbacher, P.R. 35
Avila, D. 34
Ayers, D.A. 7

Bachman, L.F. xiii, xv, xvi, 60, 78, 80,
    81, 89, 92, 111, 115, 116, 122, 125,
    128, 135, 136, 142, 144, 168, 169,
    179, 228, 231, 232, 234, 238, 250,
    255, 257, 265, 275, 277, 282, 308,
    325, 326, 328
Backlund, P.A. 31–33
Baddeley, A.D. 202
Bailey, K.M. 294, 297, 329
Bain, B.A. 217
Baker xvii, 29
Baker, C. 165
Baker, E. 327
Baker, R. 247
Baldauf, R.B. 180, 183
Ballard, P. 5
Bamford, R. 318
Banerjee, J. xv, xvi, 42, 81, 135, 175,
    232, 283
Bardovi-Harlig, K. 57
Barker, L.L. 22–24
Barlow, S.M. 212
Barnwell, D. 77, 78
Barrs, M. 151, 153, 154, 166, 171
Bartlett, E. 194
Barton, M.A. 228
Bassett, R.E. 31
Bassich, C.J. 220
Batstone, R. 88, 93, 94
Beach, R. 189
Beal, C.R. 194
Beard, R. 45
Beason, L. 196
Beaton, A.E. 238
Becker 22
Behnke, R.R. 23
Beier, E. 22
Bejarano, Y. 80
Beland, A. 232
Bentler, P.M. 234, 260
Berberich, F. 147
Bereiter, C. 190, 195
Bernhardt, E.B. 41, 42
Berry, V. 280, 327
Berwick, R. 277, 281
Bhaskar, R. 324
Birenbaum, M. 238
Black, L. 16
Blanche, P. 181
Blaye, A. 195
Bloom, L. 214, 228

343

TABLE OF CONTENTS

VOLUME 1: LANGUAGE POLICY AND POLITICAL ISSUES IN EDUCATION

TABLE OF CONTENTS

TABLE OF CONTENTS

VOLUME 2: LITERACY

TABLE OF CONTENTS

TABLE OF CONTENTS

VOLUME 3: ORAL DISCOURSE AND EDUCATION

TABLE OF CONTENTS

TABLE OF CONTENTS

VOLUME 4: SECOND LANGUAGE EDUCATION

TABLE OF CONTENTS

TABLE OF CONTENTS

VOLUME 5: BILINGUAL EDUCATION

TABLE OF CONTENTS

TABLE OF CONTENTS

VOLUME 6: KNOWLEDGE ABOUT LANGUAGE

TABLE OF CONTENTS

TABLE OF CONTENTS

VOLUME 8: RESEARCH METHODS IN LANGUAGE AND EDUCATION

TABLE OF CONTENTS

Encyclopedia of Language and Education

Set ISBN Hb 0-7923-4596-7; Pb 0-7923-4936-9

1. R. Wodak and D. Corson (eds.): *Language Policy and Political Issues in Education.*
   1997   ISBN Hb 0-7923-4713-7
                                                 ISBN Pb 0-7923-4928-8

2. V. Edwards and D. Corson (eds.): *Literacy.* 1997   ISBN Hb 0-7923-4595-0
                                                         ISBN Pb 0-7923-4929-6

3. B. Davies and D. Corson (eds.): *Oral Discourse and Education.* 1997
                                                 ISBN Hb 0-7923-4639-4
                                                 ISBN Pb 0-7923-4930-X

4. G.R. Tucker and D. Corson (eds.): *Second Language Education.* 1997
                                                 ISBN Hb 0-7923-4640-8
                                                 ISBN Pb 0-7923-4931-8

5. J. Cummins and D. Corson (eds.): *Bilingual Education.* 1997
                                                 ISBN Hb 0-7923-4806-0
                                                 ISBN Pb 0-7923-4932-6

6. L. van Lier and D. Corson (eds.): *Knowledge about Language.* 1997
                                                 ISBN Hb 0-7923-4641-6
                                                 ISBN Pb 0-7923-4933-4

7. C. Clapham and D. Corson (eds.): *Language Testing and Assessment.* 1997
                                                 ISBN Hb 0-7923-4702-1
                                                 ISBN Pb 0-7923-4934-2

8. N.H. Hornberger and D. Corson (eds.): *Research Methods in Language and Education.* 1997   ISBN Hb 0-7923-4642-4
                                                 ISBN Pb 0-7923-4935-0

KLUWER ACADEMIC PUBLISHERS – DORDRECHT / BOSTON / LONDON